Jack O'Connell

Hemingway and His Critics
AN INTERNATIONAL ANTHOLOGY

Hemingway and His Critics

AN INTERNATIONAL ANTHOLOGY

Edited, with an introduction and a checklist
of Hemingway criticism by **Carlos Baker**

AMERICAN CENTURY SERIES

HILL AND WANG · NEW YORK

FIRST AMERICAN CENTURY SERIES EDITION MARCH 1961

SECOND PRINTING, JULY 1961

Manufactured in the United States of America by
The Colonial Press Inc., Clinton, Massachusetts

in memoriam

ALLAN HOUSTON MACDONALD

1901–1951

Prefatory Notes

The editor is very much indebted to the critics of Hemingway who have permitted their distinguished essays to appear in this volume; without their kindness such a collection could not have been made. For the checklist of criticism which concludes the volume, a particular debt is acknowledged to Professor Maurice Beebe, editor of *Modern Fiction Studies,* on whose compilation of 1955 the present listing is based, and to Mr. James Adams, who assisted materially in enlarging it and bringing it up to date. The editor also wishes to thank Joseph M. Bernstein, who translated the essays of André Maurois, Pier Francesco Paolini, and Horst Oppel; and Mrs. Ilsa Barea, who translated the essay by her late husband.

The editor and the publisher also acknowledge the permission to reprint granted by these authors and publishers:

George Plimpton, for "An Interview with Ernest Hemingway" from *The Paris Review* 18 (Spring 1958).

André Maurois, for "Ernest Hemingway" from *La Revue de Paris* 62 (March 1955).

Edmund Wilson, for "Emergence of Ernest Hemingway" from *The Shores of Light* (New York: Farrar, Straus and Cudahy, 1952).

Lionel Trilling and *Partisan Review,* for "Hemingway and His Critics" from *Partisan Review* 6 (Winter 1939).

H. E. Bates and Thomas Nelson & Sons, Ltd., for "Hemingway's Short Stories" from *The Modern Short Story* (London: Thomas Nelson & Sons, Ltd., 1942).

Mark Spilka and Wayne State University Press, for "The Death of Love in *The Sun Also Rises*" from *Twelve Original Essays on Great American Novels* (Charles Shapiro, ed.). Copyright 1958, Wayne State University Press, Detroit.

Harry Levin, for "Observations on the Style of Ernest Hemingway" from *Kenyon Review* 13 (Autumn 1951). Reprinted from *Contexts of Criticism* (Cambridge, Mass.: Harvard University Press, 1957).

Mario Praz, for "Hemingway in Italy" from *Partisan Review* 15 (October 1948). Copyright Mario Praz.

Pier Francesco Paolini, for "The Hemingway of the Major Works" from *Letterature Moderne* 6 (November–December 1956).

Deming Brown, for "Hemingway in Russia" from *American Quarterly* 5 (1953).

Ivan Kashkeen, for "Alive in the Midst of Death" from *Soviet Literature* 7 (1956).

Charles Scribner's Sons, for "Ernest Hemingway: The Missing Third Dimension," by Michael F. Moloney, reprinted with the permission of Charles Scribner's Sons from *Fifty Years of the American Novel* (Harold C. Gardiner, ed.), copyright 1951, Charles Scribner's Sons.

Frederic I. Carpenter and Philosophical Library, for "Hemingway Achieves the Fifth Dimension" from *American Literature and The Dream,* copyright 1955 by Philosophical Library, New York.

Ilsa Barea, for "Not Spain but Hemingway" by Arturo Barea, from *Horizon* [England] 3 (May 1941).

Horst Oppel and *Die Neueren Sprachen,* for "Hemingway's *Across the River and Into the Trees"* from *Die Neueren Sprachen,* Heft 11 (1952).

Dagmar Doneghy Beach, for "How Do You Like It Now, Gentlemen?" by Joseph Warren Beach, from *Sewanee Review* 59 (Spring 1951).

Melvin Backman, for "Hemingway: The Matador and the Crucified" from *Modern Fiction Studies* 1 (August 1955).

Clinton S. Burhans, Jr., for *"The Old Man and the Sea:* Hemingway's Tragic Vision of Man" from *American Literature* 31 (January 1960).

Keiichi Harada, for "The Marlin and the Shark: A Note on *The Old Man and the Sea"* from *Journal* Number 4 of the College of Literature, Aoyama Gakuin University, Tokyo.

The Editor

CARLOS BAKER is Woodrow Wilson Professor of Literature at Princeton University and the author of *Hemingway: The Writer as Artist* (1952, 1956). His other books include a critical study of Shelley; editions of Fielding, Wordsworth, Shelley, and Keats; and a novel, *A Friend in Power* (1958).

Contributing Essayists

GEORGE PLIMPTON is one of the founders and editors of *The Paris Review*.

ANDRÉ MAUROIS is a distinguished French novelist and biographer and a member of the Academie Française. His works include lives of Shelley, Byron, Disraeli, Turgenev, Proust, Hugo, and George Sand.

EDMUND WILSON, one of the leading critics in the United States, is the author of many books, including *Axel's Castle* (1931), *The Triple Thinkers* (1938), *The Wound and the Bow* (1941), and *The Shores of Light* (1952).

LIONEL TRILLING, Professor of English at Columbia University, is well known for critical studies of Matthew Arnold and E. M. Forster as well as the critical essays in *The Liberal Imagination* (1950) and *The Opposing Self* (1955).

H. E. BATES, British novelist, short-story writer, and critic, is the author of a valuable commentary, *The Modern Short Story* (1942).

MARK SPILKA teaches at the University of Michigan and frequently writes on American and English literature of the past century.

HARRY LEVIN holds a chair in Comparative Literature at Harvard University. Among his many books are studies of Christopher Marlowe, James Joyce, Stendhal, and Balzac. *The Power of Blackness* (1958) concerns Hawthorne, Poe, and Melville.

MARIO PRAZ, Professor of English Language and Literature at the University of Rome, is the author of a number of books, including *The Romantic Agony* (1933) and *The Hero in Eclipse in Victorian Fiction* (1956).

PIER FRANCESCO PAOLINI has contributed articles on modern literature to the leading Italian literary journals.

DEMING BROWN is Chairman of the Department of Slavonic Languages and Literatures at the University of Michigan.

IVAN KASHKEEN is one of the most gifted and perceptive critics of modern literature, both Russian and non-Russian, in the USSR.

The late MICHAEL MOLONEY taught literature at Marquette University.

FREDERIC I. CARPENTER, Research Associate in English, University of California at Berkeley, is the author of *American Literature and The Dream,* two books on Emerson, and a number of critical essays that have appeared in American periodicals.

The late ARTURO BAREA is known in the United States chiefly for his work on Lorca and Unamuno. After the Spanish civil war he lived for twenty years in England.

HORST OPPEL, Professor of English Literature at the University of Marburg, is the author of a recent study of Shakespearean tragedy.

The late JOSEPH WARREN BEACH taught at the University of Minnesota and was the author of many books concerning English and American literature. His works include *The Twentieth-Century Novel* (1932), *The Concept of Nature in 19th-Century English Poetry* (1936), and *American Fiction, 1920-1940* (1941).

MELVIN BACKMAN of the Clarkson College of Technology in Potsdam, New York, teaches liberal arts and writes frequently of modern literature.

CLINTON S. BURHANS, JR., is a member of the English Department at the University of British Columbia in Vancouver.

KEIICHI HARADA is Lecturer in American Literature at Aoyama Gakuin University in Tokyo. A graduate of Doshisha University in Kyoto, he also holds the M.A. degree from Syracuse University. His published work includes a translation of Melville's *Billy Budd* into Japanese, and he has written on Melville and Faulkner.

Contents

Hemingway and His Critics
AN INTERNATIONAL ANTHOLOGY

INTRODUCTION

Citizen of the World

I

For years before he won the Nobel Prize in literature at the age of fifty-five, Ernest Hemingway had been a citizen of the world. In every country of western and eastern Europe, the Middle East, Asia, and Australia, and in the northern and southern parts of America and Africa, his books were known and read. As early as 1924 he was publishing poetry and prose in little magazines in Germany, France, and the United States. On October 1, 1927, he wrote from Paris to his American editor, Maxwell Perkins, to say with a mixture of pride and astonishment that he then had "2 British, 1 Danish, 1 Swedish, 1 French, and 1 German publisher." Less than eighteen months after the first serious novel, his reputation was already international.

During the next twenty-five years, the early stream of translations swelled to a river. By 1930, Norwegians were reading *Og Solen Gar Sin Gang* and *Farvel Til Vabnene*. Germans that year could buy *Fiesta*—as *The Sun Also Rises* was called both there and in England—as well as *In Einem Andern Land,* which was the German title for *A Farewell to Arms* by ironic courtesy of Marlowe's *Jew of Malta.* In the bookstalls along the Seine a year later Parisians discovered a fresh translation of *L'Adieu aux Armes.* By the time another world war had come and gone, the name and the works were nearly everywhere: *In Unserer Zeit, Tambien el Sol se Levanta, Morte nel Pomeriggio, Les Vertes Collines d'Afrique, Der Schnee vom Kilimandscharo, Tener y No Tener, Per Chi Suona La Campana, Über den Fluss und in die Wälder, El Viejo y el Mar.* "For we have been there in the books and out of the books," wrote Hemingway at thirty-six, "and where we go, if we are any good, there you can go as we have been."

1

He had started going young. "I can remember," wrote the doctor's son from Oak Park, Illinois,

the first motor car in town and how our old pacer, Star Bright, would try (abetted by me) to not let the motor car pass him. My father, being a doctor, needed fast horses for emergencies and this pacer had been a hell of a good horse until my father bought him because he got the heaves and couldn't race.

The boy in the buggy had no such difficulty. At eighteen he was busily scribbling reporter's notes in the police courts and hospital wards of Kansas City. At nineteen, with one leg nearly destroyed by Austrian shrapnel, he was carried from a blown-up dugout near Fossalta on the Italian front to spend a long summer and autumn recuperating in the American Hospital at Milan. When he was twenty and twenty-one, he turned back, more seriously this time, to the hard trade of writing in Petoskey, Chicago, and Toronto. At twenty-two he was watching tuna fishermen off Vigo, Spain, exploring the tourist resorts of Switzerland, and discovering for the first time that colony of American expatriates which had already sprung up in the Montparnasse section of Paris.

In Thrace and Anatolia during his twenty-third year he gazed curiously at the dead men "wearing white ballet skirts and upturned shoes with pompons on them" while the Turkish armies swept the ill-equipped Greek soldiery before their charge. In steady rain which had swollen the yellow rivers to the brim, he watched the evacuation of Adrianople while steaming beasts of burden, including an occasional camel, hauled the carts of refugees through the mud of the Karagatch Road. By the age of twenty-four he had interviewed Clemenceau, Mussolini, and Lloyd George, discovered that Spanish bullfighting was more tragedy than sport, fished for trout in Swiss, French, and Italian rivers, and learned the joys of Alpine skiing. His prose and poetry had begun to appear in the *avant-garde* journals; he had assisted Ford Madox Ford in editing one of them; and "the lad with the supple look like a sleepy panther" was beginning to be heard of. His first book, *Three Stories and Ten Poems,* showed that he was already capable of making literature from subjects as diverse as steeplechasing in Auteuil, love-making on a dock in Northern Michigan, and trout-fishing out of season in Cortina d'Ampezzo. So at twenty-four he had launched a career in writing whose world-wide dimensions were still to be measured.

"Where we go . . . there you can go." With a boyish and

romantic enthusiasm he covered the face of Europe. "You can imagine," he later wrote,

the fun it was to go to the Vorarlberg where there was not one single café character but only the villagers, and [to] have all those books—Stendhal, Flaubert, and de Maupassant—to read all winter. We would go to ski at Thanksgiving and not come back until Easter. I worked wonderfully there and it was a fine healthy life.

A typical letter of that exuberant time is dated from the Hotel Taube at Schruns, February 2, 1925.

Have had some swell skiing today [he wrote]. Feel tired. . . . Wish you were here and we could uncork a bottle. You'd have to bring it tho from Paris. No good hootch in Mittel Europa. But great beer—38 different kinds—swell beer from here to Budapest, then it gets bum again until you hit Constantinople. The Boche were there so long that they instituted real German suds factories—the real Bavarian kind. From here we can ski into Bavaria and back without a visa. . . .

Soon, he went on, he was planning to ski over into Italy, sending his baggage ahead by train and working his way down through the Dolomites. It was necessary for him "to see some guys in Milan and Rapallo," although the rising tide of fascism was an unpleasant prospect. "By gad," he wrote, "Mussolini is running a disgraceful business. Lead pipe government and everybody that squeals gets bumped off." He knew Milan well from seven years before. Later he would recall the game dangling from hooks outside the Milanese butcher shops. "Snow powdered in the fur of the foxes and the wind blew their tails. The deer hung stiff and heavy and empty, and small birds blew in the wind and the wind turned their feathers." He would remember Rapallo in the rains of the spring, with the dripping palm trees and the bright stucco walls of the seaside hotels darkening in the wet, and the cat that crouched to keep dry under one of the glistening green tables in the garden situated on the seaward side.

"I had loved country all my life," he would write ten years later, thinking back to a Christmas Day in his beloved Schruns, with the snow blinding in the winter sun, "smooth to see as cake frosting" as it stretched out on either side of the "sleigh-smoothed urine-yellowed road along the river." Going to Bludenz to buy presents, he remembered taking the steep drop onto the icy road behind the inn, knocking the bindings loose, "kicking the skis free and leaning them up against the wooden wall of the inn, the lamplight coming from the window where, inside, in the smoky, new-wine smelling warmth, they were playing the accordion."

His long memories of France would include the Rhone Valley in spring, "with the moonlight on the fields of narcissus" and the chestnut trees in conical bloom "like waxen candelabras." Another chestnut tree spread its branches over the roof of the upstairs pavilion at 113, rue de Notre Dame des Champs while the buzz saw whined in the mill nearby and the mad woman complained in the rooms downstairs. He would remember walks in that neighborhood between the bouts of writing: up the hill to Observatory Square where the fountain water rippled thinly down the green bronze of the sculptured horses, or taking the pleasant stroll into the entrance to the Luxembourg Gardens where children frolicked with miniature sailboats in the pools. There the bust of Flaubert, "heavy now in stone as an idol should be," gazed pensively from its pedestal among the embowering leaves or the bare branches, and the flower vendors outside the park gates spilled their purple dyes along the pavement. He would recall bicycling over the velvet-feeling asphalt of that "street that ran up toward the Pantheon . . . with the high narrow houses and the cheap tall hotel where Paul Verlaine had died." Or sitting in the room on the top floor of another cheap tall hotel, rented for sixty francs a month as a writing studio, where by the window he could glance up from his battered and machine-gun-sounding Corona to "see the roofs and chimney pots and all the hills of Paris."

Although he protested to Maxwell Perkins in 1926 that "in several ways I have been long enough in Europe," he continued to find it an excellent place to write, both in and about. Most of the miniatures in the Paris edition of *in our time,* like many of the short stories in the American edition of the following year, had been set down in various parts of Europe. In November of 1925 he turned out in a week's time his satirical *jeu d'esprit* on Sherwood Anderson, *The Torrents of Spring,* borrowing the title from Turgenev, one of the writers he had read in Sylvia Beach's Shakespeare and Company bookshop in Paris. It was, he later said, "the place I loved the best. It was out of there I read Tolstoi and Turgenev and Gogol. Chekhov and Dostoevski."

The Sun Also Rises was done in no fewer than four countries. The preparation of the first draft took forty-eight days, beginning in Valencia and ending in Paris; the revision, which was extensive, was accomplished in Austria and New York. He regularly found that he worked well in Spain. There was even a day in May, 1926, when snow had compelled cancellation of the bullfights in Madrid, during which he managed to complete three short stories between morning and evening. When they appeared, along with eleven others, in the *Men Without Women* collection in the fall of 1927, Hemingway was still in Europe, once again hard at work on a new novel.

The magnetic hold of the Continent was still apparent even after 1928, when Hemingway had established residence in Key West, Florida, and was beginning to frequent the happy hunting grounds of Wyoming. It was in Paris that March that he began to write *A Farewell to Arms,* and though much of the book was composed in Arkansas, Missouri, and Wyoming, it was back in Paris that he completed the final draft in the spring of 1929. That summer and again in 1931 he spent much time and labor in Spain, gathering materials and pictures for *Death in the Afternoon.* Nearly half the stories in *Winner Take Nothing,* his next book, were European in origin and scene, and the book had been out in New York for less than three weeks when Hemingway was once more back in Paris, dining on pheasant and venison with James and Nora Joyce the night before he sailed from Marseilles on the way to fresh pastures farther south.

A few months later he would be eating lunch beside the Sea of Galilee and watching the grebes swimming and diving offshore. But this was less important to him than the fact that in the meantime he had added a new continent to his widening world—or at least as much of it as could be discovered at Mombasa and Nairobi in Kenya, and the plain and hill territory of Tanganyika. From the mountains of Wyoming in 1930 he had written Maxwell Perkins that he was dreaming of a trip to Africa. Now he actualized the long dream on safari across the Serengetti Plain and into the highlands south of Ngorongoro Crater and the Rift Escarpment. He found that he loved the country and felt at home in it. Some of the prospects from the high places reminded him of the American West, others suggested New England, and still others looked oddly like parts of Galicia and Aragon. Nothing he had previously read in the travel literature gave any idea, he said, of what Africa was really like or of how much game could still be found there. Although the book he wrote about the safari is scarcely comparable as a work of art with such novels as *A Farewell to Arms* and *For Whom the Bell Tolls,* nevertheless it is a superb piece of construction and observation which wonderfully communicates the sense of how it was to hunt big game in Africa in the winter of 1933-

1934, and for a number of years after that. As he had done with *The Sun Also Rises,* and as he would do with *The Bell,* Hemingway deliberately set about composing *Green Hills of Africa* while his memory of those hills was still green.

In Africa he had dreamed of Aragon and Navarre. The Civil War which began in 1936 drew him back once more to Spain, the country he had called in 1926 "much the best . . . left in Europe." Between the two Februaries of 1937 and 1939 he made four extended journeys into the brave but hapless nation which had begun to serve the foreign dictators as a proving ground for untried warplanes and weapons in preparation for their forthcoming effort in the Second World War. Chiefly in his ancient haunts around Madrid but also often in the field, Hemingway lived and wrote during the greater part of the struggle. Out of these experiences came a play and a novel of which he has said, "I think *The Fifth Column* is probably the most unsatisfactory thing I ever wrote. . . . It was an attempt to write under what you could honestly call impossible writing conditions. After it, and after we were beaten in Spain, I came home and cooled out and disciplined myself and wrote *For Whom the Bell Tolls.*" This last, which in the long run is likely to seem his fictional masterpiece of the middle years, was completed in eighteen months after his return to Cuba.

Although his trip to Hong Kong in the spring of 1941 was neither lengthy nor productive of any piece of genuine literature, it added the Far East to his tally of regions and gave him an opportunity to observe yet another war at first hand. Before the year was out, the Japanese attack on Pearl Harbor would bring him one further chance to be an eyewitness of *los desastres de la guerra.* His thick volume of 1942, *Men at War,* was an editorial interlude. He was barely established in his new home at Finca Vigia, San Francisco de Paula, outside Havana, Cuba, when he entered on thirty-six months of wartime activity, first in the Caribbean aboard an armed, submarine-hunting launch, then as air observer over his erstwhile European stamping grounds, and in the final year of the war as correspondent with the invading Allied armies in France and Germany. Although he was ostensibly a noncombatant, he could not escape involvement of a kind in the small fights which took place between Rambouillet and Paris. He taught his friends among the *maquis* a fighting song which derived from his own life in Paris twenty-odd years earlier. It was one he had made his son John commit to memory as a child so that he could find his way home again:

Dix bis Avenue des Gobelins,
Dix BIS Avenue des GOBELINS,
DIX BIS AVENUE DES GOBELINS,
THAT'S WHERE MY BUMBY LIVES.

Although the *maquis* did not know its source, they accepted it happily as they moved in on occupied Paris. There, fittingly enough, Hemingway assisted in the liberation of the Travellers' Club, considered doing the same for the Guaranty Trust Company of New York at 4, place de la Concorde, from which they were deterred both by its sturdy doors and by the concentration of German fire from the Ministry of Marine just across the rue Royale, and then went by way of the place de la Concorde through the Tuileries to the place Vendôme where, as Hemingway jocularly said, they "liberated" the Ritz Hotel. Before the German snipers had been silenced he crossed the river to see his old friend Sylvia Beach at her Shakespeare and Company bookshop. But the war was not over for him. In the months that followed he accompanied the American forces as far eastward as Hürtgenwald and the Rhine.

II

"Some men," wrote an old friend of Hemingway's, "are just natural expatriates, belonging everywhere or nowhere; the citizens of that other *Tir na n'Og,* the Land of 'God Knows Where'. That may be the reason for the quality of youth" in him. When Hemingway returned to Paris in 1944, he bore very little resemblance physically to the lithe and pantherlike young man who had formerly inhabited the pavilion in the rue de Notre Dame des Champs or the apartment at 10 bis avenue des Gobelins. With the bush-bearded and well-grizzled countenance, and the heft of an aging athlete, he seemed outwardly more like a bear than a panther. At forty-five the wheel of time was coming full circle on one phase of his expatriate life, as it would do again in Venice when he was fifty, and yet again in Stockholm (though he was not personally present) in his fifty-fifth year. The man who had served as the young ambulance driver on the Piave, the young war casualty in Milan, the young journalist in Thrace and Anatolia, the young *aficionado* in Pamplona and Madrid, the young winter-sportsman in the Austrian Vorarlberg, and the young expatriate writer in Paris, was now beginning to double back upon his earlier life, for all the world as if he were writing a personal sequel to Dumas's story of d'Artagnan twenty years after.

If he was indeed a citizen of *Tir na n'Og,* it was becoming clear that he did not propose to renounce the fixed habits and the unfixed residences of the 1920s and the 1930s. Of course it was true that much of what he had earlier known and loved was changed and gone. Although he had had too much experience to expect it to be otherwise, he was often rueful over places he had liked and lost— or seen wrested from him by what we sometimes refer to as progress. "When my father built his house in Oak Park," he once wrote,

there was nothing but the North Prairie that ran all the way to the Des Plaines River. Now it is residential developments, cheap subdivisions, filling stations. So when Ford Madox Ford went to visit the scene of the crime he formed the impression that I was brought up in cheap subdivisions and weaned in a filling station.

Even the farm "where we could go out any afternoon with a shotgun for wild guineas, lots of quail, and snipe in the bogs along the creek" had long ago succumbed to the rapacity of the real-estaters. "The first year we went back to Italy," he said,

I wouldn't go to Milano because I wanted to remember how it was. Finally I had to go through it and it was really ruined. Not from bombing: from cupidity. In Valencia they built big apartment buildings in the park that was the heart and breathing space of the city. . . . This isn't complaint. It is just comment. But where the hell does a man go now? I guess it is best to just take it a day at a time. The sea is still O.K. And the unpopular mountains. The name-mountains are overrun.

Perhaps, indeed, he *was* taking it a day at a time as he began once more to move through a temporarily warless Europe in the period after 1945. Because of his alliance with the Popular Front in Spain in the late 1930s, he did not return for some years to the country where Franco ruled. But natives of other European countries now began to see again the familiar face with the brown eyes, the bump on the left side of the forehead, the short, wide-flanged, pugnacious nose, and the gradually whitening hair. Sometimes the bearded mouth would be lit by a wide smile reminiscent of Teddy Roosevelt in the Bull Moose campaign; sometimes the eyes peered gravely through steel-rimmed glasses at what their owner might well have called *Tir na n'Og.* He reappeared in Cortina d'Ampezzo, blinking at noon in the glare of snow; or stood erect and burly in a Venetian gondola in one of the reaches of the Grand Canal; or dined, chewing slowly, at a corner table in one of the Right Bank hotels: the citizen of the world enjoying himself between the bouts of writing, spending the foreign royalties on *Las Verdes Colinas de Africa, Addio alle Armi,* or *En Avoir ou Pas.*

"I used to wish," he wrote about this time, that "I lived in the old days before all the books had been written and all the stories told for the first time. In those days it was no disgrace to drink and fight and be a writer, too." If he had long since abandoned this nostalgic dream, he did not choose to leave the old days wholly behind him. "Because of his absolute youthfulness," said one of his oldest and most admiring friends,

he regards old-growing as an utter and complete tragedy, as it is of course, the only true tragedy, [and] he is not going to degrade himself by maturing or anything absurd of that sort. All the same, since he has a sense of costume, he will emphasize his decline in all its hopelessness by sprouting a white beard and generally acting the part of *senex.* We are going to get a lot of this inverted youth from [him] henceforth.

Hemingway's own explanation of the beard was much less romantic. "When you have a slight case of skin cancer from the rays of the sun off the sea," he said, "you grow a beard and quit shaving." But whatever the degree of truth in his friend's jocose analysis, the process of the backward look had begun some time before the adoption of the white beard and the role of fatherly counselor. For years he had enjoyed the odd overlay of the past upon the present, as the flashbacks in *Green Hills of Africa* amply prove. Personal reminiscences somewhat fictionized had appeared also in a few of the italicized portions of "The Snows of Kilimanjaro" and in several stories in the *Winner Take Nothing* volume of 1937. Already, in short, before he was forty, he was beginning to emphasize the changes time inevitably brings and to make fictional capital from the remembrance of things past.

As he approached his fiftieth year he began, like Conrad before him, to employ a fictional method by which the turning wheel of time could not only be harnessed but also made to produce light and power. Postwar revisitations to the scenes of his youth were at least partly responsible for setting the machinery in motion, and among these was the city of Venice, which had long been one of his favorite wheel hubs—a place, as he said, which "I always feel that I have been in all my life and that maybe I came from." To a noninitiate such an idea might well seem silly. For the veteran Hemingway it was "a very strong feeling"—strong enough to en-able him to "go out to Torcello in a fog" even when the Venetian boatman wished to turn back, strong enough so that Torcello seemed as familiar as his "own house, barefooted at night in the dark."

Inverted youth? Perhaps, but the term was slightly off-center. What underlay his writing of *Across the River and into the Trees* in Cortina, Cuba, Paris, and Venice in 1949-1950 could better be described as youth recollected and then placed into dramatic contiguity, almost as in a palimpsest, with advancing age. For when the dying professional soldier Cantwell returns to the scenes of his youth for a few last hours before his personal time-wheel stops turning for good, it soon becomes evident that the confrontation between youth and age is one of the major thematic devices of the novel.

The device reappeared in *The Old Man and the Sea*. Again the superannuated man derived courage and strength from the contemplation of the man he had once been, achieving thereby such a degree of reinvigoration that he was able at least to equal, and probably to surpass, the levels of previous attainments. For years Hemingway had known the story of the heroic old fisherman who conquered a huge marlin only to see it destroyed by sharks. In 1936 he wrote a 200-word summary; in 1939 he mentioned it to his editor as a future writing project. As the story matured in his mind it began to take on the dimensions of a parable: the stoic individual who knowingly pits his powers against overwhelming odds in the attempt to win once more something of what he has won— and lost—so many times before. When he felt at last prepared to undertake the task of narration, the story of Santiago had gone far beyond the fishing anecdote of 1936. "In the period between Jan. 12 and yesterday," he wrote from Cuba on February 17, 1951, "I worked every day but two and completed 25,000 and up words of as good prose as I can write." In the process he made use of something more than twenty years' experience on the sea. "I knew," he said, "about a man in that situation with a fish. I knew what happened in a boat, in a sea, fighting a fish. So I took a man I knew for twenty years and imagined him under those circumstances." What Hemingway's imagination led him to was a fable of struggle, victory, and loss in which the empowering effects of memory were an essential—in many ways *the* essential—element.

Despite his temerity in going "too far out" in pursuit of his enormous quarry, Santiago staves off defeat through his recurrent memory of the boy Manolo, who comes to stand in his mind, by a not impenetrable mystique, as a living image of his own former youth and strength. Through the course of his agony the image sustains him, setting a moral standard of power and endurance which he strives to reach and in striving attains. It is one of the uses of the past that the memory of our own previous performances, as well as those of others, may help us to emulate or even to surpass them in the continuing tests which the present thrusts upon us.

As if Hemingway were subconsciously setting out in pursuit of pastness to see what light it could be made to throw upon the present, other revisitations ensued in the period after the completion of *The Old Man and the Sea*. Nearly thirty years after the events recorded in *The Sun Also Rises* he returned to Spain in the summer of 1953 and "put in the usual rough seven days" at the Pamplona fiesta. The homecoming contained certain elements of anticlimax, the weather being bad, the performances poor, and the former air of romance at least somewhat dissipated. The trip to Africa that winter followed by exactly twenty years the experiences recorded in the *Green Hills*. Once more he sought the delights which had so much moved him at an earlier epoch, landing at Mombasa and going inland to the region around Kilimanjaro and the Rift Escarpment. Once more the homecoming was marred. Two airplane accidents late in January hurt him severely and spoiled the fun before it was properly over. Newspapers throughout the world carried premature stories of his decease, but he shortly emerged from the bush to set down a record of the journey and its nearly fatal climax in three articles for *Look* magazine. "Where the hell does a man go now?" he had ruefully asked in 1951, recalling the incursions of cupidity in such places as Milan and Valencia where he had once felt at home. By 1953 he had accumulated further evidence that one couldn't go home again. Yet he remained singularly undaunted. In the return to Africa, as in the previous returns to Venice and Pamplona, he might well have been echoing the view of Thomas Mann, that "to be poised against fatality, to meet adverse conditions gracefully, is more than simple endurance; it is an act of aggression, a positive triumph."

Yet another confrontation of youth and age still lay ahead. The brightest event of the otherwise disappointing summer of 1953 was Hemingway's first meeting with a young matador named Antonio Ordoñez, a son of Niño de la Palma, called Cayetano, of whom he had painted a memorable portrait as the young bullfighter hero, Pedro Romero, in *The Sun Also Rises*. Successive visits to Spain in 1954, 1956, 1959, and 1960 deepened Hemingway's paternal friendship with the young Ordoñez, and led to his writing of "The Dangerous Summer" (excerpted in *Life* magazine in the fall of 1960). It was partly a second-generation sequel to *Death in the Afternoon,* and mainly an account of the intense rivalry between Ordoñez and Luis Miguel Dominguin, another matador of great prowess, during the summer of 1959. It is at least a possible surmise that Ordoñez—this dark young Spanish athlete, lithe as a panther, brave as a lion, a genuine champion in his profession— had come to stand in Hemingway's mind *in loco filii,* assuming a functional role in the imaginative search for things past which had been for years one of the demonstrable preoccupations of the old-growing citizen of *Tir na n'Og.*

III

Although no year has passed without praise of his work from one quarter or another, the critical disparagement of Hemingway began while he was still in his twenties and has continued sporadically ever since. A typical early objection centered on the short stories which made up *Men Without Women* (1927). It held that the young writer's interests were low in level and narrow in scope. One reviewer spoke of his "fascinated fixation" with such social dregs as "bullfighters, bruisers, touts, gunmen, professional soldiers, prostitutes, hard drinkers, [and] dope fiends." Another deplored his continuing preoccupation with "sordid little catastrophes in the lives of very vulgar people."

This accusation of parochialism, if not in geographical setting then in choice of subject, is itself a parochial view of Hemingway's work, even that much of it which had appeared by 1927. Yet it is common enough to merit some examination. The record shows that, after "Fifty Grand," he wrote no formal fiction about prize fighters, and after "My Old Man" nothing of any significance about horse racing. Skiing is incidental in two or three stories, dope-taking appears in one, and prostitutes, though they come in occasionally elsewhere, are central characters only in that comic tour de force, "The Light of the World." Murder by hoodlums is the subject of "The Killers" and provides a prominent motif in *To Have and Have Not.* In short, despite the continuing bibulousness of some of his people, it is fair to say that Hemingway's "fascinated fixation" on "very vulgar people" has not continued, however important it may once have seemed to the reviewers.

Four subjects which have always fascinated Hemingway are fishing, hunting, bullfighting, and war, all of which show certain international aspects, and in all of which the qualities of courage and perseverance, grace under pressure and respect for moral codes of behavior, physical athleticism and mental control are naturally of great importance. War puts in an early appearance among the miniatures and short stories of both the Paris and the New York editions of *in our time*. It is at once a horror and a perennial challenge to the characters of *A Farewell to Arms, The Fifth Column, For Whom the Bell Tolls,* and *Across the River,* to say nothing of some dozen later short stories and the observations on the natural history of the dead in *Death in the Afternoon.* Since Hemingway was concerned as observer or participant in five separate wars between 1917 and 1945, the "fixation" is scarcely surprising. Nor has he surrendered, despite a twenty-year hiatus, his interest in the bullfight. Beginning with some early miniatures on such matadors as Maera and Villalta, and the memorable account of Garcia in "The Undefeated," he used the subject in three further short stories. It likewise elicited the climactic passages of *The Sun Also Rises;* occasioned the weighty handbook, *Death in the Afternoon;* infiltrated some parts of *For Whom the Bell Tolls;* and reappeared, after a long lapse of time, in "The Dangerous Summer." The lapse was partly necessitated by his leftist political sympathies during the Spanish Civil War, which led to a long absence from Spain. During the interregnum, Hemingway has explained, he grew away from "spectator sports," lost much of his "old feeling for the bullfight," and even "resolved never to have a bullfighter for a friend again" because he suffered too much vicariously when they succumbed to fear, to gorings, or to death. At least some of the old feeling clearly returned, for reasons already outlined, during the summer of 1959.

His lifelong avocation of fishing has resulted in such triumphant stories as "Big Two-Hearted River," the Burguete episode of *The Sun Also Rises,* and *The Old Man and the Sea,* to name only the best. The love of hunting is reflected in several early short stories, reaches a crescendo in the kudu chase of the *Green Hills of Africa* and "The Short Happy Life of Francis Macomber," and fades to a diminuendo in the duck-shooting passages of *Across the River.* As Edmund Wilson long ago suggested, it is still true that "from the point of view of life as a sport, all that seems most painful in it is somehow very closely bound up with what [Hemingway] finds to be most enjoyable." Yet it ought to be added that "life as a sport" is neither Hemingway's only point of view nor even, all writings considered, his central one.

Another persistent accusation in Hemingway criticism is that of anti-intellectualism. Fostered by Wyndham Lewis and Aldous Huxley in England, and echoed by Max Eastman and others in America, this opinion appeared early and is still audible. It is partly the result of Hemingway's persistent refusal to employ literary or historical allusions as a modus operandi in getting his stories told. One finds, of course, a few exceptions, like the reference to Circe in *The Sun;* the mention of Mantegna in *A Farewell;* the discussions of writers and artists in *Death in the Afternoon* and the *Green Hills;* or Cantwell's discourses on Venetian history and Italian painting in *Across the River*. In general, however, the learned reference is exceptional. To the extent that its absence betokens anti-intellectuality, adverse critics can continue to make a case.

Yet the case must always consider certain elements of Hemingway's esthetic position. One of these, formulated specifically as a reply to the animadversions of Huxley, says that

If the people the writer is making talk of old masters; of music; of modern painting; of letters; or of science then they should talk of those subjects in the novel. If they do not talk of those subjects and the writer makes them talk of them he is a faker. . . . A writer who appreciates the seriousness of writing so little that he is anxious to make people see he is formally educated, cultured, or well-bred, is merely a popinjay.

Another point is Hemingway's assertion that "every so many years the intellectuals lose contact with both the world and the language." To one who insists upon keeping in constant touch with both the world as it is and the language as it is spoken, any abstractionist tendency among the "intellectuals" is obviously something to resist. His resistance to it enabled the Italian critic Emilio Cecchi to observe of his writing that it gives us "the illusion of his having hit upon a literature which has nothing to do with literature, which is not spoiled and weakened by literature." It is precisely this illusion that Hemingway's esthetic is designed to promote.

Associated with the opinion that he is anti-intellectual is the persistent view that Hemingway's primary allegiance, both as writer and thinker, is to the naturalistic mode of expression and belief. Once again the idea originated early and for years gained acceptance as the central fact about his place in modern literature.

His obvious interest in seeing objects as they are in themselves, together with his often-reiterated assertion that a writer's job is to tell the truth, helped to perpetuate the view and led critics to the observation that his was an art of "surfaces and anecdotes." Those who had found that his work lacked breadth could now add that it was also deficient in depth, leaving it, dimensionally speaking, with nothing but its growing length to recommend it.

Two pioneers in the critical art of depth perception in the work of Hemingway were Malcolm Cowley and Edmund Wilson. By examining such stories as "Big Two-Hearted River" and "Alpine Idyll" these critics were able to discern the operation of an emotional-moral dimension whose existence had not hitherto been seriously suspected. At any prior time, of course, the author could have conducted what he humorously spoke of to George Plimpton as "guided tours through the more difficult country of his work." But he had consistently held that it was "not the writer's province to explain" the effects he had achieved or attempted. Once when the present editor asked him to comment on the synoptic use of a bullfight metaphor in the massacre-sequence of *For Whom the Bell Tolls,* Hemingway replied: "I try to do these things. But it is not for me to point them out."

To borrow a phrase from Keats, the symbolic in Hemingway's writings must come as naturally as the leaves to a tree or it had better not come at all. He seems early to have rejected the arbitrary importation of symbols which are not strictly germane to the action in hand, thus agreeing with Coleridge's assertion—though in a way different from what Coleridge meant—that the symbol "always partakes of the reality which it renders intelligible." For this reason he has scornfully denied the allegation by one critic that "the leopard in 'The Snows of Kilimanjaro' is from Dante and the mountain from a letter by Flaubert." Instead of ransacking other arts and literatures for viable symbols, he chose rather to allow the object or scene or person whose function was to be symbolic to gather its meanings through a process of association strictly within the terms of the ongoing narrative.

When asked his views on symbolism in *The Old Man and the Sea,* he replied that "no good book has ever been written that had in it symbols arrived at beforehand and stuck in." What he did not deny was that natural objects or scenes may be made to acquire the unifying power of symbols in the actual process of writing. To make such an achievement even more difficult, this "endowment" must occur in such a way that the artist does not violate the integrity of the symbol in its "actual" or nonsymbolic aspect. This is part of what he had in mind when he said of the story of Santiago: "I tried to make a real old man, a real boy, a real sea and a real fish and real sharks. But if I made them good and true enough they would mean many things."

Having penetrated to this "more difficult country of his work," we are so to speak *in einem andern Land* than that which the naturalistic critics have found in Hemingway. Ethically speaking, it is very far from being that *Tir na n'Og* to which we are led by the naturalistic morality as evidenced, for example, in the work of Theodore Dreiser. What we are likely to find in Hemingway is a complex associational process in which the artist is playing on our psychological responses for a moral end. If he uses his symbolic landscape, as Hemingway does, to convey emotions of repulsion, setting up an atmosphere like the retreat scenes in *A Farewell to Arms* from which we instinctively recoil—an atmosphere colored by loneliness, fear, disgust, frustration, guilt, or pain—it immediately affects the reader with a reaction of rejection which is essentially moral in nature. If, on the other hand, he uses the symbolic landscape to convey emotions of pleasure, or freedom, or the right love of woman—and in the absence or virtual absence of the various modes of disquiet—he can evoke from us not only a pleasurable response but also a vicarious embracement of those values which he has introduced into our imaginations. Once again, this response is in its essence a moral one.

Turning now to the question of Hemingway's religious belief, we may be reminded of the late Professor Moloney's argument that he does not in fact ever achieve "the third dimension"—if by the term one would signify the break-through, however momentary, into the realm of spirit. A subliminal or conscious skepticism, it is suggested, has persuaded him not to make, even fictionally, a truly religious affirmation. The most that can be maintained in the face of this view is that Hemingway's people—Barnes, Henry, Jordan, Anselmo, Santiago, and even Cantwell—speculate with some frequency on supernal matters. They often act, too, as if they believed that some higher power—whether it is the malignantly pluralistic *They* of *A Farewell* or the beneficently monistic *It* which sustains from within the sea-universe of Santiago—does indeed actually concern itself, however enigmatically, with human experience.

One cannot predict how, on balance, this question will be resolved once Hemingway's total work is before us. A good interim summation, written by an Italian Catholic, is that of Marcello Camilucci, contributed to *L'Osservatore Romano* in January, 1953. Santiago and the sea on which he works are, says Camilucci, "two terms emblematic of the history of the world." First there is *Man*, "who has lived long, learned much, but is substantially disarmed before the mystery if he attempts to dominate instead of worshiping it, asking to be received by it." Second, there is *Nature*, "which, though ransacked through all its laws and forms, delivers itself only to those who make of it a path to that love from which springs everything which makes the life of creatures beautiful and precious." Hemingway's engagement of these two emblematic terms gives his novel the quality of a fable. It carries "the profound weight of wisdom, a little secret and hard to grasp, exactly as in the fables which come to us down the broad river of time, like stones worn smooth by the flow of centuries, yet in whose veins fire exists and which gleam at night, like stars, along the banks of streams."

A survey of the now voluminous criticism shows what might have been expected: that Hemingway has had, and still has, admirers and detractors in every country where his works are read, not excluding the Italy of Signor Camilucci where he had, in his nineteenth year, a first experience of European civilization. If by nothing else, his world citizenship would be proved by the very intensity with which his faults and virtues have been critically debated in scores of different languages. More than most American writers of his approximate stature, he has managed to write in such a way that the impact of his work carries easily across national boundaries, irrespective of the idiosyncratic "genius" of the country it enters. The young Berliner who opens *In Einem Andern Land* and reads, "Im Spätsommer jenes Jahres lebten wir in einem Hause in einem Dorfe, das über den Fluss und die Ebene bis zu den Bergen hinübersah," is having almost precisely the same imaginative experience as the old Roman who opens *Addio alle Armi* and reads, "Sul finire dell'estate di quell'anno eravamo in una casa in un villaggio che di là del fiume e della pianura guardava le montagne." And at the end, taking leave of the dead Catherine, the young Neapolitan who reads "Fu come salutare una statua" knows exactly the same response as the aged Hannoverian who reads "Es war, als ob man einer Statue Lebewohl sagt." Some such notion was perhaps in the mind of Signor Camilucci when he remarked, apropos of *The Old Man and the Sea,* that the people and events in Hemingway, "while remaining in their time and their space, become universal emblems of the story of man," rising as it were "spontaneously up to the level of symbolism which is all the more suggestive for its not being transformed into an allusive heraldry, but is poured completely into whatever it impregnates as the sea does with a sponge." At his best, this is the nature of Hemingway's achievement, as it is the best of reasons for calling him a citizen of the world.

Carlos Baker

Princeton, New Jersey
October, 1960

GEORGE PLIMPTON

An Interview with Ernest Hemingway

HEMINGWAY: You go to the races?
INTERVIEWER: Yes, occasionally.
HEMINGWAY: Then you read the *Racing Form* . . . there you have the true Art of Fiction.

—Conversation in a Madrid café, May, 1954

Ernest Hemingway writes in the bedroom of his home in the Havana suburb of San Francisco de Paula. He has a special workroom prepared for him in a square tower at the southwest corner of the house, but prefers to work in his bedroom, climbing to the tower room only when "characters" drive him up there.

The bedroom is on the ground floor and connects with the main room of the house. The door between the two is kept ajar by a heavy volume listing and describing "The World's Aircraft Engines." The bedroom is large, sunny, the windows facing east and south letting in the day's light on white walls and a yellow-tinged tile floor.

The room is divided into two alcoves by a pair of chest-high bookcases that stand out into the room at right angles from opposite walls. A large and low double bed dominates one section, oversized slippers and loafers neatly arranged at the foot, the two bedside tables at the head piled seven high with books. In the other alcove stands a massive flattop desk with two chairs at either side, its surface an ordered clutter of papers and mementos. Beyond it, at the far end of the room, is an armoire with a leopard skin draped across the top. The other walls are lined with white-painted bookcases from which books overflow to the floor, and are piled on top amongst old newspapers, bullfight journals, and stacks of letters bound together by rubber bands.

It is on the top of one of these cluttered bookcases—the one against the wall by the east window and three feet or so from his bed—that Hemingway has his "work desk"—a square foot of cramped area hemmed in by books on one side and on the other

19

by a newspaper-covered heap of papers, manuscripts, and pamphlets. There is just enough space left on top of the bookcase for a typewriter, surmounted by a wooden reading board, five or six pencils, and a chunk of copper ore to weight down papers when the wind blows in from the east window.

A working habit he has had from the beginning, Hemingway stands when he writes. He stands in a pair of his oversized loafers on the worn skin of a lesser kudu—the typewriter and the reading board chest-high opposite him.

When Hemingway starts on a project he always begins with a pencil, using the reading board to write on onionskin typewriter paper. He keeps a sheaf of the blank paper on a clipboard to the left of the typewriter, extracting the paper a sheet at a time from under a metal clip which reads "These Must Be Paid." He places the paper slantwise on the reading board, leans against the board with his left arm, steadying the paper with his hand, and fills the paper with handwriting which in the years has become larger, more boyish, with a paucity of punctuation, very few capitals, and often the period marked with an x. The page completed, he clips it face down on another clipboard which he places off to the right of the typewriter.

Hemingway shifts to the typewriter, lifting off the reading board, only when the writing is going fast and well, or when the writing is, for him at least, simple: dialogue, for instance.

He keeps track of his daily progress—"so as not to kid myself" —on a large chart made out of the side of a cardboard packing case and set up against the wall under the nose of a mounted gazelle head. The numbers on the chart showing the daily output of words differ from 450, 575, 462, 1250, to 512, the higher figures on days Hemingway puts in extra work so he won't feel guilty spending the following day fishing on the Gulf Stream.

A man of habit, Hemingway does not use the perfectly suitable desk in the other alcove. Though it allows more space for writing, it too has its miscellany: stacks of letters, a stuffed toy lion of the type sold in Broadway nighteries, a small burlap bag full of carnivore teeth, shotgun shells, a shoehorn, wood carvings of lion, rhino, two zebras, and a warthog—these last set in a neat row across the surface of the desk—and, of course, books. You remember books of the room, piled on the desk, bedside tables, jamming the shelves in indiscriminate order—novels, histories, collections of poetry, drama, essays. A look at their titles shows their variety. On the shelf opposite Hemingway's knees as he stands

up to his "work desk" are Virginia Woolf's *The Common Reader,*
Ben Ames Williams' *House Divided, The Partisan Reader,* Charles
A. Beard's *The Republic,* Tarlé's *Napoleon's Invasion of Russia,*
How Young You Look by one Peggy Wood, Alden Brook's
Shakespeare and the Dyer's Hand, Baldwin's *African Hunting,*
T. S. Eliot's *Collected Poems,* and two books on General Custer's
fall at the battle of the Little Big Horn.

The room, however, for all the disorder sensed at first sight,
indicates on inspection an owner who is basically neat but cannot
bear to throw anything away—especially if sentimental value is
attached. One bookcase top has an odd assortment of mementos:
a giraffe made of wood beads, a little cast-iron turtle, tiny models
of a locomotive, two jeeps and a Venetian gondola, a toy bear
with a key in its back, a monkey carrying a pair of cymbals, a
miniature guitar, and a little tin model of a U.S. Navy biplane (one
wheel missing) resting awry on a circular straw place mat—the
quality of the collection that of the odds and ends which turn up
in a shoebox at the back of a small boy's closet. It is evident,
though, that these tokens have their value, just as three buffalo
horns Hemingway keeps in his bedroom have a value dependent
not on size but because during the acquiring of them things went
badly in the bush which ultimately turned out well. "It cheers me
up to look at them," Hemingway says.

Hemingway may admit superstitions of this sort, but he prefers
not to talk about them, feeling that whatever value they may have
can be talked away. He has much the same attitude about writing.
Many times during the making of this interview he stressed that
the craft of writing should not be tampered with by an excess of
scrutiny—"that though there is one part of writing that is solid
and you do it no harm by talking about it, the other is fragile, and
if you talk about it, the structure cracks and you have nothing."
As a result, though a wonderful raconteur, a man of rich humor,
and possessed of an amazing fund of knowledge on subjects which
interest him, Hemingway finds it difficult to talk about writing—
not because he has few ideas on the subject, but rather that he
feels so strongly that such ideas should remain unexpressed, that
to be asked questions on them "spooks" him (to use one of his
favorite expressions) to the point where he is almost inarticulate.
Many of the replies in this interview he preferred to work out on
his reading board. The occasional waspish tone of the answers is
also part of this strong feeling that writing is a private, lonely
occupation with no need for witnesses until the final work is done.

This dedication to his art may suggest a personality at odds with the rambunctious, carefree, world-wheeling Hemingway-at-play of popular conception. The point is, though, that Hemingway, while obviously enjoying life, brings an equivalent dedication to everything he does—an outlook that is essentially serious, with a horror of the inaccurate, the fraudulent, the deceptive, the half-baked.

Nowhere is the dedication he gives his art more evident than in the yellow-tiled bedroom—where early in the morning Hemingway gets up to stand in absolute concentration in front of his reading board, moving only to shift weight from one foot to another, perspiring heavily when the work is going well, excited as a boy, fretful, miserable when the artistic touch momentarily vanishes—slave of a self-imposed discipline which lasts until about noon when he takes a knotted walking stick and leaves the house for the swimming pool where he takes his daily half-mile swim.

INTERVIEWER: Are these hours during the actual process of writing pleasurable?

HEMINGWAY: Very.

INTERVIEWER: Could you say something of this process? When do you work? Do you keep to a strict schedule?

HEMINGWAY: When I am working on a book or a story I write every morning as soon after first light as possible. There is no one to disturb you and it is cool or cold and you come to your work and warm as you write. You read what you have written and, as you always stop when you know what is going to happen next, you go on from there. You write until you come to a place where you still have your juice and know what will happen next and you stop and try to live through until the next day when you hit it again. You have started at six in the morning, say, and may go on until noon or be through before that. When you stop you are as empty, and at the same time never empty but filling, as when you have made love to someone you love. Nothing can hurt you, nothing can happen, nothing means anything until the next day when you do it again. It is the wait until the next day that is hard to get through.

INTERVIEWER: Can you dismiss from your mind whatever project you're on when you're away from the typewriter?

HEMINGWAY: Of course. But it takes discipline to do it and this discipline is acquired. It has to be.

INTERVIEWER: Do you do any rewriting as you read up to the

place you left off the day before? Or does that come later, when the whole is finished?

HEMINGWAY: I always rewrite each day up to the point where I stopped. When it is all finished, naturally you go over it. You get another chance to correct and rewrite when someone else types it, and you see it clean in type. The last chance is in the proofs. You're grateful for these different chances.

INTERVIEWER: How much rewriting do you do?

HEMINGWAY: It depends. I rewrote the ending to *Farewell to Arms,* the last page of it, thirty-nine times before I was satisfied.

INTERVIEWER: Was there some technical problem there? What was it that had stumped you?

HEMINGWAY: Getting the words right.

INTERVIEWER: Is it the rereading that gets the "juice" up?

HEMINGWAY: Rereading places you at the point where it *has* to go on, knowing it is as good as you can get it up to there. There is always juice somewhere.

INTERVIEWER: But are there times when the inspiration isn't there at all?

HEMINGWAY: Naturally. But if you stopped when you knew what would happen next, you can go on. As long as you can start, you are all right. The juice will come.

INTERVIEWER: Thornton Wilder speaks of mnemonic devices that get the writer going on his day's work. He says you once told him you sharpened twenty pencils.

HEMINGWAY: I don't think I ever owned twenty pencils at one time. Wearing down seven No. 2 pencils is a good day's work.

INTERVIEWER: Where are some of the places you have found most advantageous to work? The Ambos Mundos hotel must have been one, judging from the number of books you did there. Or do surroundings have little effect on the work?

HEMINGWAY: The Ambos Mundos in Havana was a very good place to work in. This *finca* is a splendid place, or was. But I have worked well everywhere. I mean I have been able to work as well as I can under varied circumstances. The telephone and visitors are the work destroyers.

INTERVIEWER: Is emotional stability necessary to write well? You told me once that you could only write well when you were in love. Could you expound on that a bit more?

HEMINGWAY: What a question. But full marks for trying. You can write any time people will leave you alone and not interrupt you. Or rather you can if you will be ruthless enough about it. But the best writing is certainly when you are in love. If it is all the same to you I would rather not expound on that.

INTERVIEWER: How about financial security? Can that be a detriment to good writing?

HEMINGWAY: If it came early enough and you loved life as much as you loved your work it would take much character to resist the temptations. Once writing has become your major vice and greatest pleasure only death can stop it. Financial security then is a great help as it keeps you from worrying. Worry destroys the ability to write. Ill health is bad in the ratio that it produces worry which attacks your subconscious and destroys your reserves.

INTERVIEWER: Can you recall an exact moment when you decided to become a writer?

HEMINGWAY: No, I always wanted to be a writer.

INTERVIEWER: Philip Young in his book on you suggests that the traumatic shock of your severe 1918 mortar wound had a great influence on you as a writer. I remember in Madrid you talked briefly about his thesis, finding little in it, and going on to say that you thought the artist's equipment was not an acquired characteristic, but inherited, in the Mendelian sense.

HEMINGWAY: Evidently in Madrid that year my mind could not be called very sound. The only thing to recommend it would be that I spoke only briefly about Mr. Young's book and his trauma theory of literature. Perhaps the two concussions and a skull fracture of that year had made me irresponsible in my statements. I do remember telling you that I believed imagination could be the result of inherited racial experience. It sounds all right in good jolly post-concussion talk, but I think that is more or less where it belongs. So until the next liberation trauma, let's leave it there. Do you agree? But thanks for leaving out the names of any relatives I might have implicated. The fun of talk is to explore, but much of it and all that is irresponsible should not be written. Once written you have to stand by it. You may have said it to see whether you believed it or not. On the question you raised, the effects of wounds vary greatly. Simple wounds which do not break bone are of little account. They sometimes give confidence. Wounds which do extensive bone and nerve damage are not good for writers, nor anybody else.

INTERVIEWER: What would you consider the best intellectual training for the would-be writer?

HEMINGWAY: Let's say that he should go out and hang himself

because he finds that writing well is impossibly difficult. Then he should be cut down without mercy and forced by his own self to write as well as he can for the rest of his life. At least he will have the story of the hanging to commence with.

INTERVIEWER: How about people who've gone into the academic career? Do you think the large numbers of writers who hold teaching positions have compromised their literary careers?

HEMINGWAY: It depends on what you call compromise. Is the usage that of a woman who has been compromised? Or is it the compromise of the statesman? Or the compromise made with your grocer or your tailor that you will pay a little more but will pay it later? A writer who can both write and teach should be able to do both. Many competent writers have proved it could be done. I could not do it, I know, and I admire those who have been able to. I would think though that the academic life could put a period to outside experience which might possibly limit growth of knowledge of the world. Knowledge, however, demands more responsibility of a writer and makes writing more difficult. Trying to write something of permanent value is a full-time job even though only a few hours a day are spent on the actual writing. A writer can be compared to a well. There are as many kinds of wells as there are writers. The important thing is to have good water in the well and it is better to take a regular amount out than to pump the well dry and wait for it to refill. I see I am getting away from the question, but the question was not very interesting.

INTERVIEWER: Would you suggest newspaper work for the young writer? How helpful was the training you had with the *Kansas City Star*?

HEMINGWAY: On the *Star* you were forced to learn to write a simple declarative sentence. This is useful to anyone. Newspaper work will not harm a young writer and could help him if he gets out of it in time. This is one of the dustiest clichés there is and I apologize for it. But when you ask someone old tired questions you are apt to receive old tired answers.

INTERVIEWER: You once wrote in the *transatlantic review* that the only reason for writing journalism was to be well paid. You said: "And when you destroy the valuable things you have by writing about them, you want to get big money for it." Do you think of writing as a type of self-destruction?

HEMINGWAY: I do not remember ever writing that. But it sounds silly and violent enough for me to have said it to avoid having to bite on the nail and make a sensible statement. I certainly do not think of writing as a type of self-destruction though journalism, after a point has been reached, can be a daily self-destruction for a serious creative writer.

INTERVIEWER: Do you think the intellectual stimulus of the company of other writers is of any value to an author?

HEMINGWAY: Certainly.

INTERVIEWER: In the Paris of the twenties did you have any sense of "group feeling" with other writers and artists?

HEMINGWAY: No. There was no group feeling. We had respect for each other. I respected a lot of painters, some of my own age, others older—Gris, Picasso, Braque, Monet, who was still alive then—and a few writers: Joyce, Ezra, the good of Stein. . . .

INTERVIEWER: When you are writing, do you ever find yourself influenced by what you're reading at the time?

HEMINGWAY: Not since Joyce was writing *Ulysses*. His was not a direct influence. But in those days when words we knew were barred to us, and we had to fight for a single word, the influence of his work was what changed everything, and made it possible for us to break away from the restrictions.

INTERVIEWER: Could you learn anything about writing from the writers? You were telling me yesterday that Joyce, for example, couldn't bear to talk about writing.

HEMINGWAY: In company with people of your own trade you ordinarily speak of other writers' books. The better the writers the less they will speak about what they have written themselves. Joyce was a very great writer and he would only explain what he was doing to jerks. Other writers that he respected were supposed to be able to know what he was doing by reading it.

INTERVIEWER: You seem to have avoided the company of writers in late years. Why?

HEMINGWAY: That is more complicated. The further you go in writing the more alone you are. Most of your best and oldest friends die. Others move away. You do not see them except rarely, but you write and have much the same contact with them as though you were together at the café in the old days. You exchange comic, sometimes cheerfully obscene and irresponsible letters, and it is almost as good as talking. But you are more alone because that is how you must work and the time to work is shorter all the time and if you waste it you feel you have committed a sin for which there is no forgiveness.

INTERVIEWER: What about the influence of some of these people—your contemporaries—on your work? What was Gertrude

Stein's contribution, if any? Or Ezra Pound's? Or Max Perkins'?
HEMINGWAY: I'm sorry but I am no good at these post-mortems.
There are coroners literary and nonliterary provided to deal with
such matters. Miss Stein wrote at some length and with considerable inaccuracy about her influence on my work. It was necessary
for her to do this after she had learned to write dialogue from a
book called *The Sun Also Rises*. I was very fond of her and
thought it was splendid she had learned to write conversation. It
was no new thing to me to learn from everyone I could, living or
dead, and I had no idea it would affect Gertrude so violently. She
already wrote very well in other ways. Ezra was extremely intelligent on the subjects he really knew. Doesn't this sort of talk
bore you? This backyard literary gossip while washing out the
dirty clothes of thirty-five years ago is disgusting to me. It would
be different if one had tried to tell the whole truth. That would
have some value. Here it is simpler and better to thank Gertrude
for everything I learned from her about the abstract relationship
of words, say how fond I was of her, reaffirm my loyalty to Ezra
as a great poet and a loyal friend, and say that I cared so much
for Max Perkins that I have never been able to accept that he is
dead. He never asked me to change anything I wrote except to
remove certain words which were not then publishable. Blanks
were left, and anyone who knew the words would know what they
were. For me he was not an editor. He was a wise friend and a
wonderful companion. I liked the way he wore his hat and the
strange way his lips moved.

INTERVIEWER: Who would you say are your literary forebears
—those you have learned the most from?

HEMINGWAY: Mark Twain, Flaubert, Stendhal, Bach, Turgenev,
Tolstoi, Dostoevski, Chekhov, Andrew Marvell, John Donne,
Maupassant, the good Kipling, Thoreau, Captain Marryat, Shakespeare, Mozart, Quevedo, Dante, Vergil, Tintoretto, Hieronymus
Bosch, Breughel, Patinier, Goya, Giotto, Cézanne, Van Gogh,
Gauguin, San Juan de la Cruz, Góngora—it would take a day to
remember everyone. Then it would sound as though I were claiming an erudition I did not possess instead of trying to remember
all the people who have been an influence on my life and work.
This isn't an old dull question. It is a very good but a solemn
question and requires an examination of conscience. I put in
painters, or started to, because I learn as much from painters about
how to write as from writers. You ask how this is done? It would
take another day of explaining. I should think what one learns

from composers and from the study of harmony and counterpoint
would be obvious.

INTERVIEWER: Did you ever play a musical instrument?

HEMINGWAY: I used to play cello. My mother kept me out of
school a whole year to study music and counterpoint. She thought
I had ability, but I was absolutely without talent. We played
chamber music—someone came in to play the violin; my sister
played the viola, and mother the piano. That cello—I played it
worse than anyone on earth. Of course, that year I was out doing
other things too.

INTERVIEWER: Do you reread the authors of your list—Twain,
for instance?

HEMINGWAY: You have to wait two or three years with Twain.
You remember too well. I read some Shakespeare every year,
Lear always. Cheers you up if you read that.

INTERVIEWER: Reading, then, is a constant occupation and
pleasure.

HEMINGWAY: I'm always reading books—as many as there are.
I ration myself on them so that I'll always be in supply.

INTERVIEWER: Do you ever read manuscripts?

HEMINGWAY: You can get into trouble doing that unless you
know the author personally. Some years ago I was sued for pla-
giarism by a man who claimed that I'd lifted *For Whom the Bell
Tolls* from an unpublished screen scenario he'd written. He'd read
this scenario at some Hollywood party. I was there, he said, at
least there was a fellow called "Ernie" there listening to the reading, and that was enough for him to sue for a million dollars. At
the same time he sued the producers of the motion pictures *North-
West Mounted Police* and the *Cisco Kid,* claiming that these, as
well, had been stolen from that same unpublished scenario. We
went to court and, of course, won the case. The man turned out
to be insolvent.

INTERVIEWER: Well, could we go back to that list and take one
of the painters—Hieronymus Bosch, for instance? The nightmare
symbolic quality of his work seems so far removed from your own.

HEMINGWAY: I have the nightmares and know about the ones
other people have. But you do not have to write them down. Anything you can omit that you know you still have in the writing
and its quality will show. When a writer omits things he does not
know, they show like holes in his writing.

INTERVIEWER: Does that mean that a close knowledge of the
works of the people on your list helps fill the "well" you were

speaking of a while back? Or were they consciously a help in developing the techniques of writing?

HEMINGWAY: They were a part of learning to see, to hear, to think, to feel and not feel, and to write. The well is where your "juice" is. Nobody knows what it is made of, least of all yourself. What you know is if you have it, or you have to wait for it to come back.

INTERVIEWER: Would you admit to there being symbolism in your novels?

HEMINGWAY: I suppose there are symbols since critics keep finding them. If you do not mind I dislike talking about them and being questioned about them. It is hard enough to write books and stories without being asked to explain them as well. Also it deprives the explainers of work. If five or six or more good explainers can keep going why should I interfere with them? Read anything I write for the pleasure of reading it. Whatever else you find will be the measure of what you brought to the reading.

INTERVIEWER: Continuing with just one question on this line: One of the advisory staff editors wonders about a parallel he feels he's found in *The Sun Also Rises* between the dramatis personae of the bull ring and the characters of the novel itself. He points out that the first sentence of the book tells us Robert Cohn is a boxer; later, during the *desencajonada,* the bull is described as using his horns like a boxer, hooking and jabbing. And just as the bull is attracted and pacified by the presence of a steer, Robert Cohn defers to Jake who is emasculated precisely as is a steer. He sees Mike as the picador, baiting Cohn repeatedly. The editor's thesis goes on, but he wondered if it was your conscious intention to inform the novel with the tragic structure of the bullfight ritual.

HEMINGWAY: It sounds as though the advisory staff editor was a little bit screwy. Who ever said Jake was "emasculated precisely as is a steer"? Actually he had been wounded in quite a different way and his testicles were intact and not damaged. Thus he was capable of all normal feelings as a *man* but incapable of consummating them. The important distinction is that his wound was physical and not psychological and that he was not emasculated.

INTERVIEWER: These questions which inquire into craftsmanship really are an annoyance.

HEMINGWAY: A sensible question is neither a delight nor an annoyance. I still believe though that it is very bad for a writer to talk about how he writes. He writes to be read by the eye and no explanations nor dissertations should be necessary. You can be sure that there is much more there than will be read at any first reading and having made this it is not the writer's province to explain it or to run guided tours through the more difficult country of his work.

INTERVIEWER: In connection with this, I remember you have also warned that it is dangerous for a writer to talk about a work in progress, that he can "talk it out" so to speak. Why should this be so? I only ask because there are so many writers—Twain, Wilde, Thurber, Steffens, come to mind—who would seem to have polished their material by testing it on listeners.

HEMINGWAY: I cannot believe Twain ever "tested out" *Huckleberry Finn* on listeners. If he did they probably had him cut out good things and put in the bad parts. Wilde was said by people who knew him to have been a better talker than a writer. Steffens talked better than he wrote. Both his writing and his talking were sometimes hard to believe, and I heard many stories change as he grew older. If Thurber can talk as well as he writes he must be one of the greatest and least boring talkers. The man I know who talks best about his own trade and has the pleasantest and most wicked tongue is Juan Belmonte, the matador.

INTERVIEWER: Could you say how much thought-out effort went into the evolvement of your distinctive style?

HEMINGWAY: That is a long-term tiring question and if you spent a couple of days answering it you would be so self-conscious that you could not write. I might say that what amateurs call a style is usually only the unavoidable awkwardnesses in first trying to make something that has not heretofore been made. Almost no new classics resemble other previous classics. At first people can see only the awkwardness. Then they are not so perceptible. When they show so very awkwardly people think these awkwardnesses are the style and many copy them. This is regrettable.

INTERVIEWER: You once wrote me that the simple circumstances under which various pieces of fiction were written could be instructive. Could you apply this to "The Killers"—you said that you had written it, "Ten Indians" and "Today Is Friday" in one day—and perhaps to your first novel *The Sun Also Rises*?

HEMINGWAY: Let's see. *The Sun Also Rises* I started in Valencia on my birthday, July 21st. Hadley, my wife, and I had gone to Valencia early to get good tickets for the *feria* there which started the 24th of July. Everybody my age had written a novel and I was still having a difficult time writing a paragraph. So I started the book on my birthday, wrote all through the *feria,* in bed in the morning, went on to Madrid and wrote there. There was no *feria* there, so we had a room with a table and I wrote in great luxury on the table and around the corner from the hotel in a beer place in the Pasaje Alvarez where it was cool. It finally got too hot to write and we went to Hendaye. There was a small cheap hotel there on the big long lovely beach and I worked very well there and then went up to Paris and finished the first draft in the apartment over the sawmill at 113 rue Notre Dame des Champs six weeks from the day I started it. I showed the first draft to Nathan Asch, the novelist, who then had quite a strong accent and he said "Hem, vaht do you mean saying you wrote a novel? A novel huh. Hem, you are riding a trahvel buch." I was not too discouraged by Nathan and rewrote the book, keeping in the travel (that was the part about the fishing trip and Pamplona) at Schruns in the Vorarlberg at the Hotel Taube.

The stories you mention I wrote in one day in Madrid on May 16 when it snowed out the San Isidro bullfights. First I wrote "The Killers," which I'd tried to write before and failed. Then after lunch I got in bed to keep warm and wrote "Today Is Friday." I had so much juice I thought maybe I was going crazy and I had about six other stories to write. So I got dressed and walked to Fornos, the old bullfighters' café, and drank coffee and then came back and wrote "Ten Indians." This made me very sad and I drank some brandy and went to sleep. I'd forgotten to eat and one of the waiters brought me up some bacalao and a small steak and fried potatoes and a bottle of Valdepeñas.

The woman who ran the pension was always worried that I did not eat enough and she had sent the waiter. I remember sitting up in bed and eating, and drinking the Valdepeñas. The waiter said he would bring up another bottle. He said the señora wanted to know if I was going to write all night. I said no, I thought I would lay off for a while. Why don't you try to write just one more, the waiter asked. I'm only supposed to write one, I said. Nonsense, he said. You could write six. I'll try tomorrow, I said. Try it to-night, he said. What do you think the old woman sent the food up for?

I'm tired, I told him. Nonsense, he said (the word was not non-sense). You tired after three miserable little stories. Translate me one.

Leave me alone, I said. How am I going to write it if you don't leave me alone. So I sat up in bed and drank the Valdepeñas and thought what a hell of a writer I was if the first story was as good as I'd hoped.

INTERVIEWER: How complete in your own mind is the conception of a short story? Does the theme, or the plot, or a character change as you go along?

HEMINGWAY: Sometimes you know the story. Sometimes you make it up as you go along and have no idea how it will come out. Everything changes as it moves. That is what makes the movement which makes the story. Sometimes the movement is so slow it does not seem to be moving. But there is always change and always movement.

INTERVIEWER: Is it the same with the novel, or do you work out the whole plan before you start and adhere to it rigorously?

HEMINGWAY: *For Whom the Bell Tolls* was a problem which I carried on each day. I knew what was going to happen in principle. But I invented what happened each day I wrote.

INTERVIEWER: Were the *Green Hills of Africa, To Have and Have Not,* and *Across the River and into the Trees* all started as short stories and developed into novels? If so, are the two forms so similar that the writer can pass from one to the other without completely revamping his approach?

HEMINGWAY: No, that is not true. The *Green Hills of Africa* is not a novel but was written in an attempt to write an absolutely true book to see whether the shape of a country and the pattern of a month's action could, if truly presented, compete with a work of the imagination. After I had written it I wrote two short stories, "The Snows of Kilimanjaro" and "The Short Happy Life of Francis Macomber." These were stories which I invented from the knowledge and experience acquired on the same long hunting trip one month of which I had tried to write a truthful account of in the *Green Hills. To Have and Have Not* and *Across the River and into the Trees* were both started as short stories.

INTERVIEWER: Do you find it easy to shift from one literary project to another or do you continue through to finish what you start?

HEMINGWAY: The fact that I am interrupting serious work to answer these questions proves that I am so stupid that I should be penalized severely. I will be. Don't worry.

INTERVIEWER: Do you think of yourself in competition with other writers?

HEMINGWAY: Never. I used to try to write better than certain dead writers of whose value I was certain. For a long time now I have tried simply to write the best I can. Sometimes I have good luck and write better than I can.

INTERVIEWER: Do you think a writer's power diminishes as he grows older? In the *Green Hills of Africa* you mention that American writers at a certain age change into Old Mother Hubbards.

HEMINGWAY: I don't know about that. People who know what they are doing should last as long their heads last. In that book you mention, if you look it up, you'll see I was sounding off about American literature with a humorless Austrian character who was forcing me to talk when I wanted to do something else. I wrote an accurate account of the conversation. Not to make deathless pronouncements. A fair per cent of the pronouncements are good enough.

INTERVIEWER: We've not discussed character. Are the characters of your work taken without exception from real life?

HEMINGWAY: Of course they are not. *Some* come from real life. Mostly you invent people from a knowledge and understanding and experience of people.

INTERVIEWER: Could you say something about the process of turning a real-life character into a fictional one?

HEMINGWAY: If I explained how that is sometimes done, it would be a handbook for libel lawyers.

INTERVIEWER: Do you make a distinction—as E. M. Forster does—between "flat" and "round" characters?

HEMINGWAY: If you describe someone, it is flat, as a photograph is, and from my standpoint a failure. If you make him up from what you know, there should be all the dimensions.

INTERVIEWER: Which of your characters do you look back on with particular affection?

HEMINGWAY: That would make too long a list.

INTERVIEWER: Then you enjoy reading over your own books—without feeling there are changes you would like to make?

HEMINGWAY: I read them sometimes to cheer me up when it is hard to write and then I remember that it was always difficult and how nearly impossible it was sometimes.

INTERVIEWER: How do you name your characters?

HEMINGWAY: The best I can.

INTERVIEWER: Do the titles come to you while you're in the process of doing the story?

HEMINGWAY: No. I make a list of titles *after* I've finished the story or the book—sometimes as many as 100. Then I start eliminating them, sometimes all of them.

INTERVIEWER: And you do this even with a story whose title is supplied from the text—"Hills Like White Elephants," for example?

HEMINGWAY: Yes. The title comes afterwards. I met a girl in Prunier where I'd gone to eat oysters before lunch. I knew she'd had an abortion. I went over and we talked, not about that, but on the way home I thought of the story, skipped lunch, and spent that afternoon writing it.

INTERVIEWER: So when you're not writing, you remain constantly the observer, looking for something which can be of use.

HEMINGWAY: Surely. If a writer stops observing he is finished. But he does not have to observe consciously nor think how it will be useful. Perhaps that would be true at the beginning. But later everything he sees goes into the great reserve of things he knows or has seen. If it is any use to know it, I always try to write on the principle of the iceberg. There is seven eighths of it under water for every part that shows. Anything you know you can eliminate and it only strengthens your iceberg. It is the part that doesn't show. If a writer omits something because he does not know it then there is a hole in the story.

The Old Man and the Sea could have been over a thousand pages long and had every character in the village in it and all the processes of how they made their living, were born, educated, bore children, etc. That is done excellently and well by other writers. In writing you are limited by what has already been done satisfactorily. So I have tried to learn to do something else. First I have tried to eliminate everything unnecessary to conveying experience to the reader so that after he or she has read something it will become a part of his or her experience and seem actually to have happened. This is very hard to do and I've worked at it very hard.

Anyway, to skip how it is done, I had unbelievable luck this time and could convey the experience completely and have it be one that no one had ever conveyed. The luck was that I had a good man and a good boy and lately writers have forgotten there still are such things. Then the ocean is worth writing about just as man is. So I was lucky there. I've seen the marlin mate and know about that. So I leave that out. I've seen a school (or pod) of more than fifty sperm whales in that same stretch of water and once harpooned one nearly sixty feet in length and lost him. So I left that out. All the stories I know from the fishing village I leave out. But the knowledge is what makes the under-water part of the iceberg.

INTERVIEWER: Archibald MacLeish has spoken of a method of conveying experience to a reader which he said you developed while covering baseball games back in those *Kansas City Star* days. It was simply that experience is communicated by small details, in-timately preserved, which have the effect of indicating the whole by making the reader conscious of what he had been aware of only subconsciously. . . .

HEMINGWAY: The anecdote is apocryphal. I never wrote base-ball for the *Star*. What Archie was trying to remember was how I was trying to learn in Chicago in around 1920 and was searching for the unnoticed things that made emotions such as the way an outfielder tossed his glove without looking back to where it fell, the squeak of resin on canvas under a fighter's flat-soled gym shoes, the gray color of Jack Blackburn's skin when he had just come out of stir and other things I noted as a painter sketches. You saw Blackburn's strange color and the old razor cuts and the way he spun a man before you knew his history. These were the things which moved you before you knew the story.

INTERVIEWER: Have you ever described any type of situation of which you had no personal knowledge?

HEMINGWAY: That is a strange question. By personal knowl-edge do you mean carnal knowledge? In that case the answer is positive. A writer, if he is any good, does not describe. He invents or *makes* out of knowledge personal and impersonal and some-times he seems to have unexplained knowledge which could come from forgotten racial or family experience. Who teaches the homing pigeon to fly as he does; where does a fighting bull get his bravery, or a hunting dog his nose? This is an elaboration or a condensation on that stuff we were talking in Madrid that time when my head was not to be trusted.

INTERVIEWER: How detached must you be from an experience before you can write about it in fictional terms? The African air crashes, for instance?

HEMINGWAY: It depends on the experience. One part of you sees it with complete detachment from the start. Another part is very involved. I think there is no rule about how soon one should write about it. It would depend on how well adjusted the indi-vidual was and on his or her recuperative powers. Certainly it is valuable to a trained writer to crash in an aircraft which burns. He learns several important things very quickly. Whether they will be of use to him is conditioned by survival. Survival, with honor, that outmoded and all-important word, is as difficult as ever and as all-important to a writer. Those who do not last are always more beloved since no one has to see them in their long, dull, unrelenting, no quarter given and no quarter received, fights that they make to do something as they believe it should be done before they die. Those who die or quit early and easy and with very good reason are preferred because they are understandable and human. Failure and well-disguised cowardice are more human and more beloved.

INTERVIEWER: Could I ask you to what extent you think the writer should concern himself with the sociopolitical problems of his times?

HEMINGWAY: Everyone has his own conscience and there should be no rules about how a conscience should function. All you can be sure about in a political-minded writer is that if his work should last you will have to skip the politics when you read it. Many of the so-called politically enlisted writers change their politics frequently. This is very exciting to them and to their political-literary reviews. Sometimes they even have to rewrite their viewpoints . . . and in a hurry. Perhaps it can be respected as a form of the pursuit of happiness.

INTERVIEWER: Has the political influence of Ezra Pound on the segregationalist Kasper had any effect on your belief that the poet ought to be released from St. Elizabeth's Hospital? [1]

HEMINGWAY: No. None at all. I believe Ezra should be released and allowed to write poetry in Italy on an undertaking by him to abstain from any politics. I would be happy to see Kasper jailed as soon as possible. Great poets are not necessarily girl guides nor scoutmasters nor splendid influences on youth. To name a few: Verlaine, Rimbaud, Shelley, Byron, Baudelaire, Proust, Gide, should not have been confined to prevent them from being aped in their thinking, their manners or their morals by local Kaspers. I am sure that it will take a footnote to this paragraph in ten years to explain who Kasper was.

INTERVIEWER: Would you say, ever, that there is any didactic intention in your work?

---

[1] As this issue went to press a Federal Court in Washington, D.C., dismissed all charges against Pound, clearing the way for his release from St. Elizabeth's. [April 18, 1958—ED.]

HEMINGWAY: Didactic is a word that has been misused and has spoiled. *Death in the Afternoon* is an instructive book.

INTERVIEWER: It has been said that a writer only deals with one or two ideas throughout his work. Would you say your work reflects one or two ideas?

HEMINGWAY: Who said that? It sounds much too simple. The man who said it possibly *had* only one or two ideas.

INTERVIEWER: Well, perhaps it would be better put this way: Graham Greene said in one of these interviews that a ruling passion gives to a shelf of novels the unity of a system. You yourself have said, I believe, that great writing comes out of a sense of injustice. Do you consider it important that a novelist be dominated in this way—by some such compelling sense?

HEMINGWAY: Mr. Greene has a facility for making statements that I do not possess. It would be impossible for me to make generalizations about a shelf of novels or a wisp of snipe or a gaggle of geese. I'll try a generalization though. A writer without a sense of justice and of injustice would be better off editing the year book of a school for exceptional children than writing novels. Another generalization. You see; they are not so difficult when they are sufficiently obvious. The most essential gift for a good writer is a built-in, shockproof, shit detector. This is the writer's radar and all great writers have had it.

INTERVIEWER: Finally, a fundamental question: namely, as a creative writer what do you think is the function of your art? Why a representation of fact, rather than fact itself?

HEMINGWAY: Why be puzzled by that? From things that have happened and from things as they exist and from all things that you know and all those you cannot know, you make something through your invention that is not a representation but a whole new thing truer than anything true and alive, and you make it alive, and if you make it well enough, you give it immortality. That is why you write and for no other reason that you know of. But what about all the reasons that no one knows?

George Plimpton

Ernest Hemingway

Alain used to say: "Our first impulse is to kill." And Simone Weil said: "When you know it is possible to kill without blame or punishment, you kill; or at least you lavish encouraging smiles on those who kill. If by chance you feel a little disgust, you keep quiet about it and soon you stifle it, for fear of appearing to lack manliness." These two quotations, terrible and true, must be offered as epigraphs, at the outset of an article on a body of work completely devoted to violence and death.

Ernest Hemingway is a great writer. Archibald MacLeish wrote of him:

> Veteran out of the wars before he was twenty:
> Famous at twenty-five; thirty a master
> Whittled a style for his time from a walnut stick . . .

He used this hard style, carved in hard wood, to tell hard stories. Bloodied prize fighters, hired killers, disemboweled bullfighters, crippled soldiers, hunters of wild animals, deep-sea fishermen—Hemingway's favorite characters are men who deal in death and accept its risk. Let us try to understand how the events in a man's life formed this style and temperament and gave birth to this obsession.

I

Oak Park, Illinois, is a suburb of Chicago. There, at the end of the last century, Dr. Clarence E. Hemingway practiced medicine. The bearded doctor was highly respected in town, known for his keen eyesight and his great skill at hunting and fishing. His wife, very religious, read the Bible, sang in the church choir, and kept a close, overstrict watch on the spiritual life of her husband whom she did not understand. They had six children. Ernest, the second child, was born on July 21, 1899. Relations between his parents, compatible only on the surface, made his childhood unhappy. His mother nudged him toward music, preferably church music; his father put a fishing rod in his hand at the age of three, and a rifle at ten. Male solidarity soon asserted itself. In one of Hemingway's first short stories,[1] we read:

"Your mother wants you to come and see her," the doctor said. "I want to go with you," Nick said. ". . . I know where there's black squirrels." "All right," said his father. "Let's go there."

Nick Adams is the hero created by Hemingway to depict himself. Nick's youth is wild and free; he spends his summers in Michigan among the Indians, where he sees life in the raw. An Indian girl, with brown legs, flat belly, and hard little breasts, initiates him sexually at a very young age. He witnesses his doctor-father perform a Caesarean operation with a jackknife. He cuts a freshly caught trout into pieces and uses the chunks as bait to catch more trout. His is a savage world of sacrificed animals, such as Victor Hugo knew at his childhood home of Les Feuillantines. And these are years of apprenticeship for a boy who wants to be strong yet has his weaknesses—specifically, an equivocal attitude toward his father. Nick (Hemingway) is grateful to the doctor for the rifle and hunting lessons; but he resents his father's weakness toward his mother and his conventional ideas about "sex." Nick's father "was sentimental, and like most sentimental people, he was both cruel and abused. . . . If he wasn't a coward, he would have stood up to that woman and not let her bully him. . . ." All sentimental people are betrayed. "Nick could not write about him yet, although he would, later."

At school in Oak Park Hemingway showed a fondness for literature and was an editor of the weekly school paper. His schoolmates admired his talent but had no liking for him as a person; they confirmed in him the idea that in life one must be hard, that only the tough-skinned survive. A "loner," he took boxing lessons and fought so strenuously that he had his nose broken and one eye severely injured. Loving neither family nor school, he ran away twice. For several months he led the life of a vagrant, coming face to face with violence and evil "on the road." He worked on farms, washed dishes in restaurants, hopped freights: in short, he tasted of that adventurous kind of life "on

[1] "The Doctor and the Doctor's Wife" in *In Our Time*.

the bum" which seems to shape many a young American writer, in contrast to our youthful French bohemians of the Café des Deux Magots or the Café Flore.

In 1917 the United States entered World War I. Hemingway tried to enlist but was rejected because of his bad eye. For six months he worked as a reporter on the *Kansas City Star,* one of the biggest newspapers in the Middle West. He "covered" local crime news and accidents. Then he found a way to leave for Europe as an ambulance driver with the American Red Cross. Sent to the Italian front, he soon found himself in the midst of bloody battles in which he served with distinction. He was severely wounded and decorated with the Italian *al Valore Militare* medal.

This wound left deep marks on him. He still bears its actual scars along the entire length of one leg. And for a time it scarred his soul as well. He was up in front of the trenches at Fossalta di Piave, when fragments from an Austrian trench mortar hit him. "I died then," he said. Two Italian soldiers with him were killed; a third had his legs blown off. When Hemingway regained consciousness, he carried the legless, screaming Italian on his back toward a first-aid dugout. As he stumbled on, a searchlight spotted him and a machine gun opened fire. He was wounded twice more, in the foot and the knee. When he got back, his Italian was dead and he himself close to death. Twenty-eight steel fragments were taken out of his leg.[2]

For a long time he could not forget that hell. He was in a state of shock. He found it hard to fall asleep and, when he did succeed, he would dream of that exploding trench mortar and awake with a start.

I myself did not want to sleep because I had been living for a long time with the knowledge that if I ever shut my eyes in the dark and let myself go, my soul would go out of my body. I had been that way for a long time, ever since I had been blown up at night and felt it go out of me and go off and then come back. I tried never to think about it, but it had started to go since, in the nights, just at the moment of going off to sleep, and I could only stop it by a very great effort.[3]

For a while he lived in Chicago, where he came to know some good writers—Sherwood Anderson and his friends. He fell in

[2] The actual number of fragments was in excess of one hundred.—ED.
[3] "Now I Lay Me," *The Fifth Column and The First Forty-Nine Stories,* New York: 1938, p. 461.—ED.

love with Hadley Richardson, a young newspaperwoman, married her in September, 1921, and then left with her to cover the Greek-Turkish War.[4] Despite his bad memories—perhaps because of them—battlefields seemed to summon him. There was a morbid attraction to places where there was killing. He saw other terrible things there. After the war he came to Paris, with a letter of introduction from Sherwood Anderson to Gertrude Stein. He could not have picked a better person to learn from.

"At that moment," he has told us,

I was trying to write and I found that my greatest difficulty (apart from that of knowing what you truly felt, rather than what you were supposed to feel, or what you had been taught to feel) was to note what really happened in action, what the actual things were which produced the emotion which you experienced. . . . So I was trying to learn to write, commencing with the simplest things. . . .

Gertrude Stein, a massive monolith of a person who had voluntarily expatriated herself from the United States, was a writer with good sense who understood the virtue of everyday words, the power of repetition, and the rhythm of spoken language. These were all things that Hemingway was trying to master. So a kind of craft intimacy developed between the two experimenters. Hemingway could often be found at Gertrude Stein's house, Number 27, rue de Fleurus, the walls covered by her many Cézannes and Picassos; sometimes she would come to the Place du Tertre and read through the young American's manuscripts. He did not write in clichés; he used the plainest and shortest words. She recognized a style after her own heart.

What was Hemingway trying to say? He wanted to purge himself of violence by expressing it:

"Your psychoanalyst?"
"A portable Corona, No. 3."

Hadley Hemingway had a suitcase filled with her husband's first manuscripts stolen from her. It was a terrible blow. Besides, Hadley was pregnant and wanted to go back to the United States, to give birth to her child on American soil. All was not well with the married couple. Nevertheless, they had a definite program: "Have the baby, then return to Paris, and write a novel." Meanwhile Hemingway wrote short stories. They were hard as nails.

[4] The first Mrs. Hemingway was not a newspaperwoman, nor did she accompany her husband to Thrace.—ED.

One of them, "Fifty Grand," told the story of a prize fighter who, feeling himself washed up, bets against himself and wins. It was a sharp-edged story, all in dialogue. Nothing was said outright; everything was suggested. Reading it, one is reminded of the best of Kipling. Hemingway never speaks of Kipling, and perhaps he never read him. The fact is, a writer rarely talks about the true sources of his inspiration. He mentions those that are the most flattering, or the least obvious. The influential *Atlantic Monthly* accepted "Fifty Grand" for publication. Seasoned readers recognized a new master. This twenty-page short story launched Hemingway on his writing career.

After that, all the magazines asked him for stories. The Hearst newspaper chain offered him a contract. Hemingway refused. He was not opposed to the idea of making money, but that—in his eyes—was not the main thing. Above all, he wanted to remain a *serious* writer, in the Flaubertian sense of the word. "All I want is to write as well as I can." To write well, at his own hours— and so no contract with Hearst. As he put it, integrity in a writer was like virginity in a woman; once lost, it was never recovered. Often during his stay in Paris, he allowed himself only five sous a day for a plate of fried potatoes—so he could write solely in his own way and according to his own ideas.

His reputation began to spread among the expatriates. Gertrude Stein, Ezra Pound, F. Scott Fitzgerald, expected big things from him. James Joyce became his friend. Often the two men went out in the evening to drink together. "Once," according to Hemingway,

Joyce told me he was afraid his writings would become suburban, that maybe it would be better for him to get around a little and see the world. Joyce was afraid of lots of things: of thunder, of lightning, but he was a wonderful man. His wife, who was listening, said: "Yes, a bit of lion-hunting would certainly do James no harm."

But Joyce, nearsighted as a mole, was hardly equipped for lion-hunting. Hemingway, on the other hand, needed hunting as he needed war.

In 1923 Hemingway brought out a little book, *Three Stories and Ten Poems,* published in Dijon by the Contact Publishing Company. Then there appeared, in 1924, *in our time,* in which episodes alternate with short prose poems, all of them evoking dreadful memories, without comment. Naked, blood-covered facts. Here is an example:

They shot the six cabinet ministers at half-past six in the morning against the wall of a hospital. There were pools of water in the court-yard. There were wet dead leaves on the paving of the courtyard. It rained hard. All the shutters of the hospital were nailed shut. One of the ministers was sick with typhoid. Two soldiers carried him down-stairs and out into the rain. They tried to hold him up against the wall but he sat down in a puddle of water. The other five stood very quietly against the wall. Finally the officer told the soldiers it was no good trying to make him stand up. When they fired the first volley he was sitting down in the water with his head on his knees.[5]

Technically, this is excellent writing. The scene is described with cold precision; and its horror stands out all the more against the dull background. Mérimée knew that device—over a century ago. The title *in our time* was undoubtedly ironical. It suggested "Peace in our time, O Lord," from the Common Prayer Book. "Peace in our time, O Lord" . . . when dying men are shot; when crowds insist that bullfighters risk disembowelment; when wounded soldiers groan and bleed in front of trenches; when ropes are coldly slipped around men's necks, in prisons. It was a silent protest against violence; at the same time a masochist's delight in describing that violence; and a liberation from it. I quote again:

"Your psychoanalyst?"
"A portable Corona, No. 3."

The child and the man had seen too much. He belonged to a sick generation, a poisoned generation.

II

In 1927 Hadley left him. He discussed their break, with his usual objectivity, in a curious story, "Homage to Switzerland," in which he pictures himself chatting with three porters in a Swiss railway station, explaining that he is getting a divorce:

"And it is really the first time you've been divorced?" asked the porter.
"Absolutely. . . ."
"And is it very expensive?"
"Ten thousand francs."
"Swiss money?"

[5] *in our time,* Chapter V.

"No, French money."

"Oh, yes. Two thousand francs Swiss. All the same it's not cheap."

"No."

"And why does one do it?"

"One is asked to."

"But why do they ask that?"

"To marry someone else."

Hemingway himself remarried, that same year: his second wife was Pauline Pfeiffer, an attractive editor at *Vogue* magazine. The next year, 1928, he suffered a heavy blow. His father, Clarence Edmonds Hemingway, committed suicide. Why? It is hard to say. "He had much bad luck, and it was not all of it his own. He had died in a trap that he had helped only a little to set." Now the son harbored a new obsession: Had the doctor become frightened? Fear was destined to be one of Hemingway's great themes.

Heretofore his volumes of short stories, though excellent, had been financial failures. With *The Sun Also Rises,* a novel about expatriates in Paris—Americans, Greeks, Englishmen—he joined the best-seller list for the first time. His hero, Jake Barnes, wounded in World War I, moves from bar to bar, from shabby hotel to shabby hotel, from France to Spain, in love yet no longer capable of making love. The woman he loves, Lady Brett Ashley, sleeps with a boxer, then with a matador. Brett and Jake suffer— but without talking about it. Romanticism? Yes, in a sense, but a silent romanticism, drowned in cocktails and champagne.

This long cinemalike sequence of hotel nights, dismal drinking bouts, bartenders, prostitutes, and bedroom scenes achieves a tragic effect. Rarely has any human group been so detached from all society. Everything seems pointless. The sun also rises—and just as futilely. The postwar mood of despair was sufficiently widespread for the book to touch the most vibrant chord in "the lost generation." Americans, Englishmen, and Frenchmen admired the rawness of the style. This was something new. A Hemingway novel was to the traditional novel what functional architecture is to ornate architecture.

A short-story collection (*Men Without Women*) brought these qualities to a high point. A short story such as "The Killers" is literally a masterpiece. As Paul Valéry said: "You can recognize a masterpiece by the fact that nothing in it can be changed." One enters abruptly into the story—there are no lengthy preliminaries à la Balzac. The reader has to imagine the setting and characters. At the beginning he doesn't even know what the latter are talking about. They repeat the same words—over and over again. Little by little the picture emerges from this chaos. What a magnificent story!

Around 1928 Hemingway left Europe and came to live on the ocean front at Key West, Florida. There he acquired a paunch, a beard, and a nickname: "Papa." From his first marriage he had a son John, nicknamed "Bumby." Pauline Pfeiffer gave him two more sons: Patrick, born in 1929, and Gregory, in 1932. Books too were born in those years: in 1929, *A Farewell to Arms*, a novel about his Italian campaign; [in 1932] *Death in the Afternoon*, a long study of bullfighting; and *Green Hills of Africa* [1935], an account of a hunting trip in the heart of Africa. War, bullfighting, hunting: "To kill in order to avoid killing oneself." He had to overcome an inner despair, a disgust with human beings, that went back to his childhood. Yet during that same period Hemingway wrote for *Esquire,* just as the French critic Taine contributed to *La Vie Parisienne.* American critics have reproached him for working on such a "slick-paper" magazine, in which his stories rubbed shoulders with erotic anecdotes and drawings. What of it? He liked eroticism, and the magazine had literary standards. Thomas Mann and André Gide wrote for it.

Nevertheless, everything seems to indicate that in 1936 Hemingway felt dissatisfied with himself. In Africa he had hunted with very rich people (although "they were dull and they drank too much, or they played too much backgammon"). He had drunk much too much himself ("so much that he blunted the edge of his perceptions"). Seven lean years had passed since he had written a good book: *A Farewell to Arms* (and "you made an attitude that you cared nothing for the work you used to do, now that you could no longer do it"). Two marriages had finished badly; he felt that he was being criticized for his association with *Esquire. . . .* "He had destroyed his talent by not using it, by betrayals of himself and what he believed in, by drinking so much . . . by laziness, by sloth, and by snobbery, by pride and prejudice. . . ." And to top it all, the thought of his own death obsessed him. With horror he realized that "it could all end like this—on an idle safari, haggling with a woman." [6] His second wife divorced him in 1940.

In 1936 the Civil War broke out in Spain. In the United States many intellectuals enlisted in the cause of the Spanish Republican government. Hemingway was among them. It was less from po-

---

[6] Quoted in Philip Young, *Ernest Hemingway,* London, 1952, p. 48.

litical conviction than from a desire to sniff the odor of blood again, and to try to believe in something. From this experience came the novel *For Whom the Bell Tolls,* whose hero, Robert Jordan, personifies Hemingway himself—as, previously, was the case with Nick Adams. A hero without political faith and whose sacrifice is gratuitous. Maria, the lovely young Spanish girl, is talking to Jordan:

> "Are you a communist?"
> "No I am an anti-fascist."
> "For a long time?"
> "Since I have understood fascism."

Actually, what were Jordan's political beliefs? "He had none now, he told himself. . . . He fought now in this war because it had started in a country he loved and he believed in the Republic. . . ." As in *A Farewell to Arms,* a love story is grafted onto a wartime adventure—but it is love Hemingway-style, sensual, short-lived, stillborn.

In 1940 at Cheyenne, Wyoming, Hemingway married the writer Martha Gellhorn. Together they took a trip to China, then settled down in Cuba, not far from Havana. In 1942 he offered his yacht *Pilar* to the United States Navy and volunteered to serve as a one-man suicide squadron. He would cruise by himself to attract enemy submarines; then, when one of them stopped him, he would blow up the submarine and himself. It is easy to see why this romantic idea attracted him. The Navy refused, and Hemingway managed to get himself sent to England as a war correspondent. After D-day in June, 1944, he made contact with the French Resistance forces and formed a unit of irregulars of which he was the commanding general—or captain. His exact status was unclear. He was "Papa," and the men under him realized in a vague sort of way that he was someone of importance. His headquarters were at Rambouillet. Loaded down with guns, field-glasses in a sling, a vermouth on one side and a gin on the other, he proved to be an old hand and adept at war. The Resistance fighters respected him; the army tolerated him. Entering Paris by a different road from the one taken by General Leclerc's division, he headed immediately for the Ritz Hotel to liberate it. The symbolism is obvious. At the Place Vendôme he stationed a guard at the hotel entrance with a notice: *Papa took good hotel, Plenty stuff in cellar.* . . . Then he left for Germany with a division of his own choice. He was a curious war correspondent, always way up in front, calling for tanks to protect his flanks, firing in violation of the Geneva and other conventions, at times threatened with court-martial, at times praised for his bravery.

An American artist, John Groth, described him in the Hürtgen forest. "Everybody knew his jeep. Out of the dark woods you could hear hundreds of voices saying, one after another: 'Good morning, Mr. Hemingway.' It was like a royal progress." Most of the soldiers called him "Papa." Groth tells how one evening, near the German lines, he was having dinner with Hemingway and several officers when enemy shells began to rain down on their command post. All the officers put on their helmets and sprawled on the ground. When the candles were lit again, they saw that Hemingway had remained at the table, bareheaded, his back to the German batteries, still eating his dinner all alone. It was the courage of a man who had known fear and overcome it. He had been through the mill: beneath the mask of toughness, the face had become like the mask.

After World War II he stayed at a hotel in Venice, where he hoped to write a book about the war. Interrupted by illness (an eye infection which developed during a hunting trip), he gave up that work to write a shorter novel: *Across the River and into the Trees,* which is the story of a bitter, aging colonel's last love affair, with a young woman of nineteen. The critics, weary of praising, pounced on this book and tore it to shreds. In it Hemingway indulged in some digressions on military strategy, in the course of which he attacked Field Marshal Montgomery—hence the irritation of many British readers. In reality, the critics were unfair; the novel was not unworthy of its author. It is not his best, to be sure, but far superior to the best of other writers.

Meanwhile, Hemingway had married for the fourth time. His new wife was Mary Welsh, a *Time* magazine correspondent. With her he now lives in a house near Havana called *Finca Vigia* (Lookout Farm). He has chosen to live there because he loves Cuba and feels a little more at peace there than elsewhere. He has had a constant stream of visitors—from Hollywood stars to Spanish grandees. Hemingway, looking like a sacred idol with his white beard, his sun-tanned and deeply lined face, gets up at five-thirty in the morning and works. He writes his descriptive passages in pencil, his dialogues on the typewriter. In the afternoon, weather permitting, he fishes with his sailor-navigator. He still believes that the writer must keep in touch with nature by some form of action. If he withdraws from life, his style wastes away.[7] He remains as ardent a fisherman today as when his father put his first fishing rod in his hands.

In 1952 he proved the truth of his idea that the writer *must* keep in touch with life: he wrote *The Old Man and the Sea,* a short narrative that was received with unanimous praise. After *Across the River and into the Trees,* someone had said, wrongly: "Papa is finished." In *The Old Man and the Sea* Papa was never in better form. It is a fine book: fine in its literary craftsmanship, in its knowing treatment of deep-sea fishing, and in its warm humanity. There is vividness and genuineness of feeling in this story of the old Cuban fisherman Santiago, fighting stubbornly and courageously to land the biggest fish in his life, only to see it devoured by the sharks, who leave him nothing but a naked white skeleton of bones. I cannot help feeling that in this there is a symbol, perhaps an unconscious one. The giant marlin is the big novel Hemingway thought he would come up with and which the critics tore to pieces. This personal feeling, this smart of a burning wound, gives *The Old Man and the Sea* its bitter and moving overtones.

After this revenge Hemingway's war against his time was won. This time the old fisherman kept his catch intact. The world applauded when the Nobel Prize for literature was awarded him in 1954. There could not have been a fairer choice. Hemingway has really given literature a new style, the style of our century. At the beginning of that year, for a few hours he was thought dead. While he was hunting in Africa, his plane crashed in the Sudan jungle near the Nile—a region of man-eating animals. Newspapers hastily brought obituary notices out of their morgues. The stories were flattering. But Papa got up a trifle bruised, reached the Nile, and boarded a passing boat. "My luck is still very good," he told a press conference hastily summoned to his camp in the brush. Thus near-tragedy was miraculously transformed into world-wide publicity for the writer.

Hemingway did not go to Stockholm to receive his Nobel Prize. "My wounds, you know." The main reason, however, was that he was busily at work on a big novel. "It was going very well, you know, better than for a long time, when that prize came. . . . And when it goes well, if a writer stops, God knows when it will come back." But he sent to Sweden a message that was read by the United States Ambassador. He apologized for not

[7] See *The Fifth Column and The First Forty-Nine Stories,* New York: 1938, p. vii.—ED.

prose. His is as different from Flaubert's as jazz differs from
Mozart—but all music is music. He praises Stendhal, which
should not surprise us. But his real predecessors are Americans:
Ambrose Bierce, Stephen Crane, and especially Mark Twain.
Hemingway has stated: "All modern American literature comes
from one book by Mark Twain called *Huckleberry Finn*. . . .
It's the best book we've had."

Mark Twain was the first to attempt to give beauty and form
to the everyday language of the ordinary American. To Hemingway, the other great American writers of the past are "colonial"
writers, that is, English writers who happened to have been born
in America. He recognizes Edgar Allan Poe's skill, "but he is
dead." He dislikes the rhetoric in Melville; he cannot read
Thoreau. As for Emerson, Hawthorne, Whittier, and company,
they were "English Colonials . . . who did not know that a new
classic does not bear any resemblance to classics that have preceded it." I question this point of view. Even though a new classic
may not imitate the older ones, it is indebted to them. Hemingway himself is the best proof of that. He absorbed the simplicity
of rhythm, syntax, and vocabulary which constituted Mark
Twain's freshness. But he set his own stamp on these borrowings.

As for his philosophy, I have said above that it owes much to
that of Rudyard Kipling—either accidentally or by genuine affinity. The world which, from their childhood, unfolded to both
men, was not a Sunday-school world. Force and deceit dominated
it. The hero can do nothing about that: the universe is as it is.
Only man, within this world without moral laws, can set up a
code and observe it. A code of honor and courage "which, in a
life of tension and pain makes a man a man and distinguishes
him from the people who follow random impulses, let down their
hair, and are generally messy, perhaps cowardly, without inviolable rules for how to live holding tight." [8]

The inviolable rules are not exactly moral rules; or at least
they are not those of middle-class, puritan morality. A boxer, a
gambler, or a thief can satisfy Hemingway's code, provided that
they live up to their contract, which is not made with society
but with their chosen companions. "There is honor among pick-
pockets and honor among whores. It is simply that the standards
differ."

The capital sin is to yield to fear. One must not be afraid. Fear
comes, most often, from an inability to suspend the functioning

[8] In Philip Young, *op. cit.*, p. 36.

being a public speaker. And he added: "Writing at its best is
lonely life. . . . How simple the writing of literature would H
if it were only necessary to write in another way what has alread
been well written. It is because we have had such great writers
the past that a writer is driven far out past where he can go, o
to where no one can help him. I have talked too long for a writ
A writer must write what he has to say, not speak it. I that
you."

On the day of the ceremony in Stockholm, Hemingway
fishing off Cojimar, the Cuban village which is the setting
The Old Man and the Sea. He was with Gregorio Fuentes,
sailor, in his black and green boat *Pilar,* a forty-two footer
two Chrysler engines. The fish were biting and the sea smile
the old man. A *Time* magazine editor who was with him j
down his remarks. Even if he could, Hemingway would not
to change either his life or his writings. "It's enough for you
it once for a few men to remember you. But if you do *it*
after year, then many people remember you and they tell
their children, and their children and grandchildren rem
and, if it concerns books, they can read them. And if it's
enough, it will last as long as there are human beings." W
the only prize a writer really wants.

III

"He looks like a modern," Gertrude Stein said of hi
smells of the museums." She meant her comment, writt
time when they had quarreled, to be malicious—in reality
an involuntary tribute and mark of high praise. A grea
however modern, is always bound to some tradition. T
taught person, who starts from scratch, rarely gets far.
is no thought which is not about thinkers." There is
which disregards the stylists. Hemingway, although
writer, read much—if only to go beyond what he rea
over, Gertrude Stein herself read and borrowed a great
Hemingway. I am not criticizing; I am simply stating a

Who are Hemingway's teachers? He has said: "Tha
learned to write—by reading the Bible." Not *only* that
the Bible teaches the storyteller the art of simple nar
power of repetition, and poetry. Hemingway says tha
much to Flaubert, and it is easy to see what: the sens
pline, the search for the right word, the need for rhy

of the imagination. Nervous persons are more fearful than those without nerves. There is no crime in that; it is merely a question of human nature. But the code demands that the timid soul must not yield to fear. On this theme Hemingway has written a marvelous short story, "The Short Happy Life of Francis Macomber." The hero is a wealthy American who has gone to Africa with his wife in order to hunt wild animals. Then, when he faces his first lion, he is seized with irresistible panic. Robert Wilson, an Englishman and professional hunter whom he has hired as guide, has developed a polite contempt for Macomber. The latter's wife, Margot, a beautiful woman, is ashamed of her husband. The night after the encounter with the lion she goes into the Englishman's tent and gives herself to him because he is brave. Wilson accepts his good luck without any outward show of surprise: rich people are crazy, and it's all part of the game.

Mad with jealousy as the unfaithful Margot returns to their marital tent, Macomber feels something happen inside himself. The English guide's stolidity, and the strictness of his sportsman's code which says that he must not endanger the lives of the native gun-bearers or make the wild animals suffer, even at the risk of his own life, leave their mark on the American.

Macomber says to Wilson: "You know I don't think I'd ever be afraid of anything again."

And it is true. It is as if his mind has suddenly been cleansed. After all, what can a lion do to you? Kill you. But a man can only die once. Wilson quotes Shakespeare:

" '. . . we owe God a death and let it go which way it will he that dies this year is quit for the next.' "

So, by a mere snap of the trigger, Macomber has become a brave man—and a radiantly happy one.

"You know," he says to his wife, "something did happen to me. I feel absolutely different."

His wife "eyed him strangely." A little later, when her husband bravely stands up to a rampaging buffalo, she fires toward the animal and hits Macomber at the base of his skull. He dies instantly. Was it an accident? No; Margot Macomber, accustomed to dominating, felt that once her husband Francis had become a brave man he would no longer be a compliant husband. So she got rid of him—coldly, with no risk to herself.

To Hemingway, as to Kipling, woman is both an obstacle and a temptation. She respects the strong man, the man of the code,

but she cannot resist the need to dominate the weak man. Captain
Gadsby, in Kipling, became both a good husband and a bad
officer. In Hemingway's play *The Fifth Column*, Philip, who has
come to Spain to fight in the International Brigade and has hero-
ically carried out counterespionage missions, is tempted by
Dorothy, the attractive young American blonde:

Dorothy. Philip, let's go away from here. I don't have to stay
here. . . . We could go to that place near Saint Tropez. . . . Then
afterwards we could go to ski.

Philip [*very bitterly*]. Yes, and afterwards to Egypt and make love
happily in all the hotels, and a thousand breakfasts come up on trays
in the thousand fine mornings of the next three years; or the ninety
of the next three months; or however long it took you to be tired of
me, or me of you. And all we'd do would be amuse ourselves. We'd
stay at the Crillon, or the Ritz, and in the fall when the leaves were
off the trees in the Bois and it was sharp and cold, we'd drive out to
Auteuil steeplechasing, and keep warm by those big coal braziers in
the paddock, and watch them take the water jump and see them coming over the bullfinch and the old stone wall. That's it. And nip into
the bar for a champagne cocktail and afterwards ride back in to
dinner at La Rue's and weekends go to shoot pheasants in the Sologne.
Yes, yes, that's it. And fly out to Nairobi and the old Mathaiga Club,
and in the spring a little spot of salmon fishing. Yes, yes, that's it.
And every night in bed together. Is that it?

Dorothy. Oh, darling, think how it would be! . . .

Philip. You can go if you like. I'll draw you up an itinerary.

Dorothy. But why can't we go together?

Philip. You can go. But I've been to all those places and I've left
them all behind. And where I go now I go alone, or with others who
go there for the same reason I go.

Dorothy. And I can't go there?

Philip. No.

Dorothy. And why can't I go wherever it is? I could learn and I'm
not afraid.

Philip. One reason is I don't know where it is. And another is I
wouldn't take you.

Dorothy. Why not?

Philip. Because you're useless, really. You're uneducated, you're
useless, you're a fool and you're lazy.

Dorothy. Maybe the others. But I'm not useless.

Philip. Why aren't you useless?

Dorothy. You know—or you ought to know. [*She is crying*.]

Philip. Oh, yes. *That*.

Dorothy. Is that all it means to you?

Philip. That's a commodity you shouldn't pay too high a price for.

So love does not exist? Yet sensuality seems to be the very essence of Hemingway's heroes. Physical love, yes; but one mustn't pay too high a price for it. The modern warrior's woman is one who gives herself generously, between two battles, and knows that afterward she will be forgotten. All she will remember of her love-making will be a hotel room, some empty bottles, tips to the chambermaids and elevator operators, and some shells whistling in the night. This is a time of pleasures indulged in on the run.

For a few years this code was valid for many men and women —in all countries. It was the law of the jungle; the law of a world at war in which fear, courage, and, at bottom, despair, held sway. For a time this was the world of all of us; it remains that of a great many among us. And, if we do not watch out, it may well be the world of tomorrow. Its entire morality is based on the manner in which one behaves in the presence of death. In this constant state of alarm, there are two solutions. One is to forget. Hemingway's characters, like their models in real life, drink and make love to numb their senses. The other and nobler solution is a stoicism which accepts as normal this reprieve for those who are doomed to die. Man walks in the midst of ruins, always ready for the final explosion, trying to forget his nightmares and searching, among the casualties, for "passionate idyls." "Love, like hunting or war, or drinking, all acts of violence and excess, conceals from us the presence of *nada*—it is a moment, an all-too-brief moment." [9]

This world is more terrible than that of Kipling, and more terrible than the real world of which it is only an aspect. We know hundreds of towns, thousands of homes, in which hard-working men, devoted women, and fun-loving children live in peace and happiness. Not all human beings need to forget. Obsession with death is a real psychosis—only too real—and yet most human beings do not suffer from it. They too deserve to be described. But after two hellish interludes of war, and in the face of even greater potential suffering, Hemingway's anguish is legitimate. This hell is the one we have dwelt in, and in which our children may dwell tomorrow. By contrast with it, the anguish of a Proust seems mild.

This world is saved by form. To escape "the senselessness of a world without values," there is a finer way out than drunkenness

⁹ John Brown: *Panorama de la littérature contemporaine aux Etats-Unis*, Paris: Gallimard, 1954, p. 129.

or sensual satisfaction. It is creation. Here Hemingway rejoins Proust. The latter sought to surround the simplest things with "rings of a beautiful style." Hemingway relies less on images. His style is objective and bare. He describes the worst horrors with classic sobriety. This restraint in describing the monstrous is precisely what style is. As the sportsman makes his gestures of force with grace, so Hemingway—seeking to paint "the darkness at noon" which in his eyes the universe appears to be—has found a style as clean and hard, in the words of Ford Madox Ford, "as pebbles fresh from a brook."

Above all, to understand the universe Hemingway resorts to vast symbols rather than metaphors—such as the symbol of the old man Santiago and his fish. A world is not wholly without values when it recognizes esthetic values. The writer, like the hunter and the soldier, respects his code; and, by his word magic, succeeds not in recapturing Time—which to Hemingway would mean recapturing horror—but in killing it. It may well be that the word of the universe is *nada*—nothingness; but in this nothingness, the writer's code and craft dimly outline the shadows of something.

André Maurois

Translated from the French by Joseph M. Bernstein

Emergence of Ernest Hemingway

On October 21, 1923, the following note appeared in Burton Rascoe's *A Bookman's Daybook*, a feature of the Sunday edition of the New York *Tribune*, of which Rascoe was at that time literary editor:

Called upon Mary and Edmund Wilson late in the afternoon, and Wilson called my attention to some amusing stuff by Ernest Hemingway in the new issue of the *Little Review*.[1] [Lewis] Galantière sent me a copy of Hemingway's *Three Stories and Ten Poems*, which was published in Paris, and said that I would find it interesting, but I have not yet got around to reading it. Wilson was ill with a cold and complained that the difficulty with New York is that it is hard to keep feeling well here, that it ties one up nervously and residents of Manhattan are always having colds.

I presently had the following letter from Hemingway, who was then working on a newspaper in Canada:

November 11, 1923

Dear Mr. Wilson:

In Burton Rascoe's Social and Literary Notes I saw you had drawn his attention to some writing of mine in the *Little Review*.

I am sending you *Three Stories and Ten Poems*. As far as I know it has not yet been reviewed in the States. Gertrude Stein writes me she has done a review but I don't know whether she has gotten it published yet.

You don't know anything in Canada.

I would like to send out some for review but do not know whether to put a dedication, as compulsory in France, or what. Being an unknown name and the books unimposing they would probably be received as by Mr. Rascoe, who has not yet had time, after three months, to read the copy Galantière sent him. (He could read it all in an hour and a half.)

---

[1] These contributions were *in our time,* comprising six of the little vignettes that afterward appeared in the two books of that title, and a satirical prose poem called *They Made Peace—What Is Peace?*

The Contact Publishing Co. is McAlmon. It has published Wm. Carlos Williams, Mina Loy, Marsden Hartley and McAlmon.

I hope you like the book. If you are interested could you send me the names of four or five people to send it to to get it reviewed? It would be terribly good of you. This address will be good until January when we go back to Paris.

Thanking you very much whether you have the time to do it or not.

Yours sincerely,
Ernest Hemingway

1599 Bathurst Street
Toronto, Canada

I acknowledged the book when I got it, mentioning that I might do a note on it in the *Dial*, and had from him the following reply:

November 25
1599 Bathurst Street
Toronto

Dear Mr. Wilson:

Thank you ever so much for the letter. It was awfully good of you.

The book is a silly size. McAlmon wanted to get out a series of small books with Mina Loy, W. C. Williams, etc., and wanted me in it. I gave him the stories and poems. I am glad to have it out and once it is published it is back of you.

I am very glad you liked some of it. As far as I can think at the minute yours is the only critical opinion in the States I have any respect for. Mary Colum is sometimes sound. Rascoe was intelligent about Eliot. There are probably good ones that I don't know.

No I don't think "My Old Man" derives from Anderson. It is about a boy and his father and race horses. Sherwood has written about boys and horses. But very differently. It derives from boys and horses. Anderson derives from boys and horses. I don't think they're anything alike. I know I wasn't inspired by him.

I know him pretty well but have not seen him for several years. His work seems to have gone to hell, perhaps from people in New York telling him too much how good he was. Functions of criticism. I am very fond of him. He has written good stories.

Would it perhaps be better to postpone the "Briefer Mentions" in the *Dial* until *In Our Time* comes out sometime next month and I will send it to you? You can get from it what I am trying to get at and the two of them together could make one review.

I am awfully glad you liked the *In Our Time* stuff in the *Little Review* and it is where I think I have gotten hold of it.

There is no use trying to explain it without the book.

It is very sporting of you to offer to help me get a book before the publishers. I don't know any of them.

Edward O'Brien wrote me the other day asking formal permission to reprint "My Old Man" in his *Best Short Stories of 1923* and asking if he could dedicate the book to me. As the book isn't out that is confidential. He prints bum ones and good ones. He asked me if I had enough stories for a Boni and Liveright book. I don't know whether that means he could get them to publish it. I will write and ask you about it when the time comes if you don't mind.

E. E. Cummings' *Enormous Room* was the best book published last year that I read. Somebody told me it was a flop. Then look at *One of Ours.* Prize, big sale, people taking it seriously. You were in the war weren't you? Wasn't that last scene in the lines wonderful? Do you know where it came from? The battle scene in *Birth of a Nation.* I identified episode after episode, Catherized. Poor woman she had to get her war experience somewhere.

The thing in the *L.R.* was a joke.[2] I wrote it in the *wagon-restaurant* going back to Lausanne, had been at a very fine lunch at Gertrude Stein's and talked there all afternoon and read a lot of her new stuff and then drank a big bottle of Beaune myself in the dining car. Facing opening the wire again in the morning I tried to analyze the conference.

Her method is invaluable for analyzing anything or making notes on a person or a place. She has a wonderful head. I would like to write a review of an old book of hers sometime. She is where Mencken and Mary Colum fall down and skin their noses.

Please excuse this very long letter and thanks again ever so much for your letter and the good advice. I would like to see you very much when we go through N.Y.

> Very sincerely,
> Ernest Hemingway.

He looked me up on his next visit to New York and sent me the first *In Our Time* (lower-cased *in our time*), which was published in the spring of 1924 in an edition of a hundred and seventy copies by the Three Mountains Press in Paris. This contained only eleven of the fifteen stories that appeared in the Boni and Liveright edition of 1925.

I wrote a review of *in our time* and *Three Stories and Ten Poems,* which appeared in the *Dial* of October, 1924. Though it is not of much interest in itself, I am proud of it because it is, so far as I know, the first criticism of Hemingway that appeared in print.[3] (It is not, however, listed by Louis Henry Cohn in his *Bibliography of the Works of Ernest Hemingway.* The first article

[2] *They Made Peace—What Is Peace?*

[3] I have learned, since the above was written, that my review of *in our time* was not the first. An earlier review, signed M.R., had appeared in the April, 1924, issue of *the transatlantic review,* published in Paris by Ford Madox Ford.

noted by him is of November, 1925: a review by Burton Rascoe
of the expanded *In Our Time.*)

Mr. Hemingway's Dry-Points

Three Stories and Ten Poems. By Ernest Hemingway. 12mo. 58
pages. Contact Publishing Company. Paris. $1.50.
In Our Time. By Ernest Hemingway. 12mo. 30 pages. The Three
Mountains Press. Paris. $2.

Mr. Hemingway's poems are not particularly important, but his
prose is of the first distinction. He must be counted as the only American writer but one—Mr. Sherwood Anderson—who has felt the genius
of Gertrude Stein's *Three Lives* and has evidently been influenced by
it. Indeed, Miss Stein, Mr. Anderson, and Mr. Hemingway may now
be said to form a school by themselves. The characteristic of this school
is a naïveté of language, often passing into the colloquialism of the
character dealt with, which serves actually to convey profound emotions and complex states of mind. It is a distinctively American development in prose—as opposed to more or less successful American
achievements in the traditional style of English prose—which has ar-
tistically justified itself at its best as a limpid shaft into deep waters.
Not, however, that Mr. Hemingway is imitative. On the contrary,
he is rather strikingly original, and in the dry compressed little vignettes
of *In Our Time,* has almost invented a form of his own:

"They shot the six cabinet ministers at half-past six in the morning
against the wall of a hospital. There were pools of water in the courtyard. There were dead leaves on the paving of the courtyard. It rained
hard. All the shutters of the hospital were nailed shut. One of the
ministers was sick with typhoid. Two soldiers carried him downstairs
and out into the rain. They tried to hold him up against the wall but he
sat down in a puddle of water. The other five stood very quietly
against the wall. Finally the officer told the soldiers it was no good
trying to make him stand up. When they fired the first volley he was
sitting down in the water with his head on his knees."

Mr. Hemingway is remarkably successful in suggesting moral values
by a series of simple statements of this sort. His more important book
is called *In Our Time,* and, behind its cool objective manner, it constitutes a harrowing record of the barbarities of the period in which
we live: you have not only political executions, but hangings of
criminals, bullfights, assassinations by the police, and the cruelties and
horrors of the war. Mr. Hemingway is unperturbed as he tells us about
these things: he is not a propagandist even for humanity. His bullfight
sketches have the dry sharpness and elegance of the bullfight litho-
graphs of Goya. And, like Goya, he is concerned first of all with making a fine picture. Too proud an artist to simplify in the interests of

conventional pretenses, he is showing you what life is like. And I am inclined to think that his little book has more artistic dignity than anything else about the period of the war that has as yet been written by an American.

Not perhaps the most vivid book, but the soundest. Mr. Hemingway, who can make you feel the poignancy of the Italian soldier deciding in his death agony that he will "make a separate peace," has no anti-militarist *parti pris* which will lead him to suppress from his record the exhilaration of the men who had "jammed an absolutely perfect barricade across the bridge" and who were "frightfully put out when we heard the flank had gone, and we had to fall back." It is only in the paleness, the thinness, of some of his effects that Mr. Hemingway sometimes fails. I am thinking especially of the story called "Up in Michigan," which should have been a masterpiece, but has the curious defect of dealing with rude and primitive people yet leaving them rather shadowy.

In Our Time has a pretty and very amusing cover designed from scrambled newspaper clippings. The only objection I have to its appearance is that the titles are printed throughout without capitals— thus: "in our time by ernest hemingway—paris." This device, which had a certain effectiveness when the modernists used it first to call attention to the newness of what they were offering, is now becoming a bore. The American advertisers have taken it over as one of their stock tricks. And it is so unsightly in itself that one does not like to see it become—as in the case of Mr. Hemingway's book and Mr. Hueffer's[4] *trans-atlantic review*—a kind of badge for all that is freshest and most interesting in contemporary writing.

October, 1924

In connection with this review, Hemingway wrote me the following letter:

113 Rue Notre Dame des Champs
Paris VII
October 18, 1924

Dear Wilson:

Thank you so much for writing the review in the October *Dial*. I liked it very much. You are very right about the lack of capital letters —which seemed very silly and affected to me—but Bird had put them in and as he was printing the *In Our Time* himself and that was all the fun he was getting out of it I thought he could go ahead and be a damn fool in his own way if it pleased him. So long as he did not fool with the text.

I'm awfully glad you liked it.

How are you anyway? and did you ever get Chaplin for your ballet?

[4] Ford Madox Ford, who changed his family name from Hueffer.

We have lived very quietly, working hard, except for a trip to Spain, Pamplona, where we had a fine time and I learned a lot about bull-fighting, the inside-the-ring scene. We had a lot of minor adventures.

I've worked like hell most of the time and think the stuff gets better. Finished the book of 14 stories with a chapter of *In Our Time* between each story—that is the way they were meant to go—to give the picture of the whole between examining it in detail. Like looking with your eyes at something, say a passing coastline, and then looking at it with 15X binoculars. Or rather, maybe, looking at it and then going in and living in it—and then coming out and looking at it again.

I sent the book to Don Stewart[5] at the Yale Club about three weeks ago. When he was here he offered to try and sell it for me. I think you would like it, it has a pretty good unity. In some of the stories since the *In Our Time* I've gotten across both the people and the scene. It makes you feel good when you can do it. It feels now as though I had gotten on top of it.

Will you get over here this winter do you think? We will probably be in Paris all winter. Not enough money to get out. The baby is very well and husky. Hadley is working on the piano.

She sends her best regards to you and Mrs. Wilson.

Hope everything is going well with you and that you have a good winter. I would like to hear from you and I did appreciate the review. It was cool and clear minded and decent and impersonal and sympathetic. Christ how I hate this terrible personal stuff. Do you remember my writing from Toronto wanting some reviews and publicity? and then got some and it turned me sick.

I think there's nothing more discouraging than unintelligent appreciation. Not really discouraging; but just driving something back inside of you. Some bright guy said *In Our Time* was a series of thumbnail sketches showing a great deal of talent but obviously under the influence of Ring Lardner. Yeah! That kind of stuff is fine. It doesn't bother. But these wordy, sentimental bastards. You are the only man writing criticism who or whom I can read when the book being criticized is one I've read or know something about. I can read almost anybody when they write on things I don't know about. Intelligence is so damn rare and the people who have it often have such a bad time with it that they get bitter or propagandistic and then it's not much use.

With best wishes to you and to your wife,

Very sincerely,
Ernest Hemingway.

Is this *What Price Glory?* really a good play? I don't mean a good *play*—it sounds fine over here.

Edmund Wilson

[5] Donald Ogden Stewart.

Hemingway and His Critics

Between *The Fifth Column*, the play which makes the occasion for this large volume,[1] and *The First Forty-Nine Stories*, which make its bulk and its virtue, there is a difference of essence. For the play is the work of Hemingway the "man" and the stories are by Hemingway the "artist." This is a distinction which seldom enough means anything in criticism, but now and then an author gives us, as Hemingway gives us, writing of two such different kinds that there is a certain amount of validity and at any rate a convenience in making it. Once made, the distinction can better be elaborated than defined or defended. Hemingway the "artist" is conscious, Hemingway the "man" is self-conscious; the "artist" has a kind of innocence, the "man" a kind of naivety; the "artist" is disinterested, the "man" has a dull personal ax to grind; the "artist" has a perfect medium and tells the truth even if it be only *his* truth, but the "man" fumbles at communication and falsifies. As Edmund Wilson said in his "Letter to the Russians about Hemingway," which is the best estimate of our author that I know,

. . . something frightful seems to happen to Hemingway as soon as he begins to write in the first person. In his fiction, the conflicting elements of his personality, the emotional situations which obsess him, are externalized and objectified; and the result is an art which is severe, intense, and deeply serious. But as soon as he talks in his own person, he seems to lose all his capacity for self-criticism and is likely to become fatuous or maudlin.

Mr. Wilson had in mind such specifically autobiographical and polemical works as *Green Hills of Africa* (and obviously he was not referring to the technical use of the first person in fictional narrative) but since the writing of the "Letter" in 1935, we may observe of Hemingway that the "man" has encroached upon the

---

[1] *The Fifth Column and The First Forty-Nine Stories.* By Ernest Hemingway. New York: Charles Scribner's Sons. 1938. $2.75.

"artist" in his fiction. In *To Have and Have Not* and now in *The Fifth Column* the "first person" dominates and is the source of the failure of both works.

Of course it might be perfectly just to set down these failures simply to a lapse of Hemingway's talent. But there is, I think, something else to be said. For as one compares the high virtues of Hemingway's stories with the weakness of his latest novel and his first play, although one is perfectly aware of all that must be charged against the author himself, what forces itself into consideration is the cultural atmosphere which has helped to bring about the recent falling off. In so far as we can ever blame a critical tradition for a writer's failures, we must, I believe, blame American criticism for the illegitimate emergence of Hemingway the "man" and the resultant inferiority of his two recent major works.

It is certainly true that criticism of one kind or another has played an unusually important part in Hemingway's career. Perhaps no American talent has so publicly developed as Hemingway's: more than any writer of our time he has been under glass, watched, checked up on, predicted, suspected, warned. One part of his audience took from him new styles of writing, of lovemaking, of very being; this was the simpler part, but its infatuate imitation was of course a kind of criticism. But another section of his audience responded negatively, pointing out that the texture of Hemingway's work was made up of cruelty, religion, anti-intellectualism, even of basic fascism, and looked upon him as the active proponent of evil. Neither part of such an audience could fail to make its impression upon a writer. The knowledge that he had set a fashion and become a legend may have been gratifying but surely also burdensome and depressing, and it must have offered no small temptation. Yet perhaps more difficult for Hemingway to support with equanimity, and, from our point of view, much more important, was the constant accusation that he had attacked good human values. For upon Hemingway were turned all the fine social feelings of the now passing decade, all the noble sentiments, all the desperate optimism, all the extreme rationalism, all the contempt of irony and indirection—all the attitudes which, in the full tide of the liberal-radical movement, became dominant in our thought about literature. There was demanded of him earnestness and pity, social consciousness, as it was called, something "positive" and "constructive" and literal.

For is not life a simple thing and is not the writer a villain or a counterrevolutionary who does not see it so?

As if under the pressure of this critical tradition, which persisted in mistaking the "artist" for the "man," Hemingway seems to have undertaken to vindicate the "man" by showing that he, too, could muster the required "social" feelings in the required social way. At any rate, he now brought the "man" with all his contradictions and conflicts into his fiction. But "his ideas about life"— I quote Edmund Wilson again—

or rather his sense of what happens and the way it happens, is in his stories sunk deep below the surface and is not conveyed by argument or preaching but by directly transmitted emotion: it is turned into something as hard as crystal and as disturbing as a great lyric. When he expounds this sense of life, however, in his own character of Ernest Hemingway, the Old Master of Key West, he has a way of sounding silly.

If, however, the failures of Hemingway "in his own character" were apparent to the practitioners of this critical tradition, they did not want Hemingway's virtues—the something "hard" and "disturbing." Indeed, they were in a critical tradition that did not want artists at all; it wanted "men," recruits, and its apologists were delighted to enlist Hemingway in his own character, with all his confusions and naivety, simply because Hemingway had now declared himself on the right side.

And so when *To Have and Have Not* appeared, one critic of the Left, grappling with the patent fact that the "artist" had failed, yet determined to defend the "man" who was his new ally, had no recourse save to explain that in this case failure was triumph because artistic fumbling was the mark of Hemingway's attempt to come to grips with the problems of modern life which were as yet too great for his art to encompass. Similarly, another critic of the Left, faced with the esthetic inferiority of Hemingway's first play, takes refuge in praising the personal vindication which the "man" has made by "taking sides against fascism." In other words, the "man" has been a sad case and long in need of regeneration; the looseness of thought and emotion, the easy and uninteresting idealism of the social feelings to which Hemingway now gives such sudden and literal expression, are seen as the grateful signs of a personal reformation.

But the disinterested reader does not have to look very deep to see that Hemingway's social feelings, whatever they may yet become, are now the occasion for indulgence in the "man." His two recent failures are failures not only in form but in feeling; one looks at *To Have and Have Not* and *The Fifth Column*, one looks at their brag, and their disconcerting forcing of the emotions, at their downright priggishness, and then one looks at the criticism which, as I conceive it, made these failures possible by demanding them and which now accepts them so gladly, and one is tempted to reverse the whole liberal-radical assumption about literature. One almost wishes to say to an author like Hemingway, "You have no duty, no responsibility. Literature, in a political sense, is not in the least important. Wherever the sword is drawn it is mightier than the pen. Whatever you can do as a man, you can win no wars as an artist."

Very obviously this would not be the whole truth, yet saying it might counteract the crude and literal theory of art to which, in varying measure, we have all been training ourselves for a decade. We have conceived the artist to be a man perpetually on the spot, who must always report to us his precise moral and political latitude and longitude. Not that for a moment we would consider shaping our own political ideas by his; but we who of course turn for political guidance to newspapers, theorists, or historians, create the fiction that thousands—not, to be sure, ourselves—are waiting on the influence of the creative artist, and we stand by to see if he is leading us as he properly should. We consider then that we have exalted the importance of art, and perhaps we have. But in doing so we have quite forgotten how complex and subtle art is and, if it is to be "used," how very difficult it is to use it.

One feels that Hemingway would never have thrown himself into his new and inferior work if the necessity had not been put upon him to justify himself before this magisterial conception of literature. Devoted to literalness, the critical tradition of the Left took Hemingway's symbols for his intention, saw in his stories only cruelty or violence or a calculated indifference, and turned upon him a barrage of high-mindedness—that liberal-radical high-mindedness that is increasingly taking the place of thought among the "progressive professional and middle-class forces" and that now, under the name of "good will," shuts out half the world. Had it seen what was actually in Hemingway's work, it would not have forced him out of his idiom of the artist and into the idiom of the man which he speaks with difficulty and without truth.

For what should have been always obvious is that Hemingway is a writer who, when he writes as an "artist," is passionately and aggressively concerned with truth and even with social truth. And with this in mind, one might begin the consideration of his virtues with a glance at Woodrow Wilson. Hemingway has said that all genuine American writing comes from the prose of Huckleberry Finn's voyage down the Mississippi, and certainly his own starts there. But Huck's prose is a sort of moral symbol. It is the antithesis to the Widow Douglas—to the pious, the respectable, the morally plausible. It is the prose of the free man seeing the world as it really is. And Woodrow Wilson was, we might say, Hemingway's Widow Douglas. To the sensitive men who went to war it was not, perhaps, death and destruction that made the disorganizing shock. It was perhaps rather that death and destruction went on at the instance and to the accompaniment of the fine grave words, of which Woodrow Wilson's speeches were the finest and gravest. Here was the issue of liberal theory; here in the bloated or piecemeal corpse was the outcome of the words of humanitarianism and ideals; this was the work of presumably careful men of good will, learned men, polite men. The world was a newspaper world, a state-paper world, a memorial-speech world. Words were trundled smoothly o'er the tongue—Coleridge had said it long ago—

> *Like mere abstractions, empty sounds to which*
> *We join no feeling and attach no form*
> *As if the soldier died without a wound . . .*
> *Passed off to Heaven, translated and not killed.*

Everyone in that time had feelings, as they called them; just as everyone has "feelings" now. And it seems to me that what Hemingway wanted first to do was to get rid of the "feelings," the comfortable liberal humanitarian feelings: and to replace them with the truth.

Not cynicism, I think, not despair, as so often is said, but this admirable desire shaped his famous style and his notorious set of admirations and contempts. The trick of understatement or tangential statement sprang from this desire. Men had made so many utterances in such fine language that it had become time to shut up. Hemingway's people, as everyone knows, are afraid of words and ashamed of them and the line from his stories which has become famous is the one that begins "Won't you please," goes on through its innumerable "pleases," and ends, "stop talking." Not only slain men but slain words made up the mortality of the war.

Another manifestation of the same desire in Hemingway was

his devotion to the ideal of technique as an end in itself. A great
deal can go down in the tumble but one of the things that stands
best is a cleanly done job. As John Peale Bishop says in his
admirable essay on Hemingway (which yet, I feel, contributes to
the general misapprehension by asserting the evanescence of
Hemingway's "compassion"), professional pride is one of the last
things to go. Hemingway became a devotee of his own skill and
he exploited the ideal of skill in his characters. His admired men
always do a good job; and the proper handling of a rod, a gun,
an *espada,* or a pen is a thing, so Hemingway seems always to be
saying, which can be understood when speech cannot.

This does not mean that Hemingway attacks mind itself, a
charge which has often been brought against him. It is perhaps
safe to say that whenever he seems to be making such an attack,
it is not so much *reason* as it is *rationalization* that he resists;
"mind" appears simply as the complex of false feelings. And
against "mind" in this sense he sets up what he believes to be
the primal emotions, among others pain and death, met not with
the mind but with techniques and courage. "Mind" he sees as a
kind of castrating knife, cutting off people's courage and proper
self-love, making them "reasonable," which is to say dull and
false. There is no need to point out how erroneous his view
would have been were it really mind that was in question, but in
the long romantic tradition of the attitude it never really *is* mind
that is in question but rather a dull overlay of mechanical negative proper feeling, or a falseness of feeling which people believe
to be reasonableness and reasonable virtue. And when we think
how quickly "mind" capitulates in a crisis, how quickly, for example, it accommodated itself to the war and served it and glori-
fied it, revulsion from it and a turning to the life of action—reduced, to be sure, to athleticism: but skillful physical effort is
perhaps something intellectuals too quickly dismiss as a form of
activity—can be the better understood. We can understand too
the insistence on courage, even on courage deliberately observed
in its purity: that is, when it is at the service of the most sordid
desires, as in "Fifty Grand."

This, then, was Hemingway's vision of the world. Was it a
complete vision? Of course it was not. Was it a useful vision? That
depended. If it was true, it was useful—if we knew how to use
it. But the use of literature is not easy. In our hearts most of us
are Platonists in the matter of art and we feel that we become
directly infected by what we read; or at any rate we want to be

Platonists, and we carry on a certain conviction from our Tom Swift days that literature provides chiefly a means of identification and emulation. The Platonist view is not wholly to be dismissed; we *do* in a degree become directly infected by art; but the position is too simple. And we are further Platonistic in our feeling that literature must be religious: we want our attitudes formulated by the tribal bard. This, of course, gives to literature a very important function. But it forgets that literature has never "solved" anything, though it may perhaps provide part of the data for eventual solutions.

With this attitude we asked, Can Hemingway's people speak only with difficulty? and we answered, Then it surely means that he thinks people should not speak. Does he find in courage the first of virtues? Then it surely means that we should be nothing but courageous. Is he concerned with the idea of death and of violence? Then it must mean that to him these are good things.

In short, we looked for an emotional leader. We did not conceive Hemingway to be saying, Come, let us look at the world together. We supposed him to be saying, Come, it is your moral duty to be as my characters are. We took the easiest and simplest way of using the artist and decided that he was not the "man" for us. That he was a man and a Prophet we were certain; and equally certain that he was not the "man" we would want to be or the Prophet who could lead us. That, as artist, he was not concerned with being a "man" did not occur to us. We had, in other words, quite overlooked the whole process of art, overlooked style and tone, symbol and implication, overlooked the obliqueness and complication with which the artist may criticize life, and assumed that what Hemingway saw or what he put into his stories he wanted to have exist in the actual world.

In short, the criticism of Hemingway came down to a kind of moral-political lecture, based on the assumption that art is—or should be—the exact equivalent of life. The writer would have to be strong indeed who could remain unmoved by the moral pressure that was exerted upon Hemingway. He put away the significant reticences of the artist, opened his heart like "a man," and the flat literalness, the fine, fruity social idealism, of the latest novel and the play are the result.

The Fifth Column is difficult to speak of. Summary is always likely to be a critical treachery, but after consulting the summaries of those who admire the work and regard it as a notable event, it seems fair to say that it is the story of a tender-tough

American hero with the horrors, who does counterespionage in Madrid, though everybody thinks he is just a playboy, who fears that he will no longer do his work well if he continues his liaison with an American girl chiefly remarkable for her legs and her obtuseness; and so sacrifices love and bourgeois pleasure for the sake of duty. Hemingway as a playwright gives up his tools of suggestion and tone and tells a literal story—an adventure story of the Spanish war, at best the story of the regeneration of an American Scarlet Pimpernel of not very good intelligence.

It is this work which has been received with the greatest satisfaction by a large and important cultural group as the fulfillment and vindication of Hemingway's career, as a fine document of the Spanish struggle, and as a political event of significance, "a sign of the times," as one reviewer called it. To me it seems none of these things. It does not vindicate Hemingway's career because that career in its essential parts needs no vindication; and it does not fulfill Hemingway's career because that career has been in the service of exact if limited emotional truth and this play is in the service of fine feelings. Nor can I believe that the Spanish war is represented in any good sense by a play whose symbols are so sentimentally personal[2] and whose dramatic tension is so weak; and it seems to me that there is something even vulgar in making Spain serve as a kind of mental hospital for disorganized foreigners who, out of a kind of self-contempt, turn to the "ideal of the Spanish people." Nor, finally, can I think that Hemingway's statement of an antifascist position is of great political importance or of more than neutral virtue. It is hard to believe that the declaration of antifascism is nowadays any more a mark of sufficient grace in a writer than a declaration against disease would be in a physician or a declaration against accidents would be in a locomotive engineer. The admirable intention in itself is not

[2] In fairness to Hemingway the disclaimer of an important intention which he makes in his Preface should be cited. Some people, he says, have objected that his play does not present "the nobility and dignity of the cause of the Spanish people. It does not attempt to. It will take many plays and novels to do that, and the best ones will be written after the war is over." And he goes on: "This is only a play about counterespionage in Madrid. It has the defects of having been written in wartime, and if it has a moral it is that people who work for certain organizations have very little time for home life." I do not think that this exempts the play from severe judgment by those who dislike it, just as I think that those who admire it have a right to see in it, as they do, a "sign of the times."

enough and criticism begins and does not end when the intention is declared.

But I believe that judgments so simple as these will be accepted with more and more difficulty. The "progressive professional and middle-class forces" are framing a new culture, based on the old liberal-radical culture but designed now to hide the new anomaly by which they live their intellectual and emotional lives. For they must believe, it seems, that imperialist arms advance proletarian revolution, that oppression by the right people brings liberty. Like Hemingway's latest hero, they show one front to the world and another to themselves, know that within they are true proletarian men while they wrap themselves in Early American togas; they are enthralled by their own good will; they are people of fine feelings and they dare not think lest the therapeutic charm vanish. This is not a political essay and I am not here concerned with the political consequences of these things, bad though they be and worse though they will be, but only with the cultural consequences. For to prevent the anomaly from appearing in its genuine difficulty, emotion—of a very limited kind—has been apotheosized and thought has been made almost a kind of treachery; the reviewer of *The Fifth Column* to whom I have already referred cites as a virtue Hemingway's "unintellectual" partisanship of the Spanish cause. The piety of "good will" has become enough and Fascism is conceived not as a force which complicates the world but as a force which simplifies the world—and so it does for any number of people of good will (of a good will not to be doubted, I should say) for whom the existence of an absolute theological evil makes nonexistent any other evil.

It is this group that has made Hemingway its cultural hero and for reasons that need not be canvassed very far. Now that Hemingway has become what this group would call "affirmative" he has become insufficient; but insufficiency is the very thing this group desires. When Hemingway was in "negation" his themes of courage, loyalty, tenderness, and silence, tangentially used, suggested much; but now that they are used literally and directly they say far less than the situation demands. His stories showed a great effort of comprehension and they demand a considerable effort from their readers, that effort in which lies whatever teaching powers there is in art; but now he is not making an effort to understand but to accept, which may indeed be the effort of the honest political man but not of the honest artist.

An attempt has been made to settle the problem of the artist's relation to politics by loudly making the requirement that he give up his base individuality and rescue humanity and his own soul by becoming the mouthpiece of a party, a movement, or a philosophy. That requirement has demonstrably failed as a solution of the problem; the problem, however, still remains. It may be, of course, that politics itself will settle the problem for us; it may be that in our tragic time art worthy the name cannot be produced and that we must live with the banalities of *The Fifth Column* or even with less. However, if the problem will be allowed to exist at all, it will not be solved in theory and on paper but in practice. And we have, after all, the practice of the past to guide us, at least with a few tentative notions. We can learn to stop pressing the writer with the demand for contemporaneity when we remember the simple fact that writers have always written directly to and about the troubles of their own time and for and about their contemporaries, some in ways to us more obvious than others but all responding inevitably to what was happening around them. We can learn too that the relation of an artist to his culture, whether that culture be national or the culture of a relatively small recusant group, is a complex and even a contradictory relation: the artist must accept his culture and be accepted by it, but also—so it seems—he must be its critic, correcting and even rejecting it according to his personal insight; his strength seems to come from the tension of this ambivalent situation and we must learn to welcome the ambivalence. Finally, and simplest of all, we learn not to expect a political, certainly not an immediately political, effect from a work of art; and in removing from art a burden of messianic responsibility which it never has discharged and cannot discharge we may leave it free to do whatever it actually can do.

Lionel Trilling

Hemingway's Short Stories

In *Winesburg, Ohio,* Sherwood Anderson saw his characters thoughtfully, with bemused detachment, with a certain melancholy heaviness behind which glowed a constant kindliness of heart. Undetained and unguided by him, these people moved past the office windows of the young reporter, up and down the hard Chicago streets, through lives that led "out of nowhere into nothing." Anderson set down what he saw and felt about them with a kind of tender bewilderment, as if he were really as troubled by their negation and stupidity and colorless frustration as they were, in a style handled with apparent casualness, offhand, so that its charm arose from what seemed to be a studied stylelessness.

Both the rewards and the dangers of this method are obvious. By a public instructed largely in a literature where characters were stereotyped as good or bad, and the physical processes of life, and especially love, were rendered by means of a patent formula, Anderson was of course branded as immoral. This was natural, and is now irrelevant. The real danger of Anderson's method was that it lay wide open to parody, which Anderson himself accomplished to some extent in *Dark Laughter,* unintentionally, of course, and which Hemingway completed in *Torrents of Spring.* This too, I think, does not matter. In Anderson there is a weakness arising from a certain lack of self-censorship. He lacks the austerity that would prevent him from reveling in the luxury of an emotion. But it does not and cannot detract from the inspirational force of Anderson's example to the short story of his day. *Winesburg, Ohio,* is the first directional signpost of the contemporary American short story, directing the writer to turn inward to the job of establishing, out of indigenous American material, a new American tradition.

The ultimate effect of Anderson's pioneering example was a release of energy that was to have, during the next fifteen or twenty years, immense creative results. The immediate effect was its influence on Ernest Hemingway: for if Anderson stopped creating stories by the old facile methods of stereotyping, Hemingway broke up every known type face with which the American short story had ever been set, and cut for it a more austere, revolutionary, and yet more classic design than it had ever known. In doing so Hemingway brought down a hammer on all writing done to a fancy design; he stripped of its impossible periodic splendor that style of writing which reaches its limits in the intricacies of Henry James; he sheared away the literary woolliness of English as no one had ever done before.

Like Anderson, Hemingway began publishing obscurely, during the private-press vogue of the early twenties, and some of his stories appeared privately in Paris, where it is obvious that he came under the influence of Gertrude Stein. Somewhere between Stein and Anderson, however, there was a middle course, and Hemingway took it. Hemingway had sense enough to see that it might be a million years before there was a public initiated enough to read its fiction in the bony theoretical rhythms offered by Miss Stein. You cannot feed a public on fancy literary theorems, and Hemingway, who had plenty to say, wanted a public. He took the Stein method, which at its most aggravated seemed to have some appeal to mental deficiency, and, as it were, put sanity into it. For every person who read Stein, pretending to understand it whether he did or not, a potential million could read Hemingway.

His first story, "Up in Michigan," was written in Paris in 1921, and as far as I know there is no record that it caused a sensation. It was collected, together with another fifteen stories, into the volume *In Our Time*, and again I know of no record that a revolution was caused. Yet a revolution had been caused, and in these stories, less good and less famous than the contents of *Men Without Women* though they are, the Hemingway method is already in conscious and advanced production.

What is that method? Why did it cause a revolution? In the first place Hemingway was a man with an ax. For generations— it might almost be said for a hundred years or more—written English had been growing steadily more pompous, more prolix, more impossibly parochial; its continuous tendency had been towards discussing and explaining something rather than projecting and painting an object. It carried a vast burden of words which were not doing a job, and it was time, at last, to cut those words away. In the nineties Samuel Butler too had arrived with an ax, but it was an ax less against English writing than against English morality, and Butler had never dramatized the conflict except in a single book. Hemingway, looking back over what still purports to be the great age of the English novel, must have been struck by an interesting fact, of which there are most notable examples in Hardy. He must have been struck by the fact that out of the cavernous gloom of explanations, discussions, social dilemmas, and philosophizings all that emerged of permanent interest and value were the scattered bright scraps of pictorial narrative. In one generation the philosophy had grown moldy, the social dilemmas were forgotten for others, the moral currency had been changed. But the people, the narrative action, the color of scenes, remained, and could, if properly conceived and painted, never fade. So what one remembers out of Hardy, for example, is not the philosophic vaporings or the spiritual anguish, all impossibly unreal today, but the sharp bright scenes that have been painted by a man with his eye on the object—the pigsticking in *Jude*, Tess working in the winter turnip field, Tess praying with the children, the man selling his wife in *The Mayor of Casterbridge*. No changing currency of social and moral action changes these; nothing can come between them and countless generations of readers.

What Hemingway went for was that direct pictorial contact between eye and object, between object and reader. To get it he cut out a whole forest of verbosity. He got back to clean fundamental growth. He trimmed off explanation, discussion, even comment; he hacked off all metaphorical floweriness; he pruned off the dead, sacred clichés; until finally, through the sparse trained words, there was a view.

The road of the pass was hard and smooth and not yet dusty in the early morning. Below were the hills with oak and chestnut trees, and far away below was the sea. On the other side were snowy mountains.

The picture is complete. And again:

The hills across the valley of the Ebro were long and white. On this side there was no shade and no trees and the station was between two lines of rails in the sun. Close against the side of the station there was the warm shadow of the building and a curtain, made of strings of bamboo beads, hung across the open door into the bar, to keep out flies.

And here is a portrait, with background, complete:

An old man with steel-rimmed spectacles and very rusty clothes sat by the side of the road. There was a pontoon bridge across the river and carts, trucks, and men, women and children were crossing it. The mule-drawn carts staggered up the steep bank from the bridge with soldiers helping push against the spokes of the wheels. The trucks ground up and away heading out of it all and the peasants plodded along in the ankle-deep dust. But the old man sat there without moving. He was too tired to go any farther.

The pictures projected are as natural as life. There are no attempts at falsification, no superimposed colors, no rose glasses, no metaphors. Everything that could cloud or date the scene has been ruthlessly rejected. Examine by contrast:

No sooner did the rays of the rising sun shine on the dew, and fall in little fiery tongues upon their eyelids, than instinct made them strike camp and move away. All day they would journey, until the setting sun made the air to glow like a damp fire, burning the eyes while it chilled the body. The moon, like a disc of copper, hung behind them and the plain seemed dead.[1]

Here the effort to influence the reader is strenuous. Hemingway in effect says: "Here is the picture. That's all. Keep your eye on it"; and is prepared to trust the reader to absorb the proper impression. But Mr. Sitwell cannot trust the reader. The light must be changed, trick-focused, dimmed or raised for a series of effects. Each sentence has its metaphor; each metaphor is supported by some poetic archaism—"upon," "made the air to glow," "than instinct made them." The result is a decorative backcloth, looking real enough until the wind stirs it, and then suddenly ludicrous—what a Hemingway character would rightly call phony.

But Hemingway carried this purge of style beyond mere description. For a century the novel had staggered along under the weight of a colossal convention of fancy mechanics in the matter of dialogue. The novel had managed somehow to survive it; the short story had been in constant danger of collapsing. In this convention the words of a character had their intonation, flavor, emotion, or meaning underlined by the writer. Thus: "he reiterated with a manifest show of anger"; "she ventured to remark with a melancholy intonation in her voice"; "he declared haltingly"; "he stammered out in frightened accents"; "he interposed"; "he interjected with a low laugh," and so on and so on.

---

[1] Sacheverell Sitwell: *The Gothick North* (Duckworth).

Wads of this verbal padding bolstered up the conversation of every novel from Dickens down to the fourpenny paperback.

Hemingway swept every letter of that convention away. In its place he put nothing but his own ability to imply, by the choice, association, and order of the words, whether a character was feeling and speaking with anger, regret, desperation, tenderness; quickly or slowly; ironically or bitterly. All intonation and emotion lay somewhere in the apparently abrupt and casual arrangement of the words ("I feel fine," she said. "There's nothing wrong with me. I feel fine."), and Hemingway asked nothing except the cooperation of the reader in the job of capturing these intonations and emotions.

A classic example of this method will be seen in the famous story "Hills Like White Elephants." In that story a man is taking a girl to Madrid for an illegal operation. That fact is nowhere stated throughout the whole story, nor is the girl's terror and bitterness, nor in fact is any other emotion. The couple wait on the wayside station for the Madrid express; it is very hot, they drink beer, and they talk. For the girl something has crumpled up, and it is not only the past but the future. She is terrified, and the story is one of the most terrible Hemingway or anyone else ever wrote. Yet throughout the whole of it—a story largely projected through dialogue—Hemingway makes no single attempt to influence the readers' thoughts, impressions, or conclusions. He himself is never there; not for a single instant does he come between object and reader.

This story, and others like "The Killers," "The Undefeated," and "Fifty Grand," finally fixed the legend of the Hemingway method. The legend was that Hemingway was tough and unliterary, a dumb ox. The truth was the opposite. Hemingway is as conscious a literary writer as ever there was. Behind him, unless I am greatly mistaken, stand the influences of Turgenev, Maupassant, Sherwood Anderson, Stephen Crane, Defoe, and the English of the Authorized Version.[2] The legend of toughness arose from a failure to distinguish between Hemingway and his characters: the inarticulate boxers, the bullfighters, the gangsters, the soldiers. They were depicted as leading a life governed more or less without thought; they moved to oxlike instincts; the world is full of such people, and it is no use, as Hemingway knew, putting fancy

[2] It is interesting to compare Hemingway's method with that of the New Testament in Basic English, recently issued; in particular with certain narrative passages in the Acts of the Apostles.

literary thoughts into their heads. So Hemingway wrote about them in their own oxlike, instinctive, thoughtless language, well knowing that his greatest danger was sentimentalism, a danger he struggled so hard to avoid that finally he fell over backwards, as it were, into an inverted form of it. For Hemingway is a deeply emotional writer. Underneath the crust of style, apparently so hard and arid, the deepest rhythms move like warm volcanic lava. He is above all a tragic writer, haunted, repelled, and attracted by the everlasting fear of mortality.

Perhaps no Protestant can pretend to understand the Catholic mind, and it is from Catholicism, perhaps, that Hemingway's constant preoccupation with the theme of death arises. His stories appear to deal with a variety of themes: boxing, bullfighting, illegal operations, game-hunting, war, fishing; all of them physical subjects. But in reality Hemingway has only one theme—death. It is behind all but a fraction of his short stories; it is the whole subject of *Death in the Afternoon;* it is the climax towards which *A Farewell to Arms* inexorably moves. For Hemingway the twin ideas of physical activity and physical mortality are forces of a magnetism that never ceases its powerful attraction. As he remarks in *Death in the Afternoon*, "all stories, if continued far enough, end in death, and he is no true storyteller who would keep that from you." So death is the recurrent theme; the fear of it terrorizes Hemingway as the thought of being sentimental terrorizes him, until at last he is forced into it: death by gangsterism in "The Killers," the man dying of gangrene in "The Snows of Kilimanjaro," the fear of death in "Hills Like White Elephants," death for the bullfighter in "The Undefeated," death for the Spanish boy in "The Capital of the World." For a time, in some of the shorter sketches, he escapes it, but sooner or later the magnetism of the eternal paradox that the flesh lives, and yet rots, draws him back again. The melancholy of it beats with rhythmic dying fall under the shell of the prose that has earned for itself, mistakenly, the reputation of being so imperviously tough:

The boys picked up the cot and carried it around the green tents and down along the rock and out on to the plain and along past the smudges that were burning brightly now, the grass all consumed, and the wind fanning the fire, to the little plane.

Behind or beneath such a passage lies a personal rhythm that can never be imitated; the rhythm of the man, the personal inward melancholy, the deep-rooted fear of death. It was this that the thousand imitators of Hemingway on both sides of the Atlantic could never recapture: for the little Hemingways, attracted by the easy street-corner toughness of the style, sprang up everywhere, slick copyists of the surface line, not one in a thousand of them understanding that the colder and harder a man writes, as Chekhov once pointed out, the more deeply and more movingly emotional is the result likely to be. Hemingway was in reality so deeply susceptible to emotion that he strove constantly for the elimination of himself, his thoughts and feelings, from the surface of the work. For that he was taken to task by Mr. Aldous Huxley, who represented the very intellectual aridity in writing that Hemingway was out to break; Huxley accused Hemingway of belonging to a class of "intelligent and cultured people doing their best to feign stupidity and to conceal the fact that they have received an education."

Hemingway had a reply for that, and it was a good reply:

When writing a novel a writer should create living people; people not characters. . . . If the people the writer is making talk of old masters; of music; of modern painting; of letters; or of science then they should talk of those subjects in the novel. If they do not talk of those subjects and the writer makes them talk of them he is a faker, and if he talks about them himself to show how much he knows then he is showing off. No matter how good a phrase or a simile he may have if he puts it in where it is not absolutely necessary and irreplaceable he is spoiling his work for egotism.[3]

That statement is in reality as much a crack at Huxley and the archintellectuals who had become so overeducated that there was little in life that did not bore them with familiarity, as it is a defense of Hemingway himself and what he felt writing ought to be. Hemingway might have added that Huxley had never created a character, let alone a person, that was much more than a biological specimen being laid on the table for analytical dissection. He might have added that though he himself dealt largely with people who were soon to be dead, the characters of Huxley were dead before Huxley ever dealt with them. What he did add was this:

People in a novel, not skillfully constructed *characters,* must be projected from the writer's assimilated experience, from his knowledge, from his head, from his heart and from all there is of him.[4]

[3] *Death in the Afternoon,* p. 182 (Cape). American edition (Scribner), p. 191.—ED.

[4] *Ibid.,* pp. 182-83. American edition (Scribner), p. 191.—ED.

No statement of a writer's objects and intentions could be clearer; and here it seems to me is the final proof, if proof is needed, that the legend of Hemingway's toughness (i.e., emotionlessness, dumbness, thick-skinnedness, etc.) had never any basis in fact. What Hemingway realized, and what it is important all short-story writers should realize, was that it is possible to convey a great many things on paper without stating them at all. To master the art of implication, of making one sentence say two or more different things, by conveying emotion and atmosphere without drawing up a tidy balance sheet of descriptions about them, is more than half the short-story writer's business. Because he mastered that business with a new staccato slickness of style, eliminating so much of what had been considered essential literary paraphernalia, Hemingway was and still is a most important writer.

Like all iconoclasts who break in on the stuffiness of their particular age with rude disregard for accepted behavior, Hemingway was dangerous to imitate. It would be hard to assess the number of versions of "Hills Like White Elephants" received by editors during the last ten or fifteen years, but it would probably exceed the number of imitations of *Winesburg, Ohio*. One-story writers in the Hemingway-Anderson manner popped up all over America just as one-book writers in the D. H. Lawrence manner popped up all over England. Both types in turn were never heard of again, but the fertilizing influence of Hemingway and Anderson went on.

The extent of that influence has been enormous. Anderson indicated that the American short-story writer had better practice self-denial in the matter of territory—he must be content with the regional, not the national, view; Hemingway indicated that the American short-story writer should practice another kind of self-denial—the denial of irrelevant material, literary tricks, luxury emotions, literary descriptions, and literary faking.

If the writer of prose knows enough about what he is writing about he may omit things that he knows and the reader, if the writer is writing truly enough, will have a feeling of those things as strongly as though the writer had stated them.[5]

Inspired by such teaching, which incidentally achieved for the short story a new kind of commercial success, a whole generation of American short-story writers turned round to American earth, American cities, small American towns, American homes, Ameri-

[5] *Ibid.*, p. 183. American edition (Scribner), p. 192.—ED.

can politics, and American hopes and troubles, to find waiting for it the limitless untouched raw materials of a new American tradition. Writers had once shipped themselves, or had been shipped by anxious editors, to Cuba and Tahiti and Honolulu and other romantic spots in order to find something known as local color. Now suddenly they found their local color in Ohio valleys, in the fishing villages of Cape Cod, in San Francisco saloons, in Southern feuds between Negro and white, in the Middle West, on wayside hot-dog stands, on East Side New York, in Texas, indeed everywhere on their own multitongued conglomerous continent.

In writing of all this, they did something else which was significant. They took the language, which was still English, as they found it. They took it straight off the earth, the saloon floor, the café table, the factory bench, the street, and the drugstore counter, not troubling to wipe off the colloquial dirt or the spittle, the common dust or the color, the wit or the fantastically apt metaphor, the slickness or the slang. They took free speech and made it into free writing: a more flexible, more vital, more fluent writing, a braver and newer writing than ever the overintellectualized writing of Mr. Huxley's *Brave New World* had known how to be.

H. E. Bates

MARK SPILKA

The Death of Love in *The Sun Also Rises*

> She turns and looks a moment in the glass,
> Hardly aware of her departed lover;
> Her brain allows one half-formed thought to pass:
> "Well now that's done: and I'm glad it's over."
> When lovely woman stoops to folly and
> Paces about her room again, alone,
> She smoothes her hair with automatic hand,
> And puts a record on the gramophone.
>
> T. S. Eliot, *The Waste Land*

One of the most persistent themes of the twenties was the death of love in World War I. All the major writers recorded it, often in piecemeal fashion, as part of the larger postwar scene; but only Hemingway seems to have caught it whole and delivered it in lasting fictional form. His intellectual grasp of the theme might account for this. Where D. H. Lawrence settles for the shock of war on the Phallic Consciousness, or where Eliot presents assorted glimpses of sterility, Hemingway seems to design an extensive parable. Thus, in *The Sun Also Rises,* his protagonists are deliberately shaped as allegorical figures: Jake Barnes and Brett Ashley are two lovers desexed by the war; Robert Cohn is the false knight who challenges their despair; while Romero, the stalwart bullfighter, personifies the good life which will survive their failure. Of course, these characters are not abstractions in the text; they are realized through the most concrete style in American fiction, and their larger meaning is implied only by their response to immediate situations. But the implications are there, the parable is at work in every scene, and its presence lends unity and depth to the whole novel.

Barnes himself is a fine example of this technique. Cut off from love by a shell wound, he seems to suffer from an undeserved misfortune. But as most readers agree, his condition represents a peculiar form of emotional impotence. It does not involve distaste for the flesh, as with Lawrence's crippled veteran, Clifford

Chatterley; instead Barnes lacks the power to control love's strength and durability. His sexual wound, the result of an unpreventable "accident" in the war, points to another realm where accidents can always happen and where Barnes is equally powerless to prevent them. In Book II of the novel he makes this same comparison while describing one of the dinners at Pamplona: "It was like certain dinners I remember from the war. There was much wine, an ignored tension, and a feeling of things coming that you could not prevent happening." This fear of emotional consequences is the key to Barnes's condition. Like so many Hemingway heroes, he has no way to handle subjective complications, and his wound is a token for this kind of impotence.

It serves the same purpose for the expatriate crowd in Paris. In some figurative manner these artists, writers, and derelicts have all been rendered impotent by the war. Thus, as Barnes presents them, they pass before us like a parade of sexual cripples, and we are able to measure them against his own forbearance in the face of a common problem. Whoever bears his sickness well is akin to Barnes; whoever adopts false postures, or willfully hurts others, falls short of his example. This is the organizing principle in Book I, this alignment of characters by their stoic qualities. But, stoic or not, they are all incapable of love, and in their sober moments they seem to know it.

For this reason they feel especially upset whenever Robert Cohn appears. Cohn still upholds a romantic view of life, and since he affirms it with stubborn persistence, he acts like a goad upon his wiser contemporaries. As the narrator, Barnes must account for the challenge he presents them and the decisive turn it takes in later chapters. Accordingly, he begins the book with a review of Cohn's boxing career at Princeton. Though he has no taste for it, college boxing means a lot to Cohn. For one thing, it helps to compensate for anti-Semitic treatment from his classmates. More subtly, it turns him into an armed romantic, a man who can damage others in defense of his own beliefs. He also loves the pose of manhood which it affords him and seems strangely pleased when his nose is flattened in the ring. Soon other tokens of virility delight him, and he often confuses them with actual manliness. He likes the idea of a mistress more than he likes his actual mistress; or he likes the authority of editing and the prestige of writing, though he is a bad editor and a poor novelist. In other words, he always looks for internal strength in outward signs and sources. On leaving Princeton, he marries "on the rebound from the rotten time . . . in college." But in five years the marriage falls through, and he rebounds again to his present mistress, the forceful Frances Clyne. Then, to escape her dominance and his own disquiet, he begins to look for romance in far-off countries. As with most of his views, the source of this idea is an exotic book:

He had been reading W. H. Hudson. That sounds like an innocent occupation, but Cohn had read and reread "The Purple Land." "The Purple Land" is a very sinister book if read too late in life. It recounts splendid imaginary amorous adventures of a perfect English gentleman in an intensely romantic land, the scenery of which is very well described. For a man to take it at thirty-four as a guidebook to what life holds is about as safe as it would be for a man of the same age to enter Wall Street direct from a French convent, equipped with a complete set of the more practical Alger books. Cohn, I believe, took every word of "The Purple Land" as literally as though it had been an R. G. Dun report.

Cohn's romanticism explains his key position in the parable. He is the last chivalric hero, the last defender of an outworn faith, and his function is to illustrate its present folly—to show us, through the absurdity of his behavior, that romantic love is dead, that one of the great guiding codes of the past no longer operates. "You're getting damned romantic," says Brett to Jake at one point in the novel. "No, bored," he replies, because for this generation boredom has become more plausible than love. As a foil to his contemporaries, Cohn helps to reveal why this is so.

Of course, there is much that is traditional in the satire on Cohn. Like the many victims of romantic literature, from Don Quixote to Tom Sawyer, he lives by what he reads and neglects reality at his own and others' peril. But Barnes and his friends have no alternative to Cohn's beliefs. There is nothing here, for example, like the neat balance between sense and sensibility in Jane Austen's world. Granted that Barnes is sensible enough, that he sees life clearly and that we are meant to contrast his private grief with Cohn's public suffering, his self-restraint with Cohn's deliberate self-exposure. Yet, emasculation aside, Barnes has no way to measure or control the state of love; and though he recognizes this with his mind and tries to act accordingly, he seems no different from Cohn in his deepest feelings. When he is alone with Brett, he wants to live with her in the country, to go with her to San Sebastian, to go up to her room, to keep her in his own room, or to keep on kissing her—though he can never really act upon such sentiments. Nor are they merely the yearnings of a tragically impotent man, for eventually they will lead Barnes to betray his own principles and to abandon self-respect, all for the sake of Lady Ashley. No, at best he is a restrained romantic, a man who carries himself well in the face of love's impossibilities, but who seems to share with Cohn a common (if hidden) weakness.

The sexual parade continues through the early chapters. Besides Cohn and his possessive mistress, there is the prostitute Georgette, whom Barnes picks up one day "because of a vague sentimental idea that it would be nice to eat with someone." Barnes introduces her to his friends as his fiancée, and as his private joke affirms, the two have much in common. Georgette is sick and sterile, having reduced love to a simple monetary exchange; but, like Barnes, she manages to be frank and forthright and to keep an even keel among the drifters of Paris. Together they form a pair of honest cripples, in contrast with the various pretenders whom they meet along the Left Bank. Among the latter are Cohn and Frances Clyne, the writer Braddocks and his wife, and Robert Prentiss, a rising young novelist who seems to verbalize their phoniness: "Oh, how charmingly you get angry," he tells Barnes. "I wish I had that faculty." Barnes's honest anger has been aroused by the appearance of a band of homosexuals, accompanied by Brett Ashley. When one of the band spies Georgette, he decides to dance with her; then one by one the rest follow suit, in deliberate parody of normal love. Brett herself provides a key to the dizzy sexual medley. With a man's felt hat on her boyish bob, and with her familiar reference to men as fellow "chaps," she completes the distortion of sexual roles which seems to characterize the period. For the war, which has unmanned Barnes and his contemporaries, has turned Brett into the freewheeling equal of any man. It has taken her first sweetheart's life through dysentery and has sent her present husband home in a dangerous state of shock. For Brett these blows are the equivalent of Jake's emasculation; they seem to release her from her womanly nature and expose her to the male prerogatives of drink and promiscuity. Once she claims these rights as her own, she becomes an early but more honest version of Catherine Barkley, the English nurse in Hemingway's next important novel, *A Farewell to Arms*. Like Catherine, Brett has been a nurse on the Italian front and has lost a sweetheart in the war; but for her there is no saving interlude of love with a wounded patient, no rigged and timely escape through death in childbirth. Instead she survives the colossal violence, the disruption of her personal life, and the exposure to mass promiscuity, to confront a moral and emotional vacuum among her postwar lovers. With this evidence of male default all around her, she steps off the romantic pedestal, moves freely through the bars of Paris, and stands confidently there beside her newfound equals. Ironically, her most recent conquest, Robert Cohn, fails to see the bearing of such changes on romantic love. He still believes that Brett is womanly and therefore deeply serious about intimate matters. After their first meeting, he describes her as "absolutely fine and straight" and nearly strikes Barnes for thinking otherwise; and a bit later, after their brief affair in the country, he remains unconvinced "that it didn't mean anything." But when men no longer command respect, and women replace their natural warmth with masculine freedom and mobility, there can be no serious love.

Brett does have some respect for Barnes, even a little tenderness, though her actions scarcely show abiding love. At best she can affirm his worth and share his standards and perceptions. When in public, she knows how to keep her essential misery to herself; when alone with Barnes, she will express her feelings, admit her faults, and even display good judgment. Thus her friend Count Mippipopolous is introduced to Barnes as "one of us." The count qualifies by virtue of his war wounds, his invariable calmness, and his curious system of values. He appreciates good food, good wine, and a quiet place in which to enjoy them. Love also has a place in his system, but since he is "always in love," the place seems rather shaky. Like Jake and Brett and perhaps Georgette, he simply bears himself well among the postwar ruins.

The count completes the list of cripples who appear in Book I. In a broader sense, they are all disaffiliates, all men and women who have cut themselves off from conventional society and who have made Paris their permanent playground. Jake Barnes has introduced them, and we have been able to test them against his stoic attitudes toward life in a moral wasteland. Yet such life is finally unbearable, as we have also seen whenever Jake and Brett are alone together, or whenever Jake is alone with his thoughts. He needs a healthier code to live by, and for this reason the movement in Book II is away from Paris to the trout stream at Burguete and the bull ring at Pamplona. Here a more vital testing process occurs, and with the appearance of Bill Gorton we get our first inkling of its nature.

Gorton is a successful writer who shares with Barnes a love for boxing and other sports. In Vienna he has helped to rescue a splendid Negro boxer from an angry and intolerant crowd. The incident has spoiled Vienna for him, and, as his reaction suggests, the sports world will provide the terms of moral judgment from this point onward in the novel. Or, more accurately, Jake Barnes's feelings about sports will shape the rest of the novel. For, with Hemingway, the great outdoors is chiefly a state of mind, a projection of moral and emotional attitudes onto physical arenas, so that a clear account of surface action will reproduce these attitudes in the reader. In "Big Two-Hearted River," for example, he describes Nick Adams' fishing and camping activities along a trout stream in Michigan. His descriptions run to considerable length, and they are all carefully detailed, almost as if they were meant for a fishing manual. Yet the details themselves have strong emotional connotations for Nick Adams. He thinks of his camp as "the good place," the place where none of his previous troubles can touch him. He has left society behind him, and, as the story begins, there is even a burnt town at his back, to signify his disaffiliation. He has also walked miles to reach an arbitrary campsite, and this is one of the ways in which he sets his own conditions for happiness and then lives up to them. He finds extraordinary pleasure, moreover, in the techniques of making coffee and pitching camp, or in his responses to fishing and eating. In fact, his sensations have become so valuable that he doesn't want to rush them: they bring health, pleasure, beauty, and a sense of order which is sorely missing in his civilized experience; they are part of a healing process, a private and imaginative means of wiping out the damages of civilized life. When this process is described with elaborate attention to surface detail, the effect on the reader is decidedly subjective.

The same holds true, of course, for the fishing trip in *The Sun Also Rises*. As Barnes and Gorton approach "the good place," each item in the landscape is singled out and given its own importance. Later the techniques of fishing are treated with the same reverence for detail. For, like Nick Adams, these men have left the wasteland for the green plains of health; they have traveled miles, by train and on foot, to reach a particular trout stream. The fishing there is good, the talk free and easy, and even Barnes is able to sleep well after lunch, though he is usually an insomniac. The meal itself is handled like a mock religious ceremony: "Let us rejoice in our blessings," says Gorton. "Let us utilize the fowls of the air. Let us utilize the produce of the vine. Will you utilize a little, brother?" A few days later, when they visit the old monastery at Roncesvalles, this combination of fishing, drinking, and male camaraderie is given an edge over religion itself. With their English friend, Harris, they honor the monastery as a remarkable place, but decide that "it isn't the same as fishing"; then all agree to "utilize" a little pub across the way. At the trout stream, moreover, romantic love is given the same comparative treatment and seems sadly foolish before the immediate joys of fishing:

It was a little past noon and there was not much shade, but I sat against the trunk of two of the trees that grew together, and read. The book was something by A. E. W. Mason, and I was reading a wonderful story about a man who had been frozen in the Alps and then fallen into a glacier and disappeared, and his bride was going to wait twenty-four years exactly for his body to come out on the moraine, while her true love waited too, and they were still waiting when Bill came up [with four trout in his bag]. . . . His face was sweaty and happy.

As these comparisons show, the fishing trip has been invested with unique importance. By sticking closely to the surface action, Barnes has evoked the deeper attitudes which underlie it and which make it a therapeutic process for him. He describes himself now as a "rotten Catholic" and speaks briefly of his thwarted love for Brett; but with religion defunct and love no longer possible, he can at least find happiness through private and imaginative means. Thus he now constructs a more positive code to follow: as with Nick Adams, it brings him health, pleasure, beauty and order, and helps to wipe out the damage of his troubled life in Paris.

Yet somehow the code lacks depth and substance. To gain these advantages, Barnes must move to Pamplona, which stands roughly to Burguete as the swamp in "Big Two-Hearted River" stands to the trout stream. In the latter story, Nick Adams prefers the clear portion of the river to its second and more congested heart:

In the swamp the banks were bare, the big cedars came together overhead, the sun did not come through, except in patches; in the fast deep water, in the half light, the fishing would be tragic. In the swamp fishing was a tragic adventure. Nick did not want it. . . . There were plenty of days coming when he could fish the swamp.

The fishing is tragic here because it involves the risk of death. Nick is not yet ready for that challenge, but plainly it will test his manhood when he comes to face it. In *The Sun Also Rises* Barnes makes no such demands upon himself; but he is strongly attracted to the young bullfighter, Pedro Romero, whose courage before death lends moral weight to the sportsman's code.[1]

So Pamplona is an extension of Burguete for Barnes: gayer and more festive on the surface, but essentially more serious. The spoilers from Paris have arrived, but (Cohn excepted) they are soon swept up by the fiesta: their mood is jubilant, they are surrounded by dancers, and they sing, drink, and shout with the peasant crowd. Barnes himself is among fellow *aficionados;* he gains "real emotion" from the bullfights and feels truly elated afterwards. Even his friends seem like "such nice people," though he begins to feel uneasy when an argument breaks out between them. The tension is created by Brett's fiancé, Mike Campbell, who is aware of her numerous infidelities and who seems to accept them with amoral tolerance. Actually he resents them, so that Cohn (the perennial Jewish scapegoat) provides him with a convenient outlet for his feelings. He begins to bait him for following Brett around like a sick steer.

Mike's description is accurate enough. Cohn is always willing to suffer in public and to absorb insults for the sake of true love. On the other hand, he is also "ready to do battle for his lady," and when the chance finally comes, he knocks his rivals down like a genuine knight-errant. With Jake and Mike he has no trouble, but when he charges into Pedro's room to rescue Brett, the results are disastrous: Brett tells him off, the bullfighter refuses to stay knocked down, and no one will shake hands with him at the end, in accord with prep-school custom. When Brett

---

[1] Hemingway's preoccupation with death has been explained in various ways: by his desire to write about simple, fundamental things; by his "sado-masochism"; or, more fairly and accurately, by his need to efface an actual war wound, or to supplant the ugly, senseless violence of war with ordered, graceful violence. Yet chiefly the risk of death lends moral seriousness to a private code which lacks it. The risk is arbitrary; when a man elects to meet it, his beliefs take on subjective weight and he is able to give meaning to his private life. In this sense, he moves forever on a kind of imaginative frontier, where the opposition is always Nature, in some token form, where the stakes are always manliness and self-respect, and where death invests the scene with tragic implications. In *The Sun Also Rises*, Romero lives on such a frontier, and for Barnes and his friends he provides an example of just these values.

remains with Pedro, Cohn retires to his room, alone and friend-less.

This last encounter is the high point of the parable, for in the Code Hero, the Romantic Hero has finally met his match. As the clash between them shows, there is a difference between physical and moral victory, between chivalric stubbornness and real self-respect. Thus Pedro fights to repair an affront to his dignity; though he is badly beaten, his spirit is untouched by his opponent, whereas Cohn's spirit is completely smashed. From the beginning Cohn has based his manhood on skill at boxing, or upon a woman's love, never upon internal strength; but now, when neither skill nor love supports him, he has bludgeoned his way to his own emptiness. Compare his conduct with Romero's, on the following day, as the younger man performs for Brett in the bull ring:

Everything of which he could control the locality he did in front of her all that afternoon. Never once did he look up. . . . Because he did not look up to ask if it pleased he did it all for himself inside, and it strengthened him, and yet he did it for her, too. But he did not do it for her at any loss to himself. He gained by it all through the afternoon.

Thus, where Cohn expends and degrades himself for his beloved, Romero pays tribute without self-loss. His manhood is a thing independent of women, and for this reason he holds special at-tractions for Jake Barnes.

By now it seems apparent that Cohn and Pedro are extremes for which Barnes is the unhappy medium. His resemblance to Pedro is clear enough: they share the same code, they both be-lieve that a man's dignity depends on his own resources. His re-semblance to Cohn is more subtle, but at this stage of the book it becomes grossly evident. Appropriately enough, the exposure comes through the knockout blow from Cohn, which dredges up a strange prewar experience:

Walking across the square to the hotel everything looked new and changed. . . . I felt as I felt once coming home from an out-of-town football game. I was carrying a suitcase with my football things in it, and I walked up the street from the station in the town I had lived in all my life and it was all new. They were raking the lawns and burning leaves in the road, and I stopped for a long time and watched. It was all strange. Then I went on, and my feet seemed to be a long way off, and everything seemed to come from a long way off, and I could hear my feet walking a great distance away. I had been kicked in the head early in the game. It was like that crossing the square. It was like that going up the stairs in the hotel. Going up the stairs took a long time, and I had the feeling that I was carrying my suitcase.

Barnes seems to have regressed here to his youthful football days. As he moves on up the stairs to see Cohn, who has been asking for him, he still carries his "phantom suitcase" with him; and when he enters Cohn's room, he even sets it down. Cohn himself has just returned from the fight with Romero: "There he was, face down on the bed, crying. He had on a white polo shirt, the kind he'd worn at Princeton." In other words, Cohn has also regressed to his abject college days: they are both emotional adolescents, about the same age as the nineteen-year-old Romero, who is the only real man among them. Of course, these facts are not spelled out for us, except through the polo shirt and the phantom suitcase, which remind us (inadvertently) of one of those dreamlike fantasies by the Czech genius Franz Kafka, in which trunks and youthful clothes are symbols of arrested development. Yet there has already been some helpful spelling out in Book I, during a curious (and otherwise pointless) exchange between Cohn and another expatriate, the drunkard Harvey Stone. After first calling Cohn a moron, Harvey asks him to say, without thinking about it, what he would rather do if he could do anything he wanted. Cohn is again urged to say what comes into his head first, and soon replies, "I think I'd rather play football again with what I know about handling myself, now." To which Harvey responds: "I misjudged you. . . . You're not a moron. You're only a case of arrested development."

The first thought to enter Cohn's mind here has been suppressed by Barnes for a long time, but in Book II the knockout blow releases it: more than anything else, he too would like to "play football again," to prevent that kick to his head from happening, or that smash to the jaw from Cohn, or that sexual wound which explains either blow. For the truth about Barnes seems obvious now: he has always been an emotional adolescent. Like Nick Adams, he has grown up in a society which has little use for manliness; as an expression of that society, the war has robbed him of his dignity as a man and has thus exposed him to indignities with women. We must understand here that the war, the early football game, and the fight with Cohn have this in common: they all involve ugly, senseless, or impersonal forms of violence, in which a man has little chance to set the terms of his own integrity. Hence for Hemingway they represent the kinds

of degradation which can occur at any point in modern society—
and the violence at Pamplona is our current sample of such
degradation. Indeed, the whole confluence of events now points
to the social meaning of Jake's wound, for just as Cohn has reduced him to a dazed adolescent, so has Brett reduced him to a
slavish pimp. When she asks for his help in her affair with Pedro,
Barnes has no integrity to rely on; he can only serve her as Cohn
has served her, like a sick romantic steer. Thus, for love's sake,
he will allow her to use him as a go-between, to disgrace him with
his friend Montoya, to corrupt Romero, and so strip the whole
fiesta of significance. In the next book he will even run to her
rescue in Madrid, though by then he can at least recognize his
folly and supply his own indictment: "That was it. Send a girl off
with one man. Introduce her to another to go off with him. Now
go and bring her back. And sign the wire with love. That was it all
right." It seems plain, then, that Cohn and Brett have given us a
peacetime demonstration, postwar style, of the meaning of Jake's
shell wound.

At Pamplona the demonstration continues. Brett strolls through
the fiesta with her head high, "as though [it] were being staged
in her honor, and she found it pleasant and amusing." When
Romero presents her with a bull's ear "cut by popular acclama-
tion," she carries it off to her hotel, stuffs it far back in the drawer
of the bed table, and forgets about it. The ear was taken, however,
from the same bull which had killed one of the crowd a few days
before, during the dangerous bull-run through the streets; later
the entire town attended the man's funeral, along with drinking
and dancing societies from nearby communities. For the crowd,
the death of this bull was a communal triumph and his ear a
token of communal strength; for Brett the ear is a private trophy.
In effect, she has robbed the community of its triumph, as she
will now rob it of its hero. As an *aficionado,* Barnes understands
this threat too well. These are decadent times in the bull ring,
marred by false esthetics; Romero alone has "the old thing," the
old "purity of line through the maximum of exposure": his corruption by Brett will complete the decadence. But mainly the
young fighter means something more personal to Barnes. In the
bull ring he combines grace, control, and sincerity with manliness;
in the fight with Cohn he proves his integrity where skill is lacking. His values are exactly those of the hunter in "Francis Macomber," or of the fisherman in *The Old Man and the Sea.* As one of
these few remaining images of independent manhood, he offers

Barnes the comfort of vicarious redemption. Brett seems to smash this as she leaves with Pedro for Madrid. To ward off depression, Barnes can only get drunk and retire to bed; the fiesta goes on outside, but it means nothing now: the "good place" has been ruined.

As Book III begins, Barnes tries to reclaim his dignity and to cleanse himself of the damage at Pamplona. He goes to San Sebastian and sits quietly there in a café, listening to band concerts; or he goes swimming there alone, diving deep in the green waters. Then a telegram from Brett arrives, calling him to Madrid to help her out of trouble. At once he is like Cohn again, ready to serve his lady at the expense of self-respect. Yet in Madrid he learns to accept, emotionally, what he has always faintly understood. As he listens to Brett, he begins to drink heavily, as if her story has driven home a painful lesson. Brett herself feels "rather good" about sending Pedro away: she has at least been able to avoid being "one of these bitches that ruins children." This is a moral triumph for her, as Barnes agrees; but he can scarcely ignore its implications for himself. For when Brett refuses to let her hair grow long for Pedro, it means that her role in life is fixed: she can no longer reclaim her lost womanhood; she can no longer live with a fine man without destroying him. This seems to kill the illusion which is behind Jake's suffering throughout the novel: namely, that if he hadn't been wounded, if he had somehow survived the war with his manhood intact, then he and Brett would have become true lovers. The closing lines confirm his total disillusionment:

"Oh, Jake," Brett said, "we could have had such a damned good time together."
Ahead was a mounted policeman in khaki directing traffic. He raised his baton. The car slowed suddenly pressing Brett against me.
"Yes," I said. "Isn't it pretty to think so?"

"Pretty" is a romantic word which means here "foolish to consider what could *never* have happened," and not "what can't happen now." The signal for this interpretation comes from the policeman who directs traffic between Brett's speech and Barnes's reply. With his khaki clothes and his preventive baton, he stands for the war and the society which made it, for the force which stops the lovers' car, and which robs them of their normal sexual roles. As Barnes now sees, love itself is dead for their generation.

Even without his wound, he would still be unmanly, and Brett unable to let her hair grow long.

Yet, according to the opening epigraphs, if one generation is lost and another comes, the earth abides forever; and according to Hemingway himself, the abiding earth is the novel's hero. Perhaps he is wrong on this point, or at least misleading. There are no joyous hymns to the seasons in this novel, no celebrations of fertility and change. The scenic descriptions are accurate enough, but rather flat; there is no deep feeling in them, only fondness, for the author takes less delight in nature than in outdoor sports. He is more concerned, that is, with baiting hooks and catching trout than with the Irati River and more pleased with the grace and skill of the bullfighter than with the bull's magnificence. In fact, it is the bullfighter who seems to abide in the novel, for surely the bulls are dead like the trout before them, having fulfilled their roles as beloved opponents. But Romero is very much alive as the novel ends. When he leaves the hotel in Madrid, he "pays the bill" for his affair with Brett, which means that he has earned all its benefits. He also dominates the final conversation between the lovers, and so dominates the closing section. We learn here that his sexual initiation has been completed and his independence assured. From now on, he can work out his life alone, moving again and again through his passes in the ring, gaining strength, order, and purpose as he meets his own conditions. He provides no literal prescription to follow here, no call to bullfighting as the answer to Barnes's problems; but he does provide an image of integrity, against which Barnes and his generation are weighed and found wanting. In this sense, Pedro is the real hero of the parable, the final moral touchstone, the man whose code gives meaning to a world where love and religion are defunct, where the proofs of manhood are difficult and scarce, and where every man must learn to define his own moral conditions and then live up to them.

Mark Spilka

HARRY LEVIN

Observations on the Style of Ernest Hemingway

I

"The most important author living today, the outstanding author since the death of Shakespeare," is Ernest Hemingway. So we have lately been assured by John O'Hara in *The New York Times Book Review*. We should have to know what Mr. O'Hara thinks of the various intervening authors, of Shakespeare himself, and indeed of literature, in order to get the full benefit of this evaluation. It might be inferred, from his review of *Across the River and into the Trees,* that he holds them well on this side of idolatry. Inasmuch as Hemingway's latest novel tends regrettably to run certain attitudes and mannerisms to the ground, merely to describe it—if I may use an unsportsmanlike simile—is like shooting a sitting bird. Mr. O'Hara's gallant way of protecting this vulnerable target is to charge the air with invidious comparisons. His final encomium should be quoted in full, inasmuch as it takes no more than two short words, which manage to catch the uncertainty of the situation as well as the strident unsteadiness of Mr. O'Hara's tone: "Real class." That interesting phrase, which could be more appropriately applied to a car or a girl, carries overtones of petty snobbery; it seems to look up toward an object which, it admits in wistful awe, transcends such sordid articles of the same commodity as ordinarily fall within its ken. To whistle after Hemingway in this fashion is doubtless a sincerer form of flattery than tributes which continue to be inhibited by the conventions of literary discourse. Had Mr. O'Hara been a French symbolist poet, he might have said: *Tout le reste est littérature.*

Yet Hemingway too, one way or another, is literature. If his preoccupation has been mortality, his ambition—spurred perhaps by having easily won such rewards as contemporaries offer—is nothing less than immortality. He doesn't speak of building a

93

monument or even burning a candle, but he sometimes refers to
playing in the big league or writing something that will not soon go
bad. Shakespeare, as Colonel Cantwell acknowledges in *Across
the River,* is "the winner and still the undisputed champion." But
Mr. O'Hara's buildup seems to suggest that Hemingway is training for the title bout. At least there are confirmatory signs, to
state the matter in milder and more bookish terms, that he is
becoming a classic in his time. He has just become the subject of
"a critical survey" which should be welcomed as the first of its
kind, with the expectation that its shortcomings will probably be
made good by a long shelf of future volumes devoted to *Heming-
wayforschung.*[1] Since the present volume has been pasted together
from other publications, it does not pretend to originality; it offers
a readable and typical selection of twenty-one reviews and articles.
This sort of symposium, especially when it concentrates upon so
compact a body of material, is bound to cross and recross familiar
territory. It is no discredit to the contributors—in fact it rein-
forces their positions—that they do not diverge from each other
more variously. However, it raises questions reflecting upon the
judgment and knowledge of the anthologist.

He does not seem to have cast a very wide net. Given the scope
and impact of his author, we might fairly expect international
representation. But, except for one Soviet contribution, the table
of contents is one hundred per cent American, thereby excluding
such significant essays as the almost classical polemic of Wyndham
Lewis or the more recent appreciation of Claude-Edmonde Magny.
Closer to home, it is hard to see how the editor—whose introduction strives to counterbalance the negative emphasis of so much
criticism—could have overlooked the handsome tribute and
prescient revaluation by Robert Penn Warren, which appeared in
The Kenyon Review (Winter, 1947). Yet sins of omission, with
anthologies, should always be considered venial; and we need not
question the individual merits of the editor's inclusions. Some of
them justify their place by being too little known and not readily
accessible: notably Lincoln Kirstein's sensitive review of *Death in
the Afternoon* and Edward Fenimore's informative article on the
language of *For Whom the Bell Tolls.* But others, though not less
notable, are not so readily justified: chapters from volumes still
in print by Edmund Wilson, Alfred Kazin, and W. M. Frohock.
It should also be pointed out that Malcolm Cowley has published

[1] *Ernest Hemingway: The Man and His Work,* edited by John K. M.
McCaffery. World Publishing Company, 1950.

better pieces on Hemingway than the profile that Mr. McCaffery reprints from *Life*. The editor might have done a more useful job by collecting Hemingway's unreprinted writings. These are not touched upon by the bibliography, which is therefore inadequate; and there are no notes to identify the contributors, though several of them require identification. Since the chronological arrangement is based on dates of books, rather than periodical publication, it is somewhat misleading.

Yet when these cavils have been duly registered, it should be acknowledged that the book remains faithful to its protagonist. Its qualities and defects, like his, are journalistic—and I use that term in no deprecatory spirit, for journalism has more often than not been the school of our ablest writers, from Mark Twain to Hemingway himself. I simply refer to the losing race that fiction runs against fact, the hot pursuit of immediate reality in which the journalist outstrips the novelist, and also the risks—artistic as well as physical—that the imaginative writer takes by competing on the reporter's ground. For one thing, the successful reporter is seldom content to remain a good observer; give him a by-line, and he starts writing about himself; and he ends by making news for his professional colleagues, the gossip columnists. From all accounts, including his own, it would seem that, as a correspondent in the last war, Hemingway saw action in more ways than one. It may be that his refusal to draw the line between actor and spectator is one of the secrets of his vitality. Herein it is reported by John Groth that "Hemingway's jeep driver knew him as Hemingway the guy, rather than Hemingway the famous writer." And Mr. McCaffery devotes his particular enthusiasm to "Hemingway as a man among men." We see him plain; we hear and applaud his feats as soldier, traveler, sportsman, athlete, and playboy; and sooner or later we find ourselves asking why this consummate extrovert should have taken the trouble to become a famous writer.

If he was, as we are informed, "an okay joe" to his comrades in arms, he is something more complex to his fellow writers. Their collected opinions range from grudging admiration to fascinated suspicion. Though most of them make their separate peace with him, they leave a total impression which is fairly consistent and surprisingly hostile. The exception that proves the rule, in this case Elliot Paul, is the warm admirer who demonstrates his loyalty by belaboring Hemingway's critics. Few of them are able to maintain the distinction, premised by Mr. McCaffery's subtitle, between "the man" and "his work." Curiously

enough, the single essay that undertakes to deal with craftsmanship is the one that emanates from Marxist Russia. The rest,
though they incidentally contain some illuminating comments on
technique, seem more interested in recapitulating the phases of
Hemingway's career, in treating him as the spokesman of his
generation, or in coming to grips with a natural phenomenon.
All this is an impressive testimonial to the force of his personality.
Yet what is personality, when it manifests itself in art, if not style?
It is not because of the figure he cuts in the rotogravure sections,
or for his views on philosophy and politics, that we listen to a
leading *Heldentenor*. No contemporary voice has excited more admiration and envy, stimulated more imitation and parody, and had
more effect on the rhythms of our speech than Hemingway's has
done. Ought we not then, first and last, to be discussing the characteristics of his prose, when we talk about a man who—as Archibald MacLeish has written—"whittled a style for his time"?

II

Mr. Hemingway, in his turn, would hardly be himself—which he
is, of course, quite as consciously as any writer could be—if he
did not take a dim view of criticism. This is understandable and,
as he would say, right: since criticism, ever seeking perspective,
moves in the very opposite direction from his object, which has
been immediacy. His ardent quest for experience has involved
him in a lifelong campaign against everything that tends to get
in its way, including those more or less labored efforts to interpret and communicate it which may be regarded—if not disre-
garded—as academic. Those of us who live in the shelter of the
academy will not be put off by his disregard; for most of us have
more occasion than he to be repelled by the encrustations of
pedantry; and many of us are predisposed to sympathize with
him, as well as with ourselves, when he tells us what is lacking in
critics and scholars. That he continues to do so is a mark of attention which ought not to go unappreciated. Thus currently, in
introducing a brilliant young Italian novelist to American readers,
he departs from his subject to drive home a critical contrast:[2]

The Italy that [Elio Vittorini] learned and the America that the American boys learned [writes Ernest Hemingway, making a skillful transi-
tion] has little to do with the Academic Italy or America that periodi-

[2] *In Italy*, by Elio Vittorini, translated by Wilfrid David, introduction by
Ernest Hemingway. New Directions.

cally attacks all writing like a dust storm and is always, until everything shall be completely dry, dispersed by rain.

Since Hemingway is sparing in his use of metaphors, the one he introduces here is significant. "Dryasdust" has long been the layman's stock epithet for the results of scholarly inquiry; while drouth, as evoked by T. S. Eliot, has become a basic symbol of modern anxiety. The country that seems to interest Hemingway most, Spain, is in some respects a literal wasteland; and his account of it—memorably his sound track for the Joris Ivens film, *The Spanish Earth*—emphasizes its dryness. Water, the contrasting element, for Hemingway as for his fellow men, symbolizes the purification and renewal of life. Rain beats out a cadence which runs through his work: through *A Farewell to Arms,* for example, where it lays the dust raised by soldiers' boots at the outset, accompanies the retreat from Caporetto, and stays with the hero when the heroine dies—even providing the very last word at the end. It is rain which, in a frequently quoted paragraph, shows up the unreality of "the words sacred, glorious, and sacrifice and the expression in vain." In the present instance, having reduced the contemporary situation to a handful of dust, as it were, Hemingway comes back to that sense of reality which he is willing to share with Vittorini. In the course of a single sentence, utilizing a digressive Ciceronian device, paraleipsis, he has not only rounded up such writers as he considers academic; he has not only accused them of sterility, by means of that slippery logical short cut which we professors term an enthymeme; but, like the veteran strategist he is, he has also managed to imply that they are the attackers and that he is fighting a strictly defensive action.

The conflict advances into the next paragraph, which opens on the high note that closed the previous one and then drops down again anticlimactically:

Rain to an academician is probably, after the first fall has cleared the air, H_2O with, of course, traces of other things.

Even the ultimate source of nature's vitality is no more than a jejune scientific formula to us, if I may illustrate Hemingway's point by paraphrasing his sentence. Whereas—and for a moment it seems as if the theme of fertility would be sounded soon again—but no, the emphasis waxes increasingly negative:

To a good writer, needing something to bring the dry country alive so that it will not be a desert where only such cactus as New York literary reviews grow dry and sad, inexistent without the watering of their benefactors, feeding on the dried manure of schism and the dusty taste of disputed dialectics, their only flowering a desiccated criticism as alive as stuffed birds, and their steady mulch the dehydrated cuds of fellow critics; . . .

There is more to come, but we had better pause and ruminate upon this particular mouthful. Though we may or may not accept Hemingway's opinion, we must admit that he makes us taste his distaste. Characteristically, he does not countercriticize or state the issue in intellectual terms. Instead he proceeds from agriculture to the dairy, through an atmosphere calculated to make New Yorkers uncomfortable, elaborating his earthy metaphor into a barnyard allegory which culminates in a scatological gesture. The gibe about benefactors is a curious one, since it appears to take commercial success as a literary criterion, and at the same time to identify financial support with spiritual nourishment. The hopeful adjective "alive," repeated in this deadening context, is ironically illustrated by a musty ornithological specimen: so much for criticism! Such a phrase as "disputed dialectics," which is unduly alliterative, slightly tautological, and—like "cactus"—ambiguously singular or plural, touches a sphere where the author seems ill at ease. He seems more sure of his ground when, after this muttered parenthesis, he returns to his starting point, turns the prepositional object into a subject, and sets out again toward his predicate, toward an affirmation of mellow fruitfulness:

. . . such a writer finds rain to be made of knowledge, experience, wine, bread, oil, salt, vinegar, bed, early mornings, nights, days, the sea, men, women, dogs, beloved motor cars, bicycles, hills and valleys, the appearance and disappearance of trains on straight and curved tracks, love, honor and disobey, music, chamber music and chamber pots, negative and positive Wassermanns, the arrival and non-arrival of expected munitions and/or reinforcements, replacements or your brother.

These are the "other things" missed by the academician and discerned by the "good writer"—whether he be Vittorini or Hemingway. It is by no means a casual inventory; each successive item, artfully chosen, has its meaningful place in the author's scheme of things. Knowledge is equated with experience, rendered concrete by the staple fare of existence, and wet down by essential liquids redolent of the Mediterranean; bed, with its double range of elementary associations, initiates a temporal cycle which revolves toward the timeless sea. Men, women, and dogs follow each other in unrelieved sequence; but the term of endearment, "beloved," is reserved for motor cars; while wavering alternatives suggest the movement of other vehicles over the land. Then come the great abstractions, love and honor, which are undercut by a cynical negation of the marriage ceremony, "disobey." Since chamber music sounds high-brow, it must be balanced against the downright vulgarity of chamber pots. The pangs of sex are scientifically neutralized by the reference to Wassermann tests, and the agonies of war are deliberately stated in the cool and/or colorless jargon of military dispatches. The final choice, "replacements or your brother," possibly echoes a twist of Continental slang (*et ton frère!*); but, more than that, it suddenly replaces a strategic loss with a personal bereavement.

The sentence, though extended, is not periodic: instead of suspending its burden, it falls back on anacoluthon, the rhetoric of the gradual breakdown and the fresh start. Hence, the first half is an uncharacteristic and unsuccessful endeavor to complete an elaborate grammatical structure which soon gets out of control. The second half thereupon brings the subject as quickly and simply as possible to its object, which opens up at once into the familiar Hemingway catalogue, where effects can be gained seriatim by order rather than by construction. After the chain of words has reached its climactic phrase, "your brother," it is rounded out by another transitional sentence:

All these are a part of rain to a good writer along with your hated or beloved mother, may she rest in peace or in pieces, porcupine quills, cock grouse drumming on a basswood log, the smell of sweet grass and fresh smoked leather and Sicily.

This time love dares to appear in its primary human connection, but only in ambivalence with hatred, and the hazards of sentimentality are hysterically avoided by a trite pun. And though the final images resolve the paragraph by coming back to the Sicilian locale of Vittorini's novel, they savor more of the northern woods of Hemingway's Upper Peninsula. Meanwhile the digression has served its purpose for him and for ourselves; it has given us nothing less than his definition of knowledge—not book knowledge, of course, but the real thing. Thus Robert Jordan decides to write a book about his adventures in Spain: "But only about the things he knew, truly, and about what he knew." Such a book is Hemingway's novel about him, *For Whom the Bell Tolls;* and

what he knew, there put into words, is already one remove away
from experience. And when Hemingway writes about Vittorini's
novel, unaccustomed though he is to operating on the plane of
criticism, he is two removes away from the objects he mentions
in his analysis—or should I call it a hydroanalysis? Critics—and
I have in mind Wyndham Lewis—have called his writing "the
prose of reality." It seems to come closer to life than other prose,
possibly too close for Mr. Lewis, yet for better or worse it happens to be literature. Its effectiveness lies in virtually persuading
us that it is not writing at all. But though it may feel like walks in
the rain or punches in the jaw, to be literal, it consists of words
on the page. It is full of half-concealed art and self-revealing
sacrifice. Since Hemingway is endlessly willing to explicate such
artful and artificial pursuits as bullfighting and military tactics,
he ought not to flinch under technical scrutiny.

III

Hemingway's hatred for the profession of letters stems quite
obviously from a lover's quarrel. When Richard Gordon is re-
viled by his dissatisfied wife in *To Have and Have Not,* her most
embittered epithet is "you writer." Yet Hemingway's writing
abounds in salutes to various fellow writers, from the waitress's
anecdote about Henry James in *Torrents of Spring* to Colonel
Cantwell's spiritual affinity with D'Annunzio. And from Nick
Adams, who takes Meredith and Chesterton along on fishing trips,
to Hemingway himself, who arranges to be interviewed on American literature in *Green Hills of Africa,* his heroes do not shy
away from critical discussion. His titles, so often quoted from
books by earlier writers, have been so apt that they have all but
established a convention. He shows an almost academic fondness,
as well as a remarkable flair, for epigraphs: the Colonel dies with
a quotation on his lips. Like all of us, Hemingway has been influenced by T. S. Eliot's taste for Elizabethan drama and metaphysical poetry. Thus Hemingway's title, "In Another Country,"
is borrowed from a passage he elsewhere cites, which he might
have found in Marlowe's *Jew of Malta* or possibly in Eliot's "Portrait of a Lady." *A Farewell to Arms,* which echoes Lovelace's
title, quotes in passing from Marvell's "To His Coy Mistress,"
echoed more recently by Robert Penn Warren, which is parodied
in *Death in the Afternoon.* Hemingway is no exception to the rule
that makes parody the starting point for realistic fiction. Just as

Fielding took off from Richardson, so Hemingway takes off from
Sherwood Anderson—indeed his first novel, *Torrents of Spring,*
which parodies Anderson's *Dark Laughter,* is explicit in its ac-
knowledgments to *Joseph Andrews.* It has passages, however,
which read today like a pastiche of the later Hemingway:

Yogi was worried. There was something on his mind. It was spring,
there was no doubt of that now, and he did not want a woman. He had
worried about it a lot lately. There was no question about it. He did
not want a woman. He couldn't explain it to himself. He had gone to
the Public Library and asked for a book the night before. He looked
at the librarian. He did not want her. Somehow she meant nothing to
him.

A recoil from bookishness, after a preliminary immersion in it,
provided Fielding's master, Cervantes, with the original impetus
for the novel. In "A Banal Story" Hemingway provides us with
his own variation on the theme of *Don Quixote,* where a writer
sits reading about romance in a magazine advertisement, while in
far-off Madrid a bullfighter dies and is buried. The ironic contrast
—romantic preconception exploded by contact with harsh reality
—is basic with Hemingway, as it has been with all novelists who
have written effectively about war. The realism of his generation
reacted, not only against Wilsonian idealism, but against Wilsonian
rhetoric. Hence the famous paragraph from the Caporetto episode
describing Frederic Henry's embarrassment before such abstract
words as "glory" and "honor," which seem to him obscene beside
the concrete names of places and numbers of roads. For a Spaniard, Hemingway notes in *Death in the Afternoon,* the abstraction
may still have concreteness: honor may be "as real a thing as
water, wine, or olive oil." It is not so for us: "All our words from
loose using have lost their edge." And "The Gambler, The Nun,
and The Radio" brings forward a clinching example: "Liberty,
what we believed in, now the name of a Macfadden publication."
That same story trails off in a litany which reduces a Marxist
slogan to meaninglessness: "the opium of the people" is everything
and nothing. Even more desolating, in "A Clean, Well-Lighted
Place," is the reduction of the Lord's prayer to nothingness: "Our
nada who art in nada . . ." Since words have become inflated
and devalued, Hemingway is willing to recognize no values save
those which can be immediately felt and directly pointed out. It
is his verbal skepticism which leads toward what some critics
have called his moral nihilism. Anything serious had better be

said with a smile, stranger. The classic echo, "irony and pity," jingles through *The Sun Also Rises* like a singing commercial.

There is something in common between this attitude and the familiar British habit of understatement. "No pleasure in anything if you mouth it too much," says Wilson, the guide in "The Short Happy Life of Francis Macomber." Yet Jake, the narrator of *The Sun Also Rises,* protests—in the name of American garrulity—that the English use fewer words than the Eskimos. Spanish, the language of Hemingway's preference, is at once emotive and highly formal. His Spanish, to judge from *Death in the Afternoon,* is just as ungrammatical as his English. In "The Undefeated" his Spanish bullfighters are made to speak the slang of American prize fighters. Americanisms and Hispanisms, archaic and polyglot elements, are so intermingled in *For Whom the Bell Tolls* that it calls to mind what Ben Jonson said of *The Faerie Queen:* "Spenser writ no language." Hemingway offers a succinct example by translating *"Eras mucho caballo"* as "Thou wert plenty of horse." It is somewhat paradoxical that a writer, having severely cut down his English vocabulary, should augment it by continual importation from other languages, including the Swahili. But this is a facet of the larger paradox that a writer so essentially American should set the bulk of his work against foreign backgrounds. His characters, expatriates for the most part, wander through the ruins of Babel, smattering many tongues and speaking a demotic version of their own. Obscenity presents another linguistic problem, for which Hemingway is not responsible; but his coy ways of circumventing the taboos of censorship are more of a distraction than the conventional blanks. When he does permit himself an expression not usually considered printable, in *Death in the Afternoon,* the context is significant. His interlocutor, the Old Lady, requests a definition and he politely responds: "Madam, we apply the term now to describe unsoundness in abstract conversation or, indeed, any overmetaphysical tendency in speech."

For language, as for literature, his feeling is strongly ambivalent. Perhaps it could be summed up by Pascal's maxim: *"La vraie éloquence se moque de l'éloquence."* Like the notorious General Cambronne, Hemingway feels that one short spontaneous vulgarism is more honest than all those grandiloquent slogans which rhetoricians dream up long after the battle. The disparity between rhetoric and experience, which became so evident during the First World War, prompted the twenties to repudiate the genteel stylistic tradition and to accept the American vernacular as our norm of literary discourse. "Literary" is a contradiction in terms, for the resultant style is basically oral; and when the semi-literate speaker takes pen in hand, as Hemingway demonstrates in "One Reader Writes"—as H. L. Mencken demonstrated in "A Short View of Gamalielese"—the result is even more artificial than if it had been written by a writer. A page is always flat, and we need perspective to make it convey the illusion of life in the round. Yet the very fact that words mean so much less to us than the things they represent in our lives is a stimulus to our imaginations. In "Fathers and Sons" young Nick Adams reads that Caruso has been arrested for "mashing," and asks his father the meaning of that expression.

"It is one of the most heinous of crimes," his father answered. Nick's imagination pictured the great tenor doing something strange, bizarre, and heinous with a potato masher to a beautiful lady who looked like the pictures of Anna Held on the inside of cigar boxes. He resolved, with considerable horror, that when he was old enough he would try mashing at least once.

The tone of this passage is not altogether typical of Hemingway. Rather, as the point of view detaches itself affectionately and ironically from the youth, it approximates the early Joyce. This may help to explain why it suggests a more optimistic approach to language than the presumption that, since phrases can be snares and delusions, their scope should be limited to straight de-notation. The powers of connotation, the possibilities of oblique suggestion and semantic association, are actually grasped by Hemingway as well as any writer of our time. Thus he can retro-spectively endow a cheap and faded term like "mashing" with all the promise and poetry of awakening manhood. When Nick grows up, foreign terms will hold out the same allure to him; like Frederic Henry, he will seek the actuality that resides behind the names of places; and Robert Jordan will first be attracted to Spain as a professional philologist. But none of them will find an equivalence between the word and the thing; and Hemingway, at the end of *Death in the Afternoon,* laments that no book is big enough to do final justice to its living subject. "There was so much to write," the dying writer realizes in "The Snows of Kilimanjaro," and his last thoughts are moving and memorable recollections of some of the many things that will now go unwritten. Walt Whit-man stated this challenge and this dilemma, for all good writers, when he spoke of expressing the inexpressible.

IV

The inevitable compromise, for Hemingway, is best expressed by his account of Romero's bullfighting style: "the holding of his purity of line through the maximum of exposure." The maximum of exposure—this throws much light upon the restlessness of Hemingway's career, but here we are primarily concerned with the holding of his purity of line. It had to be the simplest and most flexible of lines in order to accommodate itself to his desperate pursuit of material. His purgation of language has aptly been compared, by Robert Penn Warren, to the revival of diction that Wordsworth accomplished with *Lyrical Ballads*. Indeed the question that Coleridge afterward raised might once again be asked: why should the speech of some men be more real than that of others? Today that question restates itself in ideological terms: whether respect for the common man necessitates the adoption of a commonplace standard. Everyone who writes faces the same old problems, and the original writers—like Wordsworth or Hemingway—are those who develop new ways of meeting them. The case of Wordsworth would show us, if that of Hemingway did not, that those who break down conventions tend to substitute conventions of their own. Hemingway's prose is not without precedents; it is interesting to recall that his maiden effort, published by *The Double Dealer* in 1922, parodied the King James Bible. He has his forerunners in American fiction, from Cooper to Jack London, whose conspicuous lack was a style as dynamic as their subject matter. The ring-tailed roarers of the frontier, such as Davy Crockett, were Colonel Cantwell's brothers under the skin; but, as contrasted with the latter's tragic conception of himself, they were mock-heroic and seriocomic figures, who recommend themselves to the reader's condescension. Mark Twain has been the most genuine influence, and Hemingway has acknowledged this by declaring—with sweeping generosity—that *Huckleberry Finn* is the source of all modern American literature.

But Mark Twain was conducting a monologue, a virtual tour de force of impersonation, and he ordinarily kept a certain distance between his narrative role and his characters. And among Hemingway's elder contemporaries, Ring Lardner was a kind of ventriloquist, who made devastating use of the vernacular to satirize the vulgarity and stupidity of his dummies. It remained for Hemingway—along with Anderson—to identify himself wholly with the lives he wrote about, not so much entering into them as allowing them to take possession of him, and accepting—along with their sensibilities and perceptions—the limitations of their point of view and the limits of their range of expression. We need make no word count to be sure that his literary vocabulary, with foreign and technical exceptions, consists of relatively few and short words. The corollary, of course, is that every word sees a good deal of hard use. Furthermore, his syntax is informal to the point of fluidity, simplifying as far as possible the already simple system of English inflections. Thus "who" is normally substituted for "whom," presumably to avoid schoolmarmish correctness; and "that," doing duty for "which," seems somehow less prophetic of complexity. Personal pronouns frequently get involved in what is stigmatized, by teachers of freshman composition, as faulty reference; there are sentences in which it is hard to tell the hunter from his quarry or the bullfighter from the bull. "When his father died he was only a kid and his manager buried him perpetually." So begins, rather confusingly, "The Mother of a Queen." Sometimes it seems as if Hemingway were taking pains to be ungrammatical, as do many educated people out of a twisted sense of *noblesse oblige*. Yet when he comes closest to pronouncing a moral, the last words of Harry Morgan—the analphabetic hero of *To Have and Have Not*—seem to be half-consciously fumbling toward some grammatical resolution: "A man . . . ain't got no hasn't got any can't really isn't any way out. . . ."

The effectiveness of Hemingway's method depends very largely upon his keen ear for speech. His conversations are vivid, often dramatic, although he comes to depend too heavily upon them and to scant the other obligations of the novelist. Many of his wisecracks are quotable out of context, but as Gertrude Stein warned him: "Remarks are not literature." He can get his story told, and still be as conversational as he pleases, by telling it in the first person. "Brother, that was some storm," says the narrator, and the reader hears the very tone of his voice. In one of Hemingway's critical digressions, he declares that he has always sought "the real thing, the sequence of motion and fact which made [*sic*] the emotion. . . ." This seems to imply the clear-cut mechanism of verbal stimulus and psychological response that Eliot formulates in his theory of the objective correlative. In practice, however, Hemingway is no more of a behaviorist than Eliot, and the sharp distinction between motion and emotion is soon blurred. Consider his restricted choice of adjectives, and the heavy load of subjective implication carried by such uncertain monosyllables as "fine" and "nice." From examples on nearly every page, we are struck by one which helps to set the scene for *A Farewell to Arms:* "The town was very nice and our house was very fine." Such descriptions—if we may consider them descriptions—are obviously not designed for pictorial effect. When the Colonel is tempted to call some fishing boats picturesque, he corrects himself: "The hell with picturesque. They are just damned beautiful." Where "picturesque" might sound arty and hence artificial, "beautiful"—with "damned" to take off the curse—is permissible because Hemingway has packed it with his own emotional charge. He even uses it in *For Whom the Bell Tolls* to express his esthetic appreciation of gunfire. Like "fine" and "nice," or "good" and "lovely," it does not describe; it evaluates. It is not a stimulus but a projected response, a projection of the narrator's euphoria in a given situation. Hemingway, in effect, is saying to the reader: *Having wonderful time. Wish you were here.*

In short, he is communicating excitement; and if this communication is received, it establishes a uniquely personal relationship; but when it goes astray, the diction goes flat and vague. Hemingway manages to sustain his reputation for concreteness by an exploring eye for the incidental detail. The one typescript of his that I have seen, his carbon copy of "The Killers" now in the Harvard College Library, would indicate that the arc light and the tipped-back derby hat were later observations than the rest. Precision at times becomes so arithmetical that, in "The Light of the World," it lines up his characters like a drill sergeant: "Down at the station there were five whores waiting for the train to come in, and six white men and four Indians." Numbers enlarge the irony that concludes the opening chapter of *A Farewell to Arms* when, after a far from epic invocation, a casual introduction to the landscape, and a dusty record of troops falling back through the autumn, rain brings the cholera which kills off "only seven thousand." A trick of multiplication, which Hemingway may have picked up from Gertrude Stein, is to generalize the specific episode: "They always picked the finest places to have the quarrels." When he offers this general view of a restaurant—"It was full of smoke and drinking and singing" —he is an impressionist if not an abstractionist. Thence to expressionism is an easy step: ". . . the room whirled." It happens that, under pressure from his first American publishers, the author was compelled to modify the phrasing of "Mr. and Mrs. Elliott." In the original version, subsequently restored, the title characters "try to have a baby." In the modified version they "think of having a baby." It could be argued that, in characterizing this rather tepid couple, the later verb is more expressive and no more euphemistic than the earlier one; that "think," at any rate, is not less precise or effectual than "try." But, whereas the sense of effort came naturally, the cerebration was an afterthought.

If we regard the adjective as a luxury, decorative more often than functional, we can well understand why Hemingway doesn't cultivate it. But, assuming that the sentence derives its energy from the verb, we are in for a shock if we expect his verbs to be numerous or varied or emphatic. His usage supports C. K. Ogden's argument that verb forms are disappearing from English grammar. Without much self-deprivation, Hemingway could get along on the so-called "operators" of Basic English, the sixteen monosyllabic verbs that stem from movements of the body. The substantive verb *to be* is predominant, characteristically introduced by an expletive. Thus the first story of *In Our Time* begins, and the last one ends, with the storyteller's gambit: "there was," "there were." In the first two pages of *A Farewell to Arms* nearly every other sentence is of this type, and the third page employs the awkward construction, "there being." There is—I find the habit contagious—a tendency to immobilize verbs by transposing them into gerunds. Instead of writing *they fought* or *we did not feel,* Hemingway writes "there was fighting" and "there was not the feeling of a storm coming." The subject does little more than point impersonally at its predicate: an object, a situation, an emotion. Yet the idiom, like the French *il y a,* is ambiguous; inversion can turn the gesture of pointing into a physical act; and the indefinite adverb can indicate, if not specify, a definite place. Contrast, with the opening of *A Farewell to Arms,* that of "In Another Country": "In the fall the war was always there, but we did not go to it any more." The negative is even more striking, when Frederic Henry has registered the sensations of his wound, and dares to look at it for the first time, and notes: "My knee wasn't there." The adverb is *there* rather than *here,* the verb is *was* rather than *is,* because we—the readers—are separated from the event in space and time. But the narrator has lived through it, like the Ancient Mariner, and now he chooses his words to grip and transfix us. *Lo!* he says. *Look! I was there.*

V

Granted, then, that Hemingway's diction is thin; that, in the technical sense, his syntax is weak; and that he would rather be caught dead than seeking the *mot juste* or the balanced phrase. Granted that his adjectives are not colorful and his verbs not particularly energetic. Granted that he commits as many literary offenses as Mark Twain brought to book with Fenimore Cooper. What is behind his indubitable punch, the unexampled dynamics of Hemingway's style? How does he manage, as he does, to animate this characteristic sentence from "After the Storm"?

I said "Who killed him?" and he said "I don't know who killed him but he's dead all right," and it was dark and there was water standing in the street and no lights and windows broke and boats all up in the town and trees blown down and everything all blown and I got a skiff and went out and found my boat where I had her inside of Mango Key and she was all right only she was full of water.

Here is a good example of Hemingway's "sequence of motion and fact." It starts from dialogue and leads into first-person action; but the central description is a single clause, where the expletive takes the place of the observer and his observations are registered one by one. Hence, for the reader, it lives up to Robert Jordan's intention: "you . . . feel that all that happened to you." Hemingway puts his emphasis on nouns because, among parts of speech, they come closest to things. Stringing them along by means of conjunctions, he approximates the actual flow of experience. For him, as for Marion Tweedy Bloom, the key word is *and,* with its renewable promise of continuity, occasionally varied by *then* and *so.* The rhetorical scheme is polysyndeton—a large name for the childishly simple habit of linking sentences together. The subject, when it is not taken for granted, merely puts us in touch with the predicate: the series of objects that Hemingway wants to point out. Even a preposition can turn this trick, as "with" does in this account of El Sordo waiting to see the whites of his enemy's eyes:

Come on, Comrade Voyager . . . Keep on coming with your eyes forward . . . Look. With a red face and blond hair and blue eyes. With no cap on and his moustache is yellow. With blue eyes. With pale blue eyes. With pale blue eyes with something wrong with them. With pale blue eyes that don't focus. Close enough. Too close. Yes, Comrade Voyager. Take it, Comrade Voyager.

Prose gets as near as it can to physical conflict here. The figure enlarges as it advances, the quickening impression grows clear and sharp and almost unbearable, whereupon it is blackened out by El Sordo's rifle. Each clipped sentence, each prepositional phrase, is like a new frame in a strip of film; indeed the whole passage, like so many others, might have been filmed by the camera and projected on the screen. The course of Harry Morgan's launch speeding through the Gulf Stream, or of Frederic Henry's fantasy ascending the elevator with Catherine Barkley, is given this cinematographic presentation. *Green Hills of Africa* voices the long-range ambition of obtaining a fourth and fifth dimension in prose. Yet if the subordinate clause and the complex sentence are the usual ways for writers to obtain a third dimension, Hemingway keeps his writing on a linear plane. He holds the purity of his line by moving in one direction, ignoring sidetracks and avoiding structural complications. By presenting a succession of images, each of which has its brief moment when it commands the reader's undivided attention, he achieves his special vividness and fluidity. For what he lacks in structure he makes up in sequence, carefully ordering visual impressions as he sets them down and ironically juxtaposing the various items on his lists and inventories. "A Way You'll Never Be" opens with a close-up showing the debris on a battlefield, variously specifying munitions, medicaments, and leftovers from a field kitchen, then closing in on the scattered papers with this striking montage effect: ". . . group postcards showing the machine-gun unit standing in ranked and ruddy cheerfulness as in a football picture for a college annual; now they were humped and swollen in the grass. . . ." It is not surprising that Hemingway's verse, published by *Poetry* in 1923, is recognizably imagistic in character—and perhaps his later heroics are foreshadowed by the subject of one of those poems, Theodore Roosevelt.

In her observant book, *L'Age du roman américain,* Claude-Edmonde Magny stresses Hemingway's "exaltation of the instant." We can note how this emphasis is reflected in his timing, which—after his placing has bridged the distance from *there* to *here*—strives to close the gap between *then* and *now*. Where Baudelaire's clock said "remember" in many languages, Robert Jordan's memory says: "Now, *ahora, maintenant, heute*." When death interrupts a dream, in "The Snows of Kilimanjaro," the ultimate reality is heralded by a rising insistence upon the word "now." It is not for nothing that Hemingway is the younger contemporary of Proust and Joyce. Though his time is neither *le temps perdu* nor the past nostalgically recaptured, he spends it gathering roses while he can, to the ever-accelerating rhythm of headlines and telegrams and loud-speakers. The act, no sooner done than said, becomes simultaneous with the word, no sooner said than felt. Hemingway goes so far, in "Fathers and Sons," as to render a sexual embrace by an onomatopoetic sequence of adverbs. But, unlike Damon Runyon and Dickens, he seldom narrates in the present tense, except in such sporting events as "Fifty Grand." Rather, his timeliness expresses itself in continuous forms of the verb and in his fondness for all kinds of participial constructions. These, compounded and multiplied, create an ambience of overwhelming activity, and the epithets shift from El Sordo's harassed feelings to the impact of the reiterated bullets, as Hemingway recounts "the last lung-aching, leg-dead, mouth-dry, bullet-spatting, bullet-cracking, bullet-singing run up the final slope of the hill." More often the meaning takes the opposite turn, and moves from the external plane into the range of a character's senses, proceeding serially from the visual to the tactile, as it does when the "Wine of Wyoming" is sampled: "It was very light and clear and good and still tasted of the grapes."

When Nick Adams goes fishing, the temperature is very tangibly indicated: "It was getting hot, the sun hot on the back of his neck." The remark about the weather is thereby extended in two directions, toward the distant source of the heat and toward its immediate perception. Again in "Big Two-Hearted River," Nick's fatigue is measured by the weight of his pack: ". . . it was heavy. It was much too heavy." As in the movies, the illusion of movement is produced by repeating the same shot with further modification every time. Whenever a new clause takes more than one step ahead, a subsequent clause repeats it in order to catch up. Repetition, as in "Up in Michigan," brings the advancing narrative back to an initial point of reference. "Liz liked Jim very much. She liked it the way he walked over from the shop and often went to the kitchen door to watch him start down the road. She liked it about his moustache. She liked it about how white his teeth were when he smiled." The opaque verb "like," made increasingly transparent, is utilized five more times in this paragraph; and the fumbling preposition "about" may be an acknowledgment of Hemingway's early debt to Gertrude Stein. The situation is located somewhere between a subjective Liz and an objective Jim.

The theme of love is always a test of Hemingway's objectivity. When Frederic kisses Catherine, her responses are not less moving because they are presented through his reflexes; but it is her sentimental conversation which leaves him free to ask himself: "What the hell?" At first glance, in a behavioristic formula which elsewhere recurs, Colonel Cantwell seems so hard-boiled that motions are his only emotions: "He saw that his hand was trembling." But his vision is blurred by conventionally romantic tenderness when he contemplates a heroine whose profile "could break your . . . or anyone else's heart." Hemingway's heroines, when they aren't bitches, are fantasies—or rather, the masculine reader is invited to supply his own, as with the weather in Mark Twain's *American Claimant*. They are pin-up girls.

If beauty lies in the eye of the beholder, Hemingway's purpose is to make his readers beholders. This is easily done when the narration is conducted in the first person; we can sit down and drink, with Jake Barnes, and watch Paris walk by. The interpolated chapters of *In Our Time*, most of them reminiscences from the army, employ the collective *we;* but, except for "My Old Man," the stories themselves are told in the third person. Sometimes, to strengthen the sense of identification, they make direct appeal to the second person; the protagonist of "Soldier's Home" is "you" as well as "he"—and, more generally, "a fellow." With the exception of Jake's confessions, that is to say *The Sun Also Rises,* all of Hemingway's novels are written in the *style indirect libre*—indirect discourse which more or less closely follows the consciousness of a central character. An increasing tendency for the author to intrude, commenting in his own person, is one of the weaknesses of *Across the River*. He derives his strength from a power to visualize episodes through the eyes of those most directly involved; for a page, in "The Short Happy Life of Francis Macomber," the hunt is actually seen from the beast's point of view. Hemingway's use of interior monologue is effective when sensations from the outer world are entering the stream of a character's consciousness, as they do with such a rush at El Sordo's last stand. But introspection is not Hemingway's genre, and the night thoughts of *To Have and Have Not* are among his least successful episodes. His best are events, which are never far to seek; things are constantly happening in his world; his leg-man, Nick Adams, happens to be the eyewitness of "The Killers." The state of mind that Hemingway communicates to us is the thrill that Nick got from skiing in "Cross Country

Snow," which "plucked Nick's mind out and left him only the wonderful, flying, dropping sensation in his body."

VI

If psychological theories could be proved by works of fiction, Hemingway would lend his authority to the long-contested formula of William James, which equates emotion with bodily sensation. Most other serious writers, however, would bear witness to deeper ranges of sensibility and more complex processes of motivation than those he sees fit to describe. Some of them have accused Hemingway of aggressive anti-intellectualism: I am thinking particularly of Aldous Huxley. But Huxley's own work is so pure an example of all that Hemingway has recoiled from, so intellectual in the airiest sense, and so unsupported by felt experience, that the argument has played into Hemingway's hands. We have seen enough of the latter to know that he doesn't really hate books —himself having written a dozen, several of which are, and will remain, the best of their kind. As for his refusal to behave like a man of letters, he reminds us of Hotspur, who professes to be a laconic philistine and turns out—with no little grandiloquence— to be the most poetic character in Shakespeare's play. Furthermore, it is not Hemingway, but the sloganmongers of our epoch, who have debased the language; he has been attempting to restore some decent degree of correspondence between words and things; and the task of verification is a heavy one, which throws the individual back on his personal resources of awareness. That he has succeeded within limits, and with considerable strain, is less important than that he has succeeded, that a few more aspects of life have been captured for literature. Meanwhile the word continues to dematerialize, and has to be made flesh all over again; the firsthand perception, once it gets written down, becomes the secondhand notation; and the writer, who attains his individuality by repudiating literary affectation, ends by finding that he has struck a new pose and founded another school.

It is understandable why no critique of Hemingway, including this one, can speak for long of the style without speaking of the man. Improving on Buffon, Mark Schorer recently wrote: "[Hemingway's] style is not only his subject, it is his view of life." It could also be called his way of life, his *Lebenstil*. It has led him to live his books, to brave the maximum of exposure, to tour the world in an endless search for wars and their moral equivalents.

It has cast him in the special role of our agent, our plenipotentiary, our roving correspondent on whom we depend for news from the fighting fronts of modern consciousness. Here he is, the man who was there. His writing seems so intent upon the actual, so impersonal in its surfaces, that it momentarily prompts us to overlook the personality behind them. That would be a serious mistake; for the point of view, though brilliantly intense, is narrowly focused and obliquely angled. We must ask: who is this guide to whom we have entrusted ourselves on intimate terms in dangerous places? Where are his limitations? What are his values? We may well discover that they differ from our assumptions, when he shows us a photograph of a bullfighter close to a bull, and comments: "If there is no blood on his belly afterwards you ought to get your money back." We may be ungrateful to question such curiosity, when we are indebted to it for many enlargements of our vicarious knowledge; and it may well spring from the callowness of the tourist rather than the morbidity of the voyeur, from the American zest of the fan who pays his money to reckon the carnage. When Spain's great poet García Lorca celebrated the very same theme, averting his gaze from the spilling of the blood, his refrain was *"Que no quiero verla!"* ("I do not want to see it!")

Yet Hemingway wants to see everything—or possibly he wants to be in a position to tell us that he has seen everything. While the boy Nick, his seeing eye, eagerly watches a Caesarean childbirth in "Indian Camp," the far from impassive husband turns away; and it is later discovered that he has killed himself. "He couldn't stand things . . ." so runs the diagnosis of Nick's father, the doctor. This, for Nick, is an initiation to suffering and death; but with the sunrise, shortly afterward, youth and well-being reassert themselves; and the end of the story reaffirms the generalization that Hazlitt once drew: "No young man ever thinks he shall die." It is easy enough for such a young man to stand things, for he is not yet painfully involved in them; he is not a sufferer but a wide-eyed onlooker, to whom the word "mashing" holds out mysterious enticements. Hemingway's projection of this attitude has given his best work perennial youthfulness; it has also armed his critics with the accusation that, like his Robert Cohn, he is "a case of arrested development." If this be so, his plight is generalized by the Englishman Wilson, who observes that "Americans stay little boys . . . all their lives." And the object of Wilson's observation, Francis Macomber, would fur-

nish a classic case history for Adler, if not for Freud—the masculine sense of inferiority which seeks to overcome itself by acts of
prowess, both sanguinary and sexual. Despite these two sources
of excitement, the story is a plaintive modulation of two rather
dissonant themes: *None but the brave deserves the fair* and *The
female of the species is deadlier than the male.* After Francis
Macomber has demonstrated his manhood, the next step is death.
The world that remains most alive to Hemingway is that stretch
between puberty and maturity which is strictly governed by the
ephebic code: a world of mixed apprehension and bravado before the rite of passage, the baptism of fire, the introduction to
sex.

Afterward comes the boasting, along with such surviving ideals
as Hemingway subsumes in the word *cojones*—the English
equivalent sounds more skeptical. But for Jake Barnes, all passion
spent in the First World War, or for Colonel Cantwell, tired and
disgruntled by the Second, the aftermath can only be elegiac. The
weather-beaten hero of *Across the River*, which appears in 1950,
is fifty years old and uneasily conscious of that fact; whereas "the
childish, drunken heroics" of *The Sun Also Rises* took place just
about twenty-five years ago. From his spectacular arrival in the
twenties, Hemingway's course has paralleled that of our century;
and now, at its mid-point, he balks like the rest of us before the
responsibilities of middle age. When, if ever, does the *enfant du
siècle,* that *enfant terrible,* grow up? (Not necessarily when he
grows a beard and calls himself "Mr. Papa.") Frederic Henry
plunges into the Po much as Huck Finn dived into the Mississippi,
but emerges to remind us even more pointedly of Fabrice del
Dongo in Stendhal's *Chartreuse de Parme,* and of our great contemporary shift from transatlantic innocence to Old-World experience. Certain intimations of later years are present in Hemingway's earlier stories, typically Ad Francis, the slap-happy
ex-champ in "The Battler." Even in "Fifty Grand," his most contrived tale, the beat-up prizefighter suffers more than he acts and
wins by losing—a situation which has its corollary in the title
of Hemingway's third collection, *Winner Take Nothing*. The ultimate article of his credo, which he shares with Malraux and
Sartre, is the good fight for the lost cause. And the ultimate
protagonist is Jesus in "Today Is Friday," whose crucifixion is
treated like an athletic feat, and whose capacity for taking punishment rouses a fellow feeling in the Roman soldiers. The stoic or
masochistic determination to take it brings us back from Heming-

way to his medium, which—although it eschews the passive voice —is essentially a receiving instrument, especially sensitized for recording a series of violent shocks.

The paradox of toughness and sensitivity is resolved, and the qualities and defects of his writing are reconciled, if we merely remember that he was—and still is—a poet. That he is not a novelist by vocation, if it were not revealed by his books, could be inferred from his well-known retort to F. Scott Fitzgerald. For Fitzgerald the rich were different—not quantitatively, because they had more money, but qualitatively, because he had a novelistic interest in manners and morals. Again, when we read André Gide's reports from the Congo, we realize what *Green Hills of Africa* lacks in the way of social or psychological insight. As W. M. Frohock has perceived, Hemingway is less concerned with human relations than with his own relationship to the universe— a concern which might have spontaneously flowered into poetry. His talents come out most fully in the texture of his work, whereas the structure tends to be episodic and uncontrived to the point of formlessness. *For Whom the Bell Tolls*, the only one of his six novels that has been carefully constructed, is in some respects an overexpanded short story. Editors rejected his earliest stories on the grounds that they were nothing but sketches and anecdotes, thereby paying incidental tribute to his sense of reality. Fragments of truth, after all, are the best that a writer can offer; and, as Hemingway has said, ". . . Any part you make will represent the whole if it's made truly." In periods as confusing as the present, when broader and maturer representations are likely to falsify, we are fortunate if we can find authenticity in the lyric cry, the adolescent mood, the tangible feeling, the trigger response. If we think of Hemingway's temperamental kinship with E. E. Cummings, and of Cummings' "Buffalo Bill" or "Olaf glad and big," it is easy to think of Hemingway as a poet. After the attractions and distractions of timeliness have been outdated, together with categorical distinctions between the rich and the poor, perhaps he will be remembered for a poetic vision which renews our interrupted contact with the timeless elements of man's existence: bread, wine, bed, music, and a few more concrete-universals. When El Sordo raises his glance from the battlefield, he looks up at the identical patch of blue sky that Henry Fleming saw in *The Red Badge of Courage* and that looked down on Prince Andrey in *War and Peace*.

Harry Levin

Hemingway in Italy

I must apologize if, speaking of the influence of modern American authors on Italian fiction, I begin by quoting myself. The first article that ever appeared in Italy on Hemingway was published in the Turin daily paper *La Stampa* in June, 1929, with my signature. Hemingway's first important book, *In Our Time*, had been published five years before, in 1924, so the Italian press was not doing badly this time in keeping the public informed of literary events in the Anglo-Saxon world. I won't say that twenty years is the usual time the light of a foreign star takes to travel as far as Italy, but literary vogues usually did take more than five years to reach us in the twenties, and usually came via France. There was no question of a French intermediary this time. The circumstances in which I came to know of Hemingway rob my "discovery" a little of its glamour. At that time I was teaching in an English university, and, whenever I was in London, I used to see T. S. Eliot and the people of the *Criterion,* of which I was a contributor, and I think I owe to Eliot my first acquaintance with Hemingway's work. My reaction was immediate, and the article I wrote in *La Stampa*, with the title *"Un giovane narratore americano,"* contained a challenge which was not left unanswered by the Italian literary press. This was what I said:

Our present period seems to mark the triumph of narrative art. I do not only speak of France and England, where the traditions of the novel and the short story can be traced back to a distant date, but even Italy teems with skillful storytellers. Nowadays, nearly everybody in Italy seems to know how to write a plausible story. It is the gold reserve of narrative genius accumulated during the last century which allows so much paper currency in our time. Because, after all, we live on the crumbs of the banquet of the great French, Russian, and English novelists of the nineteenth century; and today's stories are well contrived, and convincing, because their authors have learned a lesson either from Chekhov, or from Henry James, or from Proust. It is not even strictly necessary that young authors should take the trouble of reading the classics of the novel: their lesson is in the air. The short story has reached its moment of perfection and saturation just as the sonnet had done in the sixteenth century, when sonnets, so to say, got written by themselves, so saturated was the air with Petrarchan strains. And as in the sixteenth century even grammarians knew how to polish off a pretty sonnet, so nowadays even critics know how to write a plausible short story. One wonders what is going to survive out of so much fecundity. The case of the sixteenth-century sonneteers, all perfect and interchangeable—seldom if ever read by posterity—is a warning.

Now Ernest Hemingway has a new accent in this multitude of storytellers; it would be next to impossible to find in him an echo of the current recipes. Maybe because he is an American, and America may be considered relatively virgin soil, so far as literary traditions are concerned. If you have to think of somebody else, you may think of Defoe, who in *Moll Flanders* causes his heroine to talk in a sublimated version of the style of a maidservant's letter. Nothing, at first, seems simpler than Hemingway's technique: he confines himself to repeating speeches almost dryly, to describing the scene with the barest particulars. His style adheres to the outlines of things with an almost impersonal firmness. If one can talk of an objective style, it is his. There is nothing in him of that cerebral tendency which cannot do away with certain standards and categories, and no sooner contemplates an object than it deforms and judges it, so as to give an artificial, rhetorical, vision of the world. . . . It would be difficult to imagine a more elementary style than Hemingway's: the greatest possible economy of means, as in a natural process. He wraps things round by a repeated verbal contact; he seems to possess the spontaneous wisdom of the dowser, who divines the presence of underground water. Hemingway relates half a sentence, sketches the expression of a face, a twitching of the lips, a nothing; but this nothing throws light on a whole situation: a maximum of evocation with a minimum display of means. One may object that this can be said of the art of every great storyteller; but the novelty consists in this, that the austere fitness which in a European is, as a rule, the result of a laborious process of simplification, seems to exist naturally in this American. He cannot help adhering to the things he describes, so much so that a sophisticated reader may find his way of approach monotonous in the long run. Any subject is good for Hemingway: a fishing party, a conversation overheard in a military hospital or in a sleeping car or in a bar, a boxing match, a bullfight. He has a definite propensity for subjects of this latter description, since he seems sometimes to identify "life" with the display of violence and brutality, so that blows and blood appear occasionally to be regarded as high human values. But Hemingway has not read Pirandello, so that his boxers are not suffering from metaphysical languors. And he knows next to nothing about the history of religions, so that his *matadores* in the act of stabbing the bull between its horns are not reminded, like

Montherlant's, of Mithra's sacrifice. One is indeed at a loss to imagine what his readings may have been. Hemingway's point of view has so little in common with the esthete's that occasionally it may even appear strictly utilitarian. He singles out details of a practical character with the humdrum precision of the man in the street.

I am quoting extensively from my 1929 article, not because of the originality of my remarks, but because I presented Hemingway to the Italian public as an opposite case of whatever they knew in the way of narrative art. I tried to convey what D. S. Savage has said much more forcibly in the London literary miscellany *Focus*:

Hemingway is, within very narrow limits, a stylist who has brought to something like perfection a curt, unemotional, factual style which is an attempt at the objective presentation of experience. A bare, dispassionate reporting of external actions is all that Hemingway as a rule attempts, in presenting his characters and incidents. His typical central character, his "I," may be described generally as a bare consciousness stripped to the human minimum, impassively recording the objective data of experience. He has no contact with ideas, no visible emotions, no hopes for the future, and no memory. He is, as far as it is possible to be so, a *depersonalized* being.

These words express admirably what I wanted to convey to a public of Italian writers and readers, steeped in the delicious sea of Proust. I did not try to see behind the façade, to reveal what view of life was behind that depersonalized style. This has been done, however, in Mr. Savage's essay, where he shows how the entire extrusion of personality into the outward sensational world makes Hemingway's characters the inwardly passive victims of a meaningless determinism; how the profound spiritual inertia, the inner vacuity and impotence, which is a mark of all Hemingway's projected characters, ends in a deadening sense of boredom and negation which can only be relieved by violent, though still essentially meaningless, activity; how the final upshot of it all is the total absence of a sense of life, so that life is brought into a sensational vividness only by contrast with the nullity of death.

I did not try to see through Hemingway's world; what interested me was the aspect hinted at in these words of Savage: "A novelist, of admitted literary merit, who lacks all the equipment generally expected of a practitioner of his art except a certain artistic scrupulousness and poetic sense, is something of a phenomenon." For Savage, Hemingway represents "a special form of that which might be termed the *proletarianization* of literature: the adapta-

tion of the technical artistic conscience of the subaverage human
consciousness." To a literature overripe with culture, as ours was
in the twenties, so much so that it seemed quite natural to compare us with Petrarch's followers, I offered as a curative the example of an art which seemed to spring from virgin soil. A return to nature has been, every now and then, the infallible remedy
for a too sophisticated society. Now Italian literature, at the time
I wrote that article, had preciosity and traditionalism as its
dominant characteristics, its main currents being still the same
ones which had prevailed in the nineteenth century, and which
can be conveniently described by the epithet: Biedermeier. Italian
narrative was then, and is still to a large extent, steeped in a
Biedermeier atmosphere: realism, bourgeois or peasant life in the
provinces, avoidance of sharp contrasts, Christian resignation,
genre painting, conversation pieces. In short, such characteristics
which fit to a nicety what German critics have defined as *Biedermeierkultur,* from the name of the humble schoolmaster whose
homely poems were burlesqued in *Fliegende Blätter* in the 1850s.

The Biedermeier world is a small world of common sense and
healthy habits, delights of the home, the cult of a tamed and
well-groomed nature, observance of sound principles, love for
the concrete, along with, every so often, a flight on the wings of a
sweet, and often gently sad, dream: a world of bourgeois ethics
and bourgeois art, shrinking from extremes, half-classical, half-
romantic—the world which in England is called Victorian. It has
been said that there never was an Italian romantic movement in
the true sense of the word; that same common sense and well-
balanced taste which kept Italy free from the raptures and excesses of romanticism (not even Leopardi, for all his pessimism, is
a romantic), made her the ideal country for a blossoming of
Biedermeierkultur. I cannot speak here of the whole course of
Italian literature in the last century; but every student of Italian
abroad knows at least two Italian books of the nineteenth century:
Manzoni's *I promessi sposi* and De Amicis' *Cuore*: the traditional
ethics and quiet humor of the former, the sentimentality border-
ing on mawkishness of the latter, are typically bourgeois, or
Biedermeier, products. Croce's four volumes of *La letteratura
della nuova Italia* offer a gallery of portraits of typically Biedermeier artists. Indeed, if one considers the whole of Italian literature, its representative genius is not Dante, but Ariosto, *"Ludo-
vico della tranquillità"*: the bourgeois poet whose uneventful life
culminated in the building of his little house in Ferrara—*"parva*

sed apta mihi"—who had no "message," but delighted in a pageant of fantastic adventures, tempering the superhuman with the humorous, reducing everything to a golden level of harmony; a writer of tales which could appeal equally to the courtier and to the gondolier. It is usual to refer to the provincial character of Italy (where there is no predominant cultural center) when accounting for the output of short stories and novels which formed in the twenties, and still forms in the forties, the bulk of her literary production. Books whose best portions deal as a rule with the childhood of the protagonist (a thin disguise of the author himself) spent in some little town far away from the modern world, simple stories of family troubles with a mother up front; half-yearning, half-melancholy, conjuring up streets and squares undisturbed by modern traffic—sad experiences made beautiful in recollection, love for concrete detail, no pretense of metaphysical complications—how many books of this kind, generally written in very good Italian, have been appearing year after year, enjoying a moderate success and a still more moderate sale, to recede finally into the background where their features dissolve in the uniform Biedermeier color!

To this kind of storytelling, the influence of Proust and, less evidently, of Henry James, has added a spice of *intimismo,* a precious intricacy of pattern, stressing a shade of sensibility here, deepening the sense of the past there, and altogether leaving the imprint of a dulcet cadence, as in a Petrarchan sonnet. Joyce and Virginia Woolf have favored a still deeper preciosity, the *stile allusivo,* flights of fancy too remote to be traced by the lay reader, and prose has often vied with poetry in the *trobar clus,* as the Provençal poets used to say, or *ermetismo,* as modern critics have termed this exquisite, but unsociable, tendency, the *ultima Thule* of individualism. I shall only mention one name, in order to make you realize what kind of Italian storyteller I had in mind when I held up the example of Hemingway to our writers: Gianna Manzini, born in Siena at the beginning of this century, the author of *Tempo innamorato* (1928). As an instance of Hemingway's style I quoted in my article a long passage from "Cat in the Rain," and advised a study of "Big Two-Hearted River."

My article in *La Stampa* was resented in certain quarters: it was said, among other things, that long ago Italian literature had gone through the phase represented by Hemingway's stories; one must not forget that those were the years of the Fascist rule, and nationalism was rampant, so much so that when, in 1936, I

wrote about Hemingway's *Green Hills of Africa*, the Fascist censorship must have been caught napping when it allowed the article
to appear at all: Hemingway's name was taboo among us because
of his attitude during the Abyssinian campaign.

In the meantime, however, other critics had been speaking of
Hemingway with praise, chiefly on account of his novel about the
Italian front, *Farewell to Arms*; and what information the Italians
could not get from their own literary reviews they gathered from
French magazines, always widespread in our country. By 1941,
Hemingway's work was not only so well known but so widely
imitated that one of our leading critics, Emilio Cecchi (who had
helped to acquaint the Italian public with Hemingway) wrote in
the *Corriere della sera*: "We keep stumbling everywhere against
this type of dialogue, whether we read a short story or a reporter's
correspondence."

Among the first to learn from Hemingway, as well as from
other American novelists, Elio Vittorini became known in the
thirties through his translations of D. H. Lawrence as well as
original short stories and impressions of places (*Piccola borghesia,
Nei Morlacchi*): he was then a Fascist and had himself photographed with the front page of the *Corriere della sera* under his
eyes, with the "Discorso del Duce" well in evidence: he was then
very young. In 1941 he wrote his best book, *Conversazione in
Sicilia*; in the previous year he had published a selection of short
stories by William Saroyan (*Che ve ne sembra dell'America?*).
Hemingway and Saroyan are the evident literary sponsors of the
book which he published in 1945, *Uomini e no*: from the very
title, which sounds very quaint in Italian until one realizes that
the model has been supplied for it by Hemingway's *To Have and
Have Not*, combined with Steinbeck's *Of Mice and Men* (*Uomini
e topi* in the Italian translation).

Uomini e no claims to be the novel of the Italian resistance
and partisan war: the Italian counterpart of *For Whom the Bell
Tolls*. Vittorini has come out of the war a blossoming Communist, the editor of the Communist review *Il Politecnico*, which
tries to imitate Russian weeklies even in the external appearance.
Vittorini and another Sicilian, the painter Guttuso, both proletarian artists, are, together with Silone, the only names international literary correspondents have got hold of in present-day
Italian art and letters. In a recent English miscellany *New Road*
(No. 4), I read with no little amusement the title of an essay by
Paul Potts, "Not since Dante: Ignazio Silone, A Footnote," ex

plained in the course of the article by the curious statement that
no one has done so much as Silone to lead Italian literature back
towards that glory it has not known since the days of Dante and
Guido Cavalcanti. And when Stephen Spender came to Rome, the
only name of a young Italian writer he seemed to have heard was
that of Vittorini: he and Guttuso were the prominent figures in a
gossipy piece on Italian art and letters which appeared in *Vogue*.

The reader has not long to search in *Uomini e no* to discover its
secret. The lyrical tone obviously goes back to Saroyan, but the
continuous dialogues, the tough manner, the delineation of characters, the crudity of certain episodes, could not have existed without the example of Hemingway, particularly of *For Whom the
Bell Tolls*. The minute narration of the torture of the peddler
Giulaj, on whom a German officer sets his dogs, finds a counterpart in the description in Hemingway's novel of the massacre of
all the fascists of a small town, done to death between two lines
of peasants armed with flails. Enne 2, the protagonist of Vittorini's book, is in love with a girl, Berta; they go to the house
of an old woman, Selva, who belongs to the movement. Now
Selva's behavior to the lovers reminds one immediately of the behavior of elderly Pilar, the partisan woman, to the couple, Robert
Jordan and Maria. Both elderly women push the young ones into
the arms of the young men, and at the same time are jealous of
their youth and beauty. A passage from Vittorini's novel will also
illustrate the peculiar mannerisms of his dialogue, a subject to
which I shall have to return in a moment:

"Do you think it is odd?" Selva said. "It isn't odd. We've never seen
you with a companion, and we want you to have a companion. Can't
we want you to have a companion?"

She fixed glowing eyes on the man and the woman.

"Can't we want this for a man who is dear to us? A man is happy
when he has a companion. Shouldn't a man be happy?"

"Thank you," Enne 2 said. "Thank you, Selva. But——"

"To hell with 'but,' " old Selva said. "Can't we want a man to be
happy? We work in order that men may be happy. What good would it
do to work if it didn't serve to make men happy? That's why we work.
Isn't that why we work?"

"That's why," Enne 2 said.

"Then it is why!" Selva said.

And she kept on fixing her eyes on the man and the woman.

"God!" she said. "Men must be happy. What sense would our work
make if men couldn't be happy? You tell me, young woman. Would
our work make any sense?"

"I don't know," Berta replied.

And it was as if she hadn't replied, she was very serious; and she lifted her face a moment, but it was as if she hadn't lifted it.

"Would any of our work make sense?"

"No, Selva, I don't think it would."

"Would it make sense? No, it wouldn't make any sense at all."

"It wouldn't make sense. Nothing on earth would make sense."

"Nothing on earth would make sense. Isn't it so, young woman?"

"I don't know," Berta replied again.

"Or would something make sense then?"

"No," Enne 2 replied, "I do not think so."

"Would our clandestine newspapers make sense? Would our plots make sense?"

"I don't think so."

"And our men who get shot? Would they make sense? No, they would not make any sense."

"No, they wouldn't make sense."

"Would anything in the world make sense? Would our bombs make sense?"

"I don't think anything would make sense."

"Nothing would make sense. Or would the enemies we kill make sense?"

"Not even they. I don't think they would."

"No, no. Men must be happy. Everything makes sense only if men can be happy. . . ."

Later on, Selva is alone with Berta:

Selva got up and went behind the table. She looked to see if the water was boiling.

"I hoped you were his companion," she said.

She broke off, but still she did not let Berta speak. She went on: "A man has to have his companion. Even more so if he's one of ours. He must be happy. What can he know of what men need if he isn't happy? We are fighting for this. For men to be happy."

She turned around, leaning on the table with both hands. "Do you follow what I'm saying?"

"It's simple," Berta replied.

"Very simple," Selva said. "A man who is fighting in order that men may be happy should know what men need in order to be happy. And he must have a companion. He must be happy with his companion."

"Hasn't he a companion?" Berta asked.

Selva looked again to see if the water was boiling. "You ask me? I hoped you were. . . . I never knew that he had one." She came around the table with the teapot and two cups. "The first time I saw you," she said, "I thought immediately that you ought to be his com-

panion. You are just what he would want a woman to be. But you,"
she asked, "do you believe what I am saying?"

"Why not?" Berta said.

"If I were young," Selva continued, "I would like to have been his
companion. But I might be his mother. But when I saw you I thought
that you must be the one."

If we read after this the various passages in *For Whom the
Bell Tolls* where old Pilar eggs the two lovers on, we shall find a
similarity of situations, of atmosphere, of treatment, although no
single passage of Vittorini can be said to imitate Hemingway
closely. In both authors the scenes consist almost exclusively of
dialogues. But the passage from Vittorini's novel illustrates a
peculiarity of his dialogues as compared with Hemingway's. True,
there are repetitions in Hemingway's dialogues, as there are in
ordinary life, but we very seldom get from them the impression
of exercises in conversation (such as we might find, with all the
cases and tenses and moods, in a foreign-language grammar).
There are pages and pages of Vittorini which read like such
exercises. The nucleus of his dialogues is a triplet. First a statement, then the same repeated with a query, then repeated again as
a stronger asseveration:

—*Lui ora non ha da fare con molte compagne.*
—*Lui ha da fare con molte compagne?*
—*Non ha più da fare con molte compagne.*

Very frequently the echo extends beyond the triplet:

—*Sembra che si vedano le montagne.*
—*Sembra? Si vedono. Sono le montagne.*
—*Sono le montagne?*
—*Sono le montagne.*
—*Si vedono le montagne da Milano?*
—*Non le vedi? Si vedono.*
—*Non sapevo che si vedessero.*

Thus Hemingway's technique, devised to carry the impression
of actual life by reproducing word by word a dialogue of short
sentences, becomes in Vittorini a mannerism, because he is not
such an impassive onlooker and listener as Hemingway, but invests everything with a lyrical mood, or merely with a rhetorical
emphasis. The effect is very curious. Starting from Hemingway,
Vittorini comes near certain effects of Charles Péguy, whose ex-
asperating repetitions give the impression of a person seized with
the symptoms of general paralysis. Péguy had caught the rhythm

of peasants' talk, and tried to couch it in an artistic pattern; Vittorini does the same with the talk of the man in the street. But Hemingway never tries to impose a pattern on his dialogues: hence their impression of freshness, even in monotony. Thus the lesson of simplicity and directness of Hemingway has been lost on a writer hopelessly predisposed to mannerism. This does not mean, however, that the lesson is not there. A fake postulates the genuine thing. Vittorini's tone rings false, affected, childishly rhetorical, but his model is still recognizable. The whole thing looks as absurd as an eighteenth-century European imitation of Chinese art, or as a Japanese picture of Napoleon as a prisoner in St. Helena, with the English soldiers in the garb of samurai. Vittorini's partisans talk more like the shepherds in Theocritus's *Idyls* than like the men who fought in Milan against the Germans: *Uomini e no* stands to *For Whom the Bell Tolls* in the same relation as Callimachus to Homer, if for a moment we could call Hemingway a Homer and Vittorini a Callimachus. If to us the result of Vittorini's effort seems therefore to be a new preciosity, we may consider with amusement how far he has traveled from his original intention, which must obviously have been a proletarianization of literature, the adaptation of the technical artistic conscience to the subaverage human consciousness, according to D. S. Savage's definition which I have already quoted.

The influence of American fiction, particularly of Hemingway, is also apparent in another Italian war book which has caused a certain stir—Giuseppe Berto's *Il cielo è rosso*. This novel is the story of a group of Italian adolescents whom the bombardment of a northern Italian town has deprived of their parents and homes. Tullio, Carla, Giulia, and a half-witted little girl live in the ruins of a devastated area; they are joined by Daniele, who has come out of a priests' college to find his home destroyed and himself alone in the world. Tullio is the chief of a gang of boys who live by stealing and blackmail: part of their profit is destined to the relief of the poor and to the funds of their party (they're Communists): in a word, he reincarnates the type of the generous outlaw which is a well-known figure of early romanticism. Carla is also a type one comes across in romantic literature, the kind-hearted prostitute: though only fifteen, with the connivance of her lover, Tullio, she earns her living as a whore. To this depraved, though not repulsive, couple, is contrasted the pair Daniele and Giulia, who are essentially honest and good, and find it very hard to adapt themselves to the new circumstances: they pathetically succumb, Giulia by dying of consumption, Daniele by committing suicide. And then Tullio is killed in the course of an unlucky gangsters' expedition. The whole novel is steeped in a profoundly melancholy atmosphere, from the description of the lazy, marshy riverland and the provincial Venetian town at the beginning to the shooting party in the marshes, which forms the only idyllic episode of the whole book, and on to Daniele's suicide under a train in the end. *Il cielo è rosso* is certainly one of the saddest novels ever written, and, for all its American influence, is tinged with a typical Latin sentimentalism. Italian readers have been reminded of De Amicis' *Cuore*; if one wants to sum up one's impressions, one could say that *Il cielo è rosso* is Murger's *Vie de bohème* translated into terms of a modern American novel. (American influence on Berto, incidentally, is not merely bookish; he was made a prisoner in the Tunis campaign and spent two years in the United States.) Yet, whatever strictures one may make, the novel remains one of the most remarkable books written in Europe in the postwar period.

One of the most obvious signs of American influence on Berto is again the abundance and character of the dialogues. It would naturally be preposterous to ascribe every example of dialogue to Hemingway's example. But whenever you come across what purports to be a faithful reproduction of conversation, with all its repetitions and apparently meaningless expletives, with its short sentences falling like drops in a vacuum, creating an atmosphere almost by the significance of the pauses, by barely hinted gestures and actions—whenever you come across this, you may depend on it that an American influence is at hand. Take for instance this passage in *Il cielo è rosso*:

"They're obstinate," Tullio said. "The most obstinate people I ever saw. Sometimes they stand in front of the town hall or in front of the military command and wait. They wait from morning to night. They don't ask them what they want any more; they'll go on waiting all the same. Maybe some day something will turn up, because they are so obstinate."

Or this:

"Then there is the girl's father," Tullio said. "He's a druggist, the owner of a big pharmacy. The girl will be a druggist too, like her father. I do not know how many years she still has to study, but she's sure to become a druggist, because she's a clever girl. She helps out now once in a while in the store."

A single word is the keynote of both these passages: it is repeated over and over again, so as to give the listener the maximum impact. The bare word is occasionally used in incantation, as if, by sheer repetition, it could take on all the life of the thing itself. Passages like these I have been quoting may not be typical in themselves: but the repetitions, the short sentences, give in the long run the impression of simplicity, of elementariness, of closeness to nature, which we associate with American novels, in particular Hemingway's. An episode of the American soldiers who are distributing food to a crowd of beggars is too long to quote, but a small portion of it will indicate some characteristics of Berto's prose:

"Whom have you got at home?" the sergeant asked.

"Two sisters," replied the boy. "They're smaller than me. They'll be very happy if I bring home some white bread."

"You've no father?" the sergeant asked.

"He died in the bombardment," the boy said. "My mother died in the bombardment, also."

The sergeant came over to the boy and put his hand on his head, then sat down on the box on which the old man had been sitting. "Sit down," he said. The boy sat down again. The sergeant did not speak, and he felt a little embarrassed. "They're singing," he said.

"Yes," said the sergeant.

The melancholy song of the soldiers, with a few notes of a guitar, reached their ears.

"They want to go back home," the sergeant said. "That's why they're singing."

"What do the words mean?" the boy asked.

"That there's a happy country somewhere, far away," the sergeant said.

"It's nice," said the boy.

They listened in silence until the song was over. Then the boy asked again: "Tell me what I have to do."

"Nothing," the sergeant said. "Nothing this evening. Tomorrow, come here at seven."

"O.K.," said the boy. He was still holding the dirty mess tin in his hand and asked: "Should I wash the mess tin?"

"Yes, wash it up," the sergeant said.

The boy went to where the water casks were, and washed the mess tin by rubbing it with earth. A soldier who saw him gave him a piece of soap, and he washed the mess tin again with soap. Then he went back to the sergeant. "I would like to dry it," he said, "but I haven't anything to dry it with."

"You don't have to dry it," the sergeant said. He seemed absent-minded, as if he was thinking of something else. The soldiers at the end of the courtyard were still singing.

This spareness of contours, this bare presentation of things, this reproduction of details which seem unessential, are certainly uncommon in Italian literature. Berto is very fond of describing practical occupations in their minute details. For instance:

Giulia smiled, but, finding nothing else to say, got up and did not sit down again. She gave a few more pulls to the pump . . . and busied herself with the preparations for the meal. She took some canned meat and some eggs out of the box, she lifted a pan off its hook on the wall, and put everything on a table placed against the wall. She opened the can, broke the eggs, and poured everything in the pan. Then she began to mix. Her gestures were slow, unstudied. Daniele looked at her, and looked also at the door to see whether Carla would come back. She had been gone a long time. Then Giulia took the pot off the fire and began to pour out the vegetables. Daniele went to help her, and took in his hand a tin plate with many holes, which was used to drain the vegetables.

Giulia smiled at him with gratitude. "Don't scald yourself," she said. She cautiously poured out the contents of the pot. The vegetables rested on the perforated tin plate, and the water dropped into a basin underneath. A thick white vapor rose, full of the smell of the boiled vegetables.

"Shall I go and throw the water away?" Daniele asked.

"No," Giulia said, "we can use it to wash the dishes."

Now, I won't try to prove that such minute cooking operations have never before been described in Italian literature, though I would be at a loss to quote anything like them. But open any book of Hemingway, and you will find the model. Take for instance this passage from "Big Two-Hearted River":

Nick was hungry. He did not believe he had ever been hungrier. He opened and emptied a can of pork and beans and a can of spaghetti into the frying pan.

"I've got a right to eat this kind of stuff, if I'm willing to carry it," Nick said. His voice sounded strange in the darkening wood. He did not speak again.

He started a fire with some chunks of pine he got with the ax from a stump. Over the fire he stuck a wire grill, pushing the four legs down into the ground with his boot. Nick put the frying pan on the grill over the flames. He was hungrier. The beans and spaghetti warmed. Nick stirred them and mixed them together. They began to bubble, making little bubbles that rose with difficulty to the surface. There was a good smell. Nick got out a bottle of tomato catchup and cut four slices of bread. The little bubbles were coming faster now. Nick sat down beside the fire and lifted the frying pan off. He poured about half the contents out into the tin plate. It spread slowly on the plate. Nick knew it was too hot. He poured on some tomato catchup. He knew the beans and spaghetti were still too hot. He looked at the fire, then at the tent, he was not going to spoil it all by burning his tongue. For years he had never enjoyed fried bananas because he had never been able to wait for them to cool. His tongue was very sensitive.

I said before that I cannot remember anything like this kind of description in Italian literature, and I may as well say, in any other literature I know. If such minute operations have ever been described before, there was no emphasis on them; they were not meant to stand out like something particularly significant. With Hemingway they have ceased to be part of the background; they are presented as important episodes. And the same has happened with the seemingly insignificant details of ordinary conversation. Before Hemingway, dialogues in fiction or on the stage were the result of a selection: all immaterial portions were left out; questions and answers followed a more or less rigid pattern dictated by art. The utmost artificiality prevailed in the stichomythy of the Greek tragedies, as in Alexandrian couplets of the French plays, or the witty repartees of Restoration comedy; but even the dialogues in the novels of the naturalist school of the nineteenth century, for all they pretended to be copied from real life, are arranged so that, so far as the author can help, there is nothing superfluous. Hemingway has shown the value of the apparently superfluous, the strange beauty of the commonest things when seen from a certain angle, so as to deserve almost the praise Baudelaire gave to the great seventeenth-century French sculptor Puget: *"Toi qui sus ramasser la beauté des goujats."* Thus he represents the extreme limit of proletarianization so far reached by literature.

At first only kings were considered fit characters for tragedies: at first only great events were to be a theme for narration: then Montaigne appeared and the apparently insignificant shades of humor and sensibility were brought into literary expression; then landscapes, bourgeois interiors, still lifes formed subjects for independent pictures; and so little by little the humble sides of society and of life have been given attention, until they have come nowadays to the limelight. *Un Cœur simple* is only an episode, though one of the greatest, in Flaubert's career: Hemingway's, on the other hand, is a world of simple hearts and simple minds, simple-looking even if they are complex: in him we see the return to primitivism in an age of great technical development, the standard being set by the man in the street as it once used to be set by the court. His influence on the two Italian authors I have discussed, both of whom once belonged to the left wing of the Fascist party (one is now a prominent Communist), is telltale enough.

Mario Praz

PIER FRANCESCO PAOLINI

The Hemingway of the Major Works

Surely it would be neither wrong nor overbold to see the best of Hemingway in his short stories—more precisely, in a certain number of them varying in length between twenty and fifty pages, with a good deal of white space in the dialogue portions. We may even recognize in these major stories a kind of "Hemingwayism in its pure state" and reconstruct from them— "The Snows of Kilimanjaro," "The Short Happy Life of Francis Macomber," "My Old Man," "The Undefeated," "The Killers," "Fifty Grand," "The Gambler, The Nun, and The Radio," "The Capital of the World," together with a few others and, finally, with the novella *The Old Man and the Sea*—a complete and sharply defined Hemingway world, harmonious in its parts and symmetrical in the classical sense of the word.

Indeed, despite the variety of their themes, this ensemble of stories reveals closely knit cohesion, if only we clear away some of the obstacles thrown up by an apparently widespread prejudice which insists that we concern ourselves solely with the marginal aspects, the "extemporaneous" art, of Hemingway the writer. (Sometimes this is even reduced to an idyllic inability to move forward, flowing from what Emilio Cecchi has branded as "the abdication to the ineffable of the American mind.") Just the opposite is true: an apparently heterogeneous mass of material can be fitted into a vast logical process; a system does emerge, based on rules of rational dialectic. These rules may appear to be scholastically rigid, but I hope to make them fulfill their function as a corrective and a stimulus to thought.

What is the "geographic" location of the great stories? They are ideally equidistant from the vague hazy atmosphere, lit up briefly by occasional flashes as of some falling star, of the brief "one-celled" stories and from the architecture of the novels, soaring spirelike toward a sky of greater clarity.

Those that rarely preserve the classic stamp of the story—and there are fine ones among them too—seem to spring hastily from the keys of the typewriter so as not to miss the fugitive moment of grace; and they have an impetus of immediate, often indefinable, perception. Or they are born as the echo of a faint suggestion in the surrounding atmosphere; or they barely emerge with a nervous thrust when the curtain suddenly closes over them, but their musical vibrations linger (stories such as "Hills Like White Elephants" and "The Sea Change" are the best examples of this kind); or they crystallize around some grim news item; or they may even take shape as variations on a single sentence, a phrase repeated like a refrain. Only rarely do they burst forth with a surprise ending, as in "An Alpine Idyll" or "A Canary for One." Here let me say that the typical Hemingway manner is to interpose a buffer, to delay the outcome, between the title and the ending of the story.

The novels, on the other hand, reveal an ambitious design, a striving to orchestrate the actions of individuals and to discover the laws governing their relations; they attest to a constant, progressive effort, at times spontaneous, at times rebelling against itself, to go higher. Or, as Alfred Kazin, referring to *For Whom the Bell Tolls*, calls it, to escape from the vainly pursued self.

Of course, the boundary lines are not clear and sharply defined. A good many of the stories center about a single person, Nick Adams. They seem to be searching for a kind of continuity, as if they were fragments of a loosely autobiographical novel. Thus, too, we find specific sections in the novels that strongly suggest self-contained short stories. This is obvious, for example, in *To Have and Have Not,* a kind of *sectional work* in this sense: three stories with a single hero, and in the third story the development of a parallel set of circumstances, and the insertion of four or five typical stories dealing with the guests on the yachts anchored in the harbor. In *For Whom the Bell Tolls* the retrospective narration entrusted to Pilar is another example; while the last part of *A Farewell to Arms*, the "duet" between Frederic Henry and his wife in Switzerland, is almost a novella in itself. This may well be the most solid external limit of Hemingway the novelist; at the same time, it is a confirmation of how, on the technical level, he finds his best rhythm, his smoothest pace, in the flow and development of a medium-length story.

Hemingway's internal limit is just as solid but in a different way. When he strives for complete harmony, attempting to enclose in a circle his "brilliant half-vision of life" (Cecchi), he is caught in a deep and unresolved antagonism: the antithesis between the "self" and the "anti-self." This occurs where the anti-self is represented by Society (as Kazin puts it: in Hemingway's works the self and Society do not succeed in meeting); whereas in cases more typically Hemingwayan it is blindly shut up within the self itself. (This reminds one of Ludwig Lewisohn's phrase about the spiritual desperation of those who squander their own lives.)

The moral conclusion of *To Have and Have Not*, even though it remains a little apart, is in the words of the dying Morgan: "A man . . . a man alone." That is all he can utter in his final delirium, but it may easily be construed as a condemnation of individualism. Here it is really the author speaking. It took him a long time to pronounce those words; it had taken him a whole lifetime to learn them.

It has been aptly pointed out that *For Whom the Bell Tolls* was meant to signify, on the hero's part, the acquisition of this important knowledge, and the bell was to sound the call to an *engagement* that would triumph over the nihilism which threatened to engulf everything in its flood. But it is likewise true, we must add, that the lumbering material and innate anarchism did not permit the effective conversion that in theory should have occurred.

The same contradiction, but developed in an opposite direction, was at the heart of *A Farewell to Arms*. The leading character, Frederic Henry, at first participated in a common adventure, war; but then, by deserting, he struck out on his own. His individual adventure ended with a bleak vision of man, defeated by a supreme fate by which he was perhaps doomed. And so, as in the climax of a Chaplin film, he shuffles off with sagging shoulders in the rain. But the "farewell" in the title shows us the precise point at which an irreparable break in the novel's structure occurs.

Consider a passage such as the following:

You died. You did not know what it was about. You never had time to learn. They threw you in and told you the rules and the first time they caught you off base they killed you. Or they killed you gratuitously. . . .

Or this dialogue:

"The coward dies a thousand deaths, the brave but one?"
"Of course. Who said it?"
"I don't know."

"He was probably a coward. . . . The brave dies perhaps two thousand deaths if he's intelligent. He simply doesn't mention them."
"I don't know. It's hard to see inside the head of the brave."

Such passages remain as if suspended in the novel's hard-boiled atmosphere; the material is not penetrated in depth. They appear like great wedges which, unable to split the tree trunk, remain imprisoned in the knotty wood. True, similar passages are found in the major short stories. There, however, they are deeply embedded in the wood—they are developed in dramatic terms, in terms of poetry.

But every page of Hemingway offers illuminating insights into the inner workings of his moral world, just as a molecule contains within itself all the physicochemical properties of the substance of which it is made. This may be the reason for "that tone as if of esthetic exaggeration" which Cecchi claims to find in every word and line of Hemingway. It also helps us to understand Hemingway as a writer obsessed with a certain basic idea from which all the other ideas develop by sporogenesis—with each image leading to another, each example logically linked to still others. On the other hand, it is virtually impossible to understand a single incident or a single work in isolation from all the others. By this criterion, therefore, we observe that the fundamental Hemingway antithesis (self and anti-self) is resolved, in the most conspicuous and interesting cases, in two ways: now in the conflict between nihilism and social consciousness, now in the conflict between opposing conceptions. These are personified on the one hand by the "professional," on the other by the "dilettante."

As for the great antithesis: *nihilism* vs. *engagement* (commitment), Hemingway reflects in his own way a phenomenon of far-reaching proportions in the American literature of a specific period. The contrast is striking if we compare the anarchic tendencies of the 1920s with the search for social content characteristic of the following decade. As John Chamberlain astutely pointed out in an article in *Life* magazine:[1]

Certainly the twenties abounded in the symbols of negation, despair, and disbelief. There was poet T. S. Eliot's *The Waste Land*. . . . There was poet Archibald MacLeish's sonnet about the spectators at the human circus: when "quite unexpectedly a top blew off"—leaving the people staring up at "nothing, nothing, nothing—nothing at all."

[1] September 1, 1947.

In another book title Scott Fitzgerald waxed rhetorical about *All the Sad Young Men.* "You are all a lost generation," so Gertrude Stein told Ernest Hemingway who sang his own dirge to nothingness which, in good expatriate fashion, he preferred to call by its Spanish name of *nada.* . . . Viciousness, hypocrisy, irresponsibility and a lackluster acceptance of the Freudian death-wish characterized many of the literary "heroes" of the twenties. . . . Against this backdrop of negation and silliness, critics like Geismar and Kazin pose the growing "social consciousness" of the authors of the thirties. The symbols of despair and disbelief officially go by the board, and in their place we discover a happy proletarian chorus singing the curative value of revolution.

Considering now what we have defined as the "golden zone" in Hemingway's work, we believe that it is marked by surprising harmony. The clash of opposing forces has not caused a rent or left behind any gaping wounds. Here the inner leitmotiv is precisely that antithesis between professionalism and dilettantism, interpreting these two opposing concepts in their broadest and universal sense. For the Hemingway man (*homo hemingwaianus*) to belong to the category of "professionals" implies a choice— either by instinct or as a result of a series of experiences; it means he has taken up a solid strategic position in the life-war which by its very nature can no longer be stormed by the enemy or engulfed in the abyss of *nada.* The choice determines whether life is worth living and fighting for, or is "a nothing and then nothing and then nothing." Hence the "dilettante" is a failure: he has failed in his duty, in the true categorical imperative of the conscience; he has wasted his talents and energies. The other category is that of the "undefeated," the winners, even when they win nothing, even when they seem to be routed. It is in these terms that Hemingway advances and solves the dilemma of "to be or not to be," in which "nonbeing," probably deriving from the mysticism of the Slav writers, is both an obstacle and a calamity to "being." Let us now examine this question more closely.

What strikes one above all is the feeling of annoyance, even disgust, engendered in certain Hemingway characters through doing the same thing too long. It may be by waiting too long for death, as in "The Snows of Kilimanjaro":

> I'm getting as bored with dying as with everything else, he thought.
> "It's a bore," he said out loud.
> "What is, my dear?"
> "Anything you do too bloody long."

Or it may simply be that one has stayed somewhere for too long, as in "An Alpine Idyll":

> "You oughtn't to ever do anything too long."
> "No. We were up there too long."
> "Too damn long. . . . It's no good doing a thing too long."

We encounter these same words, "too bloody long," in other stories (e.g., "Today Is Friday"), or at least we hear their echo. In them we can always recognize a definite symptom of the tragic or ironic dissatisfaction of the "dilettantes," the Hemingway failures. It is just this weariness with having too long carried on his hide-and-seek with death which impels Ole Andreson in "The Killers" to give up the struggle. For a long time he has run away, has hid, has defended himself; now there comes the moment when, lying on the bed in the dingy rooming house, with his face to the wall, he waits for the killers to come and murder him "because he double-crossed somebody." When young Nick Adams arrives to warn him, the Swede replies: "No, I'm through with all that running around." These words are the very heart of the famous story; to understand them in their true sense, they must be placed side by side with the line in "The Snows of Kilimanjaro": "It was strange how easy being tired made it [i.e., dying]." In the inability to endure what lasts "too bloody long" (cf. also "She loved anything that involved a change of scene"; or, from "Hills Like White Elephants": "That's all we do, isn't it—look at things and try new drinks?"), we see an important aspect of the inner struggle in a person who has not fully committed himself to anything, yet is sufficiently aware and intelligent to show the anguished signs of that struggle.

Superficiality is a manifestation of the timorous nonentity triumphant; boredom can push even the person who has understood but not heeded the voice of duty into the murky swamp of superficiality. In the stream-of-consciousness passages in "The Snows of Kilimanjaro" we attain the high point in this confrontation of two conceptions of life: Harry, the main character, lying on a cot near death, faces the bitter, deeply disturbing evidence of his failure. He was born to be a professional, a real writer, and instead

he had destroyed his talent by not using it, by betrayals of himself and what he believed in, by laziness, by sloth, and by snobbery. . . . It was never what he had done, but always what he could do. And he had chosen to make his living with something else instead of a pen or a pencil.

If he—representing the "negative" quintessence of the Hemingway man—had "lived by a lie" and, at least on the surface, "should try to die by it," the hero in "The Short Happy Life of Francis Macomber," on the other hand, lives long enough to feel his veins pulsate with the rhythm of genuine living, if only for a brief space of time. There is undoubtedly a kind of parallelism between these two stories written at short intervals from each other. Francis Macomber too had long lived in an atmosphere of deceptive wealth, of "sloth and snobbery." During a lion hunt he reveals himself as a coward. A coward like many other human beings, who do not bother overmuch about it. But the ordinary rules do not apply to Hemingway characters, as they do not apply to Conrad characters (cf. *Lord Jim*). Thus, to Macomber, the lion represents the crisis in his life, the "moment of truth."

Face to face with this dilettante and contrasting with him is the professional Robert Wilson. He is the "white hunter" who, behind the rather cynical mask of someone who does something because he is paid to do it ("You don't have to go in, of course," he said. "That's what I'm hired for, you know. That's why I'm so expensive"), is in his own way a genuine humanitarian ("For one thing he's [i.e., the lion] certain to be suffering. For another, someone else might run onto him"). Macomber's wife Margot, with the fierce primal instincts of a she-wolf leading the pack, reviles her husband for his weakness ("You *are* a bitch."—"Well, you're a coward"). Then, when Macomber redeems himself and, in a happy moment, a fatal moment, feels he is beginning a new life ("For the first time in his life he really felt wholly without fear. Instead of fear he had a feeling of definite elation"), she cold-bloodedly shoots him. If this is a triumph of death—and here let us again cite the passage in *A Farewell to Arms*: ". . . the first time they caught you off base they killed you . . . gratuitously"—it is also and above all an exaltation of man's moral values. Hence the skepticism in the phrase: "They threw you in and told you the rules," loses the hardness of "You did not know what it was about"; it is replaced by a ripened awareness, a Conradian concept of responsibility toward one's conscience. It is from that angle, therefore, that we can best follow the main lines of Hemingway's ethical development.

In "The Capital of the World"—a story in which the various elements are arranged as in a stage set and according to a procedure used also in *To Have and Have Not*, which quickens the dramatic pace—the same theme may be observed, or rather glimpsed, from a different perspective. In the soul of the boy Paco, who "himself would like to be a good Catholic, a revolutionary, and have a steady job like this, while, at the same time, being a bullfighter," we see the first vague and contradictory stirrings of a conscience that is still dull and benighted. But when he wants to prove his courage to himself, that is, seriously face the danger that lures him, he dies playing at bullfighting, stabbed by two heavy-bladed meat knives tied to the legs of a chair. He dies "full of illusions," for "he had not had time in his life to lose any of them."

On the other hand, the hero of "The Undefeated" holds fast to his illusions of being a great bullfighter, to the very end—which is his way of getting revenge on adversity. To the old and unlucky Manuel Garcia there is no problem as to what he has to do. He has solved that from the outset, once and for all. In his self-determination, in his sorry fight with a bull that refuses to charge, in the midst of the crowd's indifference and subsequent jeers, shall we see only an esthetic passion—as does Kazin? If so, it would be more correct to see the exact counterpart of *estheticism,* a "Hemingway coefficient," in *utilitarianism,* a "Conradian coefficient," with the same crushing concept of duty. (Note Conrad's marvelous utilitarianism, thanks to which his simple-minded heroes, "devoid of imagination," such as Captain McWhirr, perform great tasks. Perhaps this sheds some light on the inner reasons for the Polish-born writer's fondness for the fellow countrymen of Jeremy Bentham!) Furthermore, in "The Snows of Kilimanjaro" Hemingway uses the express words: ". . . and it was *his duty* to write it."

But a magnificently constructed story like "The Undefeated" is not only built on a sure foundation of naturalism; it also presents an idealistic problem in its most virilely positive solution. When Garcia, just out of the hospital, comes to see the bullfight promoter, his "professional" attitude is immediately revealed:

"Why don't you get a job and go to work?" he said.
"I don't want to work," Manuel said. "I am a bullfighter."

These words stand out as an act of faith, coming from the emaciated figure who utters them. He is there with the stuffed bull on the wall grimly looking down at him—the same bull that nine years ago killed his brother. When the picador Zurito asks him why he doesn't quit the bull ring for good, Manuel replies with the same stubborn simplicity: "I don't know. I got to do it." Even on the operating table he summons up enough strength to rebel as they try to cut off his *coleta,* symbol of his profession and his illusions. Finally, all he says about his last bullfight is this: "I was going good. I didn't have any luck. That was all."

This reference to "bad luck" recurs with surprising insistence. Perhaps it is this expression, repeated so frequently, with such stark simplicity and as if mysteriously, which offers us an insight into Hemingway's "pessimism"—at first complete pessimism, then gradually becoming less preconceived and blind. "Bad luck," a dark force, is perhaps also one aspect of *nada,* but at the same time a mastery of it. It is like an enemy who, remaining in the shadows, has nevertheless assumed concrete shape; or like a sickness that has been localized in the body. It is a superstitious, fatal entity that plays an important part in Hemingway's stories. Its entering wedge into the heart of the anguished problem of being and nothingness is described to us by Cayetano Ruiz, the gambler in "The Gambler, The Nun, and The Radio":

"I am a professional gambler but I like to gamble. I really gamble. For real gambling you need luck. I have no luck."

"Never?"

"Never. I am completely without luck. . . . When I make a sum of money I gamble and when I gamble I lose."

"Why continue?"

"If I live long enough the luck will change. I have had bad luck now for fifteen years." . . .

"And what is there to do?"

"Continue, slowly, and wait for luck to change."

There is nothing to add to this passage: the deep concept of *professionalism* encounters the subtle, quasi-mystical one of *bad luck.* But we have an even clearer example in *The Old Man and the Sea* where the contrast between misfortune and patient merit is expressed in highly ethical terms:

". . . Only I have no luck any more. But who knows? Maybe today. Every day is a new day. It is better to be lucky. But I would rather be exact. Then when luck comes you are ready."

So the "professional," whose personality is most clearly defined when he faces bad luck, is the one who "keeps on waiting," or who, if he doesn't live long enough, has the profound satisfaction of flinging in death's face words such as Manuel Garcia's "I was going great"—the supreme boast of the esthete and the supreme defiance of *nada*. Thus, overcoming hopeless pessimism, man finds in himself his own unit of measurement. And all those who, for good or ill, on a moral plane or a criminal level, shift their total destruction to the theoretical plane, find phrases of the Elizabethan John Ford—"perseverance in action" and "endurance in perseverance"—admirably applicable to themselves. Here, then, is a positive answer to Hamlet's tortured questioning: "Whether 'tis nobler in the mind to suffer/The slings and arrows of outrageous fortune. . . ."

Hemingway's *The Old Man and the Sea* offers an abundance of analogies with "The Undefeated." It seems significant that after so many years of silence, embittered perhaps by some failures, Hemingway returned to one of the stories which in all probability "he had saved to write." But the old theme has been notably enriched.

Like Manuel, just out of the hospital, old Santiago the fisherman returning empty-handed after eighty-four days of fishing, is dogged by bad luck. The one has Zurito, the other the boy Manolin to console him; both suffer the same hunger and misery; they have the same faith, the same desire to prove their own worth in spectacular fashion. Their adversaries, the bull and the fish, show unexpected stubbornness—they have both been raised to symbols. Although there is a kind of reversal in their respective roles—with Manuel charging the weakened bull and Santiago defending the dead fish against the sharks—there are many other points of contact. The very title "The Undefeated" is echoed in the old fisherman's words: "But man is not made for defeat. A man can be destroyed but not defeated." Of course "man" here means "hero," "professional"; and when Santiago says "I cannot betray myself," this assertion should be contrasted with the "betrayals of myself" in "The Snows of Kilimanjaro." For in a way *The Old Man and the Sea* is the *summa* of all the themes hitherto enunciated: "I will show him what a man can do and what he can bear." But there is something more: a profoundly religious sense, a feeling of the harmony in nature. Santiago wants to show how a man *and* a fish can suffer. This is the vital point: a broadening out toward the contemplation of the infinite forms of life and struggle. He may lose one eye or both—but he will go on fighting like a gamecock. In fact, what we have here is a sentiment we may properly call "Franciscan": "I am as clear as the stars that are my brothers"; "to live on the sea and kill our true brothers." I will not even dwell on the accents and rhythm of prayer in the author's style. No doubt the root of these traits is also to be found in Hemingway's preceding work: nature, for instance, plays a preponderant part in a story such as "Big Two-Hearted River." But the fresh, serene landscape revealed in that story of wanderings along trout-filled streams is related to the vast, moving, almost pantheistic representation of nature in *The Old Man and the Sea* in the way that a "vacation" is related to a professionally occupied life, or an idyl to an epic.

But man's isolation is not overcome. Santiago, like Harry Morgan, is alone in the midst of the sea; and Morgan's words in his delirium find their counterpart in Santiago's phrase, repeated with bitterness: "I wish the boy were here . . . I wish I had the boy!" Or: "No one should ever remain alone, as an old man. But it is inevitable." So there is also resignation here; and this is in perfect accord with that merging of human anguish into universal harmony, that dilution of war itself into cosmic harmony.

Manuel dies and Santiago bows his head. But if these two humble protagonists say anything to us, it may be summed up in the one word: *endure*.

Now, returning to "The Gambler, The Nun, and The Radio," we note that the story is without any real dramatic development as such but is full of suggestions and hints of suggestions. It is easy to identify the three symbols—they are side by side in the title itself. Sister Cecilia, who freely confesses her dream of becoming a saint and prays day and night for that consummation, represents naïve faith. The Mexican Cayetano Ruiz also has faith. He possesses a manly "undespairing pessimism." (Is this not perhaps an apt recipe for Hemingway's own pessimism?) Frankly avowing himself a professional gambler, he reveals a force of character and a stoicism worthy of a greater cause. The third character, Frazer, is a faceless man, disillusioned, apathetic, finding a cheap opiate for himself in the radio; he is the "dilettante" in the simplest and most sordid sense of the term. And what is Frazer's admiration for Ruiz, for the man dedicated to a single aim for which he renounces women and all else; what is Frazer's eagerness to understand if not Hemingway's own impulses of deep sympathy for the great "professionals"?

In "Fifty Grand" we witness an inner conflict between pro-

fessional pride and shady dealings. Jack Brennan is a boxer on
the downgrade. He is getting old, suffers from insomnia, and
cannot endure the rigors of training. Through two crooked individuals he has bet fifty thousand dollars at two to one against
himself. He was sure he was going to lose—but it was the way in
which he had to lose that caused the crisis within him. "He knew
he couldn't beat Walcott. He wasn't strong any more. [Thus he
reasons with himself when, after several rounds, he seems to be
weakening.] He was all right though. His money was all right and
now he wanted to finish it off right to please himself. He didn't
want to be knocked out." But his opponent Walcott also wants to
lose the fight, and he hits Brennan below the belt so as to be
disqualified. Despite excruciating pain, Brennan refuses to claim
the foul. He continues the bout and in turn hits a low blow,
knocking Walcott out. So he is disqualified. One doesn't really
know whether he has won or lost the fight—perhaps both together. In the last fight of his career Jack Brennan finds himself involved in a sordid "fix" yet manages, by a supreme effort
and a show of uttermost physical endurance, to maintain the
fierce pride of a professional boxer.

A somewhat analogous situation occurs, on a lesser scale, in
"My Old Man." Butler the jockey, unable to find work, goes
from track to track with his son Joe. He receives a "hot tip" about
a "fixed" race in which the great favorite Kzar is not going to win.
But here is how his son reacts:

> "Honest, watching the race I'd forgot how much my old man had
> bet on Kircubbin. I'd wanted Kzar to win so damned bad. But now it
> was all over it was swell to know we had the winner."

Later Butler takes up jockeying again, but he is forced to ride
in fixed races. The second time he races he breaks his neck going
over the water jump with his horse and is brought in dead. At
the exit to the track Joe hears disgruntled bettors say that Butler
was a crook and had it coming to him. Chronologically, the
jockey Butler is the first of the Hemingway professionals. "My
Old Man," in which the influence of Sherwood Anderson (cf. his
"I Want to Know Why") is discernible, is one of the transitional
stories leading to that restoration of values climaxed by the exaltation of the sense of duty in the last great stories.

But even in stories of lesser scope we get partial reflections of
the far-reaching ethical conflict. In "The End of Something,"
for example, we see in the adolescent the groping prelude of the

crisis that will beset the mature adult, the first vague signs of pain, like a chrysalis that dies without having given birth to the butterfly. In Nick Adams' words: "I feel as though everything was gone to hell inside of me. I don't know. . . . I don't know what to say." An irrational reflection of this conflict, expressed in a downright paradox and arising from a moment of deep discouragement, may be seen in the words of the Italian major in "In Another Country": "If he should lose everything, he should not place himself in a position to lose that. He should not place himself in a position to lose. He should find things he cannot lose." Elsewhere the "pure" sense of emptiness prevails—the slow decline without reason, consolation, or escape—as in "A Clean, Well-Lighted Place," which is a Magna Charta of nihilism in its most acute phase: "It was a nothing that he knew too well. It was all a nothing and a man was nothing too. It was only that. . . ." Or it is the clinging to the *only* reason for living, to memory, to regret, as in "Old Man at the Bridge" ("I was only taking care of animals"); or in "The Light of the World" (the whore building a superstructure of ideal love on a lie: ". . . I belong to him right now and always will and all of me is his"). Or there is a frustrated sadness, the failure of ideals only barely glimpsed, behind a screen of bourgeois comfort and smugness, as in "Soldier's Home": "He had tried so to keep his life from being complicated. Still, none of it had touched him. . . . He would go to Kansas City and get a job. . . . He wanted his life to go smoothly." Krebs, in the last-named story, is another typical Hemingway "dilettante" because his way is adjustment, not choice.

In Hemingway's major works society means, more than anything else, lack of understanding. The crowd that jeers Manuel; the disappointed bettors who deride Butler's memory; the tourists who see the backbone of Santiago's great fish and casually comment: "I didn't know sharks had such handsome, beautifully formed tails"; the Mexicans who come to see Ruiz in the hospital ("You gentlemen are friends of Cayetano?" . . . "No, we are friends of he who wounded him")—these are all examples of the hostility, the superficiality, the scorn, the lack of understanding, surrounding the "hero," victim of "outrageous fortune," in his loneliness of sorrow, death, disbelief, self-annihilation, and esthetic self-exaltation.

Yet over against these expressions of hostility there are always the warm, friendly, affectionate gestures of a Zurito, a Frazer; of George Gardner telling Joe: "Your old man was one swell guy"; of the boy Manolin; of the writer's wife: "I'm only a middle-aged woman who loves you"; of Nick risking a bullet in his head to warn the Swede Ole Andreson; and Robert Wilson's belated admiration for Macomber: "I'd begun to like your husband." [2]

The human solidarity of the "understanding" characters is rooted in the heart and defined by the emotions. *The Old Man and the Sea,* highest expression of human worth and misfortune, of heroic perseverance and endurance, signifies, as compared to *For Whom the Bell Tolls,* man's creative integration in the drama and mystery of Nature—following what was at bottom the failure of his political efforts at *commitment* in society. Santiago, the hero of that novella, expresses himself in terms of "looking forward," the symbolic value of which must not escape us: "There is only the boy to worry, of course. But I am sure he would have confidence. Many of the older fishermen will worry. Many others too, he thought. I live in a good town."

Pier Francesco Paolini

Translated from the Italian by Joseph M. Bernstein

[2] The same may be said of that "Franciscanism in reverse," as it is defined in *Death in the Afternoon,* since what was stated simply and crudely there has here ripened in expression.

Hemingway in Russia

Ernest Hemingway was first published in Russia in 1934. His rise to popularity was so rapid that in 1937, when the editors of a Russian literary magazine asked fifteen leading Soviet writers to name their favorite non-Russian author, nine of them named Hemingway. There were no new Soviet printings of his books from 1939 to 1955, and during the last ten years of this period, largely because of the tensions of the cold war, he was rarely mentioned in the Soviet press. Yet he has always ranked high among Western authors with Russian readers, and today he is once more openly and warmly lauded.

Prior to 1934, Hemingway had been practically unknown in Russia. A small circle of professionals had heard of his growing international reputation, and a few of them had read him in English. In the absence of translations, however, the general impression of him was vague, and he was usually cited merely as a symbol of "decadence" in contrast to the "revolutionary" Dos Passos. But by 1934, following the cultural famine of the First Five-Year Plan, Soviet editors and publishers had decided that the time was ripe to expose the Russian reader to Hemingway.

This was done in three ways in that year. First, a work of his appeared in an anthology of American short stories. Second, his stories began to come out in magazines. Finally, a collection made up of selections from four of his books was published under the title, *Death in the Afternoon*.[1] From then until 1939, his stories were printed with great frequency in Soviet magazines. *The Sun Also Rises* was published in 1935, and in 1936 the first of four editions of *A Farewell to Arms* came out. *To Have and Have Not* was translated in 1938, and was followed by a volume entitled *The Fifth Column and the First Thirty-Eight Stories* in 1939. There were also several serial publications of the novels in these years.

[1] This book had little in common with the American work published under the same title.

145

The sudden publication of Hemingway in 1934, several years after his American reputation had been established, indicates that the Russian discovery of the author was calculated. Hemingway was an active antifascist, and the Soviet Union was particularly anxious to lend a helping hand to those whom it considered its potential friends. Although he was certainly aware of their interest in him, and corresponded with one of their best critics, Ivan Kashkeen, Hemingway remained immune to the Russians' blandishments. Nevertheless, the Russians stated their case with extreme thoroughness. Not only did Soviet editors turn out carefully translated editions of Hemingway; they also encouraged literary critics to examine him meticulously. In the course of six years, in dozens of articles, these critics devised an interpretation of his career which was intended both to explain his deficiencies and to encourage his leftward growth.

According to the tenets of socialist realism, a writer must approach his art as a materialist, a rational optimist, and a collectivist. He must be firmly anticapitalist in his political convictions, and must dedicate his writing, either implicitly or by direct appeal, to revolutionary socialism. Consequently, his themes must be clearly social, and his heroes must be socially engaged. These "positive heroes" must act upon the conviction that man, and not some external force, shapes the collective destiny by understanding his physical and social environment and by reshaping it. Examining Hemingway from this point of view, Soviet critics found that his most notable characteristic was a development away from individualism, pessimism, and the aimless cultivation of artistic craftsmanship—toward collectivism, optimism, and the dedication of his art to socially constructive ends. According to their scheme, his attitudes were first of all a product of his experiences in the First World War. Here was the genesis of the themes which were to run through most of his works to 1936; an obsession with death, and a consequent feeling of hopelessness, fatalism, and passivity; an attitude of disillusionment, characterized by a hurt, defensive mistrust of ideals and a general skepticism; an attitude of political and social indifference, in which the only values are individual values; and concentration on the various means of flight from reality.

Soviet critics were particularly fascinated by his treatment of death. Comparing him to Ambrose Bierce in this respect, the critic Nemerovskaya wrote:

War impregnated him with hopeless pessimism, war prompted in him
a terror in the face of death. . . . Despair before the impotence of life
is interwoven with despair before the all-powerfulness of death. War is
not an arena for heroism, for the snatching of glory for self and
country; it is a struggle for the preservation of one's life, for the overcoming of one's own fear of death.[2]

And the critic Miller-Budnitskaya found that "fear of death is the
key to Hemingway's entire personal and creative biography, to
his whole system of images and style." [3] This fixation drove the
artist to fruitless self-laceration, a kind of grim game in which
he sedulously sought out situations, both in his life and in his
art, in which to face the horror of death and to struggle with it.
This accounted for his passion for bullfighting, big-game hunting,
and violent sports, and for exploring the details of the death
process, as in "The Snows of Kilimanjaro" and *To Have and Have
Not*.[4]

But the obsession with death was only part of a larger com-
posite of desolation in Hemingway. Accompanying this morbid,
vigorous probing at the ultimate terror was a feeling of futility, an
all-embracing attitude of indifference and passivity. The critic
Abramov pointed out that his "rough, athletic style" and the
"masculinity" of his themes were a mask covering a "weariness,
skepticism, spiritual and artistic impotence." [5] Kashkeen argued
that his tremendous mental and physical energy, in combination
with his emotional and intellectual pessimism, had created the
peculiar synthesis of a full-blooded zest for the acts of living
within an omnipresent consciousness of morbid futility. And as
this attitude continued to develop, Kashkeen declared,

It has become increasingly clear that his vigor is pretended, that it is
dissipated by him and by his heroes little by little. Hemingway's sharpness of sight has led up to this, that as the most deformed and terrible
qualities in man appeared in his writing, it became all the more clear
that his vigor is the aimless vigor of a man trying in vain not to think,
that his virility is the aimless virility of a despair, that Hemingway all

[2] Olga Nemerovskaya, "Sudba amerikanskoi novelly," *Literaturnaya
uchyoba*, No. 5 (1935), p. 102.
[3] R. Miller-Budnitskaya in O. Berestov, "Vecher E. Khemingueya," *Rezets,*
No. 7 (1939), p. 24.
[4] Olga Nemerovskaya, "V poiskakh geroizma," *Znamya*, No. 6 (1938),
p. 277.
[5] Al. Abramov, "Molodost veka," *Internatsionalnaya literatura,* No. 6
(1935), p. 141.

the more inexorably seizes upon the temptation of death, that again and again he writes only of the end—the end of relationships, the end of life, the end of hope and everything. . . . Strength itself, unapplied and unnecessary, becomes a weakness and a burden. . . . Action turns into its reverse, into the passive pose of the stoic, into the courage of despair.[6]

The war affected Hemingway even more strongly, the Russians felt, by shattering his personal and social beliefs. Perceiving the senselessness of the war, he was shocked by the human degradation it involved—the destruction of the dignity of the individual and the feeling of moral and intellectual emptiness it left with those who had experienced it. An equally important shock was his return, with heightened sensitivity, to the spiritually empty bourgeois world. The necessity of returning to life in these decadent surroundings, so the Soviet interpretation goes, solidified the feeling of moral devastation in the author. Acutely perceiving the ugliness and purposelessness of existence under the conditions of capitalism, he became the prey of a chronic and bottomless skepticism, denying all ideals, and insisting on the futility of value judgments. In his writing this feeling took the form of a pose of ironic indifference, of an unwillingness to go beneath the surface of things, a mistrust of emotions, passions, and speculative thought. Endowed with an appetite for the joys of living and an acute sense of beauty, he had become spiritually stupefied in perceiving the hollowness of the postwar world.

. . . he passionately loves life, because life—for all its deformity and unhappiness—is nevertheless beautiful and gives man an inexhaustible source of delight and joy. But these pleasures are poisoned, since bourgeois society is a rotten swamp, in which natural feelings and aspirations become putrefied.[7]

As a result, his outlook was one of tense reluctance to give himself up to pleasure and healthy emotion, for fear that it was all a lie, that through it he might become a prisoner of the general slow death about him. This had its effect on the development of his writing technique:

The unique objective manner of Hemingway, his conscious dispassionate fixation of facts and his stinginess of detail, which he has brought to the level of a high technique, arose from the soil of his

[6] I. Kashkeen, "Ernest Hemingway: a Tragedy of Craftsmanship," *International literature,* No. 5 (1935), p. 75.

[7] Nemerovskaya, "V poiskakh . . . ," p. 276.

disillusioned, skeptical consciousness. This is characteristic of the crisis of contemporary bourgeois thought in general, which is more inclined toward the empirical stating of facts than to their explanation and generalization. Devoid of genuine pathos, unfulfilled by any personal emotional participation of the author in the world he describes, it leads to spiritless, passionless, artistic glitter, which does not move or infect the reader and impresses one only by its splendid craftsmanship. But behind this craftsmanship is heard the voice of a despondent skeptic, weary of his own skepticism, but knowing no means of overcoming it.[8]

Kashkeen pointed out that the feeling of hopelessness in Hemingway was not accompanied by a loss of ideals or integrity. Instead, it had driven him to individualism:

Not to save the world, but to see it and to remake at least a tiny part of it, that's what Hemingway wants and calls upon others to do. *Il faut cultiver notre jardin,* he seems to repeat after Candide and as his aim he selects the attainment of craftsmanship.[9]

Within this narrowed perspective which Hemingway defensively set for himself, he had become preoccupied with problems of literary style. He had developed a passion for simplicity, but in the process of simplification his writing had grown capricious and cynical. He had begun presenting death, horror, and perversion in such primitive tones that his pseudo-simplicity had developed into a desperate complication. He had devoted his energies to art for art's sake, and had reached the point of frustration and perpetual floundering.

A corollary of this stunned suspension of belief and emotion was his indifference to political and social problems. For the author had purposely constricted his field of vision to protect himself from the possibility of further shocks. As a realist, he could not avoid reflecting the objective facts of twentieth-century civilization in his writing. There was a backdrop of war, revolution, and social unrest in his stories. These phenomena, however, were not important in themselves, but served merely as devices for underlining the feeling of personal disillusionment which he sought to project. Of his treatment of war in *A Farewell to Arms,* Nemerovskaya writes:

Hemingway perceived war through separate military episodes, through the single persons with whom he came into direct contact. He

[8] Nemerovskaya, "Sudba . . . ," p. 104.
[9] Kashkeen, "Ernest Hemingway . . . ," p. 78.

did not and did not want to look into the reasons for the rise of war, he did not look for the real hero of military action—the massed millions of soldiers who were transformed into cannon fodder.[10]

And the critic Dinamov complained that the love story occupied too large a place in the novel, since it did not permit the author "to turn to more significant phenomena." [11]

Another sign of Hemingway's fundamental lack of concern with large social problems was his concentration on the theme of isolation and flight. His heroes all repudiated society, considering themselves as something apart from the world about them. They refused to relate their problems to those of the rest of humanity, and tried to solve them as individuals. The critic Mingulina complained of the hero of *A Farewell to Arms,* that:

. . . Fred Henry is an enemy of imperialist war, but he does not stop to consider the possibility of fighting against it. Henry is a "passive" pacifist. He deserts not only from the front, he deserts from society and tries to win from fate only his own personal happiness.[12]

Another critic pointed out that Hemingway's heroes flee from thought itself:

Behind the insistent attention of Hemingway's heroes to little, everyday details there hides a fear of everything that is important, fundamental and decisive; people are afraid to recall anything grave or terrifying, they fear thought as they would fear an unbearable pain.[13]

Even the "healthy" tendencies in his writing sprang from the urge to escape, since "the proclivity for nature, for sports—have led him along the path of severance from the world which surrounds him." [14]

Despite their distress over these motifs of pessimism, disillusionment, fear, and flight, Soviet critics saw many good things in Hemingway's art of this period. In the blackest, most despairing and passive of his attitudes, they perceived strong strains of hardihood, honesty, courage, and clear vision, and a passionate longing for truth and beauty. They admired his deep, persistent,

[10] Nemerovskaya, "V poiskakh . . . ," p. 275.

[11] S. Dinamov, "Roman Khemingueya o voine," *Internatsionalnaya literatura,* No. 7 (1936), p. 165.

[12] A. Mingulina, "Ernest Kheminguei," *Kniga i proletarskaya revolyutsiya,* No. 8 (1937), p. 125.

[13] Ya. Frid, "Rasskazy Khemingueya," *Literaturnoye obozreniye,* No. 18 (1939), p. 49.

[14] Nemerovskaya in Berestov, *op. cit.,* p. 24.

unchanging honesty in facing the problems with which he tortured himself. His heroes might try to run away from reality, but the tragic dispassionateness with which the author comprehended their fruitless attempts to escape bespoke a firm resolve not to delude himself. Beneath the skepticism and seeming indifference, the critics observed a moral bravery and integrity, and an intellectual perseverance that compelled admiration. As one critic stated it:

The force of all of Hemingway's things is precisely in the bravery which is welded to his despair, the fact that he does not give in to his despair, but finds within it the ability to struggle against it.[15]

Another wrote:

Depicting even the most tragic moments in human life, he is able to show the health in man, his belief in the worth of humanity, of which there is so little in Western European literature.[16]

Allied to these qualities of courage and integrity was a largeness of soul. With his vigorous love of life and his haunting dread of death, he understood well the dignity and nobility of human passions and suffering. This quality led the critic Startsev to remark with deep respect on his treatment of the love story in *A Farewell to Arms*,[17] and caused the writer Kaverin to observe that he was "one of the most tender of writers," although his prose was genuinely masculine.[18] Others remarked on his democratic sentiments and his thirst for justice.[19] And even Dinamov, who was particularly fond of accusing American authors of "selling out," found that Hemingway, though "a victim of the bourgeois world," was nevertheless an honorable writer.[20]

In this period of his writing Hemingway was considered the prisoner of a destructive ideology. Yet he had a strong insight into the nature of bourgeois society. Thus, *A Farewell to Arms* was "not a patriotic bourgeois book," since it demonstrated the folly of imperialist war.[21] Likewise, his high intelligence and

[15] Adimoni in Berestov, *op. cit.*, p. 24.

[16] A. Korneichuk, "Literatura velikovo amerikanskovo naroda," *Internatsionalnaya literatura,* No. 7-8 (1939), p. 236.

[17] A. Startsev, "Novoye dekadentstvo," *Literaturnaya gazeta,* October 20, 1936.

[18] V. Kaverin in Berestov, *op. cit.*, p. 23.

[19] Konst. Fedin, "O knigakh Khemingueya," *Internatsionalnaya literatura,* No. 7-8 (1939), p. 217.

[20] Dinamov, "Roman Khemingueya . . . ," p. 169.

[21] *Ibid.*, p. 167.

instinctively healthy sense of human values prevented him from becoming a party to the decadence of the "lost generation." Kashkeen asserts that he was "at one and the same time a part of the lost generation and above it," [22] that he was "internally hostile" to it, despised its Bohemianism, and, after a period of experimentation, had even repudiated the decadent influence of its literary gods.[23] Another critic pointed out that his interest in nature and sports was in itself a repudiation of bourgeois society:

> Hemingway likes to write about people who justify their lives in struggle, in stubborn daily competition. Despising the "competition" of the bourgeoisie, the struggle of capital with capital, and of capital against poverty, Hemingway passionately studies those rare events in bourgeois society when only the naked abilities of people compete, their wills, intelligence, strength, skills and sharp-sightedness. . . .[24]

Finally, and perhaps the most important of the "positive" qualities which shone through the ideologically uncongenial works which Hemingway wrote before the middle thirties was the charm of his prose. Commenting on "The Killers" in 1934, Kashkeen wrote:

> The stinginess and reticence of Hemingway, which forces the reader to complete the saying of that which inevitably flows out of what the author has told, his tendency to sharpen the perception of the reader, to teach him alertness, to focus his eyes to unaccustomed angles—all this demands thoughtful, creative reading. And Hemingway deserves this.[25]

There were almost no objections to the effort which Hemingway demands of his readers. His disciplined, laconic, and economical narrative technique was consistently praised, by critics and writers alike. At various times he was compared to Tolstoi, Chekhov, Mayakovski, and even Pushkin. Kashkeen, who made the most thorough study of his style, stressed the variety of his verbal gifts, which made it possible for him to suggest depths of emotion and a wide range of psychological shadings through change of pace and rhythm, and through the manipulation of purely objec-

[22] I. Kashkeen, "Ernest Kheminguei," *Internatsionalnaya literatura*, No. 7-8 (1939), pp. 319-20.

[23] *Ibid.*, p. 322.

[24] Frid, p. 49.

[25] Ivan Kashkeen, "Dve novelly Khemingueya," *Internatsionalnaya literatura*, No. 1 (1934), p. 93.

tive detail.[26] Others stressed his precision and simplicity. The writer Kaverin remarked:

In the artistic manner of Hemingway one is struck by one point—accuracy, not only the astonishing accuracy of description, but the unusual faithfulness of intonation in the transmission of the most intimate things.[27]

His seemingly reticent, dispassionate manner was found to be capable of extraordinarily sharp and powerful dramatic effects. Perhaps the greatest tribute to Hemingway as a craftsman was made by the critic who said, simply:

Hemingway describes descending a mountain on skis with amazing plasticity—not a single contemporary prose writer has told about movement with such precision, energy, grace, and simplicity.[28]

It might be concluded, despite the obvious fondness for Hemingway, that Soviet critics would consider him hopelessly mired in a doomed ideology, destined to end his days as a prisoner of his own sensitivity. But when Soviet criticism saw worth in a writer, it was always eager to prescribe solutions for his psychological and ideological problems. So it was in the case of Hemingway. In spite of their distress at his subjectivity and his passive attitude toward the social, economic, and political problems of the world he so loathed, they saw hope in his freedom from bourgeois ideals. The key to his dilemma, they contended, was his self-absorption. The prescription was clear. He must cease his personal brooding over insoluble problems and employ his marvelous energy and intelligence and his high sensitivity to questions which *were,* in Soviet opinion, capable of solution. He must transform his concern over individual destiny into a concern for social destiny.

The critic Grinberg discussed the tragic lovers of *A Farewell to Arms,* with their dream of simple, sequestered happiness, and remarked that Hemingway should understand that "besides these little and unattainable dreams there exists a large dream which will be attained, a large dream which will win out in battle." [29] Miller-Budnitskaya wrote that:

[26] Kashkeen, "Ernest Kheminguei," pp. 321-22.
[27] Kaverin in Berestov, *op. cit.,* p. 23.
[28] Frid, p. 48.
[29] I. Grinberg, "Chto zhe dalshe?" *Zvezda,* No. 3 (1937), p. 190.

The tragedy of Hemingway the artist is in his huge longing to create an epic art and his inability to find genuine material for it in his surroundings. . . . The epic art of the twentieth century cannot be built on the material of the imperialist war of 1914 or of future wars of the peoples of the capitalist world. This is because one of the indispensable prerequisites of a great epos and the great theme of the most powerful epic creations of the past is the struggle for social revolution.[30]

Dinamov felt that one of Hemingway's chief difficulties was the inability to find a positive hero, since the class which he stubbornly persisted in writing about—the bourgeoisie—was incapable of supplying such a hero.[31] Again, the solution was obvious:

A remarkable master of detail, a fine observer of particulars, an attentive investigator of the little lives of empty people—Hemingway in the name of art must tear himself away from the bourgeois world.[32]

Soviet critics first saw the symptoms of ideological change in Hemingway in activities that were not precisely literary. In 1935 he wrote a bitter article for *New Masses,* concerning the responsibility of the United States government for the deaths of unemployed war veterans whom it had sent to the Florida Keys in hurricane months. The article was immediately translated and printed in the Russian edition of *International Literature,* with the following editorial footnote:

We insert the article by Ernest Hemingway as one of the most important documents of the development of revolutionary literature in America. Hemingway—the most powerful American writer—has never taken part in any sort of social action of writers and has consciously stood aside from the revolutionary movement.[33]

The critic Silman remarked approvingly that Hemingway was beginning to release himself from the shackles of "absolute neutrality" by seeking ways of effective protest against bourgeois society.[34]

[30] R. Miller-Budnitskaya, "Ernest Kheminguei," *Internatsionalnaya literatura,* No. 6 (1937), p. 219. For a discussion between Edmund Wilson and the Russians on this point, see Kashkeen, "Ernest Hemingway . . . ," *op. cit.* and Edmund Wilson, "Pismo sovetskim chitatelyam o Khemingueye," *Internatsionalnaya literatura,* No. 2 (1936), pp. 151-54.

[31] Dinamov, "Roman Khemingueya . . . ," p. 169.

[32] *Ibid.,* p. 170.

[33] Footnote to title of Hemingway's "Kto ubil veteranov voiny vo Floride?" *Internatsionalnaya literatura,* No. 12 (1935), p. 56.

[34] T. Silman, "Ernest Kheminguei," *Literaturny sovremennik,* No. 3 (1936), pp. 181-82.

The first artistic evidence of fundamental change in Hemingway, however, came in 1937,[35] with the American publication of *To Have and Have Not*. Soviet critics stressed that here, for the first time, the author had decisively come to grips with economic and social problems and had taken pains to point out sharp class contrasts,[36] although one reviewer felt that he had done this somewhat "mechanically." [37] All critics perceived that the hero of this novel, Harry Morgan, was less individualistic than Hemingway's previous heroes. Unlike his predecessors, Harry faces problems which are basically economic, brought on by the depression in the America of the thirties. The critic Platonov felt that Harry displayed most of the traits of a real proletarian hero, and Nemerovskaya tentatively suggested that he might even be considered a "positive hero." [38] There was a major shortcoming, however:

He lacks the ability to seek his salvation in cooperation with other proletarians. . . . He does not have enough of that which cognizant proletarians have—an understanding that one must ally oneself with all workingmen.[39]

Kashkeen insisted that Hemingway was still lost in his "pessimistic blind alley." [40] Nemerovskaya agreed:

To his general dissatisfaction with capitalistic reality, Hemingway has added a protest against the social order. But this protest, which discloses no perspective, remains sterile and merely aggravates the pessimistic character of his work. The novel *To Have and Have Not* belongs among his most gloomy and hopeless things.[41]

---

[35] Two critics in 1939 looked back to the stories "The Short Happy Life of Francis Macomber" and "The Snows of Kilimanjaro," both published in 1936, and found evidence of impending change. Kashkeen, "Ernest Kheminguei," *op. cit.*, p. 330 and Frid, *op. cit.*, p. 51.

[36] V. Druzin, "V poiskakh nastoyashchevo cheloveka," *Rezets*, No. 18 (1938), p. 22; Nemerovskaya, "V poiskakh . . . ," p. 286; Kashkeen, "Ernest Kheminguei," p. 329; Frid, p. 51.

[37] "Ot redaktsii," *Internatsionalnaya literatura*, No. 4 (1938), p. 23. This was the only reviewer who objected strongly to the book on esthetic grounds. Druzin took issue with this review, and contended that "in the Soviet press this novel has received unanimously positive evaluation." Druzin, *op. cit.*, p. 22.

[38] Nemerovskaya, "V poiskakh . . . ," p. 278.

[39] A. Platonov, "Navstrechu lyudyam," *Literaturny kritik,* No. 11 (1938), p. 171.

[40] Kashkeen, "Ernest Kheminguei," p. 329.

[41] Nemerovskaya, "V poiskakh . . . ," p. 286.

Nevertheless, Kashkeen felt that there was great collective significance in Harry's dying verdict that "no matter how, a man alone ain't got no bloody chance." [42] And the overwhelming number of critics shared the opinion of Kaverin that,

Two points are distinctly visible in the creative path of Hemingway: *The Sun Also Rises*—this nonintervention in tragedy; and *To Have and Have Not*—an intervention in it. Gradually, just as gradually as his heroes approach the turning point in their understanding, Hemingway himself has come to an understanding of his obligation to the people, to world art.[43]

Hemingway's departure for Spain shortly after the beginning of the Civil War was widely heralded in the Soviet Union. It was decided that at last he had accomplished a decisive political act, which in turn might bring about a reshaping of his art. Upon learning that he was writing a book on Spanish themes, one critic wrote:

We believe that this book will tear Hemingway away from his devastated, confused heroes. We believe that Hemingway will understand that heroism consists not in fearless single combat with bulls in a circus arena or in pursuing wild beasts in Africa. Because if Hemingway recognizes that in the present moment the duty of every honorable man, of every writer, is to raise his voice against the unbridled might of world reaction, then he will find the answer to the question which torments Jake Barnes: how to live in this world.[44]

The chief product of his experiences in Spain to reach Soviet readers, aside from his ardently antifascist reportage of the conflict, was the play *The Fifth Column*. The critics reacted to this work with complete and unanimous enthusiasm.[45] One of them stressed Hemingway's understanding of the complicated psychology of a fighter, and his appreciation of the fact that a positive ideology can be molded in a man in the process of struggle. Another wrote:

[42] Kashkeen, "Ernest Kheminguei," p. 330.
[43] Kaverin in Berestov, *op. cit.*, p. 23.
[44] Nemerovskaya, "V poiskakh . . . ," p. 287.
[45] B. Pesis, "Pyataya kolonna," *Literaturnoye obozreniye,* No. 11 (1939), pp. 33-36; M. Bleiman, "Poeziya borby i gumanizma," *Iskusstvo i zhizn,* No. 5 (1939), pp. 15-17; A. Abramov, "Novoye v amerikanskoi dramaturgii," *Teatr,* No. 2-3 (1939), pp. 39-50; I. Grinberg, "Geroi beryotsya za oruzhiye," *Rezets,* No. 9-10 (1939), pp. 28-30; introduction to "Pyataya kolonna," *Internatsionalnaya literatura,* No. 1 (1939), pp. 99-100.

. . . the experiences of the past two years have taught Hemingway much, have compelled him to make a definite conclusive choice, have forced him to understand that humanity, in the face of attack by the fascist barbarians, has, in the words of Hemingway himself, only one path—"fight, fight for the right to a life worthy of humanity." [46]

Kashkeen concluded that,

The problem of the personal and the social, the anarcho-individualistic and the pacifistic, which he treated a decade ago in *A Farewell to Arms,* has taken a 180-degree turn, in correspondence with Hemingway's changed view of a new, just war. In *A Farewell to Arms*—flight from the social to the personal; here—from the personal to social duty.[47]

For Whom the Bell Tolls has never been published in the Soviet Union. The novel is by no means unknown in Russia, however. The manuscript of a Russian translation has been widely circulated in the Soviet literary world, and a few copies of the American editions can be found in public libraries. One can only speculate on the reasons for withholding its Russian publication. Certainly, there are serious ideological deficiencies in the book, in Soviet eyes. Its hero, Robert Jordan, has found a social cause in the fight for the Spanish Republic against fascism, and he pursues the fight with the usual Hemingway vitality. But in spite of this the feeling of cosmic purposelessness remains dominant in his nature, and Kashkeen has pointed out that his death is a meaningless act of stoical sacrifice, dictated by a purely subjective code.[48] Further, the novel's pronounced disparagement of certain highly placed Comintern figures would be enough to prevent its issuance in Russia. A few remarks made by the critic Mendelson in 1947 help to explain its suppression. Mendelson complained that Hemingway had proved incapable of dealing with "advanced ideas," and that he had "perverted the meaning of many of the most important events of the Civil War in Spain." He had made Jordan the protagonist of the "American ideals of agrarian democracy of the middle of the past century." Hemingway's only genuinely positive characters, according to Mendelson, were his

[44] Abramov, "Novoye . . . ," *op. cit.,* p. 39.

[47] Kashkeen, "Ernest Kheminguei," *op. cit.,* p. 333.

[48] Ivan Kashkeen, "Perechityvaya Khemingueya," *Inostrannaya literatura,* No. 4 (1956), p. 200.

Spanish partisans. And his treatment of André Marty and other "international fighters" was "absolutely distorted." [49]

In 1955, after a period of sixteen years in which there were no new translations of Hemingway and no reprintings, *The Old Man and the Sea* was published in the magazine *Inostrannaya Litera-tura*. The story created a sensation among Soviet readers; once more Hemingway was their favorite living American author. No doubt he had never lost first place in the hearts of many of them, but now the official sanction of an appearance in print made it possible to admire him openly again. Clearly this story, with its message of rugged courage and quiet, dogged heroism, held something special for them. There was disagreement, however, on what that something special was. Three students of Moscow University, presumably representative of the reading public, were inclined to accept the story primarily as a parable of unflagging bravery in the face of adversity. In an open letter to Hemingway in *Inostrannaya Literatura* they gave it this interpretation:

Everywhere people struggle for happiness, for a life worthy of man. They do not always win: they must experience both misfortune and defeat. But he who, like the old man, is capable of daily feats, who *knows how* to seize victory, does not despair after the most grievous failure. He does not despair—and continues the struggle.[50]

Like these students, all the critics agreed that the author had shown deep sympathy and respect for the dignity of Santiago, his simple fisherman hero, and that Santiago's solitary exploit against nearly impossible odds was inspiring. What disturbed them, however, was that both Santiago's symbolic victory in triumphing over the giant marlin and his defeat in losing it to sharks took place in a tenuous social context. In the words of the critic Lvov, the story contained "all the winds of the sea," but lacked "a feeling of the winds of history." [51] The critic Drobyshevski clumsily provided a historical ingredient by reading the story of Santiago as a tragedy of man's loneliness in the capitalist world. It was an "optimistic tragedy," since the old man, in "all the beauty of his healthy soul and healthy body," is the kind who "will not submit to

[49] M. Mendelson, "Amerikanskaya literatura v poiskakh obraza nastoya-shchevo cheloveka," *Znamya*, No. 3 (1947), pp. 176-77.

[50] V. Agrikolyanski, A. Krasnovski, and D. Rachkov, "Pismo studentov Ernestu Khemingueyu," *Inostrannaya literatura*, No. 1 (1956), p. 233.

[51] Sergei Lvov, "Mesto cheloveka v zhizni," *Literaturnaya gazeta*, October 27, 1955, p. 2.

the dollar and will not lower his head before the cannon's mouth." [52] Lvov replied, however, that a man's *lone* struggle, however valiant, is not a source of optimism:

It seems to me that one must seek conflict in those causes which turned the life of Santiago into a mortal combat face to face with the elements and beasts of the sea. One must seek conflict in the social sphere. And however the struggle ends, this conflict will not be removed. The very circumstance that the old man has no sort of other perspective than a naked, primitive struggle for existence—this is the sum total of his life. And that is the dramatic conflict between the magnificent human qualities of Santiago and the inhuman life he lives. Hemingway senses the existence of this conflict, but he does not know a way out.[53]

In a retrospective article on Hemingway in 1956, Kashkeen pointed out that in this story, as in the novel *Across the River and into the Trees,* the writer had reemphasized his early personal themes of fate and death. Formerly, however, he had explored the weaknesses and vulnerability of strong people; now he wrote of the "moral strength of a decrepit old man," and in doing so had asserted "more faith in man and respect for him." Kashkeen thought it significant that although Santiago is physically defeated by circumstances of fate, his moral victory does not cost him his life. Nevertheless, there was fatalism in the old man's words to the fish: "Come on and kill me. I do not care who kills who." Brooding and closely identified with his hero, Hemingway had "directed life itself into the narrow, immediate surroundings of a lonely old man." Although he deeply admired the story, Kashkeen still felt that, like the unsuccessful novel that had preceded it, this was a "muttered conversation," a fragment, an etude, an attempt to work out a limited problem—"scarcely the sum of Hemingway's reflections on postwar reality." For the writer had attempted to evade the "postwar contradictions" of the capitalist world by taking up a "pan-human theme." He still refused to write about America, and this was a silent protest against his own, now alien culture. But as long as he continued to fight shy of contemporary social problems, "his attempt to avoid looking at much, and of thinking about much, limits and impoverishes his creative possibilities." [54]

[52] Vladislav Drobyshevski, "Nepobedimy," *Zvezda,* No. 5 (1956), p. 166.
[53] Sergei Lvov, "Replika kritiku Vladislavu Drobyshevskomu," *Zvezda,* No. 8 (1956), p. 189.
[54] Kashkeen, "Perechityvaya . . . ," *op. cit.,* p. 194.

Well over a million copies of Hemingway's works, in book or periodical form, have circulated among the Soviet public. It is obviously impossible to measure accurately his impact on Russian readers as a whole. Certainly his influence extends far beyond the small circle of writers and critics whom I have cited here. Russian readers may view him from a perspective quite different from that of the professional critics, who are influenced by the ideological discipline of Socialist Realism and must respect the political realities of the Party line. The judgments of the critics, while interesting in themselves, may in fact present a distorted picture of the general Russian reaction to Hemingway.

Despite the critics' disapproval of his preoccupation with themes of desolation, it is probable that many readers have appreciated him precisely because he offers a forlorn picture of life. Although there has been a concerted attempt to exorcise attitudes of pessimism, disillusionment, hopelessness, and skepticism from the Soviet scene, these emotions undoubtedly exist in abundance in Russia. Particularly in the twenties, but certainly continuing to some extent even to the present, Russia has had her own "lost generation," intellectual and spiritual casualties of the Revolution who must feel a strong affinity for Jake Barnes and Brett Ashley. Paradoxically, Hemingway's morbid picture of life in the "decadent" West may also appeal to yet another group of Russians—those who ardently support the Soviet regime—by reinforcing their feeling of cultural superiority.

On the other hand, Hemingway's realism lacks the documentary quality which is so prominent in such realists as Sinclair, Dos Passos and Theodore Dreiser. In general, his writing is much more philosophical and psychological than sociological in its emphasis. Despite his marvelous ability to reconstruct the world of people and things, he is much more concerned with eternal, abstract problems than with those of immediate social, political, or economic interest. Ultimately, to like Hemingway, one must sympathize with his approach to the large personal issues which trouble and will continue to trouble everyone, everywhere. This would suggest that in insisting that he cease exploring the problem of death and deemphasize the element of love, the critics were subscribing more to official doctrine than to their own feelings. For Russians are still awed by death, and Russians still fall in love.

Other aspects of Soviet criticism probably indicate the readers' response more accurately. For one thing, readers must admire Hemingway's narrative gifts. If his style conceals, as Kashkeen suggested, a "desperate complication," it is nevertheless simple and intelligible. It moves swiftly, and it is exciting. In this respect, the Soviet reader probably appreciates him for the same qualities that have made him a best seller in America. Likewise, his vigorous love of nature, sports, combat, and adventure must appeal to the Russians. This clean, rugged outlook on life (despite its elements of bravado, of which the critics took due note) strikes the same chord in the Russian heart as do the stories of London. In the Russians there is a strong love of the primitive, and a comparable distaste for the sophisticated, which amounts at times to a puritanical attitude toward the "decadent" trappings of civilization. The unmistakable longing for a simpler, more pure and elemental life which rings in Hemingway's stories must find response in this part of the Soviet reader's nature. Ultimately it is Hemingway's profound understanding of the natural aspirations of men which appeals to the Russian public.

Deming Brown

Alive in the Midst of Death: Ernest Hemingway

In January, 1954, Ernest Hemingway had been hunting big game in Central Africa. His plane crashed in an out-of-the-way place near the border of the Belgian Congo. For a time Hemingway was believed to have lost his life, and when he returned safely to Nairobi he found, along with other boons of civilization, heaps of newspapers containing reports of his death. "In all obituaries, or almost all, it was emphasized that I had sought death all my life," Hemingway wrote, adding that, to judge from the reports, after his "constant efforts to court death" death had caught up with him in the neighborhood of Kilimanjaro. For a while Hemingway was amused and even indulged in "that strange vice of reading his own obituaries." But soon he lost patience and declared: "Can one imagine that if a man sought death all his life he could not have found her before the age of fifty-four? It is one thing to be in the proximity of death, to know more or less what she is, and it is quite another thing to seek her. She is the most easy thing to find that I know of." In the same passage Hemingway asserted that in his dreams at least he saw himself as "a very gay and witty person," to which it may be added that, to all appearances, he is fond of life and of good people, of his sons and his wife "Miss Mary," of hunting, of good books, of a strong drink and a merry yarn.

Yet the numerous allusions in the "obituaries" to Hemingway's taste for the theme of death and violence were not accidental. They echoed a number of articles whose nature is revealed in their titles—for instance, "Canon of Death," "Mr. Hemingway und der Tod," "Torches of Violence" (all three in 1932), "Violence and Discipline" (1947)—or in their basic concept as "Une œuvre toute consacrée à la violence et à la mort" (André Maurois, 1955). The critics were influenced not only by such titles of Hemingway's stories as "The Killers," *Death in the Afternoon,* "Who Killed the Veterans in Florida?," but also by their essence. In them Hemingway seems to recognize that "in the midst of life

we are in death." He cannot but feel death in the life that surrounds him, and death for him, at least as an onlooker, is one
of the main themes of modern decadent art. It is but natural that
this should cast a shadow on his work. Who then is right, Hemingway or the authors of the "obituaries"?

A first impression might suggest that it is the latter who are
right. The theme of violence and death is seldom absent from
Hemingway's work. That may be because Hemingway took part
in two world wars and two smaller wars (though one of them
was of world-wide importance inasmuch as it was the first battle
with fascism, in Spain). War made Hemingway see death without disguise or heroic illusions, and, gazing at its grim face, he
began to treat organized death as a social phenomenon inherent
in the world that surrounded him. It was at the front that Hemingway got to know the harsh world that wants to solve all conflicts
by war, a world of wolves where everyone wars on everyone else.

The years following the First World War saw the revolt, the
breaking away and the partial return to the parental home, of
the so-called "Lost Generation." Crippled and frustrated by
their wartime experiences, depressed by the fear of the coming
crisis, they fell victims to the social disease of the age. Tired and
empty-hearted, they were haunted by "the end of something,"
the end of hope, the dulling of their very perception of life. In
his books of that period Hemingway came nearest to the decadent
philosophy of some of his good-for-nothing characters. He
attained world fame as the bard of the "Lost Generation."
Whether consciously or not, he provided a model for numerous
inferior followers and snobbish imitators.

After the great success of his first book of short stories and
his two early novels, there began for Hemingway a period of
reconciliation, of "a separate peace" with the same rich loafers
whom he had so ruthlessly exposed. He frequented bullfights in
Spain, went hunting in Africa, took to fishing, settled in Florida,
and did hardly any writing for seven years.

In the early thirties, the days of the great depression, a good
many American writers turned to social themes, but Hemingway's
response to the new demands of life was very slow. There still
worked within him the poison of the "Lost Generation," of those
who have learned to shun life, which he felt contained much
that was horrible. He tried not to think of it, but to keep silent
was terribly hard, and by way of relief he talked to himself as an
artist—"He had gotten rid of many things by writing them."

And when Hemingway made an effort to understand what was happening in the world, he came to the bitter conclusion that is held in his story "The Snows of Kilimanjaro" (1936). No matter how the dying writer Harry tries to comfort himself with the idea that he is only a spy in the country of the very rich and the very dull, a place he would leave when he had written about it, he nevertheless remains a hostage in the camp of those with whom he drinks and hunts and talks of art. The realization of the price he has paid comes too late because that price is death, physical, moral, and artistic. The death of the writer Harry is a kind of symbolic purification: he sheds a skin that is dead, but still there is no way into life either for the hero or for the author.

And in the meantime life was invading Hemingway's seclusion, reminding him of fresh acts of violence. As a newsman he had already had his say both about the tragic death of the veterans in Florida and about Mussolini's Abyssinian venture, and about the initial stages of the revolutionary movement in Spain. But the fascist intervention in Spain was the last straw: when it came, Hemingway simply could not stay at his desk any longer. More than once he had tried to crush his own journalistic restlessness so it would not hinder his work as a writer. He knew from experience what deep scars may be left by hackwork for American papers asking of the reporter "to forget every day what happened the day before," to forget it in more ways than one. But Hemingway still felt the urge to take part in real life, and it was the sallies into reality that enriched him as a writer and brought him back to the great topics of the day.

Life in a world based on the sordid laws of moneygrubbing, violence, and death is a cruel affair, particularly for the underdog. What Nick Adams (the hero of his early short stories) remembered best from his childhood were manifestations of life's dire cruelty: the suicide in "Indian Camp," the lynching of the Negro, the brutal scenes of American everyday existence from the book *In Our Time*, the encounter with the "killers" after which Nick dejectedly remarks: "I am going to get out of this town." Gangsters, killers, executions, murders—all these abound both in Hemingway's early stories and in his later novels such as *To Have and Have Not* and *For Whom the Bell Tolls*. In them there is plenty of death and fear and violence, the very things that were handled by so many decadent writers from Edgar Allan Poe to Ambrose Bierce, from Faulkner to Mailer, and down to the comic strips and Mickey Spillane. The point, however, is not only *what* you write about, but *how* you do it and what stand you take.

Hemingway's work, centering on one set of problems, turned to them again and again. Slowly and persistently he molded them into concrete shapes, only to turn to them once more from a new point and, striving at ever greater clearness, to look at them with the eyes of the same hero who under various names personifies the various stages in the biography of the author and of his generation.

For Hemingway life is inseparable from death and is a fight at close quarters in which his heroes overcome not only the fear of death but the fear of life's intricacies and the disintegration threatening the individual. It is real life, work, and creative power that give him strength for the fight. The ultimate goal of the struggle may not always be clear to him, even the immediate tasks he may not always solve correctly, but the important point is that again and again the major problems of life crop up in his books. These problems include the invigorating and inspiring role of work (it was this that helped both Hemingway himself and his Jake Barnes to break loose from the vicious circle of the *Fiesta* in which the idlers of the "Lost Generation" were moving). They include, too, the struggle for a decent life, as carried on not only by individuals like Harry Morgan, Philip Rawlings, and Robert Jordan, but by the Spanish guerrillas as well. They include, too, the solidarity of honest men and women from different countries (its clearest presentation being the film script *The Spanish Earth*), and, thence, the idea that life itself should not be spared for a great cause. They include, too, the problem of apparent defeat and inner victory on the moral plane (El Sordo, Old Man Santiago), of temporary defeat and ultimate victory on the historical plane ("On the Americans Dead in Spain").

In grappling with these problems, in overcoming difficulties and doubts, Hemingway's heroes grow up, and step by step their idea of the meaning of life changes and crystallizes. The struggle of common people for a decent existence, their simple and straightforward attitude towards life and death serve as a model for Hemingway's more complex and contradictory characters. All of them alike are faced with the problems of fear, violence and death; they solve them in different ways, but the best among them look for support to life, strength, and courage. The irresponsibility of the "Lost Generation" is superseded by heroism and the sense of duty that make Jordan akin to El Sordo; the inertia of an Ole Andreson is superseded by action that makes old Santiago akin to his creator, Hemingway. Whether of his own will or in spite of it, Hemingway seeks this assertion of life in communion with nature, in the hope that you abide forever in the work of art you have created, and in the moral victory of the heroic deed that makes you immortal in the memory of man.

In a letter of 1939 Hemingway wrote:

> As long as there is a war you always think perhaps you will be killed, so you have nothing to worry about. But now I am not killed, so I have to work. And as you have no doubt discovered living is much more difficult and complicated than dying and it is just as hard as ever to write. . . . But I am going to keep on writing as well as I can and as truly as I can until I die. And I hope I never die.

These words may be interpreted in the following way: in Republican Spain the writer came in touch with conscious heroism, and now he feels strong enough to fix it forever, and his former joyless, stoical demand "Do or die" is replaced by the no less categorical "Won't die until I've done it."

In this struggle for a decent life man must have something to fall back upon: he must conquer old habits and conventions; he must keep free from gilded chains and preserve his inner freedom; he must assert life by action, as a worker, as a hero, as an artist. He must, by training his courage, overcome both the fear of death and the fear of life. Strength, sure of its right, must check the course of violence.

Let us illustrate the idea by a few examples from Hemingway's later works. In *For Whom the Bell Tolls* the Spanish peasant Andrés asks the antifascist American Robert Jordan:

> "Do you have no big proprietors?"
> "Many."
> "Then there must be abuses."
> "Certainly. There are many abuses."
> "But you will do away with them?"
> "We try to more and more. But there are many abuses still. . . ."
> "Then you will have to fight in your country as we fight here."
> "Yes, we will have to fight."
> "But are there not many fascists in your country?"
> "There are many who do not know they are fascists but will find it out when the time comes."
> "But you cannot destroy them until they rebel?"
> "No. We cannot destroy them. But we can educate the people so

that they will fear fascism and recognize it as it appears and combat it."

Hemingway had old accounts to square with the fascists. The cruel and stupid shooting by the Italian *carabinieri* of the soldiers retreating from Caporetto—which he witnessed and later described in *A Farewell to Arms*—came to Hemingway, even amid the usual military cruelty, as a foretaste of fascist methods of intimidation. But while Tenente Henry was but an "unconscientious objector," Hemingway himself and the heroes of his Spanish books are conscious fighters against fascism. In his speech at the Second Congress of American Writers Hemingway said that fascism is the lie of a great bully and that there is only one way to quell a bully and that is to thrash him.

Even when using force to fight violence, many of Hemingway's heroes are humane. Theirs is a kindness equally free from cruelty and from weakness. Anselmo the hunter finds it hard even to kill a bear, but Anselmo the guerrilla, though he weeps, shoots at the fascists.

In *To Have and Have Not* Hemingway asked himself how a simple man could hold his own, and how he could reach and join other simple folks. The Civil War in Spain showed him such people, capable of both holding their own and repulsing fascist violence. Here, too, he got a better knowledge of his friends and comrades-in-arms. They were simple, brave, and talented men— Ralph Fox, Máté Zalka, Ludwig Renn, Joris Ivens, the soldiers of the Lincoln Battalion. They were men who had embraced the just cause of the Republic, men who loved life but were ready to lose it. Here, in Spain, Hemingway at last found the right words to be said about victory over death. In recalling the men who stemmed the flood of fascist violence at the cost of their lives, he says (in the film script *The Spanish Earth*): "When you were young you gave death much importance. Now you give it none. You only hate it for the people that it takes away." Fighting death proved to be most successful when death was treated as a social phenomenon. And even in a book so contradictory and controversial as *For Whom the Bell Tolls*, for all its deficiencies of judgment and artistic drawbacks, victory over death is convincing precisely for the reason that the author gives a picture, be it ever so subjective and even distorted, of a certain part of the struggle against the scourge of humanity, fascism.

The activities of the partisans, the tragic end of El Sordo's men, the blowing up of the bridge, Andrés making his way across the lines with the dispatch, the figures of El Sordo and old Anselmo, magnificent in their simplicity, all these are done with great force and feeling. In a way, even Robert Jordan is another step in the evolution of Hemingway's hero. For Tenente Henry there is no hope or solace anywhere. Harry Morgan dies everybody's enemy, alone with his crime. He dies because he failed in one more attempt to provide for himself. Even if he feels no remorse, neither actual nor moral victory is his, nothing, save a bitter sense of being beaten and alone. And, more important, it is not one of Hemingway's beloved individualist intellectuals that arrives at Morgan's conclusion, "One man alone ain't got no . . . chance"; it is one of those simple people whose integrity attracts Hemingway but remains as yet inaccessible for him. Now, *For Whom the Bell Tolls* opens with the words of John Donne: "No man is an Iland, intire of it selfe." Jordan, like all of Hemingway's doubles, is reticent and unsociable, yet he is something more than the Aldington hero looking for refuge in the Islands of the Blessed. Jordan leaves his seclusion, he deliberately fights "for all the poor in the world," and dying alone is but the sad lot of those of his kind. The trouble with Jordan is that the burden is too much for him to bear. He is the wrong man for the part, not typical of the scene and events which Hemingway was expected to treat as an epic.

The closing words of the epigraph "never send to know for whom the bell tolls; it tolls for thee," are Donne's. But it may be that the thought of the bell was suggested to Hemingway by the emblem on the banner of the Lincoln Battalion, showing a silhouette that might be Lincoln in a tasseled Spanish cap, with a Liberty Bell for background.

It was impossible for Hemingway, for his Jordan, to keep aloof and unconcerned when from every corner of the earth simple, honest, and courageous men came flocking to the defense of the simple, honest, and courageous people of Spain. Nor can the reader feel unconcerned when Hemingway's bell tolls for Jordan, even such a Jordan as we see in the book, and even though the bell sounds cracked.

Both El Sordo and Jordan die, but how different their last moments! El Sordo does not want to die, but he knows it is necessary. And that, for him, is the end of all doubts and the beginning of his heroic work. He works on the hill with his guerrillas as he worked in his field removing weeds, seeing to it that as many

weeds as possible should go. Jordan strives to attain the same attitude, he tries to be like El Sordo and Anselmo, if only when facing
death: stop thinking, you are a bridge-blower now. And while blowing up the bridge he also works, but then things take a different turn.
The author was not bound to kill Jordan, but nevertheless Jordan
was doomed. He dies not only for Spain, not only to save the
girl Maria whom he loves, but also for his own sake and in fulfillment of a moral duty. The grim world in which he had grown
up has not broken Jordan nor forced him to a deal with his
conscience, as it did Harry Morgan. Jordan dies a moral victor,
but he never became a part either of the common victory or the
common defeat. He fought in the ranks, but he, too, dies alone.

Just remember what a full picture of life El Sordo takes away
with him:

> Whether one has fear of it or not, one's death is difficult to accept.
> Sordo had accepted it but there was no sweetness in its acceptance even
> at fifty-two, with three wounds and him surrounded on a hill. He
> joked about it to himself but he looked at the sky and at the far
> mountains and he swallowed the wine and he did not want it. If one
> must die, he thought, and clearly one must, I can die. But I hate it.
> Dying was nothing and he had no picture of it nor fear of it in his
> mind. But living was a field of grain blowing in the wind on the side
> of a hill. Living was a hawk in the sky. Living was an earthen jar of
> water in the dust of the threshing, with the grain flailed out and the
> chaff blowing. Living was a horse between your legs and a carbine
> under one leg and a hill and a valley and a stream with trees along it
> and the far side of the valley and the hills beyond.

Thus before his death El Sordo envisions everything he had
lived by—work, joy, freedom. He dies with his eyes open, but
with such an acute sense of life's completeness that he may certainly be said to be alive to the last, alive in the midst of death.

And what is life for Jordan? It would be hard to conceive it
as one image. It includes both the abstract notion "the world is a
fine place and worth the fighting for," and the wish to take part in
this fight. It includes the thoughts about the book he would like
to write. It includes what might be called rough sketches for the
future book: the sounds and the colors of life, the smells of
Cuba, of Galicia, of his native Missoula. It also includes the two
voices, keeping up an argument in his disordered mind: his
suicide father and his grandfather, the soldier in the Civil War
whom he in a way calls upon to judge his own conduct. And his
last love, so akin to pity, for yet another disinherited, the Spanish

girl Maria. And many more things, complex, contradictory, disconnected, all darkened by the joyless stoicism of an unavailing sacrifice.

Jordan knows that to live properly is impossible without "going where you have to go and doing what you have to do." So his only reward is the consciousness of duty done. And again "Winner take nothing."

For Whom the Bell Tolls was written after the defeat of the Republic. The fight ceased (for a long time, as it seemed to many then), and yesterday's fighter at once feels he is losing his bearings. Hemingway does not see what he should save Jordan's life for. He does not visualize the new world in which Jordan might try to find a place for himself. But while showing this tragedy of the lone hand, Hemingway does not ignore the heroic deeds of the many. Early in 1939, when of all the men of the International Brigades only those remained in Spain who along with Máté Zalka, Fox, and Cornford were buried in her soil, Hemingway wrote a mournful but hopeful dedication to "the Americans Dead in Spain," and sent it to the *New Masses*. The dedication rang with a faith in the future, in the people of Spain and in her earth which can never be conquered. "For the earth endureth forever. It will outlive all systems of tyranny." This heartfelt response may be reduced to the simple thought which, however, did not come easily to Hemingway: even though you died without having won, your sacrifice was not in vain, and victory shall yet be yours. Hemingway seemed to have found something worth dying for. If you die as these men did, then physical death means nothing and you can say as you breathe your last "Death, where is thy sting?" Or to use Hemingway's own words: "Those who have entered it honorably, and no man ever entered earth more honorably than those who died in Spain, already have achieved immortality."

Hemingway's road to craftsmanship was a long one. On the way he got rid of many passing infatuations. Thus, he tried and discarded the so-called telegraphic language. Less and less we heard in his stories photographic records of hyperlaconic yet protracted dialogues. The specialized terminology of bullfighting, prize fighting, or fishing disappeared from the books, giving place to descriptions, say, of a military operation such as the blowing up of a bridge, so skillful that it would deserve a place in a manual, and yet clear to anyone without recourse to a special dictionary. In short, Hemingway saw more and more clearly the need of realist selection. And where he succeeds, one can but marvel at the frugal but well-tested means he uses to achieve his aims. After Hemingway had found a way from his impasse of the middle thirties, his style became more alive. The morbid tension and strain relax, words come in a freer and broader stream, the talks now are no riddles to the reader, all is more natural and human. Not so many specific Hemingway touches, perhaps, but more of simple, mature, and realist craftsmanship, more of the "straight honest prose on human beings. . . ."

A full-blooded, optimistic humanism, whether that of a Gorki or a Hugo, implies faith in a happy future for mankind, and a way leading through trial to complete victory. Such humanists see a clear goal ahead calling them to victory at any cost. For a long time Hemingway's humanism did not involve this clearly defined aim, nor was it imbued with a faith in victory, save on the moral plane. He neither despises people nor distrusts them. He is fond of his heroes; in his own reticent way he pities them, recognizing their right to live as human beings. True, the "good luck" he wishes them always implies a hard and often tragic lot. Still, in nearly all of Hemingway's books we feel his sympathy with those who are worthy of it. And the humanist note sounds loudest, perhaps, in his latest story, *The Old Man and the Sea*.

After the Second World War the honest "winner" whom Hemingway saw fighting at the front again "took nothing," and the fruits of his victories were reaped by grasping jobbers of the type of Stefan Heym's "Crusaders." Hemingway gave vent to his anger and disappointment at the aftermath of the war in his novel *Across the River*, then he once more took shelter among the simple folks of Cuba. It was here he wrote the tale of the old fisherman Santiago. It opens with the old familiar motif of defeat. Santiago has had a spell of bad luck, and even his old sail patched with flour sacks looks like the flag of permanent defeat. The old man's mind, still lucid where his work is concerned, is dimmed by the mist of years, which in a way makes it easier for him. "He no longer dreamed of storms, nor of women, nor of great occurrences, nor of great fish, nor fights, nor contests of strength, nor of his wife." Nothing remains but providing for his daily bread, talking baseball with the boy, and dreaming of the lions in faraway Africa. The old man still holds his own. In pursuit of the great fish he even goes farther out to sea than his strength could stand.

Stubbornly, against all hope, he defends the fish he has caught from the sharks. But in this innate stubbornness of the fisherman we hear a new note. For years Hemingway had reiterated his favorite thought that once you have entered a fight you must win, even though more often than not victory has all the appearance of defeat. The old man modifies this thought: "Man is not made for defeat. A man can be destroyed but not defeated." And right on top of this a contradiction. The old man sounds fatalistic, which is unusual for Hemingway: "I do not care who kills who." This, again, to be followed by the old man's glorifying of the "great fish" which is out to kill him.

Compared with the earlier books, this one is more subdued, and gentle, and resigned. The old man lives in concord with everybody; he is loved by the simple people around him. Formerly Hemingway used to write of the weakness and vulnerability of strong men; now he writes of the moral strength of a decrepit old fisherman. Here there is more faith in, and respect for, man, but life itself has shrunk to the narrow confines of a lonely old man's vision. Curiously enough, the sharp line separating the common people he loves from his main hero is nowhere less visible than in this story. Formerly Hemingway's thoughts and feelings had been first and foremost with the intellectual who fights honestly, but with all the old doubts still weighing him down. Now he hands over part of his thoughts and feelings to Santiago. Santiago is a character more complicated than the simple people of Hemingway's earlier books. While even the writer's doubles tried to keep from thinking, Santiago thinks of many things throughout the story. Like his author, he tackles the problem of courage, and that of craftsmanship. In spite of the spell of bad luck he won't give up his fisherman's skill, he will catch only the big fish, and catch it properly. There seeps into his mind a sense of impending defeat, peculiar to Jordan rather than to El Sordo. He dreams of things the lion-hunter Hemingway might dream of. But what he loses in plausibility, Santiago gains in complexity and color, and it is Hemingway's talent that enables the reader to believe in him.

The old man looks to youth for support. The boy who takes care of him is a real support, without which the old man is helpless and doomed to destitution. Formerly Hemingway's heroes, even if they occasionally exchanged a few words with other people, mainly conversed with themselves. Now the old man has somebody to whom he can hand down his experience and his

craft, and in this sense the book opens into the future. Hemingway seems to return to his starting point, but in quite a new
way. "One generation passeth away, and another generation
cometh," yet not the earth alone abides but also man's work,
both as work performed and as craftsmanship handed down
from generation to generation. And though the story deals with
old age and infirmity, for once nobody dies. Victory, be it only
moral, is not achieved here at the cost of life.

The Old Man and the Sea may be taken as an attempt at evad-
ing the painful postwar contradictions by turning to a universal
theme almost abstracted from time and place. It is the theme of
courageous work for a "great" but strictly confined aim which
Hemingway for the moment designates only as "the great fish."
The tangible and realistic presentation of a small particle of life
as being a point to which great forces are applied, compels our
attention. But the realism of the story is marred by a haziness of
allegory which has already given rise to diametrically opposed
interpretations.

There are many indications of Hemingway's loving his country, but it is no simple love. "It had been a good country and
we had made a bloody mess of it." Hemingway is frightened by
its aging quickly in the hands of self-seeking exploiters. His
American hero always carries with him, be it only in his mind, a
parcel of his native soil. Wherever he is, Jordan remembers the
smell of his home town, Missoula. The fact that Hemingway
hardly ever lives in his own country and keeps silent about it,
that for a long time he has been looking for brave and simple
people in Spain, at the front in Italy and France, and, finally, in
Cuba, just reminding himself by way of consolation that "you
could always come back"—all these may be taken as his nonaccept-
ance of many features of present-day American life. But silence is
silence for all that. It is ambiguous even in that there are many
ways of interpreting it. Hemingway himself, in *The Snows of
Kilimanjaro*, said of his writer, Harry: "The people he knew now
were all much more comfortable when he did not work." And
anyway, by keeping silent Hemingway reduces the portion of the
world shown in his works to a very small spot indeed, no matter
what distant countries he visits in his wanderings all over the
globe.

Yet Hemingway is by no means indifferent to what is going on
at home. Every now and again some passing comment of his

shows that he does not forget about imperialism, whatever disguise it may choose to put on. Such for instance is the gibe of the wild-dog hunter Hemingway at the witch-hunter McCarthy up in arms against all opponents of "the American way of life," contained in the sketch "The Christmas Gift" (1954), or the significant remark reminding McCarthy of the fate of another senatorial demagogue, Huey Long. And wherever Hemingway may hide, in Cuba or in Africa, his former brothers-in-arms do not forget him. In his article "Happy Landing, Hemingway!" in the New York *Worker*, Joseph North recalls his meeting with Hemingway on the Ebro in 1937, winding up thus: "We had our differences then, too, but we were down on the ground together helping those who needed it. You did not ask my politics, I didn't give a damn what yours were, not at such a time. You were not on the side of the millionaire publisher whose newsroom was awaiting your story."

Hemingway's work teaches courage and loyalty to one's duty. But in the absence of a clearly realized ultimate aim Hemingway's main heroes, even if they join the common struggle, remain lonely sportsmen, sometimes no more than nine days' wonders. For the big truth of life they substitute the minor truth of fair play, the rules of a game. Hemingway has no faith in the reason and honor of bourgeois civilization, but his attacks on it are directed from the past. In his essays he turns to backward Spain and to uncivilized Africa. In *For Whom the Bell Tolls* we are shown the backwoods and the archaic, almost tribal life and speech of guerrilla peasants and hunters. *The Old Man and the Sea* deals with the ancient craft of fishing just as a means to provide for the scant needs of a lonely individual.

Hemingway denies the nakedly utilitarian standards governing modern America, and turns back to the older ethical standards. He scorns the ideal of hypocritical conventional prosperity and offers an ethical code of his own. History knows many such codes, and all of them, whether termed feudal chivalry, bourgeois respectability and common sense, soldier's faith, or fair play as Hemingway has it, sooner or later prove to be shams. In smaller things, in the simplest cases, such a moral code is indisputable. No one could object to a man being honest, or brave, or self-possessed. But no sooner are these rules mechanically applied to the bigger demands of life than it becomes obvious how relative and inadequate they are. For it is just those rules of vaunted gentlemanly "fair play" that insist on the disparaging of one's friends—they will stand anything—and on treating one's enemies with marked civility. It is those rules that demand adherence to an abstract and narrow code that is often at variance with the great truths of life.

In the novel *For Whom the Bell Tolls* we find, side by side, the record of an eyewitness and participant and an attempt to evaluate the events on second thought: to accuse or justify from a standpoint that is utterly wrong. Here, the immediate response is usually a direct hit at the enemy, while the afterthoughts as a rule hopelessly distort the same events. It is easy to see why Hemingway's former fellow fighters did not recognize themselves in the characters of the book. Much of what Jordan thinks, and the author's lenience to the enemy on the pretext that he should be given gentlemanly treatment, and plenty of unnecessary naturalistic detail, all these go to make the story turbid. Take even fascism: while Hemingway's hatred for its manifestations is strong and sincere as ever, he is as ever blind in his tolerance for its roots. That is why at the time of its first publication the novel was sternly and, on the whole, justly censured by the veterans of the International Brigades, and sharply criticized in the progressive press.

Hemingway knows how hard it is to write truly and only about the things you know. His Jordan plans to write such a book about Spain. "But I will have to be a much better writer than I am now to handle them, he thought. The things he had come to know in this war were not so simple."

Hemingway is not always willing or able to understand and accept the big truth of today. He deliberately avoids "taking sides" politically, and said as early as in 1934: "The hardest thing in the world to do is to write straight honest prose on human beings. First you have to know the subject; then you have to know how to write. Both take a lifetime to learn and anybody is cheating who takes politics as a way out. It is too easy. All the outs are too easy and the thing itself is too hard to do."

The fallacy of the statement about politics is so obvious to us that it hardly needs disputing. No work of art, however high its professional merits, will last, if created without regard to time and politics; the latter, naturally, to mean not petty intrigues but the major issues governing the life of millions of people. To ignore

these issues cannot but restrict a man's horizon. It is for this reason
that the very humanism of Hemingway's heroes is so joyless and
stoical, the defective humanism of those doomed by history.

"A writer's problem does not change . . ." Hemingway said
in his speech at the Second Congress of American Writers. "It is
always how to write truly and having found what is true, to
project it in such a way that it becomes a part of the experience
of the person who reads it." But if a writer does not take the
trouble to find out what *is* the big truth (which includes politics),
he is liable to slip to the formula: I am a soldier, politics don't
concern me—which has turned many a good but nearsighted man
into the blind agent of the evil will of others.

Long ago, in 1932, Hemingway had written: "Let those who
want to save the world if you can get to see it clear and as a
whole," and for the writer he set apart a task all by itself: "The
great thing is to last and get your work done and see and hear
and learn and understand; and write when there is something
that you know." But what to write about, and how, remained
dark, because the very term "to understand" was not made clear.

Since then Hemingway himself has taken part in saving the
world from fascism. He has himself admitted that if a bell tolls,
"it tolls for thee." And this thought, if carried further and applied to life, means: the world in which we all live is also the
only world you live and work in, and if you let it go to ruin you
will not save your work. For whom do you work, anyway? And
more, by refusing to save the world, even by only professing such
a refusal, you rob yourself of the opportunity to see it "clear
and as a whole," and bring to nought the very attempt at "learning to make it."

What Hemingway misunderstands as "truth" occasionally
makes him introduce into his works an unnatural and morbid
element, which is not only the result of his own nightmares and
mental strain but also, perhaps, an unwitting tribute to a tendency
of our time, to the decadent sway in modern American literature.
Sometimes Hemingway's sense of proportion fails him, and naturalistic touches show in his work. This is chiefly true of the early
stories, but it occurs later as well. Thus, in *For Whom the Bell
Tolls* the interlude about the killing of fascists, as directed by the
anarchistic Pablo, is needlessly cruel; it sounds untrue because of
its studied impartiality, and takes up a place out of all proportion
to the plot.

The deathlike quality of the world that Hemingway used to

write about bred a certain tenseness in artistic expression, a kind of torpor in handling his theme, a numbness of speech. The characters of Hemingway's early stories are overreticent. Their talks are "inner dialogues," a constant effort to keep back words, with everyone speaking for himself, in answer to his own thoughts. Yet so alike are the cares that obsess the talkers that they understand each other perfectly. The mental strain shows itself in too much attention to detail, in the same experiences being analyzed over and over again. They haunt the writer, and he strives to get rid of them by writing about them as clearly as possible. The first step in this direction is a painstaking presentation of the external world absolving Hemingway from the necessity of thinking. Hence, the descriptive pages, the stories dealing with professional skill, with hunting, sports, or a soldier's craft. If he still cannot keep from thinking, he flees to the lyrical monologue which also helps him to get rid of the haunting thoughts by scrupulously setting them down.

Hemingway's language is a coinage of his own, but at times he sounds like a parody of himself. Even now the living tissue of his lucid prose is marred here and there by old scars. In the two latest books there are relapses into the early strained manner. In the unsuccessful book *Across the River and into the Trees* it is again the lengthy, inarticulate dialogues, a forced and mirthless humor; and even in *The Old Man* we find again the tiresome reiterations of an endless inner monologue, a superfluity of technical detail, and alien, impressionist patches. It is only Hemingway's great and mature craftsmanship that rivets the unflagging attention of the reader to the latter tale.

In the posthumous *Meditations* of the fine Russian writer Mikhail Prishvin we read: "In art all are pupils of one another, but each one travels a path of his own." Many writers have learned from Hemingway. What was it, according to their own evidence, that drew to him such men as young Aldridge, Italo Calvino, Graham Greene, many French and Italian film producers? The fact that he can look at life without blinking; that his manner is all his own; that he is ruthlessly exacting on himself, making no allowances, and straightforward in self-appraisal; that his hero keeps himself in check, and is ever ready to fight nature, danger, fear, even death, and is prepared to join other people at the most perilous moments in their struggle for a common cause. It is precisely these things that constitute Hemingway's contribution to the common fund of literature. But even the "pupils" admit that their "teacher" is not flawless. When they tried to use his method in presenting life with all its complexities and contradictions, the attempts at once revealed how uncertain and vulnerable were both his method and his philosophy. In his interesting article "Hemingway and Us" (1954), the progressive Italian writer Italo Calvino admits that he owes much to Hemingway, but he sees that Hemingway's possibilities are limited, and his philosophy, which he describes as "the cruel philosophy of a tourist," is narrow and defective. Waves of hopeless pessimism, a cold estrangement from life, a passive surrender to bitterly cruel experience, all these move Calvino to "distrust, and sometimes even disgust." The very style of Hemingway's early books he begins to find cramped and affected.

On the other hand, Hemingway has had many snobbish followers and imitators. At different times he tried many a novel means of expression: an intentional tongue-tiedness; short, unfinished sentences; protracted dialogues in which things are implied rather than said; the endless inner monologues fixing the famous stream of consciousness; in short, all that for which Hemingway got condescending praise from the leaders of the decadent school, and which in the hands of his numerous imitators has become boring as just another empty cliché. Hemingway liked to try on an eccentric garb only to discard it, while the imitators continued for a long time to parade the clothes he had cast off.

Some of Hemingway's favorite themes are in themselves contradictory, and change as time goes on: sudden and violent death, and the immortality of an artist (which, by the way, can only be achieved on the social plane); not merely death, but the deadening foretaste of it in a living man; defeat, even when it results in moral victory; strength, not applied to any worthy object, strength in a void, and hence the tragedy of a strong man and a powerful artist, the same old tragedy of craftsmanship passionately serving art for art's sake.

But though professing to strive for supreme abstract impartiality, Hemingway cannot silence within himself the man of our time, nor can he help sifting reality through the sieve of his own social experience. Even in this, however, Hemingway is contradictory. His main hero feels drawn to all that is simple, integral, and clear, while he himself is complex, divided, and tragic. In small things (in his immediate response to events) Hemingway himself so often proves that he understands the great truth of life; while in large things (such as his social novel), he is the slave of minor truths and untruths.

There are writers—some of them virtuosos in their field—who can write of anything, and are satisfied with their performance. To these we have nothing to say. And there are others who just cannot keep from writing again and again of what for them is most important; who like the things of life "but not to interfere with their work," their work as writers, but who at the same time feel deeply wounded when life, not interfering, passes by their most perfectly finished work. To such writers Hemingway belongs.

In the face of life's intricacies some of Hemingway's heroes are "undefeated" like his Manuel Garcia, others are "baited" like his Ole Andreson. Hemingway himself is among the former. He is alive in the very midst of death.

The possibilities of talent, when it is not secluded, but is fond of life and of people, are indeed boundless. And once again we wish Hemingway "good luck and keep writing," for we firmly believe that he still has in store more than one book, truthful, powerful, and brave.

Ivan Kashkeen

MICHAEL F. MOLONEY

Ernest Hemingway: The Missing Third Dimension

The publication of the slight and flaccid *Across the River and into the Trees* (1950) will not affect Hemingway's historic position as the most considerable figure in American fiction in the past quarter of a century. Even among those whose admiration is qualified there is no inclination to doubt the sharpness of his impact on the current literary scene. Reputations, of course, may be established by various means. The endorsement of the idols of the coteries can do much to win a hearing for a young writer, and this came early to Hemingway from two of the most legendary of Olympians—Gertrude Stein and Ezra Pound. The ability to hit off the popular taste before that taste has become quite aware of itself can be a weighty factor and the myriad synthetic Hemingways who have followed in the master's wake testify to something more than the extravagance of his success. Yet, beyond cavil, the severest evaluation of this writer, if it be honest, cannot be unaware of his formidable powers.

Here is neither the place nor the moment for a lengthy excursion into critical theory, but it is perhaps permissible to restate the ancient and unchallengeable truism that every art seeks to mirror the eternal in the temporal, the generic in the specific. It does not matter whether the writer be a classicist or a romanticist by conviction. It does not even matter whether he be an intellectualist or a sensist by profession. In every true artist the *daimon* will triumph over the limitations of faith. For the true artist is an indefatigable searcher for what W. K. Wimsatt, Jr., has called "the concrete universal," that is, for the graphic illustration of that experience which, while occurring in a particular time or a particular place, has a relevance that transcends these. Only by some such theory as this can art possess perennial value; only by some such supposition can the cultural heritage of one epoch be meaningful to a succeeding epoch.

What then are some of the universals to be found in Hemingway's writing? One characteristic note which links him with authors so various as Homer and Louis Bromfield is his love of the good earth, of cool streams, of clean air, of the fresh smell of woodlands, of the challenge of the long hike, of hunger bred in the open air. It is the tug of these primeval things which annually lures yearning tens of thousands from bench and desk to the forests of Maine, the trout streams of Michigan and Wisconsin, and the mountains of Oregon. Without question, in this phenomenon there is testimony to the artificiality of modern urban life, a kind of instinctive admission that man is a creature of earth and Antaeus-like derives his strength and physical well-being from intimate contact with her.

Hemingway's treatment of the urge behind the phenomenon is, to be sure, never crudely sociological. Instead, he is a poet with fine awareness of the manifold impressions of sight and sound and smell and taste, a poet for whom the Michigan hemlock forests of his boyhood are forever at the tips of his senses. Nick Adams, in "Big Two-Hearted River," seeing ahead "the far blue hills that marked the Lake Superior height of land," smelling the crushed sweet fern under his pack straps, savoring "the juicy syrup of the apricots," listening as the buckwheat cakes "sputtered in the pan," attests to the existence of what Wordsworth called the "grand elementary principle of pleasure" in the universe.

And Nick Adams is typical of Hemingway's later heroes. His bullfighters like "the smell of the stables about the patio de caballos" and Robert Jordan revels in "the clear night air of the mountains that smelled of the pines and of the dew on the grass in the meadow by the stream." This is, without question, Hemingway's basic affirmation. I am not concerned at the moment with its inadequacy as a philosophy of life or as an esthetic principle. As far as it goes it is a positive thing and it orientates Hemingway loosely with those romantics who place their faith in the illumined senses.

A second inescapable virtue of Hemingway is his tragic sense. This may well be the weightiest factor in his craft. To possess the tragic vision is not easy for the contemporary writer. As Joseph Wood Krutch has brilliantly pointed out, the tragic fall demands of the hero a largeness of spirit, a comprehensiveness of destiny, which the scientism of the twentieth century has denied to mankind. It has been eloquently argued that tragedy is equally impossible in a culture completely dominated by the Christian view —that since the Christian vision is of man's ultimate and certain triumph it was in the nature of things for the greatest literary monument of the Christian Middle Ages to be styled a *Commedia*.

To the proponents of this theory the great age of Greece and the sixteenth-century English Renaissance were as inevitably true periods of tragedy. In the first the accepted majesty of human endeavor was overshadowed by the unanswered questions of human fate; in the second, the serenity of the Christian synthesis had been thwarted by intestine defection and external assault.

It is a tribute to Hemingway that in so hostile a period he has kept his mastery of the tragic spirit. True, he does it at the expense of obvious strain. The "hard-boiled" atmosphere of the Hemingway fiction is there very likely because the author feels the futility of tragic differentiation in subdued colors within an experiential area so limited as that of modern man. Hence his palette frequently takes on a hard, if not nightmarish, quality. But despite this he is surprisingly consistent in suggesting and in maintaining the tragic tone.

In "The Snows of Kilimanjaro" there is tragedy of a high order which is only remotely connected with the gangrenous death of the hero. This story, though greatly admired, is, perhaps, on the whole, too contrived. If the dream of the rescue at the end is a trick which comes off well, the feverish recollection of snow on Bulgarian mountains, in the Gauertal, on the Madlener-Haus, hints at too glossy a finish. But the dying hero's review of his wasted talents and wasted hopes is finely tragic in a way rare in modern literature. The heart of the matter is not that death has cut short a promising career. The true tragedy is antecedent to the hero's physical death. It is the tragedy of a man who lacked the courage to reject the world—symbolized by the life of ease he had been living—that he might save his soul—symbolized by his artistic gifts. Death brings him clarity of insight into himself and he realizes with something of the pathos of Marlowe's Dr. Faustus that the hour of repentance is past. Thus conceived, the story is a secular morality play.

Tragic, too, is the presentation of Manuel, the superannuated bullfighter in "The Undefeated," from the collection, *Men Without Women* (1927). What, after all, is the theme of this story but the man-against-time thesis which, with a thousand permutations, runs through Western literature from Homer to Herrick, from Horace to Housman. Manuel has known the great triumphs of the bull ring. He is old now. He retains the unquestioned style of the supreme artist but the coordination of hand and eye which youth alone can give has departed. Still, his is the high courage which will ask no favors and make no concessions. It cannot be very far wrong to find in Manuel's last fight Hemingway's symbol of man's endless struggle against the flux of circumstance.

For the most part, the sureness of Hemingway's tragic touch is in inverse proportion to the length of the work. In *To Have and Have Not* (1937), the end of Harry Morgan is scarcely tragic since tragedy demands awareness on the part of the protagonist and Morgan's awareness is on the instinctive rather than truly human level. In *A Farewell to Arms* (1929), likewise, there is no profound tragic appeal in the main plot. The relationship of Lieutenant Henry and Catherine Barkley in this, the most famous novel to come out of World War I, scarcely rises above the physical. Even in death Catherine is only the trapped animal. Her world is a world of two dimensions only—of muscular and nervous reaction. There is a poignancy in the famous conclusion of the book as there is in the scene where Catherine gives Lieutenant Henry the St. Anthony medal in the efficacy of which she does not believe, but poignancy is not to be identified with the tragic vision itself.

In *For Whom the Bell Tolls* (1940), the tragic tone is much better sustained. The description of the end of Robert Jordan is carefully and deftly done, but it is not the best thing in the book. And the presentation of El Sordo's last battle, marvelously good though it is in detail, strikes one reader—it may be unjustifiably—as somehow Hollywoodish in its over-all effect. But throughout the narrative there are numerous points of genuine tragic interest. The irreconcilable struggle between selfish and selfless impulses, between vanity and humility, between cowardice and courage, is of the essence of tragedy and Hemingway has portrayed that struggle vividly. His presentation of the deterioration of Pablo is one major triumph, that of the death of old Anselmo another.

Just as an enormous vitality and a grasp of the tragic dimensions of life are important elements in Hemingway's work, so his narrative gift, which like his tragic immediacy is best illustrated in his short stories, is not less significant. In an age where bad writing has been the rule rather than the exception, the contemporary short story has probably produced more sound craftsmanship than any other genre, and Hemingway has been among the most conscientious of its practitioners. Indeed, it is difficult to think of him at his best other than as a short-story writer. The longer works, on careful reading, tend to disintegrate into component parts. This is true necessarily of *The Sun Also Rises* (1926), which is picaresque in organization. It is true also of *To Have and Have Not*. *A Farewell to Arms* is likewise highly episodic. Only *For Whom the Bell Tolls* seems organically constructed and even here it is startling to see how many sections, when disengaged, can stand by themselves.

Certain peaks of Hemingway's narrative form stand out above the consistently high level of his achievement. "The Killers" has been widely anthologized, as well as adapted to cinematic treatment. "The Short Happy Life of Francis Macomber" has also drawn Hollywood's eye. "The Snows of Kilimanjaro" has been called Hemingway's "most accomplished" if not best piece of writing by Malcolm Cowley. "My Old Man" from *In Our Time* (1925) has been justly admired as has the companion piece, "Big Two-Hearted River." From the novels, Cowley has included in the *Portable Hemingway* Harry Morgan's last adventure from *To Have and Have Not*, the Caporetto episode from *A Farewell to Arms* and El Sordo on the hilltop from *For Whom the Bell Tolls*.

Several factors contribute to Hemingway's narrative power. One of the most important, unquestionably, is the clipped, athletic march of his sentences. The bare bleakness of the conversation in "The Killers" is an extreme example (here admirably adapted to the speakers) of this trait. But, in general, all of Hemingway's characters talk alike. The manner of their speech is the straightforward assertion or the simple question without syntactical qualification, whether they be gangsters or laborers or decadent aristocrats or Italian or Spanish or American soldiers. Psychologically, Hemingway is right. In real life the incipient poetry which shows beneath the speech of his Spaniards must occasionally break into circumlocution. But Hemingway's fictional world, whatever its locale, is the deadly, stale, monotonous world of modern positivism and modern industrialism from which all spiritual leaven has been removed and he is consistent in giving a universal flatness to the speech of his characters.

The simplicity of Hemingway's style, as numerous imitators have learned and as more than one critic has pointed out, is deceiving. His assumption of the illiterate pose is, of course, only a pose. Back of it lies a hard discipline which has forced intractable words to conform to a preconceived pattern. One may legitimately question the accuracy of his ear for the nuances of speech, but the fact remains that the kind of effect he wants he superbly achieves. And in passing it may be observed that when Hemingway deserts this style for Steinesque cadences, as notably in *Death in the Afternoon* (1932), or for the more ambitious roll of Ciceronian rhetoric, as in the *Green Hills of Africa* (1935), he loses his mastery. In the one his muscular muse has donned an ill-fitting dinner jacket; in the other his schoolboy oratory is rank fustian.

Closely integrated with Hemingway's syntax is his language. The assault upon poetic diction which the nineteenth-century romantics had led had been only a relative thing, for literature throughout the nineteenth century remained a matter of the genteel tradition. But World War I ended all that. For good or for bad there has since been no washing of the materials of literature through the filter of a traditional culture. The writers of today have not only decided what their own literary standards are to be but they have remade even the ancients, who have struck their fancy, in their own image. How else account for their admiration for the seventeenth-century metaphysicals so remote from them in learning, in ideals, and in technique? Hemingway as much as any other man has put the raw language of the street, the poolroom, the barracks and the brothel into modern literature. Again, on artistic grounds alone, his judgment has been admirable. The bareness of his sentences has been heightened by the starkness of his speech.

A final significant element in Hemingway's narrative appeal is his grasp of the essentially dramatic. By dramatic effect is meant his ability to keep the reader's interest steadily focused on the central characters and on the great scenes, not through technical manipulation, but through the simple inevitability with which the narrative is unfolded. Every great novelist has this dramatic gift. Of the nineteenth-century English novelists it was preeminent in Meredith and this alone will almost certainly win Meredith a rehearing despite the low ebb of his current reputation. Hardy, too, possessed it in full measure but, like Dickens, although for different reasons, he was apt to allow the dramatic to degenerate into the theatrical. Thackeray had an unerring dramatic instinct despite a temperament that led him to excesses. Of contemporary American novelists aside from Hemingway, Steinbeck and Faulkner are outstanding for this power.

With Hemingway this dramatic sense is always present. As a striking example of it, Chapter Twenty-one of *For Whom the Bell Tolls* may be cited. The time is daybreak, the scene a mountainside. The appearance of the cavalryman signalizes the end of the respite which Robert Jordan and his little band have enjoyed. What follows is recounted with superb economy. The shooting of the Navarrese, the preparations for the attack, and, in the center of the scene, Robert and Maria: the man now concerned only with war and its demands; the girl unable to understand that the grim business of killing or being killed has displaced her in his thoughts. It is possible that Hemingway's insight into the mind of neither the man nor the girl is unexceptionable, but purely as a piece of technique the chapter is magnificently executed.

These then are Hemingway's solid assets: a poet's awareness of the beauty of the universe in which man's too fleeting hour is spent; an almost exaggerated consciousness of the unending struggle, both internal and external, to which man is committed; a mastery of syntax and diction which always reveals and never beclouds his other virtues; a sure eye for the dramatic scene and an unfailing ability to reproduce it. It will be immediately evident that these virtues are heavily weighted on the technical side.

And what of Hemingway's defects? They are many and obvious and, like his virtues, they are closely related to his age. The world of which Hemingway writes is the world which has experienced a final disillusionment with the promises of Renaissance humanism. We are still close enough to a dead era to smile understandingly at the eulogy of Francis Bacon in the *Dictionary of National Biography:* "He stood, like a prophet, on the verge of the promised land, bidding men leave, without regret, the desert which lay behind them, and enter with joyfulness and hopefulness on the rich inheritance that was spread out before them." These words, written more than fifty years ago, show, by their phrasal mockery of the Scriptural promise of heavenly rewards, how superbly confident modern man then was of reentering the earthly paradise. Amid the frustrations of the twentieth century they have an ironic ring. Yet they luminously call attention to the pitiless logic of history whereby the Christian humanism of More and Erasmus shaded in the course of three hundred years into the atheistic humanism of Feuerbach and Nietzsche, from the latter of whom Hemingway would seem unquestionably to derive.

For Feuerbach God was only a myth expressing the aspirations of the human conscience. To explain his theory Feuerbach had recourse to the Hegelian concept of *alienation,* though using it in a sense quite different from Hegel's. Alienation, he explained, involves the subtraction from man, for the benefit of an illusory reality, of certain attributes belonging to his essence. Human attributes such as wisdom, will, justice, and love are objectified by man in a fantastic being, the pure product of his imagination, which he calls God.

Although Nietzsche referred contemptuously to Feuerbach, he was indebted to the latter through the mediation of Schopenhauer and Wagner. For Nietzsche, too, God was only the mirror of man. The objectification of man's noblest traits in an external Being resulted, he believed, only in the degradation of man and this degradation was pushed to the ultimate extreme in Christianity. For in Christianity all virtue, all greatness of soul, all truth are considered the gifts of grace. Nietzsche's own atheism, he insisted in his *Ecce Homo,* was instinctive, not reasoned. Be that as it may, there can be little doubt that his ecstatic enunciation of the "death of God" was an important agent in the quickening of the nihilistic forces which in two world wars reduced the old liberal world to ruins.

The philosophy of Hemingway scarcely suggests academic sources, although in such a writer—so strange a mingling of the intellectual and the sensuous—one can never be certain. But whether directly or indirectly acquired, his works reveal a rather systematic application of Nietzsche's principles. The superman in action, the conflict of the Apollonian and Dionysian ideals, the substitution of new myths for the old faith, all these find their explication in his writings.

Like the Nietzschean superman, the heroes of Hemingway live in a world beyond moral good and evil. An obvious aspect of this truth is found in the free sexual relations of his men and women. Lady Brett, of the early *The Sun Also Rises,* "common as the way between Saint Albans and London," may be taken as a convenient illustration of Hemingway's attitude toward sex. She is a creature of appetites which she makes no pretense of controlling, indeed, seems unable to control. She passes from one man to another with a casualness complete and unself-conscious. Desired by many men, she is apparently incapable of deep attachment herself. The explanation of her thwarted relation to Jake Barnes, if it is meant to motivate her actions (I do not think it is so meant) fails of its purpose. Her sexual function (like that of all of Hemingway's women including the incredible Renata of *Across the River and into the Trees*) has no deeper justification than to help while away the tedium of her possessor of the moment. It provides an instant of relief in man's all-enveloping ennui, but as such it is no more significant than the excitement of the bull ring. Liquor fails equally to break down the emotional imperviousness of Hemingway's heroes. From Jake Barnes to Robert Jordan they are heroic drinkers in a singularly joyless manner. They are little moved either by their indulgence or by the impending cirrhosis which it invites. Life may be empty but death has no terror. "Do you know that in about thirty-five years more we'll be dead?" asks Robert Cohn in *The Sun Also Rises*. "What the hell, Robert," Jake replied. "What the hell."

This callowness, one of the identifying traits of Hemingway, derives unquestionably from his experience as an ambulance driver on the Italian front in World War I and from the subsequent years in Paris, where in the 1920s a now famous group of American literary expatriates were attempting to put together the pieces of their shattered personal faiths. One of his admirers has pointed out that in no other author of this age is there "such a profusion of corpses." And Hemingway's characters, in the presence of death, observe admirably the Nietzschean, "Be hard." Lieutenant Henry's farewell to Catherine Barkley, El Sordo's last hours on the hilltop, Ole Andreson's awaiting gangland execution—these are confrontations of death which are not so much philosophically stoical as they are bestially indifferent. The Nietzschean lineage of the Hemingway supermen is clear but from them much of the Nietzschean lyric ecstasy has evaporated.

Moreover, while Hemingway's heroes have the overtones of the Nietzschean superman they also reveal the triumph of the Nietzschean Dionysus over Apollo. One of Père Henri de Lubac's good services has been to point out (in *Le Drame de L'Humanisme Athée*) that in the beginning, at the time of writing *Die Geburt der Tragödie*, Nietzsche did not see in Dionysus a symbol of a pagan religion specifically opposed to Christianity. "His perspective was then scarcely anti-Christian. It was anti-Socratic." It is in this earlier version of Nietzsche's Dionysiac-Socratic antithesis that Hemingway follows the brilliant German. His heroes are men of action rather than thinkers. For Nietzsche the opposition of Apollo and Dionysus could be fruitful. Greek tragedy was the result of the prodigious synthesis of their opposing powers—the serenity of the one and the universal energy of the other. But the Socratic *daimon* was incapable of such compromise. Greek civilization was ruined because eventually Socrates had vanquished Dionysus.

Hemingway's rejection of the Socratic reason has, very likely, no such philosophical justification. Rather, since he came to maturity in the period of World War I, his attitude is, it may be conjectured, a result of the general disillusionment of that period. The political architects of European liberalism, buttressed by the all-embracing doctrine of evolution, had for three generations prior to 1914 confidently charted the course of the future brave new world. When the charts proved illusory and the new world began to come apart at the seams, the gaudy claims of their creators became a mockery. And if reason could be so fallacious, might not the glorification of instinct have much to recommend it? To be sure, at that particular moment Nietzsche was reinforced by Freud. So it is that Hemingway's males are what they are. "I was not made to think," says the hero of *A Farewell to Arms,* but the same is true of Nick Adams and Jake Barnes and Harry Morgan.

In a famous essay written thirty years ago, Mr. T. S. Eliot warned that it is not enough for the man of letters to look in his heart and write. He must also, Mr. Eliot declared, ". . . look into the cerebral cortex, the nervous system, and the digestive tract." That Hemingway has looked into the nervous system and the digestive tract is abundantly evident. He has not, as we have seen, been so concerned with the cerebral cortex.

But even literal adherence to Mr. Eliot's three-fold admonition would not have been enough. The philosophy and literature as well as the history of the past century and a half lead to two concomitant conclusions. First, even the most frenzied romantic exaltation of the ego must finally confess the insufficiency of an egocentric world. Second, the most enthusiastic proponents of nihilistic doctrines must turn at last to some kind of affirmation. That is to say, wherever man, in the name of freedom, sacredness of personality, or whatever the catchword of the moment may be, dethrones God to eternize himself, he eventually is forced to look outside himself for the sanction of his divinity. Thus Feuerbach, who declared that the turning point of history would be the moment when man became aware that he alone was God, also insisted that man could not achieve divinity of himself but only by identifying himself with the collective being of society. That affirmation of Feuerbach's, more effectively than Auguste Comte's somewhat parallel teaching—more effective because

Engels and Marx were among his disciples—enthroned the sociological idol on the central altar of the modern pantheon.

It is interesting to note Hemingway's reaction to this *Zeitgeist*.
The testimony of his earlier works fails to reveal any spontaneous
social devotion. On the contrary, in most of his central figures
prior to *For Whom the Bell Tolls* there is more than a hint of
the antisocial. They are lonely personages who have suffered at
the hands of their fellow men and who nurse their wounds and
their resentment in a kind of Byronic (or pseudo-Byronic)
grandeur. Even Nick Adams, although not antisocial, scarcely
yearns for social integration. But like Nietzsche his master who,
to facilitate the escape from the Socratic reason, found it necessary
to take refuge in mythmaking, Hemingway, too, could not entirely escape the myth. Hence when he came to write *For Whom
the Bell Tolls* he was caught up in the antifascist crusade which
provided doctrinal affirmation for the liberals of the 1930s. The
issue here is not Hemingway's personal devotion to the Popular-
Front forces in the Spanish Civil War. But devotion to any cause
outside themselves was something new for the creatures of Hemingway's pen and the reader may well find in the over-all effect of
his most ambitious book something of the tour de force.

Here we touch upon Hemingway's basic dilemma. His delight
in brawn and ganglion has been repeated with increasing shrill-
ness and monotony. Yet death is never far away in these tales—
all his longer works are monodies—and the harsh brittleness with
which it is presented is meaningful. We have noted Jake Barnes's
swashbuckling on the subject. What is meant to be a more per-
spicacious approach is found in the comment of the narrator to
the old lady in *Death in the Afternoon:* "Madame, there is no
remedy for anything in life. Death is a sovereign remedy for all
misfortunes and we'd do best to leave off all discoursing now and
get to table." Somehow this has a hollow ring as though the
author himself were ill at ease with the subject. One recalls, by
contrast, the mournful meditation in the *Green Hills of Africa*
on the diuturnity of the Gulf Stream whose blueness the Havana
garbage scows cannot violate, and the conviction comes that here
is a longing for something more permanent in human life than the
refuse of its sewers.

The judicious reader will not censure Hemingway because the
scent of garbage, real as well as metaphorical, invades his pages
along with the clean smell of the north woods and the African hills
and plains. For man is man, that is, an animal of animals, and he

who would write truly of him cannot be unaware of his animality. But for the greatest masters of literature man has always been something more. He is also a spirit, although "a great lob of a spirit," as a philosophical friend likes to put it. The omnipresent symbolism in Hemingway's writing seems to be a confession that this is true. For the utilization of the symbol is an admission that the fact is more than a fact, that behind it lie other planes of meaning and reality. In a strictly logical system of materialistic monism there could be no symbolism.

Hence Hemingway's naturalism is always promising to break through its isolation and to link up with the world of spirit but the promise is never quite achieved. It is this failure which will weigh heaviest against him in the final summing up. He has written that a fourth and fifth dimension are possible in prose. His own prose not only lacks a fourth and fifth dimension; it lacks, for the most part, a third. The obliqueness of his characters derives from his refusal or inability (whether he is the unconscious or willing captive of his age is a nice question) to give evidence to that potential in man which either raises him above or sinks him below the rest of the animal world.

Michael F. Moloney

F. I. CARPENTER

Hemingway Achieves the Fifth Dimension

In *Green Hills of Africa,* Ernest Hemingway prophesied: "The kind of writing that can be done. How far prose can be carried if anyone is serious enough and has luck. There is a fourth and fifth dimension that can be gotten." Since then many critics have analyzed the symbols and mythical meanings of Hemingway's prose.[1] A few have tried to imagine what he meant by "a fourth and fifth dimension."[2] But most have agreed that the phrase is pretty vague.

"The fourth dimension" clearly has something to do with the concept of time, and with fictional techniques of describing it. Harry Levin has pointed out that Hemingway's style is lacking in the complexity of structure that normally describes "the third dimension," but that it offers a series of images (much like the moving pictures) to convey the impression of time sequence and immediacy. Joseph Warren Beach has suggested that "the fourth dimension" is related to an "esthetic factor" achieved by the hero's recurrent participation in some traditional "ritual or strategy"; while "the fifth dimension" may be an "ethical factor" achieved by his "participation in the moral order of the world." And Malcolm Cowley has also related "the fourth dimension" of time to "the almost continual performance of rites and ceremonies" suggesting the recurrent patterns of human experience, but has called "the fifth dimension" a "mystical or meaningless figure of speech."

But is the prophecy of a fifth-dimensional prose "a meaningless figure of speech"? Certainly Hemingway has often attacked the critics for indulging in grandiose abstractions. Perhaps in *Green*

[1] See especially Carlos Baker, *Hemingway: The Writer as Artist,* Princeton: 1952, and Philip Young, *Ernest Hemingway,* New York: 1952.
[2] Joseph Warren Beach, "How Do You Like It Now, Gentlemen?" *Sewanee Review,* LIX (Spring, 1951), pp. 311-28; Harry Levin, "Observations on the Style of Hemingway," *Kenyon Review,* XIII (Autumn, 1951), pp. 581-609; Malcolm Cowley, *The Portable Hemingway,* New York: 1944, "Introduction."

Hills of Africa, one of his poorer books, he may have lowered his guard and relaxed his muscles. "The fifth dimension," moreover, has no accepted meaning to modern physicists. But Hemingway's art has always been self-conscious, and in the years of his apprenticeship in Paris he often discussed this art with Gertrude Stein—a trained philosopher, and an admirer of Henri Bergson's theories of the two kinds of "time." [3] Finally, I think, "the fifth dimension" is too strikingly specific a figure of speech to be "meaningless," although it may be "mystical." [4]

Actually, the specific phrase "the fifth dimension" was used in 1931 (*Green Hills of Africa* was published in 1935), by P. D. Ouspensky, who defined it to mean "the perpetual now." Ouspensky, a mystic, was an admirer of Bergson and of William James. Bergson (also an admirer of James) had emphasized the difference between psychological time and physical time. And both these ideas go back to William James's philosophy of "radical empiricism" (that is, of "immediate" or "pure" experience), which Gertrude Stein (a former pupil of James) had adapted for literary purposes. There is strong internal evidence that Hemingway's philosophy and practice both of style and of structure have followed this pattern of philosophic ideas. His literary ideal has been that of "immediate empiricism." And his "fifth-dimensional prose" has attempted to communicate the immediate experience of "the perpetual now."

This mystical idea of a "fifth-dimensional" experience of "the perpetual now" might seem fantastic except that Hemingway first suggested it explicitly, and then practiced it consciously in his best fiction. *For Whom the Bell Tolls* embodies the idea both implicitly, in structure, and explicitly, in the speeches and thoughts of its characters. If this major novel is analyzed with this philosophic idea in mind, the structure and the purpose become unmistakable. The same structure (although less explicitly) informs the two great short stories which preceded this novel: "The Short Happy Life of Francis Macomber" and "The Snows of Kilimanjaro." And the writing of these three major works immediately followed Hemingway's prophecy of a "fifth dimension" to be achieved by prose.

[3] See Bergson, *Durée et Simultanéité: à propos de la théorie d'Einstein,* Paris: 1922.
[4] I use the term "mystical" in its most general sense, to describe any intense experience or "ecstasy" which results in insight or "illumination." I have defined this kind of mysticism at length in my *Emerson Handbook,* New York: 1953, pp. 113-16.

Finally, this idea of "the perpetual now," and the philosophy of immediate empiricism which underlies it, suggest an explanation for the sharp alternation of brilliant success and painful failure in Hemingway's fictional career. In its sentimental or isolated form, this idea degenerates into "the cult of sensation," [5] or of violent experience divorced from the routine of living. In this form it explains the frequent spectacular badness of *To Have and Have Not* and of *Across the River and into the Trees*. But when related to the routine experiences of life, which give the more "sensational" experiences both a frame of reference and a meaning, this philosophy suggests the heights to which human nature can rise in moments of extreme stress. No longer the cult of "sensation," it becomes the ideal of "intensity" or "ecstasy," and produces that telescoping of experience and those flashes of illumination which make the "short" life of Francis Macomber supremely "happy," and the snows of Kilimanjaro blindingly brilliant.

In the 1920s, Albert Einstein's scientific theory of relativity—with its interpretation of "time" as a fourth dimension necessary to the measurement of the space between the stars and within the atoms—spawned a generation of pseudo-scientific speculators who attempted to interpret the meaning of these physical theories for philosophic and literary purposes. The most spectacular (and the least scientific) of these was the Russian-born mystic, P. D. Ouspensky, who published his *Tertium Organum* in 1921, and *A New Model of the Universe* in 1931. Specifically, Ouspensky defined the "fifth dimension" as

a line of perpetual now. . . . The fifth dimension forms a surface in relation to the line of time. . . . Though we are not aware of it, sensations of the existence of other "times" continually enter our consciousness. . . . The fifth dimension is movement in the circle, repetition, recurrence.[6]

And at considerable length he analyzed and illustrated these pseudo-scientific ideas with reference to James's "moments of consciousness," Bergson's theory of time, and "the Eternal Now of Brahma." I do not mean to imply that Hemingway necessarily read Ouspensky's books, but his conversations with Gertrude Stein and her friends in the twenties might well have included discus-

---

[5] See R. P. Warren, "Hemingway," *Kenyon Review,* IX (Winter, 1947), pp. 1-28.
[6] *A New Model of the Universe* (first published 1931, rev. ed., New York: 1950, p. 375).

sion of them. Moreover, his specific reference to "a fifth dimension" finds partial explanation here, and Ouspensky's description of "the perpetual now" closely parallels passages in *For Whom the Bell Tolls* (as we shall see later).

With Bergson's theory of the "fourth dimension" of time, we approach firmer ground. Closer to the main stream of philosophic thought, Bergson tried to interpret Einstein's scientific theory of the relativity of time for literary purposes. In 1922 he used recent experiments measuring the speed of light, and proving that light rays are "bent" by the force of gravitation, to illustrate his own already published theories of time. If physical "time" may be distorted by motion in space and by gravitation, the measurement of psychological time may be distorted even more. Bergson had always emphasized that mechanic time could never measure the intensities of the *élan vital* in human experience, and that the human organism distorted "time" through the devices of memory and intuitional thought. Now Einstein's theory of relativity suggested that time was not a final measurement in physics, either. In human consciousness time might be telescoped, and sensation intensified, just as a passenger on a train approaching a warning signal at a road crossing hears the ringing intensified in pitch as he approaches. Again, these ideas find echoes in Hemingway's prose.

But all these ideas are speculative. The matrix from which they spring, and in which their "mysticism" finds relation to reality, is the philosophy of William James—acknowledged as "master" by Ouspensky, Bergson, and Gertrude Stein equally. Approaching philosophy by way of psychology, James had interpreted all religious and artistic experiences as empirical phenomena: he had sought to observe, report, and analyze those intense "moments of consciousness," which men of religion and of art alike have described as the most "real" and important. With James, therefore, "realism" had become psychological, and "empiricism" had expanded to include all "immediate" or subjective as well as "mediate" or objective experience. Studying under James, Gertrude Stein had developed artistic techniques for communicating this "immediate" experience in prose style. Hemingway now carried these techniques further, and incorporated their psychological and philosophic patterns (outlined by James, Bergson, and perhaps Ouspensky) in the structural forms of his fiction.

To trace the development of these philosophic ideas, and to illustrate their application to literature, a book would hardly

suffice. But to summarize: A brief, immediate experience, observed realistically, is described first as it occurred "in our time";
the protagonist is intensely moved, but remains confused, so that
the meaning of it all seems nothing, or "nada." But this immediate experience recalls individual memories of other, similar
experiences, or historic memories of parallel experiences in the
history of other nations, or mystical, "racial" memories. And
these "mediate" experiences are suggested by "flashbacks," or by
conversations, or by the suggestion of recurrent myth or ritual
patterns. And these fragmentary remembrances of similar experiences, by relating the individual to other people, places and
times, suggest new meanings and forms. Finally this new awareness of the patterns and meanings implicit in the immediate, individual experience intensifies it, and gives it a new "dimension"
not apparent at the time it actually happened.

For Whom the Bell Tolls is Hemingway's first full-length
novel to describe, and partially to achieve, this radical intensification of experience. Both explicitly and implicitly, it seeks to realize
the "fifth dimension" of an "eternal now," beyond the usual
"fourth dimension" of time. It consciously describes—as well as
subconsciously suggests—the telescoping of time involved in this
realization of immediate experience. Indeed the very explicit self-
consciousness with which it describes this idea constitutes its chief
fault. But, although the idea has been suggested before, its formal
pattern has never been clarified.

On the surface, the novel describes the tragedy of an American
volunteer, fighting for the Loyalists in the Spanish Civil War, who
is sent to dynamite a bridge and does so, but is killed as a result.
The action takes place in three days and involves a love affair
with a Spanish girl named Maria, who has been rescued by the
band of Communist guerrillas, after having been raped by the
Fascists. This love affair has been criticized as irrelevant and obtrusive, but it actually forms the core of the book. And paradoxically it seems obtrusive *because* it struggles under so heavy a
weight of conscious meaning.

The love affair begins immediately (and sensationally) when
Maria crawls into the hero's sleeping bag the first night out. She
hopes thus to exorcise the memory of the evil that has been done
to her. But, even while loving her, the hero remains conscious of
the passage of time, asking " 'what time is it now?' . . . It was
one o'clock. The dial showed bright in the darkness that the robe

made." [7] Later when he declares his love for Maria to Pilar, the gypsy mother-confessor, she warns him that "There is not much time." Because the ending is destined to be tragic, the love affair must be brief. But it will be meaningful, later.

After the second experience of love on the second day, this new meaning is suggested: ". . . and time absolutely still and they were both there, time having stopped and he felt the earth move out and away from under them." Later, thinking of this experience, the hero generalizes:

. . . Maybe that is my life and instead of it being threescore years and ten it is . . . just threescore hours and ten or twelve rather. . . .

I suppose it is possible to live as full a life in seventy hours as in seventy years; granted that your life has been full up to the time that the seventy hours start and that you have reached a certain age.

. . . So if your life trades its seventy years for seventy hours I have that value now and I am lucky enough to know it. . . . If there is only now, why then now is the thing to praise. . . . Now, *ahora, maintenant, heute.*

This telescoping of time becomes the new "value," and a universal one. Meanwhile, the hero continues to speculate about this tragic and enigmatic wisdom suggested by Pilar, the gypsy:

. . . She is a damned sight more civilized than you and she knows what time is all about. Yes, he said to himself, I think that we can admit that she has certain notions about the value of time. . . .

Not time, not happiness, not fun, not children, not a house, not a bathroom, not a clean pair of pyjamas, not the morning paper. . . . No, none of that. . . .

So if you love this girl as much as you say you do, you had better love her very hard and make up in intensity what the relation will lack in duration and in continuity.

As explicitly as possible the hero develops these new "notions about the value of time," speculating that the intense experience of a perpetual "now" may equal in value a lifetime of "duration and continuity." "It was a good system of belief," he concluded. "There is nothing else than now. . . . A good life is not measured by any biblical span."

In the ecstatic experience of perfect union with his beloved, time has stood still, and the value of intensity has been substituted for that of duration. From this experience has emerged the

---

[7] *For Whom the Bell Tolls,* New York: 1940, p. 72.

philosophy of the eternal now. Meanwhile, as the larger action of the novel approaches its climax, the hero seeks to understand the strange combination of violence and idealism which characterizes the Spanish people.

On the last night, Maria pours out to him the story of her violation. And again he generalizes:

> Those are the flowers of Spanish chivalry. What a people they have been. . . . Spain has always had its own special idol worship within the Church. *Otra Virgen más.* I suppose that was why they had to destroy the virgins of their enemies. . . . This was the only country the reformation never reached. They were paying for the Inquisition now, all right. . . .

> Maybe I have had all my life in three days, he thought.

In the hero's mind, "Maria" thus becomes a symbol of the traditional mariolatry of the Spanish Catholic Church, which "the reformation never reached"; and the violence of the Spanish Civil War becomes an intensified version of all modern history since the Reformation, compressed in symbolic time. His love for this modern Maria becomes both a symbolic fulfillment of history and a transcendence of the old "time." In a flash, the immediate experience of the eternal now becomes not only a personal "system of belief," but a philosophy of history illuminating the action of the whole novel.

Shortly after, the third and final experience of love obliterates time ("the hand on the watch moved, unseen now"), the ecstasy is complete ("not why not ever why, only this now"), and this individual experience becomes one with the experience of all mystics: "It is in Greco and in San Juan da la Cruz, of course, and in the others. I am no mystic, but to deny it is as ignorant as though you denied the telephone." And this mystic transcendence of time and of self informs the final chapters of the book, as, after being fatally wounded, the hero comforts Maria: "Thou art me too now. Thou art all there will be of me" (p. 464), and accepts his own death: "He began to accept it and let the hate go out. . . . Once you saw it again as it was to others, once you got rid of your own self, the always ridding of self that you had to do in war. Where there could be no self." Thus finally the experience of "the perpetual now" leads to the mystical experience.

This intensification of experience under the emotional stress of love or war, resulting in an ecstasy transcending the traditional limitations of time and of self, and producing a "system of belief" verging on the mystical, is the subject of *For Whom the Bell Tolls,* both implicitly and explicitly. In a sense it has always been the subject of all Hemingway's fiction. But of course the emphasis has changed over the different periods of his writing, and he has developed this "system of belief" progressively.

Hemingway's early fiction, in general, described the immediate experience, of love or war, with a minimal awareness of meaning, and a minimal experience of ecstasy; therefore the experience seemed largely "sensational," and the meaning "nada." But beginning with "The Short Happy Life of Francis Macomber" and "The Snows of Kilimanjaro," his stories began to achieve ecstasy and to imagine a transcendence of the futility of the past. The sudden illumination of the vision of snow-capped Kilimanjaro prophesied the ecstasies and the transcendence of time in *For Whom the Bell Tolls.* But this novel exaggerated perhaps the author's new consciousness of meaning, and his concern with the "system" of his belief. In *The Old Man and the Sea* the idea became at last incarnated and the mysticism completely naturalized.

But the idea of the intensified experience of the immediate "now" is not simple, nor is its mysticism traditional. Hemingway himself has suggested some of the necessary qualifications: his Robert Jordan "supposed" that the final fulfillment of life in seventy hours was possible, "granted that your life has been full up to the time that the seventy hours start, and that you have reached a certain age." That is, the intensity of experience which transcends time, and achieves a new "value" or "dimension," depends upon an earlier fullness of experience of time and the appreciation of its value. The mysticism of this fifth-dimensional experience implies no denial of the old "values" or "dimensions," but rather a fulfillment beyond them. These heroes do not seek escape from time (as do the hero and heroine of Robert Penn Warren's *World Enough and Time*), nor do they build a "tower beyond tragedy" (like the heroes of Robinson Jeffers), but rather they seek the intensified fulfillment of life within tragedy.

Further, this achievement of a new dimension of experience requires maturity—the hero must have reached "a certain age." Besides having lived a full life in the past, he must have reached a turning point, or crisis of life. So Francis Macomber—a natural aristocrat who has excelled at sports in the past—confronts the final test of courage, fails, but suddenly overcomes his fear and achieves a brief ecstasy of happiness. And the autobiographical hero of Kilimanjaro—who has prospered well enough in love and in literature—sees suddenly the ecstatic vision of supreme success, as he dies.

Finally, the achievement of this new dimension of experience, whether in "prose" or in life, is exceptional—"one must have luck." So Robert Jordan "had learned that he himself, with another person, could be everything. But inside himself he knew that this was the exception." The new experience requires a fullness of past life, a certain age, and an ecstasy which is mystical in every sense.

A fourth-dimensional sense of time (Cowley and Beach have suggested) is often achieved by a detailed description of the patterns of experience which have crystallized in rituals, ceremonies, traditions, habits of action, codes of behavior. On the level of pure realism, this may be suggested by that loving description of the techniques of any work or sport which is characteristic of all Hemingway's stories.[8] The absence of this workaday realism contributes to the failure of *Across the River,* while the exact techniques of fishing make real the occasional mysticism of *The Old Man and the Sea.* On the level of art, the patterned ritual of the bullfight and the sporting code of the big-game hunter also suggest this sense of repetition in time. While on the level of religion, mythical or symbolic actions, which sometimes seem unreal or irrational, may provide the pattern. The esthetic sense of the perfect fulfillment of some pattern of action in time is the necessary precondition for achievement of the final "magic."

The "fifth-dimensional" intensity of experience beyond time may come, finally, from a profound sense of participation in these traditional patterns of life experience. Beach's description of the fifth dimension as a "sense of participation in the moral order of the world" is suggestive. "You felt an absolute brotherhood with the others who were engaged in it," observed Robert Jordan of his Spanish Civil War. Paradoxically, love and war become supremely "moral," and the intensity of the experience they offer may communicate a mystical ecstasy. If only the sensational and the violent aspects are described, with only a traditional, third-dimensional realism, "nada" results. But these violent sensations have always been the elemental stuff, both of human tragedy and of mystical transcendence. If the red slayer think only of slaying, and if the slain think only of being slain, no fourth or fifth dimen-

[8] See Joseph Beaver, " 'Technique' in Hemingway," *College English* (March, 1953), p. 325.

sion is achieved. But Santiago in *The Old Man and the Sea,* performing realistically the ritual techniques of his trade, goes on to identify the intensity of his own suffering with that of the great fish that he is slaying. And, telling his story, Hemingway has achieved that synthesis of immediate experience and mysticism which, perhaps, is "the fifth dimension."

F. I. Carpenter

ARTURO BAREA

Not Spain but Hemingway

Ernest Hemingway's new novel, *For Whom the Bell Tolls,* was cast for the success it is now reaping along the whole front line from left-wing reviewers to Hollywood producers.

It is a tale of violence, war, and love, blood and thunder on the Spanish soil; it combines the romanticism and glamour of bull-fighting with the ugly realism of a civil war; it is heroic, sensational, sensual, lyrical, and honestly antifascist without going in for politics; it contains one set of characters—Castilian peasants—which deserve the cliché praise "sober in outline like an old woodcut," and another set of intellectually intriguing and exotic characters— Russian journalists and generals. It shows the inner problems of the author through his hero, the American scholar and Communist who is serving behind the Fascist lines, a true man of action, yet wrestling with his very un-Communistic, honest-to-God humanist soul. It describes the violence and horror of the Spanish War so that the reader who had been in love with a strange Spain of his own nostalgia sees all his vague imaginings assuming shape and life, and feels himself to be penetrating into the innermost recesses of the Spanish soul. It is written with an excellent technique of realism, and yet spares delicate feelings by putting the foulest oaths and obscenities in Spanish and italics (English readers may or may not look up the words in a dictionary; in any case they would not find half of them), thus noticeably reducing the amount of muckings, sons-of-bitches, and hells.

I myself was fascinated by the book and felt it to be honest in so far as it renders Hemingway's real vision. And yet I find myself awkwardly alone in the conviction that, as a novel about Spaniards and their war, it is unreal and, in the last analysis, deeply untruthful, though practically all the critics claim the contrary, whatever their objections to other aspects of the book:

You come to understand much of Spain which is not always, or even often, to be found in the histories.

202

Hemingway knows his Spain profoundly. . . . In miniature, Hemingway has written the war the Spanish were fighting.

. . . here, in his astonishingly real Spanish conversation, he has surpassed anything I have ever seen. . . . Mr. Hemingway understands the hierarchy of Spanish blasphemy, the proper place of each rococo phrase. . . . Horrifying and sickening, the story has nevertheless that theatrical variety of incidents, that primitive realism and capacity to catch every emotion that was felt by the people as a whole. . . .
The Spanish peasants who help him in his dangerous errand are superbly described. . . . All are alive and astonishingly themselves; Mr. Hemingway has never done anything better.

As a Spaniard, and one who has lived through the period of our war which provides Hemingway with his stage setting, I came point by point to the following somewhat different conclusions:

Reading *For Whom the Bell Tolls,* you will indeed come to understand some aspects of Spanish character and life, but you will misunderstand more, and more important ones at that.

Ernest Hemingway does know "his Spain." But it is precisely his intimate knowledge of this narrow section of Spain which has blinded him to a wider and deeper understanding, and made it difficult for him to "write the war we have been fighting."

Some of his Spanish conversations are perfect, but others, often of great significance for the structure of the book, are totally unSpanish. He has not mastered the intricate "hierarchy of Spanish blasphemy" (anyhow the most difficult thing for a foreigner in any language, since it is based on ancient taboos and half-conscious superstitions). He commits a series of grave linguistic-psychological mistakes in this book—such, indeed, as I have heard him commit when he joked with the orderlies in my Madrid office. Then, we grinned at his solecisms because we liked him.

Hemingway has understood the emotions which our "people as a whole" felt in the bull ring, but not those which it felt in the collective action of war and revolution.

Some of the Castilian peasants Hemingway has created are real and alive, but others are artificial or out of place. Although all are magnificently described, in none of them has he touched the roots.

Ernest Hemingway himself and his book are of such importance that I think it necessary to specify, and if I can, to prove and explain my objections. After all, they cover not only the literary picture of Spaniards and their war, but also the quality of Hemingway's creative work in this instance, and the problem of his realism as a whole.

The strength of his artistry makes fiction sound like distilled reality. The reader may well follow the lead of the critics; he may accept the book because it is a powerful work of art, and implicitly believe in the inner truthfulness of Hemingway's Spain. For purely Spanish reasons I want to fight against this danger of a spurious understanding of my people.

The book relates an episode in the Republican guerrilla warfare of May, 1937. It takes place in the Sierra of the province of Segovia, and the *guerrilleros* concerned come from a small town, or rather village, in the province of Ávila. (It is more appropriate to call these *pueblos* "villages" than "towns," as Hemingway does.) Both the provinces are a part of Old Castile.

The men from those Castilian mountain villages are dour and hard, poor and distrustful. They have grown up on a soil which the snow covers half of the year and the sun scorches the other half. They are walled up in their own narrow lives, each working hard on his meager bit of land and hunting the wild animals in the mountains. Their fierce self-defense against the hardships of their existence and of the very climate makes them shut the doors of their community against any stranger, beyond a momentary and generous hospitality. They do not allow the gypsies to stay overnight in their villages, but often chase them away with stones. They have come to hate their *señores*—all those who exploit them through money, position or power—and when they feel deceived by the highest power, their God, they turn against Him with the same ferocious resentment. They do not talk much, nor do they talk easily; their turns of speech are heavy, simple and direct, with the dignity of simplicity and of pride in their manly strength.

I think Hemingway has seen all this and striven to express it. Some of his *guerrilleros,* above all Old Anselmo and El Sordo, belong to that soil. Yet he does not know the foundations of their lives and minds. Indeed, how could he? This is a Spain he has seen but never lived. And thus he commits the fatal error of putting the men of a Sierra village under the leadership of two people from the Spain he knows thoroughly, from the world of the *toreros* and their hangers-on: Pilar, the old gypsy tart, and Pablo, the horse dealer of the bull ring.

Such a situation is utterly impossible. The men from a township in the Sierra of Ávila—from a place as primitive as Hemingway himself paints it—could never have admitted and accepted a Pilar and a Pablo as their leaders. The gypsy and the gypsified horse dealer might have lived, and even become local leaders, in one of those villages in the Sierra of Guadarrama, which Hemingway knows and which live on tourists and week-enders from Madrid; but then again, these villages could never have produced Hemingway's peasant *guerrilleros*. That is to say, the old gypsy whore from Andalusia with her lover, the horse dealer, grouped together with peasants from Old Castile constitute a glaring incongruity.

This lack of realism is, however, necessary for the pattern of Hemingway's book. It permits him to introduce, through Pilar, admirable descriptions of the people of the bull ring a quarter of a century ago. It also permits him to construct scenes of savage brutality built around Pablo, whose whole mind is drenched with the smell of the *plaza de toros* and who is capable of studied, deliberate cruelty. The scenes of the book which seem to have impressed themselves deeply on the minds of every non-Spanish reader as being barbarously realistic and true are thus the result of a purely artificial choice of dramatis personae.

When Hemingway decided not to describe a group of purely Castilian guerrilla fighters led by the most brutal and brave male among them, but to introduce the colorful gypsy woman and the bull-ring assassin, he blocked his own way to the reality of the Spanish War and Spanish violence.

Pilar relates in a painfully vivid narration what happened in the small Sierra township after the outbreak of the Rebellion. First she describes the assault on the barracks of the Guardia Civil, and this part of the tale is perfect in its realism. Just so it happened in many places throughout Spain. Then she tells how Pablo (who, as I must again emphasize, could never have become a leader in such a village in real life) organizes a monstrous and elaborate lynching of the local "fascists," with the underlying intention of involving the whole population in the same blood guilt. He organizes this lynching like one of the old village bull-baitings or *capeas*. The men are in the square, most of them in their festive clothes, all with their wineskins, and armed with flails, sticks, and knives. The doors of the Town Hall open to let out the prisoners one by one; they have to pass through the narrow space between a double line of men until they reach the edge of a cliff. The men in the lines, drunk with wine and cruelty, beat and knife their enemies to death, jeering at them the while. The bodies are thrown over the precipice. The women look on from the balconies, and in the end are shamefully drunk with blood and bestiality, just like the men.

Now, it happened in countless small towns and villages that un-

derfed peasants and laborers killed the local *señores* who had
starved them for years and sneered at them: "Let the Republic
feed you!" At first, there was almost everywhere some man or
other, more savage than the rest, who wanted to lynch the "fascists"
and shouted: "Let's tear their guts out!"—guts being a euphemism
in place of which Hemingway uses the crude Spanish word in
italics. Then two or three of the most hated men would be killed
in the streets, brutally, in an outbreak of blind fury; but there was
no deliberate torture. The others were shot at night on the threshing
floors in the open fields where the women could not see it, nor even
hear the shots. They were killed, and then they were buried. Often
those who had killed in revenge were naïve enough to give their
victims a burial in the cemetery so that they should rest "in hal-
lowed ground."

Hemingway must have sensed this. He had to invent his Pablo,
the crafty, potential murderer, accustomed to seeing horses slit
open in the bull ring, in order to stage-manage this collective blood
orgy. Yet even if a Pablo could possibly have organized such a
lynching, it is unthinkable that the community of a Castilian village
would have followed him to the end of the revolting butchery, and
not sooner have lynched Pablo himself. It is even more unthinkable
that the butcher could have remained the leader of honest men who
became guerrilla fighters because of their own convictions.

The brutal violence of Spaniards, which exists together with a
dark acceptance of life and death, is always individual. It draws
strength and pride from a very simple awareness of their own masculinity. In the explosion of that stored-up violence people would
agree to kill their enemies, to kill them quickly with a straight
bullet or a straight knife, without investigation or trial. Nobody—
except of course the few with diseased brains who must have
existed—thought, or could have thought, of organizing slaughter
like a *fiesta* and of putting on festive clothes to get drunk on blood.
In those village bullfights which Hemingway describes through the
daydreaming of his young *guerrillero* Andrés, the people would
finish up intoxicated with mass cruelty; yet there is still a profound
difference. Even if those *capeas* were nothing other than collective
killings, the killing was not that of a tame cow but of a wild bull.
Brutal, yes; but demanding personal bravery and the risk to life
and limb from every individual. Thousands of young men have
died in *capeas*. But if instead of the "bull of death" a milch cow
had been put in the middle of the village square, nobody would
have touched her, because a thing like that *no tiene gracia,* it would

have held no attraction. The *gracia* does not consist in killing the bull, but in knowing that he can kill you. Everything else would destroy your claim to manliness.

Hemingway has forgotten this when he describes the collective killing of defenseless enemies in a bull-ring atmosphere. And yet, this is the kind of violence the common reader would be apt to expect from Spaniards; the supreme skill of the narration makes it seem stark reality. To me, that is the worst aspect of Hemingway's fundamental mistake: he falsifies most plausibly the causes and the actual form of the tragic violence of my people—not knowing that he falsifies it, because much of what he describes does exist in the Spain of the bull ring, the Spain he understands and seeks to find in every Spaniard.

The chain of errors prolongs itself, always springing from the same main source. Hemingway balances this story of a Republican atrocity with equally realistic-sounding and equally false stories of Fascist atrocities. Again, the most important incident is one of collective violence. The heroine, Maria, has been violated by a group of Fascists, and she tells her lover about it.

At the beginning of the Civil War, Franco's Moorish soldiers committed rape. I myself knew of concrete cases. Afterwards the Spanish Fascist officers did their best to put an end to these outrages, although they themselves went on committing other forms of brutality inherent in civil war and fascist mentality. I have never heard of a collective violation by Falangists, and I do not believe it ever happened. Such a thing is contrary to Spanish psychology.[1] I want to make it quite clear that I do not deny the potential and actual bestiality of Spaniards, but I do deny the psychological possibility of a collective sexual act. The consciousness of his own virility would make it impossible for a Spaniard to want the union of his body with that of a woman still warm and moist from another male. He would loathe it physically. Again, Hemingway describes most vividly what is intrinsically wrong;

[1] While I was translating this passage into English, in 1941, A.B. said to me that the sordid fact of queues in cheap brothels, for instance in the rearguard, did not seem to him a contradiction to his thesis, because there, sexual hunger had become a blinding elemental force. He also mentioned the case of collective rape described by the novelist Pérez de Ayala. A.B. admitted the existence of such explosions by a group of Spaniards whose dammed-up hatred and sexuality found no other outlet, but he considered them psychopathological extremes, while the episode told by Hemingway was meant to be something "normal" in spite of the abnormal circumstances. (ILSA BAREA.)

again, he is wrong because he fails to understand the individual quality of Spanish violence. Since these are the crucial parts of his psychological pattern, his whole picture of the Spaniards at war is distorted and unreal.

There is, however, another group scene which is magnificent in psychology and detail. The *guerrilleros* feel that Pablo is about to turn traitor, and try to provoke him to a step which would justify killing him. Although they believe his death to be necessary for their common good, they do not attack him together and finish him off, which would be easy; they stage a discussion that proceeds from insult to insult, true to life in its ceremonial violence, and try to incite Pablo to challenge one of them. That one would then be ready to kill him face to face. He would be ready to stab the bull —if the bull accepts the fight.

There are other Spanish scenes and characters which are excellently observed. The old man Anselmo, with his grave problems of life and death, is completely genuine. The Fascist officers are real, although their actions are artificially constructed. Everything connected with the world of the bullfight is vivid and essentially truthful. El Sordo, the peasant leader of another guerrilla band operating near Pablo's, is as much in the right place as Pablo is in the wrong. As far as he is described in his brief appearances, he is typical of his kind: primitive, harsh, straight, and ingenuous, continuing to live and fight though he knows that the future holds no hope. In the end he dies with a simple, brutal, and unsentimental dignity: he dies, killing.

But even the genuine characters are curiously detached from their background. One never quite knows why they fight for the Republic; one only feels their stoic loyalty. There is no growth and no future in them. And yet it had been precisely their hope and belief in a constructive future which had set the Spanish laborers and peasants in motion.

Less relevant for Hemingway's treatment of the Spanish War, but interesting in view of his conception of the Spanish character, is the fact that the love story between the young American, Robert Jordan, and Maria is pure romancing, at least in so far as the Spanish girl is concerned. I cannot judge—for I cannot feel and associate in English—whether the love scenes are convincing. They may be good writing, though they do not seem so to me. They are certainly unrealistic in their psychology of the female partner.

A Spanish girl of the rural middle class is steeped in a tradition in which influences from the Moorish harem and the Catholic convent mix. She could not ask a stranger, a foreigner, to let her come into his bed the very first night after they had met. This, however, is what Maria does. She could not do it *and* keep the respectful adoration of the members of her guerrilla group who know the history of her violation. They would call her a bitch in heat, not because she sleeps with a foreigner, but because she offers herself to him at once without even having been asked by him. Maria's ignorance of kissing and love is another impossible fiction. Such mental innocence may be found in other layers of Spanish society, among girls who had no other contact with life but their father confessor and the Holy Sisters of their convent school. In this, the most unreal character of the book, there is also a particularly marked discrepancy between social background and excessively lyrical language. This belongs, however, to the general question of the language used by the Spaniards throughout the book.

It is here that the artificiality of Hemingway's Spain and the gaps in his actual knowledge of the Spanish mind show themselves most clearly. The Castilian peasants speak forcefully and simply. Their language can be austere, it can express a somber kind of hilarity. They often cover their resistance to expressing their own more complicated emotions by fierce blasphemy. All this has been said often, and Hemingway knows it. But when it comes to rendering the dignity and sobriety of their speech, he invents an artificial and pompous English which contains many un-English words and constructions, most of which cannot even be admitted as literal translations of the original Spanish. To prove this would require much space and would sound merely pedantic, but I want to give an example:

Agustín says: "Also I have a boredom in these mountains." (Hemingway-Jordan had commented on the fact that Spanish peasants use the abstract word *aburrimiento,* boredom; in reality, they hardly ever use it.) In such a case, the Castilian peasant would quite simply say: *"Además me aburro en estas montañas,"* or *"Estas montañas me aburren,"* of which the English equivalents are: "Also, I'm bored in these mountains," or "These mountains bore me."

The curious translation, which is no real translation, wants to impress on the reader the abstract quality of the peasant's speech. Yet it is precisely characteristic of the Castilian of the people that it shuns abstract nouns and rather expresses the abstract idea as personified concrete action, such as "the mountains bore me." Hemingway continually sins against this spirit of the language in both the choice of words and the structure of the phrases in his dialogues between Spaniards. It seems to me that poise and simplicity of language should be rendered by equally poised, simple, and natural language. The quality of dignity must flow out of directness, not out of hollow and artificial solemnity. I resent Spaniards in a serious book speaking like Don Adriano de Armado, the "fantastical Spaniard" of *Love's Labour's Lost*. As a writer, I would be unhappy if Spanish dialogue I had written were to be translated into something as affected and artificial as: "I encounter it to be perfectly normal," when all I had said in Spanish was: *Lo encuentro perfectamente normal*—"I find it perfectly normal"; or into: "You have terminated already?" when I have said: *¿Habéis terminado ya?*—"Have you finished already?"

Now, this matter of the treatment of idiomatic speech in a translation is most difficult, in any language. Yet Hemingway's solution, which sounds like utter realism, is in point of fact the very contrary. It makes the understanding of shades almost impossible to any reader who does not know Spanish, and it removes the Castilian figures to a plane of unreality where strange phrases and strange psychology run riot. The fact that genuine Spanish swearwords and idioms are copiously scattered all over the pages only adds to this unreality.

The erroneous use of blasphemy and obscene language reveals very neatly how Hemingway has failed to grasp certain subtleties of Spanish language and psychology. Instead of a long list I will give two instances, among the most striking in the book:

Robert Jordan constantly addresses Maria as "rabbit," in both English and Spanish, in intimacy and in public. Now, the Spanish word happens to be one of the more frequent and vulgar euphemisms for the female sexual organ. Jordan is described as knowing all the intricacies of Spanish double meanings. Had he really addressed his girl like this in public, it would have provoked a truly Rabelaisian outburst.

The other instance derives from a deeper misunderstanding. One of the *guerrilleros* asks Robert about Maria: "How is she in bed?" Another, who himself loves Maria and explains to Robert that she is no whore just because she slept with him, says: "And thy care is to *joder* with her all night?"

It is strictly impossible for a Spaniard to ask another man how his wife or lover is "in bed." It would break a taboo which is only lifted in the case of prostitutes. No Spaniard would use the word *joder*: the ugliest verb for the sexual act, and one which expresses not the joy but the nausea of sexual union, about a woman he respects and whom the other man loves. It would inevitably provoke a fight. But Hemingway-Jordan discusses the matter serenely, Jordan unaware that he has lost face by accepting an insult, Hemingway unaware that the use of the word by Agustín and its acceptance by Jordan gives away the fact that his own real knowledge of Spaniards is still confined to the world of *Death in the Afternoon*.

When Hemingway came to Madrid in early spring 1937, he came with the apprehensions of a man who had been hurt and twisted by the Great War, and who was now voluntarily exposing himself to bombs and shells, afraid of being afraid once more and eager to share the experience of a people's struggle. He came with the apprehensions of a man who, many years before, had found an escape from his inner helplessness in the animal brutality of the world of the Spanish bull ring, after having been scarred by the disciplined and dull violence of modern warfare, and who was afraid of having lost the Spain he knew and loved.

I remember him vividly now, as I knew him in those months: big and lumbering, with the look of a worried boy on his round face, diffident and yet consciously using his diffidence as an attraction, a good fellow to drink with, fond of dirty jokes "pour épater l'Espagnol," questioning, skeptical and intelligent in his curiosity, skillfully stressing his political ignorance, easy and friendly, yet remote and somewhat sad.

I think he had once taken Spain, the Spain of *toreros,* wealthy young *señoritos,* gypsies, tarts, tipsters, and so on, rather as one takes drugs. That colorful and purposeless game with life and death which followed rigid and ancient rules must have responded to some inner need of his. He wrote what to my knowledge is the best book on the bull ring, *Death in the Afternoon*. When he came back to Spain into our war, tired of describing and observing the flabby violence of American gangsterdom, he found few traces of the world he knew. The great *toreros* with whom he had been friends were on the side of the Fascists. The gypsies had lost their market and had disappeared, many of them to the trenches.

Hemingway mixed with the soldiers in the bars more than with the pretentious left-wing intellectuals. He made many friends, as one makes friends drinking and joking together. Yet he lived the somewhat unreal life of a war correspondent in the shell-pitted Hotel Florida, among foreign journalists, officers of the International Brigades on leave, and a motley crowd of tourists and tarts.

He could speak well with Spaniards, but he never shared their lives, neither in Madrid, nor in the trenches. The commander of the International Brigades, a man who appeared to us Spaniards the epitome of ugly Prussianism, explained to him the strategic and tactical details of the battle of Madrid and the battle of Guadalajara. Kolzov, the correspondent of *Pravda,* gave him his cynical but shrewd explanations of life behind the scenes. Hemingway had access to the strictly guarded world of the Hotel Gaylord and he came to know its inmates, the Russians and the International Communist functionaries. And he admired them, secretly skeptical, and yet with a naïve longing to share their facility of decision. He must have had a bad conscience because he could become part neither of the Spanish fight, nor of that other political fight which seemed so clear-cut to those Russians and Communists.

In *For Whom the Bell Tolls,* there is the sublimation of all those experiences. The world of the Hotel Gaylord is evoked with an astonishing accuracy of detail; the non-Spanish figures of the book are all lifelike portraits, some under their real names, such as the disastrous André Marty; others, like Kolzov, slightly idealized and thinly disguised. What Hemingway did not do but would have liked to be capable of doing, and what he actually felt, is mirrored in his hero, Robert Jordan, who is left dying at the end of the book, not so much because the inner necessity of the tale demands it, as because Ernest Hemingway could not really believe in his future.

And then there is Spain. Hemingway could describe with truthfulness and art what he had seen from without, but he wanted to describe more. He wished for a share in the Spanish struggle. Not sharing the beliefs, the life, and the suffering of the Spaniards, he could only shape them in his imagination after the image of the Spain he knew. His old obsession with violence pushed him into a track which only led him still further away from a share in that new and still chaotic Spanish life.

Thus the inner failure of Hemingway's novel—its failure to render the reality of the Spanish War in imaginative writing—seems to me to stem from the fact that he was always a spectator who wanted to be an actor and who wanted to write as if he were an actor. Yet it is not enough to look on: to write truthfully you must live, and you must feel what you are living.

Arturo Barea

Translated from the Spanish by Ilsa Barea

HORST OPPEL

Hemingway's *Across the River and into the Trees*

Showing surprising unanimity, the critics have left no doubt that Ernest Hemingway's *For Whom the Bell Tolls* (1940) is the most impressive proof of his narrative skill to date. Compared with this great novel of the Spanish Civil War, all previous creations of Hemingway's pen look technically inferior. With it the author again proved his mastery of an unmistakable, individual style. Moreover, this novel revealed a new Hemingway to us. This new Hemingway is no longer so hopelessly possessed by the skepticism and cynicism that mark the early works—in particular *The Sun Also Rises, Men Without Women, A Farewell to Arms* and *Death in the Afternoon*. Joseph Warren Beach in his well-known book *American Fiction 1920 to 1940*,[1] referring to *For Whom the Bell Tolls*, expressed this somewhat differently. This novel, he says,

is the largest in scope, the most accomplished in technique, and the strongest in effect of anything he has written. And it demonstrates that he did indeed have something to say, something positive and tonic, which he had never said before, certainly not with the explicitness and power of the present statement.

To characterize more closely this turn to the positive which we believe can be found in *For Whom the Bell Tolls*, the following might be tentatively said: Whereas previously the life of Hemingway's characters was marked by inner emptiness and utter lack of meaning, only temporarily alleviated by intoxication and a blind lust for life, now for the first time we see that Hemingway recognizes some sort of hierarchy of ethical values. In *For Whom the Bell Tolls* fear and anxiety before nothingness are at least temporarily pushed into the background. The conflict of moral interests is no longer one-sidedly resolved in favor of "the easy life" without responsibility. Here there is at least an indication of situations in which the individual as such has become unimportant because he is caught up in the community spirit. Discipline and duty

[1] New York, 1942, p. 69.

213

are no longer felt to be restraints on the individual's freedom and search for pleasure but rather as means of tying together the community, so that each individual who accepts these restraints experiences an increase in strength and security. Confidence breaks that isolation which had previously enveloped man and kept him from contact with a responsive "other person." Finally, there grows out of this soil a new sense of human dignity, revealed in devotion to others and symbolized in the conscious acceptance of sacrifice.[2]

Was this then a decisive and lasting turn in Hemingway's philosophy and view of life? Had this writer once and for all discarded nihilism and replaced it with a new faith?

This question remained long unanswered. Hemingway was silent for ten years. Only with *Across the River and into the Trees* (1950) do we have a frame of reference and a standard of comparison. From the critic's point of view there is therefore much at stake. To begin with, this new novel would decide whether Hemingway had continued to develop in the direction indicated by *For Whom the Bell Tolls*. However, it cannot be said that the expectations of the critics were fulfilled by *Across the River and into the Trees*. There was general disappointment. A few examples will suffice.

Helmut Papajewski, who gave us an erudite and reliable outline of Hemingway's development,[3] sees the author of *Across the River* as one who has retreated to "his old way of proclaiming clichés." This critic says:

The main characters remind us too much of the characters of several earlier works which were created out of an original situation and still tied to his special presentation and analysis of existence, as for example in *A Farewell to Arms* or *The Sun Also Rises*. But these newer characters do not come to life. The lack of originality in their presentation and their dependence on imitation make the characters shadowy. Their speech is distinguished by a poverty of ideas and by linguistic barrenness. What was once a conscious reduction to the simplicity of a realizable experience has become pseudo-primitivism. Action is practically nonexistent and at times . . . becomes merely a flat shifting of scenes.

Papajewski even asks the question whether this novel should not be considered symptomatic of the decay of a whole literary trend,

---

[2] Cf. the words of Robert Jordan (*For Whom the Bell Tolls*, New York, 1945, Chas. Scribner's Sons, p. 466): "You can do nothing for yourself but perhaps you can do something for another."

[3] "The Question of Meaningfulness in Hemingway" (*Anglia*, Vol. 70, 1951, pp. 186-200).

the modern American novel of "life-analysis" (*Existenzanalyse*), which proclaims with its pale repetitiveness and its return to previous concepts that its technique leads into a "sort of dead end." Helmut Uhlig[4] is also of the opinion that Hemingway returned with *Across the River* to the world of *The Sun Also Rises*.

An unrestrained glorification of impulsive living, sensuality, strength, and bravery in the face of death characterizes this bizarre novel with which Hemingway has returned to the anti-intellectual and antihumanitarian direction of his early works.

Uhlig therefore speaks of a "development opposed to that of Faulkner." In Faulkner's novel *Intruder in the Dust* (1949) the gloom of desperation begins to lift, whereas Hemingway's *Across the River* bears the stamp of its author's "hostility to civilization."

Similarly, Henry Lüdeke[5] regards the novel written in 1950 as an artistic step backward compared with *For Whom the Bell Tolls*. With it Hemingway "returned to a quiet, contemplative, almost tedious tone and extremely flat language." He thinks the writer's attempt to "build a character from the inside out" has failed. Lüdeke ends with this passage: "In the face of this new turn in his art final judgment about Hemingway must be suspended."

Let us summarize. Criticism of *Across the River* concerns the full scope of the work and deals also with the author's attitude toward life. The most important objections are these: lack of originality, poverty of ideas, barren language, pseudo-primitivism, shifting of scenes instead of development of action, glorification of sensuous living, antihumanitarian viewpoint, poor characterizations. Let us now turn to the novel itself.

The first thing that strikes us in reading it is that the action itself is quite unimportant. The content could be given in a few lines, a sort of "argument," an introduction to the book, as was done in Renaissance drama or the Baroque novel. Curiously enough, this does not impair the reader's pleasure. Obviously it is essential to this form of narrative that it should barely deal with the development of plot. This is fundamentally different from the technique Hemingway used in his previous novels. In these he was never willing to forgo suspense as a stimulus to the reader.

The content may be described as follows: we learn of the thoughts and reminiscences of a fifty-one-year-old American colo-

[4] "Amerikanische Literatur" in *Amerikakunde* (2nd edition, Frankfurt a.M., 1952), p. 424.

[5] *Geschichte der amarikanischen Literatur*, Bern, 1952, p. 516.

nel during a hunting trip in the Venetian marshes and in the course of his relationship with nineteen-year-old Contessa Renata in Venice—all this compressed into the last two days of his life. The presentation is confined to a series of scenes, consciously arranged in dialectic order.

Not only is the dramatic content sparse but we are also disappointed in the expectation that characterization and character development compensate for this failing. Colonel Richard Cantwell is merely a type. He barely has a face of his own; his name strikes one as casual also. He stands as a symbol of all who had to suffer two world wars. Or rather of all those whose entire life—to the exclusion of anything else—was filled with two world wars. Contessa Renata as well remains merely a prototype of the beloved, without expectations and demands, without the vitality of personal life, without the unmistakable tension of a personality and environment of her own. But she has that unlimited ability for giving which is so characteristic of Hemingway's fictional women.

In regard to the narrative style one must speak of a conscious and willfully selected barrenness. Nowhere is there any indication of explicit characterization. There are simply no other figures who might serve to clarify for the reader the nature of the main characters. Hemingway also spurns the frequently used device of arousing our interest and helping us to form an opinion of our own by having other characters offer contradictory or purposely faulty judgments of the heroes. Galsworthy, in drawing Irene Forsyte, created a three-dimensional character in this manner. Hemingway, however, limits himself to the absolutely essential. Only occasionally is there any indirect characterization of the heroes through words and action. Nothing unusual or new happens in the last two days of life granted the Colonel. He has no opportunity to distinguish himself in any way or to reveal any shortcomings. What he says remains totally beside the point. Mostly, he speaks in stereotyped phrases. He is little more than a phonograph record, sputtering forth out of that poor supply of words which five decades of living have left him.

Here it becomes necessary to interrupt our analysis and remember that Hemingway never claimed to be creating "characters." In his *Death in the Afternoon* Hemingway stressed: "A writer should create living people; people not characters." [6] This axiom is based on the conviction that "character" in the usual literary sense is an abstraction and a retreat from the immediacy and fullness of life.

[6] *Death in the Afternoon* (New York, 1932), p. 191.

Life grants us human beings a confusing variety of characteristics which must be artificially ordered and arranged to create them into a "character." John Dos Passos thought in a similar vein when he prefaced each chapter of his *Number One* (1944) with a free-verse section which ends in this refrain: "The people are the republic, the people are you." Obviously both writers, in substituting the word "people" for "character," wish to indicate at once that in their work the individual fate is to be understood as typical of the collective fate.

In *Across the River* Hemingway remained true to this concept of style. The Colonel and his young mistress move before us as "people," not "characters." But there are many other indications that the author has no intention of giving up his proven technique. This novel can almost serve as an example of Hemingway's distinctive literary approach.[7] Conversation dominates the narrative; the narrator, who refuses to become involved in explanations and interpretation, remains strictly in the background; there is no broadly drawn portrayal of the social, political, and moral conditions with which his heroes have to deal. And these heroes themselves, true to Hemingway's usual concept of human life, are given over to total passivity and senseless drift. There are yet more parallels to earlier works. Richard Cantwell, too, experiences the challenge of "facing death" which Hemingway regards as the most difficult of all human situations. One can hardly go wrong in assuming that in Hemingway's own experience "facing death" has a central place and can therefore be considered the basic theme of his creative effort. He expressed it in a most penetrating way in his *Death in the Afternoon* in the study of the bullfighters who constantly live in the presence of "violent death."

Thus, at first glance, *Across the River* seems to be actually no more than a repetition of stylistic forms and means of expression long familiar to us in Hemingway—forms which he seemed to have at least temporarily transcended in *For Whom the Bell Tolls*. Is it then nothing more than a retreat to old techniques and a confirmation of his earlier complete skepticism and sarcasm?

Actually, the challenge of "facing death" which is posed for Colonel Richard Cantwell differs from that of most Hemingway characters. It is a deep, inner challenge. The form of the threat is utterly altered. The death Cantwell faces is not forced upon him violently from the outside. Such was the case with the bullfighters

[7] Cf. the list of characteristics of Hemingway's style in the essay by H. Papajewski, *op. cit.*

and big-game hunters of Hemingway's earlier works, who through "living every day with death" found their own standards and attitudes toward world and people. An external danger of this kind would certainly hold few terrors for Cantwell, a soldier of thirty years' experience. Precisely because of that experience he is less prepared and armed against a softly approaching death. With courage, skill, and a little luck a man may escape a death which threatens him with external violence. But for Cantwell that possibility of escape no longer exists. When the body refuses, even a steady spirit and unbroken courage are of no avail. For Cantwell, life simply comes to an end because his spent organism refuses him further service. His body has become a rebel not subject to any discipline prescribed by the Army manual. Cantwell's last physical examination has left no doubt that another heart attack, after three preceding ones, will mean the end of his life. Cantwell is "going to die" (p. 137).[8] He is helpless against the need expressed by his beloved in her question: "Will you do your best not to die?" (p. 79). Cantwell can affirm this will to live, but he knows that he cannot affect the outcome in the least: "I know where I'm going" (p. 252).

Clearly, Colonel Richard Cantwell stands under the signs of waning life. He can no longer deny that he is "getting slow" (p. 36). He takes notice of this fact in the manner of the bullfighters and big-game hunters, for whom "getting slow" means a heightened danger. For Cantwell, of course, such considerations are meaningless. He will never again have a chance to initiate his own destruction through "slowness" on some battlefield or other. Death has moved so incredibly close to him that all his capabilities and appropriate attitudes are now beside the point. This kind of death, if it gives any warning at all, confines itself to a gentle but unmistakable shifting of perspective: "the distances are all changed" (p. 14). But that does not at all mean that everything that has meaning in Cantwell's life has been removed at one blow. As yet he has not lost his "old wild-boar truculence" (p. 62). He still lives by the old magic of the soldier's life and holds on to his questionable values, which, despite their frailty, are passionately felt and affirmative. Thus he must ask himself: ". . . why can I not suspend this trade of arms and be a kind and good man as I would have wished to be. . . . I should be a better man with less wild-boar blood in the small time which remains" (p. 57).

[8] All quotations from *Across the River* here and elsewhere [in this essay] are from the edition of Jonathan Cape, London, 1950.

Here again one may speak of a paralysis of the will, a tendency to push things aside, which has always been present in Hemingway's characters. They all avoid thinking about their attitudes and pondering their actions seriously. Despite all self-criticism, Cantwell, in these final days of his life, makes no move whatever to become aware of the hopeless void within him, nor does he seek a cure. He is satisfied to keep the small space of time he has left as free as possible from worry and harm. This explains his frequent admonitions to himself: "don't let him spoil it (p. 9)" or "keep your temper" or "I must not let him ruin it" (p. 10). He resolutely pushes aside anything which might throw even a slight shadow on his last meeting with the Contessa or on the hunting trip to the Venetian marshes. The ability to make the best of every situation, a skill he learned as a soldier, now triumphs for the last time. But this, too, is only a form of hedonism and does not represent an ethical or religious change in the face of death; it is neither a stoicism based on ethical convictions nor the peace of mind of a believer. Cantwell gives even less thought to questioning or improving his relations with his fellow men. In this respect he thinks he has done a great deal when he comes to the decision to "try to be kind" (p. 123). Neither can he be bothered with regretting his life with all its hardships, failings, and errors. He knows nothing of "remorse" or "bad dreams" (p. 105). Of course, with the lowering of vitality he, too, has to experience the first stirrings of insecurity, which deeply trouble his usually clear mind. There seems to be no escape for him—"in his wrath and his agony and his need for confidence" (p. 168)—out of this state of confusion. The obscenities and cynical jokes with which he tries to relieve himself occasionally become more forced and stiff without bringing him relief or consolation. There is, for him, no refuge in prayer. Thus, with his last strength, he clings to a love relationship of such intensity and artificially stimulated complexity that it demands all his inner resources and helps him to ignore reality. But the fact that Cantwell must surrender to a "violent death" remains as terrible as ever despite his efforts to ignore it.

Up to this point the conclusions drawn from Hemingway's total production seem confirmed: this author one-sidedly emphasizes the enjoyment of life and puts his heroes under the spell of a determinism which simply makes it impossible for them to change themselves or their lives. Unquestioning acceptance of a preordained fate seems to be the only answer he considers proper to the great mystery of existence.

However, we have not finished our analysis of *Across the River*. Beside Richard Cantwell there stands his beloved, Contessa Renata. In her relationship with this man marked by death Renata uses all her young strength toward one purpose—to change his seemingly inevitable "violent death" into a "happy death." As she expresses it: "Don't you know I want you to die with the grace of a happy death?" (p. 200). Here is something totally new in Hemingway's world. One is reminded of Robert Jordan in *For Whom the Bell Tolls*, who, in the face of death, comes to terms with his life in these words: "You have had much luck. There are many worse things than this." [9] However, the "good life" Jordan thinks of in dying is no more than the grateful acceptance that it could have been worse and that his portion of pleasure was worth the price. In *Across the River* the change from a "violent death" to a "happy death" functions on another level. More of this later.

Renata comes from one of the best and wealthiest families of the Venetian nobility. She is equipped for the task she has set herself with that naïve, unquestioning security which comes from an old and noble tradition. Despite her decision to live a life of her own, she remains within the traditional pattern of her Catholic faith. It is true that going to mass and caring for the poor have become only an empty gesture for her. But deep down, almost against her consciousness and will, she lives in a world of religious concepts. This holds to such an extent that, in her dream, the injured hand of her lover becomes the hand of the Saviour. Buttressed by the security of her own life, she fights the self-destructive scorn of all human values which Cantwell, in his bitterness, tends to express. "Don't be rough," she often urges, trying to save him from his rotten cynicism. She knows what he needs at the end of his life: "castigation" and "purgation." Not in the form of the sacrament, however. For Cantwell it cannot even be a sort of moral settling of accounts. Renata senses with unfailing instinct that for him "castigation" is only possible on his own terms. In these terms, and only in these terms, Cantwell has already experienced something of the mystery of "castigation" for himself: "He only loved people, he thought, who had fought or been mutilated. . . . You only felt true tenderness and love for those who had been there and had received the castigation that everyone receives who goes there long enough" (p. 62). Renata tries to lead the lonely and embittered man, who remains untouched by all ethical and religious values, back to this level. It is only here, if at all, that the trans-

[9] *For Whom the Bell Tolls*, p. 466.

muting power of confession and recognition can be proved to Cantwell. Therefore she urges him frequently: "Tell me about the last
war" (p. 113) or "Please tell me about combat without being too
brutal" (p. 203). Reluctantly, Cantwell starts to reveal something
of his "sad science" (p. 114), which he considers "disheartening
as hell" (p. 116). But Renata uses the most varied reasons and
excuses to keep him at it: "Will you tell me . . . some more of
war for my education?" (p. 181). Cantwell obeys. Granting her
wish, he unexpectedly finds something happening within himself
that he never before believed possible: "he was not lecturing; he
was confessing" (p. 186). With the reserve of a man who has never
in his life felt the need of such "purgation" Cantwell still resists:
"I don't need to purge" (p. 188). But Renata has a new and
irresistible argument: what he tells her ceases to be his personal
property and belongs to her also, tying them more closely together
—"Then we can share it" (p. 192). Gradually Cantwell experiences the solace that comes from his confession. Thus his sweetheart can finally ask him: "Don't you see you need to tell me
things to purge your bitterness?" (p. 200).

It certainly emphasizes the skill of Hemingway as a narrator
that the actual description of the horrors of war in *Across the
River* has been moved into the realm of quiet conversation. In order to assure that the confession of a man about to die retain the
dignity of a soliloquy overheard by no one, Hemingway makes
use of a perfectly simple device—Renata has fallen asleep at the
side of her lover. Thus he can state: "The Colonel told her all
about it; but he did not utter it" (p. 205). And elsewhere: "Then
he looked at the girl, to see that she was sleeping well enough so
even his thoughts would not hurt her (p. 211)." These thoughts
cannot hurt her, but they must be thought through if Cantwell is
to get rid of them and die at peace with himself.

Let us then summarize what the act of "castigation" and "purgation" means in this novel. We already know that it cannot be a
question of settling moral accounts or gaining absolution in the
religious sense. The process is simple enough; the thought of "retri-
bution" and "punishment" is not introduced at all. Cantwell tells
of his war experiences. But what was real and factual in his account
loses its oppressive reality as soon as it becomes conscious. The
dark, threatening terror of what has never before been spoken or
even thought through gradually disappears. We would venture to
say that Hemingway has here transformed an experience into art
which, in the more abstract language of philosophy, is termed a

"basic paradox of our existence," namely "to be able to transcend
the world only within the world." [10] Renata commends the Colonel
to his world. Only by fully experiencing this world can he hope to
transcend it. In the earlier works of Hemingway we always meet
people who cannot muster the activity and concentration necessary
in order to enter a state of contemplation. Here the American
Colonel is forced by his beloved to overcome his lazy thinking.
". . . I will think about it and get rid of it . . ." (p. 213). In this
way only can he receive what he needs most—the inner freedom
which will turn a "violent death" into a "happy death."

Moreover, through the power of "castigation" the problem of
"facing death" has turned into the problem of "facing life" for
Richard Cantwell. This is not to be understood in the sense that
the Colonel suddenly, in the face of death, is granted a philosophical or metaphysical view which has been denied him up to then.
Even now Hemingway's creatures remain without faith in immortality (p. 110), without mystery (p. 131), and especially
without belief in salvation. Still, something essential has been gained
when Cantwell in the course of his confession is able to shed the
bitterness he has accumulated in a lifetime. Facing the final consequences, he learns at least to find the proper proportion for his
life within the universal experience. In the silent conversation
with his sleeping mistress he frees himself from the constant preoccupation with his ego—self-centeredness. Cantwell speaks of
the enormous events of the war. What he puts into words is no
longer tied to his own joys and pains, his successes and failures, his
gratifications and disappointments. Now he speaks of the suffering
of the world.

For Whom the Bell Tolls raises the thought of collective absolution,[11] whereas Across the River depicts the absolution of an individual. Of course Cantwell on his own is not capable of accom-
plishing this; he needs to be tied to the "you," to the beloved. But
this is not a matter of a purely erotic relationship. Cantwell does
not drunkenly lose himself in the "you" so as to be freed at least
temporarily from the agony of his own consciousness. No, this
relationship is capable of breaking through the terror of the "ego"

---

[10] Karl Jaspers, *Vom Ursprung und Ziel der Geschichte,* Zurich, 1949.
[11] Cf. the words of Anselmo: "I think that after the war there will have
to be some great penance done for the killing. If we no longer have religion
after the war I think there must be some form of civic penance organized
that all may be cleansed from the killing or else we will never have a true
and human basis for living" (p. 196).

and elevating his consciousness to a level where it touches upon and is soothed by the eternal mystery of existence. With this "castigation" Cantwell finally opens his eyes to the world of unreserved love, of shame and honor, a world which is always basically threatened by the millstones of the ambivalent "ego."

It is remarkable that with all this Hemingway does not anywhere falsify the life and character of Colonel Richard Cantwell. He remains bound to the end to his inner law. It is true that the background of Italian culture and landscape adds a richness of color and images which does not necessarily fit in with Cantwell. At times there are references to the great painters of the Renaissance, the masters of European music, the language and visionary power of Dante. As Cantwell projects from his own experience the enormous agony of the world there is a Dantesque touch to it all: "You sound like Dante"—"I am Mister Dante. For the moment" (p. 204). Then there are verses by Whitman woven into the scene: "When lilacs last in the dooryard bloomed." T. S. Eliot is also represented with fragments of *The Waste Land*. All this reveals a human potential in Cantwell which his life has not permitted him to realize. Again the basic determinism in Hemingway's world view is revealed—the hero remains bound to the special premises of his vision, philosophy, and judgment. So that it was not a quotation from Dante, Whitman, or Eliot which furnished the title of this work, but one from General Thomas J. Jackson, popularly known as Stonewall Jackson, who at his death reputedly said: "Let us cross over the river and rest under the shade of the trees" (p. 253).

The literary value of Hemingway's *Across the River* lies in the subordinate themes, which, flowing from various directions, help highlight and emphasize the significance of certain phenomena, in this case especially that of "purgation." In the way he treats this subject Hemingway differentiates himself markedly from all other Anglo-American authors of the present day.

This type of "purgation" is not to be confused with the confession of the soul of neo-Catholic authors such as Graham Greene and Evelyn Waugh. To these writers even the worst sinner is equipped with the knowledge that he is still within reach of the eye and hand of God.[12] As these authors see it, salvation in any form is based on two premises which they consider basic to human existence and not in need of special emphasis: for one, the Christian

[12] Cf. H. Oppel, "Englische Erzählkunst: Zwischen Chaos und Erlösung" (*Die lebenden Fremdspr.*, 1951, p. 100ff.).

concept of guilt; for another, "the appalling strangeness of the mercy of God" (*Brighton Rock*). In contrast, Hemingway stakes everything on being able to get along without a final significant and significance-giving principle to explain the metaphysical.

Therefore Hemingway cannot (like Aldous Huxley in his books since *Eyeless in Gaza* and W. Somerset Maugham in *The Razor's Edge*) introduce Far-Eastern mysticism to prompt the soul-searching which will bring man to the longed-for rest and salvation— "calmness, forbearance, compassion, selflessness, continence." For Hemingway the world remains "a good place to buy in." [13] At least until such time as man can arrange not to pay too dearly for his pleasures. Behind such a viewpoint there is considerable optimism, arising from great energy and invincible vitality. Richard Cantwell in *Across the River* does not in the least regret the lifetime he has spent at the "sad science" of soldiering. He is satisfied with the statement: "You are not supposed to have a heart in this trade" (p. 116).

In this respect it might appear that the war story *Across the River* moves on the same level as the American war stories by Norman Mailer (*The Naked and the Dead*) and James Jones (*From Here to Eternity*). But it must be sharply stressed that the differences are great indeed. Mailer and Jones merely lower us to an egotistical, chaotic world driven by desire. These authors accept anything that will show the total lack of dignity of this miserable creature "man"; theirs is a sneering destruction of all human values in a wicked and dark world. In Hemingway, on the other hand, even as the Calvary of mankind across the battlefields of two wars is pictured as "disheartening as hell," there is still enough joy of life to prevent it all from ending in doom and gloom. Perhaps there is not so much vitality as there is a vast pleasure with the well-nigh inexhaustible potential of our existence.

Having delineated, however sketchily, Hemingway's position compared with that of other contemporary authors, we can now try to outline in a few words his place in the total picture of contemporary American fiction. If one compares the social and political development of America in recent years with the cultural mainstream, one notices a resurgence of "hereditary concepts" as an "expression of an inherent conservatism." In literature this development is revealed by "glances in the direction of social togetherness," by a "turn toward the democratic beginnings of the nation

[13] *The Sun Also Rises* (Albatross), p. 130.

and to a collective humanism." [14] Examples of this trend may be found more readily in the books of Thornton Wilder, Thomas Wolfe, or even Dos Passos than in Hemingway. Hemingway never attempted a comprehensive portrayal of society. The idea of "collective humanism" reverberates only occasionally and distantly in his work (as sometimes in *For Whom the Bell Tolls*). In *Across the River* Hemingway remains on the whole the radical skeptic and nihilist of his early days. But we have to understand Hemingway's nihilism properly. It is typically American, interpreted for us only recently by Herman Pongs as a nihilism "which toys with all possibilities, including the nihilistic ones, and incorporates their ambivalences." [15] That explains how Hemingway, while limiting himself strictly to the concrete and knowable, can nevertheless touch upon the mystery of "purgation."

Life-analysis (*Existenzanalyse*) is here carried on with such power and intensity in the face of death that finally there rises out of the negative aspects of an impoverished and cynically self-depreciating existence a positive side, namely, the contradictory tension between vitality and the loneliness of dying from which the individual first retreats into silence only to find salvation in a new consciousness. Certainly this consciousness, for Hemingway, is not of the kind that inspires, orders, and illuminates chaos. Rather is it a consciousness which enables man to enrich his individuality, hitherto limited to experiencing and suffering without hope, through the act of purgation—by letting it experience a sharing with the "you" ("then we can share it") and an empathy with suffering mankind. This novel, conceived out of nihilistic diminution, develops genuine depth as it goes along and attains the dignity of a parable.

Obviously, therefore, we are certainly not ready to agree with the general verdict of the critics who regard Hemingway's *Across the River* as a retreat to his early cynicism and materialism. Looked at more closely, this novel refutes all the objections raised against it. Certainly it is possible to speak of "poverty of ideas" and "barrenness of language." But it is necessary to recognize that here we are dealing with a consciously developed style which effectively serves the total purpose. Here, a commonplace background of

[14] W. Fischer, "Über einige Zusammenhänge zwischen Kultur und Literatur in den Vereinigten Staaten der Gegenwart" (*Archiv. f.d. neueren Spr.*, Vol. 189, 1952, p. 3 ff., esp. p. 21 ff.).

[15] H. Pongs, "Im Umbruch der Zeit" (*Das Romanschaffen der Gegenwart*), Göttingen, 1952, p. 169.

egotism in thought and deed highlights the travail of a lonely, embittered man without religious faith, who keeps going solely because he has retained a simple core, a sense of justice, decency, and honor.

Whether Hemingway's work actually exemplifies the outer limit of the development of the American novel of "life-analysis," is another question. There is no doubt that over the past twenty-five years the concentration on individual phenomena has been developed to a point of mastery of this genre; but in the long run it had to be paid for by a stultification of literary technique.[16] Such isolation of the individual and the particular may well produce significant works, but it neglects many possibilities traditionally open to the epic form. It is surely one of the functions of great epic works to reveal man in the fullness of life (as shown in modern times by the English novels of the eighteenth century and the fiction of France, England, Russia, and Germany in the nineteenth century). Great epics, for one, make the human quality worldly by fusing the personal dislocation with the connective tissue of landscape, nature, society, history, and the like. For another, great epics make the worldly human by arranging the unordered sphere of appearances, causes, and effects around the focus of human existence in their explanation of the world. Only the dualism of this relationship eliminates the accidental and allows things to fall into their proper places. Surely, this is what makes certain epics "world literature." Can American fiction already lay claim to such distinction? Or is it at a crucial point because it has sought to compensate for a loss of creative totality with a study in depth of the creature "man"?

Horst Oppel

Translated from the German by Joseph M. Bernstein

[16] Cf. Papajewski, *op. cit.*, p. 209.

JOSEPH WARREN BEACH

How Do You Like It Now, Gentlemen?

I

With his latest novel,[1] Ernest Hemingway has caused a good deal of embarrassment to the many eminent critics and the large body of readers who have whole-heartedly admired him and defended him against all who challenged his perfection as an artist. Indeed, he has rather put his admirers on the spot. He is making it necessary for them to pass his earlier work in review in the light of his latest performance and satisfy themselves whether the faintly disagreeable odor that emanates from *Across the River and into the Trees* is an evidence of decay already present in the work they have admired so much, or simply an accidental feature of a story turned out in a moment of weakness.

The champion of Hemingway suffers under a double handicap if he has examined the self-portrait of the author exhibited by Lillian Ross in a May number of *The New Yorker*. It is painful to find that a serious artist, in the fullness of maturity and fame, can be such a boyish—and bearish—show-off, that a distinguished manipulator of words should depend so much on mere profanity for emphasis and characterization, that an experienced man of the world should be willing to expose to the world so many intimate personal secrets, or that a man who has seen so much and thought so much about life should be so shamelessly self-confident and self-absorbed. But then one reflects that the famous man may be genuinely embarrassed by what he considers the necessity for making a public appearance, that sensitiveness to criticism may have made him self-conscious, and that the crudity of his conversational style may be a defense against those who mistake veneer for culture, or culture for "life." Besides, it is a democratic tradition for the public man, when in the public eye, to be a bit easygoing in his manner of speech. And since we are all infinitely curious about the ways

[1] *Across the River and into the Trees.* New York: Charles Scribner's Sons, 1950.

and thoughts of genius, what is expected of the noted writer is that he should talk about himself.

If there is one thing that interests Mr. Hemingway more than writing it is manly sports, and nearly everything he has to say to Miss Ross is in terms of boxing, baseball, flying, or hunting. He is interested in the techniques of all these games; he is very much interested in excellent performance; and he is equally interested in the competitive aspects of a sport. In writing, he does not pretend to compete with Tolstoi, who is *hors concours*. But he does consider that he has beat Turgenev and Maupassant at their game; he has fought two draws with "Mr. Stendhal," and he thinks he has an edge in the last one. In the United States he is much concerned with "defending the title" against all comers; though he has stated elsewhere that he does not consider himself in a class with Faulkner.

There is plenty of evidence that Hemingway is a scrupulous artist, bent on turning out the best writing he is capable of. In the days before he had proved a good seller—living in a Paris attic, and serving an apprenticeship to Ezra Pound and Gertrude Stein—he turned down magazine offers that would have supported him handsomely for years. He is certainly devoted to this game for its own sake, and he does himself an injustice spreading his tail feathers even in this half-joking way. Defending the title is a proper and manly thing to do; but it is perhaps just here that the reader has a clue to what often makes him uneasy in Hemingway. In his talk, and sometimes in his writing, one is a trifle bored by the heavy emphasis laid on *virility*. We know, of course, that *virtue* is derived from the same word—signifying adult manhood. We know that virility is a very important factor in human life, and the root of many admirable qualities. The Romans and Greeks knew this, and so did the people of the Renaissance. American writers have long since made up for the neglect of this truth on the part of the Victorians. And Mr. Hemingway has borne his part in disseminating this important knowledge. It is almost time we returned to the attitudes of Chaucer and Shakespeare and Donne, who took this thing for granted and did not think it necessary to be forever shouting it from the housetops.

And this brings us to the subject of Hemingway's latest novel.

II

Across the River and into the Trees is the pathetic "Liebestod" of a certain Colonel Cantwell, who died of heart failure in an automobile while returning from a duck hunt in the marshes near Venice. Hemingway says "the book is about the command level in the Second World War." And that is true too; for the tactical errors and all-round stupidity of the generals in that war make the chief subject of conversation between Colonel Cantwell and his girl-friend while they do their eating and drinking at the Gritti Palace Hotel, and it is this conversation that occupies most of the pages of the book. The Colonel had had the rank of general, and had been demoted as a result of the stupid orders from above which resulted in the decimation of his regiment.

Colonel Cantwell is a genuine fighting man, whose most admirable trait is the purity of his devotion to the honorable and dirty "trade" of war. But he is a down-to-earth realist, as keen in the exposure of every sort of buncombe as Captain Bluntschli in *Arms and the Man*. And the loss of rank has not made him any more indulgent toward those who direct war or talk about it without any firsthand knowledge of fighting. He speaks the rough language of the soldier, which alternately shocks and fascinates his girl-friend. She is drawn to him by his honest character, his manliness, his interesting and uneven temper, by the intensity of his love for her, and perhaps even by the fact that he is more than twice her age and that his heart condition presages a short term of life. She is nineteen, very beautiful, and a contessa. He gives a dubious air of innocence to their relation by calling her "daughter." Circumstances seem to make marriage out of the question, and the Colonel prays God he may do her no harm. But the girl's love is too strong and prevails over his good intentions.

A dozen details, big and little, make it clear to one acquainted with Hemingway's career that a large part of this story is autobiographical. The duck-shooting is a transcript of many passages in his sporting life, as when, in these same Venetian marshes, he "shot two high doubles, rights and lefts in a row," and the Italian gardener "cried with emotion." There is even the ambitious journalist wife of the Colonel, and his taking of Paris in '44. (See Malcolm Cowley's "Portrait of Mr. Papa" in *Life* for January 10, 1949.) Many of the sayings of the Colonel are borrowed from other works of Hemingway ("Better to die on our feet than to live on our knees," from *For Whom the Bell Tolls;* "If you ever fight, then you must win it. That's all that counts," from Hemingway's introduction to *Men at War*). A strong head for Martinis and champagne is a phenomenon of wide occurrence. More intimate touches are the Colonel's age, his serious illness, his lameness, the early rising of the old campaigner, and the pillbox with the champagne. We are at liberty to assume that the Contessa and the adventure in the gondola are fictive; but they would fit in well with our imaginary life of Hemingway, either as actuality or as wish fulfillment. In one point there is a startling difference between the sentiments of Hemingway and Colonel Cantwell. In 1942 Hemingway was ready to sterilize all members of Nazi party organizations in order to secure the future peace of the world. In 1950 Colonel Cantwell is very fond of both Russians and Germans: "Do we have to hate the Krauts because we kill them?" But that might be simply the difference between 1942 and 1950.

It has often been noted that the hero of Hemingway's novels is always much the same person—that Jake Barnes and Frederic Henry and Robert Jordan are grown-up versions of the boy Nick Adams of *In Our Time,* who is so obviously a rendering of the boy Ernest Hemingway. Well, Colonel Cantwell is the oldest of all these avatars of Nick Adams; but one is not sure that he is actually the most adult in his attitude toward himself. And the sense of psychological regression here is one thing that makes us hesitate to rate this book among the best of his work.

Apart from incidental talk about fighting and brass hats, the action of the story consists of three things: the love-making of Renata and the Colonel, the duck-hunt on the following day, and the death of the Colonel on his way back to Venice. It is a slight ground of substance for so long a piece. This is not the serious book about the war on which Hemingway has been at work for many years. It is something thrown off in passing. Hemingway began the present work as a short story. "Then I couldn't stop it," he says. "It went on into a novel." The question is whether he would not have been wiser to stop it. The situation of the man of fifty, with a bad heart, falling in love with a beautiful young girl, and realizing that here, too, too late, is the true love of which he has always dreamed, is entirely plausible and deeply moving. The question is whether, as it stands, this subject is big enough, strong enough, for the weight he puts upon it.

For one thing, it has proved a considerable strain on his stylistic resources, which have generally been adequate to all his needs. He has seldom allowed himself so many soft, blank-check adjectives for characterizing towns or persons or feelings. The distant view of Venice was "wonderful" and "beautiful" to the Colonel as it was when he was eighteen. It was "like going to New York the first time . . . in the old days when it was shining, white and beautiful." The author is conscious that this is a trifle cliché (and not exactly "precise"), and he tries again: "We are coming into my town, he thought. *Christ, what a lovely town.*" He probably feels that the soldier's blasphemy takes the curse off the esthete's la-di-da. And he tries it again with the fishing boats. Picturesque? *"To hell with the picturesque. They are just damned beautiful."* And so, as Miss Ross would say, "that settled that."

When it comes to the sentiment of love, the old Hemingway is still harder to find. Renata "turned her head . . . and the Colonel *felt his heart turn over inside* him, as though some sleeping animal had turned over in its burrow," etc. (Cf. May Sarton, *Shadow of a Man,* p. 221: "His heart turned over inside him.") Hemingway seems to be vaguely aware that his figure of the heart turning over, though violent enough, may have lost its force through frequent use, and he tries to take off the curse of the cliché with the added vividness of the sleeping animal in its burrow. This really distracts the reader's attention altogether from the heart and supplants the mood of the lover with that of the natural historian. But Hemingway is in love with this figure and the trick to save it. At another point: "and he looked at Renata and *his heart rolled over as a porpoise* does in the sea." And then, for the instruction of those who cannot realize the mystical importance of what he is saying, he adds: "It was a beautiful movement and only a few people in the world can feel it and accomplish it." It remains somewhat dubious whether the rare and beautiful movement in question is that of the loving heart or the porpoise in the sea.

And then there is the oft-repeated assurance of the Colonel to Renata that she is his "last and true and only love," which is not quite in the Hemingway manner. Well, you may say that in his tenderness the Colonel is whimsically adapting the words of some old ballad. (For the girl is incidentally perfecting her English.) You may say that there is a spice of conscious wit in this paradox of a *last* and *only* love. You may say, if you like, that these lovers are performing a ritual, and that repetition is of the essence of all rituals. Well, yes, but the rituals of love are for lovers, and require some cutting down in transcription.

You may say that the belated discovery of true love is a tragic circumstance, not unknown in human experience, and one that may well draw our tears. Draw our tears, yes. But whether it is correct to use the word tragic in this connection depends on one's conception of tragedy. According to Aristotle tragedy is associated with an important action and one in which the character of the participants is a main determinant in the catastrophe. Hemingway does not succeed in giving this abortive love the sort of importance that Aristotle calls for and Shakespeare exemplifies. And it is not the character of Renata or the Colonel that provokes the tragedy here, but the accidental circumstance that they have met thirty years too late. It is more exact to say that this story is *pathetic,* and that the pathos is rather too much drawn out for the happiest effect.

There is one other thing that may well be disturbing to many readers whom it would be rash to dismiss as simply prudish. In the gondola ride, in his effort to persuade us of the "truth" of this love, Hemingway feels called on to emphasize the continued virility of the aged and ailing soldier. This is a ticklish undertaking, in which he runs the risk of appealing to the ribald more than to the compassionate reader. All the more so as the display of virility on the part of the Colonel is followed so closely by his death, after the related (and perhaps symbolic) display of the same quality in the duck-shooting. There is much danger here that the frivolous reader may put the love-making and the death together and, in view of the man's condition, may be as much inclined to laugh at the old fool as to pity the true lover.

This incident is sufficiently in tone with Hemingway's earlier writing to give it a broader significance and invite us to consider it more closely. In the medieval romance of *Le Pèlerinage de Charlemagne* there is a somewhat similar incident conceived in all the liveliness of the *esprit Gaulois.* It is where the crusading knights take time off to make their boasts as to their virility as judged by purely physical tests or scores. There is here no tragedy, no pathos, nothing but the pure worship of the phallic principle. One realizes at once that this is not the stuff for a modern novel of "true love." And that, because in the modern scale of sentimental values—not to speak of the present overpopulation of the world—we are not inclined to rate so high the mere faculty of proliferousness. And even where, in Rabelaisian circles, there is a lingering trace of the old reverence for this faculty, it is not elsewhere considered polite to make it the subject of public exploitation in works of literary art.

And I do not think this is a mere question of good taste—though I would not disparage good taste as an important factor in literary criticism. Perhaps we might say that good taste is the surface manifestation of something deeply grounded in our humanity. And in the present phase of our humanity we are inclined to put a higher valuation on qualities less purely physical than virility. For the biologist virility may take precedence over all other male virtues as guaranteeing the survival of the race. But for the cultural humanist, virility, while it may have its importance as the physical basis for higher (that is, moral) values, is not to be regarded as being in itself one of them. It is like the competitive spirit in the arts. The competitive spirit may conduce to excellent performance in any line of endeavor. But it is not considered good form to insist too much on the mere defense of the title where excellence of performance is the ideal.

III

It should here be stated, at the outset, that a fresh survey of Hemingway's fiction makes clear that both the competitive spirit and the theme of virility in the rudimentary sense are in the main duly subordinated to more important values in living. The principal subject in Hemingway is manly sports, including war, with the virtues and skills connected with these. Next to this in prominence is the subject of "true love" as that term is understood in our current American culture.

In connection with sport, war, and sex, it is true that Hemingway is acutely aware of the factual and seamy side of things and disinclined to soft-pedal anything in the facts observed however disagreeable they may be to a squeamish taste. In all that he has said about writing his emphasis is on scrupulous truth-telling; his style is an attempt to render the truth with greater exactness, to get rid of the clichés and rhetorical elaborations which tended to obscure and falsify the truth in the popular writing of his time. Many of his most brilliant short stories seem to be devoted mainly to the debunking of sentimental notions. The first seven "chapters" of *In Our Time* are camera-eye shots of the horrors of war, and "A Natural History of the Dead" is an account of what happens to dead bodies as sardonically cold-blooded as Swift could have made it. With regard to bullfighting, while his main interest is in the courage and skill of the matador and the feeling of high tragic art evoked by his performance, he extenuates nothing of the messiness and painfulness of the spectacle. He is as faithful in recording the sensations of the coward and the superannuated fighter as he is in celebrating the "greatness" of his triumphant Romeros.

As a professional storyteller he is always attracted by whatever will make a "good subject." Many of his stories are incidental sketches of characters and incidents noted in his travels ("Mr. and Mrs. Elliot," "A Canary for One," "Che Ti Dice La Patria?,"

"Homage to Switzerland," "Wine of Wyoming"). These might often be labeled satirical except that the facts are set down so objectively and without comment that one misses the *saeva indignatio* of the moralist bent on exposing vice and folly.

The impulse to debunk, or merely to call attention to neglected truths, leads him to the inclusion of a number of wry footnotes to the topic of love-and-sex. "A Canary for One" is the picture of a conventional woman bringing home a singing bird to her daughter in compensation for the love match she has prevented her making; this shallow woman has so little comprehension of the importance of love that she will not let her daughter marry a "foreigner" ("American men make the best husbands"). "Mr. and Mrs. Elliot" is a picture of the futile estheticism that takes the place of love with so many "nice" people. Like other writers, Hemingway has noted instances of love-that-didn't-last ("The End of Something," "A Very Short Story," "Hills Like White Elephants"), of prostitutes capable of romantic love ("The Light of the World"), and of sexual "inversion" ("A Simple Inquiry," "A Sea Change"); and these observations, set down briefly and objectively, fall into their proper place in a well-informed view of human nature. Hemingway, it appears, had been made uneasy, in his father, the doctor, by something strained and unnatural in his attitude toward the sexual function; and he feels in conscience bound to set down in their place (as in "Fathers and Sons") certain neglected truths in regard to sexual experience in boyhood.

Here it should be observed that no one has written with more delicacy of feeling about the emotional attitudes of adolescence toward the "facts of life" and about the uneasy passage from boyhood to manhood. Among the finest stories of our age are "Indian Camp," "The End of Something," "The Three-Day Blow," "Ten Indians," and "Big Two-Hearted River." These stories are written with the cool objectivity of a man combined with a real depth of comprehension of what makes personality in a child.

IV

Because Hemingway, like most good American writers of our time, has felt impelled to do a good deal of debunking of conventional views, and because his ideal of good writing requires him largely to abjure personal comment and the sort of eloquence that was thought to give an edifying lift to the tone of a story, he has too often been labeled a "negative" or disillusioned writer. Uncritical readers know better. They have taken the wine he pours, and know how it goes to the head. Among critics there has been some attempt, in connection with his announced project of supplying a fourth (and a fifth) dimension to prose writing, to explain that what he is aiming at is a sense of greater "depth" in our experience of life than might be suggested by a mere account in plain words of the outward facts. Thus George Snell, in *The Shapers of American Fiction*, rejects the notion that Hemingway is a "realist," and associates him with Hawthorne and Melville, with their aim "to inspire a deeper consciousness of reality through an appeal to the nonobjective factors of experience." And Malcolm Cowley, in his introduction to the *Viking Portable Hemingway*, asserts that his "prose at its best gives a sense of depth and of moving forward on different levels that is lacking in even the best of his imitators, as it is in almost all the other novelists of our time."

But, so far as my reading goes, it remained for a candidate for the master's degree at the University of Illinois to suggest most nearly what it is that gives a lift to so much of Hemingway's writing and invests our "human condition" with a sense of its dignity and "glory." Robert Stevens is not satisfied with the accounts of the fourth dimension offered by Snell, Cowley, and Beach. And perhaps he does get nearer to the heart of the matter than any of these critics. He takes his start from Hemingway's statement, in *Death in the Afternoon*, of what led him to make so close a study of the art of the matador. He chose that as a subject for his experiment in writing because there it was "I could see certain definite action that would give me the feeling of life and death that I was looking for." With regard to the morality of the bullfight Hemingway wrote: "The bullfight is very moral to me because I feel very fine while it is going on and have a feeling of life and death and mortality and immortality, and after it is over I feel very sad but very fine."

Mr. Stevens develops the thesis that what in Hemingway most often puts us in a state of mind to appreciate life is the imminent presence of death, and that it is in this connection that he proves himself a positive and not a negative writer. And he adds: "It is, in my opinion, the feeling that arises from the fact of our temporary existence that Hemingway calls the fourth dimension. . . . The result of (this) experience is, if not a feeling of absolute immortality, then at least a feeling that mortality is not a curse." He then proceeds to give illustrations of this feeling in episodes from the bull ring and in scenes of fighting in *For Whom the Bell Tolls,* including the hilltop fight of El Sordo and his men.

The great thing that may be missed in the first reading of this selection is that these five men die in glory, that despite the circumstances of their death they achieve a permanent dignity, that in the fact of their certainly approaching death it was possible for El Sordo at least to be "happy as only a hunter can be."

Whether this is what Hemingway meant by the fourth dimension there is no way of determining except by asking him. Mr. Stevens' guess is as good as another's. He might have drawn even better illustrations from the experience of Robert Jordan, the young republican who actually blew the bridge. But here the "fourth-dimension" effect would be complicated by moral factors which make the primary sensation of glory harder to isolate because they would give it an extension into the *ethical* "dimension." Even with the bullfighter, the brave and skilled matador, there is an *esthetic* factor in his feeling of glory—the sense of perfection in the performance of his ritual. But with Robert Jordan, as well as certain minor characters in his story, the satisfaction taken in their meeting with death involves a large measure of consciousness that what they are risking their lives for is a social obligation and that in the act of dying they are participating in a moral order. These are men who can say of themselves in the light of the ideal they are fighting for, that they themselves are nothing and death is nothing. For this ideal

gave you a part in something that you could believe in wholly and completely and in which you felt an absolute brotherhood with the others who were engaged in it. It was something that you had never known before but that you had experienced now and you gave such importance to it and the reasons for it that your own death seemed of complete unimportance.

These sentences may not be a good example of Hemingway's writing at its best. And it is certainly not the bald statement of these sentiments that gives to the narrative and dramatic portions of this book their peculiar vibrancy and beauty. But it is in large part the active presence of these sentiments in the hearts of Robert Jordan and Pilar and Fernando and El Sordo and others in the cast as they work out together the moral as well as the strategic problems involved in their common undertaking.

There are many reasons for the special sense of splendor and weight of significance given us by this book in comparison with any other novel of Hemingway's or even with such fine stories as "The Killers," "The Short Happy Life of Francis Macomber," or "The Snows of Kilimanjaro." We know how well acquainted Hemingway was with the Spanish country, how fond he was of its people, their folkways and speech, and how he was fascinated even by the paradoxes and contradictions of the national character. We know that, in his capacity as correspondent, he had close contact with the republican leaders and an inside view of the military campaigns and the complexities of the political situation. Presumably, like Robert Jordan, he "had no politics" of his own, but was willing to leave the conduct of the war in the hands of the Communists because "here in Spain the Communists offered the best discipline and the soundest and sanest for the prosecution of the war." But he was no Communist himself, and he had a very shrewd understanding of the seamy side of revolutionary politics, whether Communist or Fascist or Republican.

His account of these matters is more realistic than that of Malraux in *Man's Hope,* with the latter's all-out political commitments. Hemingway's is indeed the best account we have of the Spanish War. But with all his realism, all the allowance he makes for barbarity and corruption in public life and in the hearts of men, what gives its peculiar strength and beauty to this story is his recognition of the generous ideal motives that governed the action of so many men. The political issues of this war were infinitely more important for him than were those of the First World War. We know that for Hemingway that World War "made no sense"; he could hardly admire the Italians for their belated decision to have their slice of the pie with the winners. And *A Farewell to Arms,* in so far as it dealt with the War, was by necessity limited to its "negative" or unattractive aspects. But Hemingway, while he "hates" war, is, as we know, passionately interested in everything connected with fighting. And in the case of the war in Spain, he could indulge this interest with a good conscience, since he was so certain that what was here at issue was nothing less than the freeing of an oppressed people from intolerable tyranny. Robert Jordan was given the task of blowing a certain bridge, and when he realized that this might mean death for himself and the aged republican Anselmo, he could say to himself:

Neither you nor this old man is anything. You are instruments to do your duty. There are necessary orders that are no fault of yours and there is a bridge and that bridge can be the point on which the future of the human race may turn. As it can turn on everything that happens in this war. You have only one thing to do and you must do it.

This may not be the sense of glory felt by the matador facing death in the form of a bull and giving us a "feeling of life and death and mortality and immortality." But it does remind us of that persistent concern with ethical values more or less latent in all Hemingway's writing. It gives these values, so often abortive, something solid to attach themselves to; it brings them into operation as the motive for positively heroic action. If the mere courageous meeting of our mortal destiny may give us "a feeling that mortality is not a curse," the meeting with death in the interest of some positive human good may even better illustrate what Mr. Stevens calls "the glory of man."

V

The reader will note that, for reasons of space, no attempt is made here to distinguish Hemingway's peculiar qualities as a prose stylist, nor for that matter to trace the elements of his ethical system. In my chapters on him in *American Fiction 1920-1940* I have dealt somewhat at length with these parallel features of his writing.

It will be obvious that I do not share the opinion of certain thoughtful critics that *For Whom the Bell Tolls* is inferior in artistry to much of his earlier work, and that this is so because, more than in his other work, Hemingway has here attempted "to force (his material) to his own ideological end—to moralize." This is the view of Mr. Ray B. West, Jr., in an essay included in William Van O'Connor's *Forms of Modern Fiction*. I cannot here do proper justice to Mr. West's subtle argument. But I might, in the case of certain examples cited by him, indicate why his argument remains for me in the main unconvincing. It is based largely on the baldness of the terms in which Robert Jordan expresses his attachment to the Republican cause, the author's failure to provide an "objective correlative" for his sentiment or to give it an ironic turn through understatement as in his best writing. In the examples cited, Mr. West seems to me to consider certain passages without due regard to the context in which they appear and to appraise them as if they were the utterances of a lyric poet and not of characters in a work of prose fiction.

He illustrates the imaginative failure of Hemingway by contrasting a character's statement of faith with those of Donne in certain famous poems, as where the paradoxical oneness of lovers in separation is objectified in the image of the twin compasses, or where the "divine mystery" of faith is represented by the poet's resort to the Church as if to a hospitable prostitute. In the last words of Jordan to Maria, Mr. West points out, his sense of their continuing oneness is flatly expressed without the aid of any poetic figure to support the emotional paradox: "Thou wilt go now, rabbit. But I go with thee. As long as there is one of us there is both of us. Do you understand?" Now, considering that this is a novel in the realistic tradition and that there is no suggestion that Robert Jordan is a metaphysical poet, one is inclined to ask whether this manner of statement on the part of the dying man is not more fitting dramatically than if he had indulged in some elaborate conceit. And one is also inclined to ask whether, under the circumstances—the urgent need to persuade the girl to save her life by going at once, and the equally urgent need to give her some word to live by— whether, I say, the effect would be improved by any note of irony or understatement.

Again, Mr. West is not satisfied with Jordan's way of formulating his reasons for going on with his probably fatal mission. "You believe in Liberty, Equality and Fraternity. You believe in Life, Liberty and the Pursuit of Happiness." Here, says Mr. West, "the author is attempting to rely on generalities which, admirable as they may be as a statement or even as symbols of democracy, are not sharp enough to carry the emotional weight put upon them." But if the reader will examine this passage in its context (in Chapter Twenty-six), he will realize that Robert Jordan is as much aware as Mr. West that he is mouthing rhetorical stereotypes, and that his emotional attachment to what lies behind these conventional symbols in spite of their inadequacy is a good example of the much-desiderated irony. Robert Jordan is, like Jake Barnes and Frederic Henry, a man suspicious of big hollow words, determined to bring all abstractions to the tests of practical experience. In a number of such passages of meditation and self-justification, he is reminding himself that, as a soldier in a good cause, he is no political theorist or dialectician, but a simple follower of the republican ideal, which is something that, as an American, he has taken in with his mother's milk. He is not responsible for the words, the slogans, but for his deeds, content to act upon the program of those who put through the French Revolution and those who drew up the basic instruments of the American commonwealth. In capitalizing these words—which is as if he put them in quotation marks —he is as obviously indulging in irony as he was when he told his Spanish associates that his father was a member of the Republican Party. But the passage should be taken in its full context. The main point of his meditation is his assurance to himself that he is not a Communist but a Republican—not a dialectician or believer in the "materialistic conception of society." "You're not a real Marxist and you know it. You believe in Liberty, etc., etc. Don't ever kid yourself with too much dialectics."

Robert Jordan is a man who knows the difference between words and things. In his moments of self-examination he is shown indulging his irony, and arguing with it, and putting it in its place. Mr. West seems to me to overlook the fact that this is a dramatic device—that it is not strictly speaking Hemingway who is here relying on "generalities," but the young man in the story sent to blow the bridge. And besides, it is not these generalities themselves, the mere slogans, on which Jordan is relying. It is the historical facts that give them force in the Spanish setting, the personal experiences that have driven these people to the mountains, including the painfully detailed experiences of Maria. It is these things that give content and meaning to the symbols which Jordan himself finds so inadequate. These are the objective correlatives to his thought—these and the immediate drama of Pilar and Pablo, of Anselmo and El Sordo.

And there is one further source of possible misunderstanding in Mr. West's account of Hemingway. He seems to imply that what Hemingway is concerned with is, like Donne, the conflict between acceptance and rejection of some article of religious faith, some religious conception of the universe; and that he has not been able to find the imaginative "correlatives" for the paradox and "mystery" of faith. It is not my impression that, either here or elsewhere, Hemingway is occupying himself with the transcendental concepts of religious faith; it seems rather that, from the start, he has given these up as beyond his scope or beyond the range of practical concern. So far as religion is concerned he would appear to be a simple agnostic. What he seems to be looking for is not objects of faith but objects of loyalty—what we call *ideals*—and what he thinks he has found, in the Spanish War, is social or moral ideals to which one can devote oneself wholeheartedly and without giving up a realistic understanding of the ways of the world.

I quite agree with Mr. West and other critics that the imaginative effects secured by Hemingway in *For Whom the Bell Tolls* are for the most part different in kind from those for which he is best known. But I see no reason on that account to question the emotional sincerity of the later work. I certainly see no more reason to question the genuineness or the profundity of his feeling in regard to the Republican cause in Spain, as some people do, than his attachment to the Allied cause in the Second World War. It was Hemingway's ideal not to "fake" feelings, and to set down only that which he had actually "seen." But there is nothing in his career to suggest that he was constitutionally incapable of seeing more than Nick Adams or Jake Barnes, or that, in the course of a crowded life, with experience and reflection, mere sights might not with him have been carried over into *insights*. But here again I think we can better appreciate his intention and his art if we give up trying to think of him as a mystic *manqué*.

VI

It is in *For Whom the Bell Tolls* that Hemingway gives the largest "dimensions" to the concept of "true love" and most plausibly associates this concept with the other major concerns of life. It is true that he feels it necessary to assert the primary importance of physical virility, both in the relations of Pilar and Pablo and in those of Robert Jordan and Maria. It is also true that, in his insistence on this theme, he thinks fit to give descriptions of the sensations of people making love which are stylistically one of the most questionable features of the book. The passages in the thirteenth and thirty-seventh chapters in which he undertakes to render the "ecstasy" of this experience are done in a style of lyrical extravagance which is like nothing else in Hemingway, and which, while it is quite different from Sherwood Anderson's style in *Dark Laughter* and *Many Marriages* so cruelly parodied by Hemingway in *The Torrents of Spring*, would be an easy mark for the shafts of some other Hemingway taking his motto (as Hemingway did) from Henry Fielding: "The only source of the true Ridiculous (as it appears to me) is affectation." The sensations of lovers in this particular moment are doubtless of primary importance in the human economy, but they are so truly "mystical" and beyond the reach of common words that Hemingway and E. E. Cummings are almost the only authors one can think of bold enough to try to render them. And it is doubtful whether these special sensations, as Hemingway describes them, can be made the basis for distinguishing, as he does, between love of the first and second grades. In any case, it has been a matter of common consent with writers in the European tradition to leave these things more to the imagination.

But this is a minor blemish on what is essentially a very fine book, which reads as well in 1950 as it did in 1940. If for a moment one is inclined to say this affair of Maria is not necessary to the story of the Spanish War—this is simply the love-interest commercially prescribed for every successful novel—there immediately comes flooding over one a realization of the many ways in which this element is functional for the plot and theme of the book and serves to raise it all to a higher level of significance. Maria stands, to begin with, as a living symbol of the way fascism not merely overrides the elementary rights of men, but brutally invades the most sacred places of the soul and deprives men of the last shreds of personal dignity and self-respect. And Robert Jordan's love for Maria, in spite of her abject state, restoring her to decency and self-respect, in its turn embodies a principle directly opposed to that of fascism. It is like a sacred ritual serving to exorcize the evil thing that has taken possession of her soul.

Again, the serious and responsible character of his love, which is that of a man for his wife, his determination to watch over her and be faithful to her, suggests the social values which are not otherwise represented in this story of guerrilla fighters in a war of liberation. Maria and Jordan stand, even in this episode of revolution, for the institution of marriage; they stand for society itself, and—as that for which, in the last analysis, men are fighting—they give a greater significance to the sacrifice these men are making for the Republican cause. His care for the woman he loves gives a much more human quality to the character of Robert Jordan, as her generous concern for Maria does to that of the formidable and foulmouthed Pilar.

One thing that puts a heavy strain on the emotions of Robert Jordan as he prepares to blow the bridge is the fear that he is endangering the lives of this band of partisans whom he likes so much. And this is raised to a higher degree of intensity with the realization, now, that these are not indifferent strangers but include the woman for whom he has so tender a passion.

Above all, perhaps, Jordan's love for Maria serves to heighten that sense of the transitoriness of life in the face of imminent death which Mr. Stevens finds to be the fourth dimension of Hemingway's *ars poetica*. It is the preciousness of life that makes death a subject of abhorrence, as it is the utter blankness of death that brings out in sharp relief the preciousness of life. But life is precious in proportion to the gratifications which it offers to the living. Before he met Maria, Robert Jordan had been content with the thought that he was performing his duty as a soldier under orders and as one fighting to make this country "a good place to live in," with the added hope that, if he came out alive, he would write a "good book" about the Spanish War. These were the gratifications that death would deprive him of. Such a thing as Maria he had thought was "the one thing that he would never have." And just as he is coming to think that he will probably not survive this campaign, he "runs into a girl like this Maria." "What a business!" as he says to himself in his studiously unheroic idiom.

But then, as he reminds himself, the satisfactions of life are not to be measured by quantity and duration.

I suppose it is possible to live as full a life in seventy hours as in seventy years. . . . So that if your life trades in its seventy years for seventy hours I have that value now and I am lucky enough to have it. And if there is not any such thing as a long time, nor the rest of our lives, nor from now on, but there is only now, well then now is the thing to praise and I am very happy with it.

This is something more than Mr. Stevens' fourth dimension—the realization of the transitoriness of life, with its corollary that "mortality is not a curse." Here is the recognition that, within the limits of mortality, it may be possible to realize *values* (it is Robert Jordan's own word) which cannot be measured by the clock.

In *The Sun Also Rises* the theme is the general disillusionment of the "lost generation." Such a thing as Maria is indeed the "one thing" that these people "will never have." Their incapacity for that is represented by the physical impotence of Jake and the sentimental futility of Brett. In *A Farewell to Arms* one has the feeling that the death of Catherine was not "inevitable," but something added by the author to underline his thesis that the cards are stacked against even the brave. In *To Have and Have Not* the pleasures of the marriage bed are a consolation prize for the valiant man who has lost out in the unfair battle of life. In *Across the River and into the Trees* the belated discovery of love by the old campaigner proves too thin a subject for a book of three hundred pages and leaves us with the feeling of having fallen into sentimental self-indulgence.

The Sun Also Rises and *A Farewell to Arms* are books strongly conceived and carried through with imaginative consistency. In *For Whom the Bell Tolls* we have a momentous episode in modern history, with action important enough to bear the weight of the emotion roused, developed in vivid and convincing detail. And it is here that Hemingway has done fullest justice to his theme of "true love," given it organic relation to the other main concerns of life, and established its place in the scale of human values.

Joseph Warren Beach

MELVIN BACKMAN

Hemingway: The Matador and the Crucified

Running through Ernest Hemingway's work, from *In Our Time* to *The Old Man and the Sea,* are two dominant motifs —the matador and the crucified. The matador represents a great force held in check, releasing itself proudly in a controlled yet violent administering of death. The crucified stands for the taking of pain, even unto death, with all of one's courage and endurance so that it becomes a thing of poignancy and nobility. Although it was not until *The Old Man and the Sea* that Hemingway achieved a perfect blending of his two themes, the continual tension and interplay between those forces represented by the matador and the crucified create a pattern in the Hemingway canon against which the individual works of fiction may be profitably studied.

In Our Time sets forth the pain and brutality of our world, recorded apparently without comment in a terse, telegraphic style. Yet underneath the tight-lipped writing a current of protest and repressed brooding threads its secretive way. This is violence caught in the stifled shock of its initial impact. The stories and interchapters have the effect of painful memories of which one must rid himself to exorcise their evil spell, to drive them from the night into the day.

Recoiling from these memories of a sick world, the discharged soldier Nick Adams sought retreat in the Big Two-Hearted River. In this story, Hemingway omits rather ominously all mention of the war and of the people and places of Nick's past, so that a strange aloneness and suspension of time are created. Nick's only function was to fish, to immerse himself so completely in the physical sensations and details of his fishing that there was no need to think. This became, therefore, a strange idyl. Nick called it "the good place," but it was the good place because of its associations with a certain part of his past—fishing and hunting, the river and the woods—which had not been excised from his life as he was trying to do with all the rest. It was as though he wanted to rub out his immediate past and begin clean again here in the woods. But even the woods had been burned over—now there were just charred stumps and black grasshoppers. Yet here amid the shelter and quiet of the trees and the river, with the sun warm on his back and his line trailing in the water, was a moment of separation, of forgetfulness, of peace.

If Nick Adams was trying to withdraw from his world in "Big Two-Hearted River," it was in "Soldier's Home" that the Hemingway protagonist was officially separated. The soldier Krebs found himself hopelessly alienated from the conventional, middle-class American town to which he returned. Living with a kind of flat despair from day to day, holding in abeyance the inevitable decision, he dwelt in uneasy isolation in the midst of his family. Pushed to action finally by family pressure, he decided to sever the last clinging thread of his filial bond. It was a curiously cold, passionless rebellion, as though he had long since worn out his emotions and given up his hope.

In cutting the human bonds that tie one to his world there is the danger of cutting into the very will to live. The threat of this infection hovers over the three stories "Mr. and Mrs. Elliot," "Cat in the Rain," and "Out of Season," each concerned with an American couple characterized by sexual sterility and impotence. Marked by a strangely bloodless discord, without intensity or love, their lives follow a drifting purposeless course. But like green wooded mountains rising abruptly out of barren plains, the descriptions of matadors (interspersed between the stories) emerge in sharp relief:

When he started to kill it was all in the same rush. The bull looking at him straight in front, hating. He drew out the sword from the folds of the muleta and sighted with the same movement and called to the bull, Toro! Toro! and the bull charged and Villalta charged and just for the moment they became one. Villalta became one with the bull and then it was over. Villalta standing straight and the red hilt of the sword sticking out dully between the bull's shoulders. Villalta, his hand up at the crowd and the bull roaring blood, looking straight at Villalta and his legs caving.

From the unvoiced fears of disintegration of Nick Adams, from the weary despair and apathy of Krebs, and from the scorn, which may mask a secret dread, of the passionless and sterile union of impotent lovers, Hemingway has turned to the violence of the matador.

The theme is developed more fully in *The Sun Also Rises*. If *In Our Time* recorded, for Hemingway, the waves of man's violence effacing the recognizable outline of the shore of one's home, *The*

Sun Also Rises depicts the human wreckage that had been left behind. The time was one of irresponsibility, drunkenness, and promiscuity. As Mike pursued his drunken way, trailing his mounting debts like a banner, Brett preceded her escort, trailing her mounting amours, like a Don Juan turned weary bitch. Jake and Bill Gorton joined in the drunken camaraderie. Yet the endless rounds of drinks seemed to be accompanied by endless rounds of useless quarrels, and the camaraderie was broken by animosities and malice. There was, nevertheless, a certain measure of fellowship, loyalty, and even gaiety. Cohn was outside of it, not merely because he did not belong but because he seemed too self-centered to participate in friendship. Friendship or not, there is no denying the essential futility of their lives. It was a life without purpose or direction, without intensity or passion, without faith in themselves or their world. Nor did they seem truly to believe in the hedonism by which they lived. It seemed that at the bottom of their hearts there lay such a cold dead despair that they drank in order not to think of it; they drank to wind themselves up, like a clock that must be wound every twenty-four hours. So they got through their days.

Whatever fault may be found, however, with the character of these people, it is Cohn for whom Hemingway reserved his most damning portrait. Cohn lacked true identity. His personality was without a core; in place of its center there was only a sickly ego expressing itself in the spurious martyrdom of the weak and self-pitying. Woman-dominated, he was without the vital maleness which Hemingway, like Lawrence, deems absolutely essential to the true man. There was no true pride, no resistance to Cohn. In his love of Brett he was childish in his possessiveness and unmanly in his abject pursuit. What a sharply contrasting picture Hemingway has painted of Pedro Romero as he paid suit to Brett by fighting his bull in front of her.

Never once did he look up. He made it stronger that way, and did it for himself, too, as well as for her. Because he did not look up to ask if it pleased he did it all for himself inside, and it strengthened him, and yet he did it for her too. But he did not do it for her at any loss to himself.

A polarity has been established between Cohn, unmanly representative of the lost generation, and the primitive, Pedro Romero. When these two fought, the hard male core of the young bullfighter could not be touched by Cohn's punches, and he reduced Cohn to a whimpering child.

Pedro was exempt from the *mal de siècle* that beset the others, for his fighting with the bulls brought him into a fundamental relationship with life, which involved the pitting of his maleness against that of the bull. It is a life and death struggle that reveals not only the steel of his young manhood but a certain passion with which he met life—an intensity, a seriousness, a dedicated quality. Pedro had a place in the scheme of existence—and a role to fulfill. With the instinctive sureness of a primitive who need never question his reason for living, he pursued his natural course. And it was this which even Brett came to recognize. There was an absolute center to him. He did not have to drink, he did not have to keep running away. His inner core was brought into a vital active relationship with life. As Jake commented, it is only a bullfighter who lives life to the hilt, bringing to his work all his courage, intelligence, discipline, and art.

The crisis for Pedro came not in the fight with Cohn but in the invasion of his world by Brett. Jake, the only one of the blighted moderns who was truly aware of this other world, served to bridge them. When he agreed to act as go-between in the proposed seduction of the primitive by this woman of the lost generation, he was knowingly betraying all that the matador represented. No wonder that Montoya, the *aficionado*, no longer acknowledged Jake as one of them, for he knew that the two worlds had to stand forever apart if the bullfight was to retain its truth. Oddly enough, it was Brett's remnant of a conscience that, touched by shamed awareness of the desecration she threatened, brought to an end this unnatural conjunction of two separate worlds.

A purer, more natural kind of love is celebrated in *A Farewell to Arms*. Less sustained in movement and less orchestrated than *The Sun Also Rises, A Farewell to Arms* is a more emotional and subjective novel. It seems to be based upon the memory of a lost love and a lost youth: one's first love, dramatized like that of Romeo and Juliet, destroyed by the "they" that Hemingway in Byronic fashion has cast as the enemy that ever seeks to crush the individual. Although there is no primitive, like Pedro Romero, in this novel, there is, in contrast to the comparatively disillusioned picture of the war, the love itself—tender and idyllic. Glowing with the first flush of the lovers' physical discovery of each other, their love overarches the lovers themselves, who remain essentially passive. Lyrically conceived by the author, it is a small fire of life dampened by a sense of doom and threatened by the cold rain of death.

In *The Sun Also Rises* and *In Our Time,* Pedro Romero and Villalta—as their swords go all the way in, the men leaning after —become one with the bull, united for a single instant by death. This is the "moment of truth." It is an intense, almost an ecstatic, moment of communion, involving an abnegation of self before the final merging. The only other experience analogous to this in Hemingway's work is sexual union. Both are experiences of controlled violence that demand a tight holding on of self until the last moment, then the yielding, merging, and flooding ecstasy. Sexual implications may be seen in the matador's domination of the bull that leads to the climax, the final thrusting of the sword; after the sword's entry the caving in of the bull suggests, by a curious transfer of roles, the collapsed tension, the deathlike state of the spent male after ejaculation. Hemingway usually describes love as the act of becoming one: both Maria and Catherine try to become one with their lovers, Robert Jordan and Frederic Henry. While the killing of the bull ends in union, the making of love, as Hemingway has often remarked, becomes a kind of killing, the good killing. The famous love passage in *For Whom the Bell Tolls,* when the earth seems to move, is so filled with death imagery that it might be taken for a description of dying:

For him it was a dark passage which led to nowhere, then to nowhere, then again to nowhere, once again to nowhere, always and forever to nowhere, heavy on the elbows in the earth to nowhere, dark, never any end to nowhere, hung on all time always to unknowing nowhere, this time and again for always to nowhere, now beyond all bearing up, up, up and into nowhere, suddenly, scaldingly, holdingly all nowhere gone and time absolutely still and they were both there, time having stopped and he felt the earth move out and away from under them.

The feeling of soaring suggests a mystic ascension and recalls the soaring of the airplane in "The Snows of Kilimanjaro" that symbolized death.

It is this twining of sex and death, both fundamental crises of life, that is central to Hemingway's work. Both killing and sexual union are basic primitive experiences in which the male asserts his will and proves his manhood. In the primitive mind, both love and death are surrounded by religious and fearful influences. Because of a sense of danger and evil attending both marriage and death, ceremonies are instituted and taboos and restrictions imposed as safeguards. And Hemingway—defying Christianity's condemnation of killing and its concept of sex as a sort of necessary sin—has presented love as a mystic ceremonial experience and killing (killing cleanly with honor, pride, and humility) as a spiritual experience.

Killing cleanly and in a way which gives the esthetic pleasure and pride has always been one of the greatest enjoyments of the human race. . . . When a man is still in rebellion against death he has pleasure in taking to himself one of the Godlike attributes; that of giving it. This is one of the most profound feelings in those men who enjoy killing. These things are done in pride and pride, of course, is a Christian sin, and a pagan virtue.

In a world from which Hemingway has sought to dissociate himself, the only sacred subjects left for him have proved to be love and death—experiences which he has sought to invest with the quality of ancient mysteries.

One remembers the cold rain of *In Our Time* associated with an evil violence, the rain of the fiesta in *The Sun Also Rises* that became part of a Walpurgis-like nightmare, the black rain of the Caporetto retreat and of the death of Catherine Barkley in *A Farewell to Arms*. But in *For Whom the Bell Tolls* there is no rain. The sun dominates the novel—the sun shining through the trees and warming the pine-needled earth. The setting—except for the occasional huddling within the cave, where the atmosphere was close, sullen, as Pablo brooded drunkenly on his lost manhood, as tempers flared darkly, and death stalked ominously—the setting is of the out-of-doors. There love was made and the soldier's death received. And there was the sun, the warm life-giving sun, the sun that heralded the coming of spring after the snow, the sun that was Maria illuminating the life of Robert Jordan. Maria is a child of the sun, with her hair "the color of ripe wheat," her face the "color of burnt gold," and her eyes "gold with the dark flecks in them." And the sun is identified with their love. On the day that Jordan and Maria made love, the hot gold of the sun commingled with the heather smell of the earth and the cropped golden hair of Maria—blending into a Van Gogh-like celebration of the sun so that the pulsing energy of the sun beat through the lovers into the earth and the earth moved. For Robert Jordan, Maria was the sun driving away the night and abolishing loneliness; she was the life that held off death. Finally love itself became a soaring union in which for a moment *la gloria* was realized, a glory like that "in Greco and in San Juan de la Cruz."

That their love should achieve some measure of mystical glory is not completely unprepared for. Maria—her very name suggests the Virgin—was the violated virgin who by the force of her love and will obliterated the violence that had been done her and recaptured her virginity. Borne by the men of Pablo's or rather Pilar's band from the scene of the train disaster, she had been restored to life by Pilar. Although Pilar was her support and protector, all had had a hand in her restoration, and all approached her with tenderness and love. And despite the Loyalists' official disapproval of the Church, it is to the Virgin that many turned in the presence of death.

When El Sordo's band, surrounded and isolated on a hill, were facing annihilation, El Sordo in his last moment thought: "Dying was nothing and he had no picture of it nor fear of it in his mind. But living was a field of grain blowing in the wind." This image of life may suggest association with the recurring description of Jordan's running his hand through Maria's close-cropped hair like the wind blowing through the tawny wheat. But Sordo did not pray; it was Joaquin—the boy who just the day before had been teasing Maria like a brother—who, as the planes swooped down, uttered a "Hail Mary" at the hour of his death. The bombs dropped, splitting the air apart, hitting the earth with a red black roar; "and the earth rolled under him with the roar. Then it came again and the earth lurched under his belly and one side of the hilltop rose into the air and then fell slowly over them where they lay." For him too the earth had moved.

After the action only the enemy was left. Lieutenant Berrendo, riding at the head of the column, thought of his friend Julian, dead on the hill, and prayed to the Virgin for the soul of his friend. At almost the same moment Anselmo caught sight of the enemy column, and frozen by fear he prayed to the "most kind, most sweet, most clement Virgin." Unknowingly these two men, pledged enemies and destined to die the next day, were united in their prayer.

It would seem, then, that while Maria is associated with the sun, and the sun generally with life, she is also associated with the Virgin,[1] and the Virgin with death. Yet in the last chapter—when all that has gone before has led us painstakingly and inevitably to the destruction of the bridge—the sun is curiously twisted together

[1] Other evidence that might be offered is the reference to the "Blessed Virgin of Pilar" in the letter of the cavalryman shot by Robert Jordan. There is also the ambiguous evidence of the Fascists' conferring of the title of "Red Bride of Christ" upon Maria, and the scene in which Maria, in the Mary Magdalen tradition, serves Jordan, "The Lord and Master."

with death. The scene is the opening of the chapter, just prior to the commencement of the Loyalist attack at dawn, the bombing to serve as signal for the blowing of the bridge. Jordan, who had always loved the coming of the sun, lay on the pine-needled earth and watched the first light of the sun dispelling the light mist that obscured the outline of the bridge. As the bridge shone clear in the morning light he heard the bombs drop, and he drew a long breath, as if to expel the lonely feeling that came with the dealing of death, and he prepared to shoot the sentry. The sentry stood in the road with the sun shining on him. "There was no mist on the road now and Robert Jordan saw the man, clearly and sharply, standing there on the road looking up at the sky. The sun shone bright on the trees." And gently Robert Jordan squeezed the trigger. After the death of the sentry came the wiring of the bridge. With the sound of shots in his ear, suspended under the trestle of the bridge, Jordan worked with a tense quick deliberateness against time, lashing the grenades to the girders. But for a moment the noise of the white bubbling stream below him drowned out the war, and looking down he saw a trout nibbling on the chip he had dropped, and through the metal of the bridge he saw the sunlight on the green slope that had been brown but three days ago. It was a green moment of peace that could not be, and it had to yield to the twisting of sun and bridge into destruction.

And the sunlight played over Fernando, the good cigar-store Indian Fernando with all his fine wooden dignity, as he lay wounded against the bank.

In front of him was one of the whitewashed stones that marked the edge of the road. His head was in the shadow but the sun shone on his plugged and bandaged wound and on his hands that were cupped over it. His legs and his feet also were in the sun. The rifle lay beside him and there were three clips of cartridges shining in the sun beside the rifle.

Then there was Anselmo—loyal Anselmo, the good old man who did not want to kill, believing that killing men was sin—with the wire pulled tight around his fist, waiting for the signal from the Inglés. The sun weighed heavy on his back. Then came the blowing of the bridge—and Anselmo lay face down behind the white marking stone, that shone in the sunlight like a common gravestone for the good and the brave.

If the sun represents the exposure that spelled death for some, for Robert Jordan it meant still more. The novel opens with Jordan lying on the pine-needled floor of the forest, planning the destruction of the bridge that arched peacefully over the stream, white in the summer sunlight. And the novel ends:

Lieutenant Berrendo, watching the trail, came riding up, his thin face serious and grave. His sub-machine gun lay across the saddle in the crook of his left arm. Robert Jordan lay behind the tree, holding onto himself very carefully and delicately to keep his hands steady. He was waiting until the officer reached the sunlit place where the first trees of the pine forest joined the green slope of the meadow. He could feel his heart beating against the pine-needle floor of the forest.

We have come full circle. The pine trees and the sun and Robert Jordan have become inextricably mingled with the giving and receiving of death. Yet there is the moving memory of the love in the hot sunlight and the love on the pine boughs in the cool nights in the sleeping bag. It is as though death in some subtle fashion has not only twisted itself about love but has become a secret forbidden attraction that the Hemingway hero finds hard to resist. But resist it he must, even if resistance requires the inflicting of violence upon others. Or it may be that by his administering of death he takes unconscious revenge for the violence inflicted upon the young manhood of Nick Adams and Jake Barnes and Frederic Henry.

Yet death in this novel is different from death in *The Sun Also Rises* or *Death in the Afternoon*. In those earlier works the dominating point of view was that of the matador, because killing was the means of proving one's manhood. The identification was chiefly with the killer; there was a deep fundamental enjoyment, Hemingway said, to be had from killing. In *For Whom the Bell Tolls*, however, there is an ambiguity of attitude. In only one instance did Robert Jordan identify himself, partially at least, with the desire to kill. This took place at the scene when Robert Jordan and Agustín, tense and still behind their guns, were watching the enemy cavalry depart. Agustín, speaking of the necessity to kill that was on him like "on a mare in heat," said that there was no stronger thing in life. Jordan, in silent thought, called it the Spanish "extra sacrament" that, repressed by Christianity, had welled forth in wars and inquisitions; and Jordan admitted that he too and "all who are soldiers by choice have enjoyed it at some time whether they lie about it or not." Yet throughout the story Jordan never killed with pleasure but always with reluctance. He could not bring himself to "assassinate" Pablo, he shot the sentry with sadness, and his defensive killing of the cavalryman initiated a long searching of his conscience in which he questioned his right to kill. (Even the old man in *The Old Man and the Sea* continues this questioning of one's right to kill.) Jordan's position seems to lie between that of Anselmo and Pablo. Although Agustín had spoken of killing as an instinct, only with Pablo had this "instinct" become an inordinate lust, revealed in the brutally sadistic executions and the blood-drunken slaughter initiated by Pablo during the taking of his town. Part of Robert Jordan—the greater part, it would seem— was in accord with Anselmo, who felt that "in those who like it [killing] there is always a rottenness." Hating to kill, Anselmo is a foil to Pablo in other respects, manifesting loyalty as against treachery, courage as against fear, gentleness as against cruelty. Something of the quality of the old man in "Old Man at the Bridge" invests Anselmo. Idealized, of course, he represents a position toward which part of Hemingway was drawn, just as the priest in *A Farewell to Arms* had served as a similar attraction for Frederic Henry.

But the most crucial experience for Robert Jordan lay not in the killing but in the preparing to be killed. Although he had to face up to his ordeal with courage and dignity, like all the Hemingway heroes who live by the "code," the reason for this code is now made clear. Submerged in the back of Jordan's mind was the guilt of his father's suicide, which compelled Jordan to live in such a manner as to annul his father's cowardice. Just as he had to rid himself of the pistol by which his father had shot himself, so had he to rid himself of his father—that is, to obliterate his father from his consciousness, as if he had never been, and to replace him with his grandfather, the soldier in the family.

Although Jordan must die to make the "code" live, to wipe out the stain of his father's cowardice, may there not be another explanation for his pain and death? Jordan, after all, is but part of a pattern into which all the Hemingway protagonists fall. At the end of *In Our Time* Nick Adams, having been initiated into a painful world, was left in a curious state of suspension; Jake Barnes resigned himself hopelessly to a miserable lot in a futile world; Frederic Henry, stripped by death of his love, was left alone with his despair and misery in a war-torn world. Always the Hemingway protagonist was left alone and always a victim, his world a torturing wheel upon which he was stretched. *Death in the Afternoon, Green Hills of Africa,* and *To Have and Have Not* recorded the seeking of violence as a means of asserting oneself in despite of the world. But Harry Morgan received only pain and death. And death came to

Robert Jordan and Richard Cantwell. This pattern of agony and death, with the protagonist as a sort of crucified victim[2]—is it not a curious complement to the matador going in for the kill? Or are these two faces to a single coin? On one side there is the matador who in his administering of death, Hemingway has said, takes on the attributes of a god. Is there an old primitive truth here: the welding of the act to the unvitiated passion, like an Oedipus rising in pure wrath to strike down his father; the godlike taking to oneself of the power to judge and punish, like a Zeus dealing out divine punishment to a transgressing Prometheus; the mingling of sadism with power, like a Moloch demanding sacrifice? On the other side there is the glorifying of the victim, the seeking of brotherhood out of weakness and life out of death, like a Prometheus transformed into helper of mankind, like a Yahweh become Christ. But Hemingway's works do not reflect any true belief in the glory of martyrdom; they reflect only the tendency to see oneself as victim and life as pain. Nor do they manifest any true desire for brotherhood, for the Hemingway protagonist is always an island, separated by his pain and despair and, in the last resort, by death. In a life that is pain, death may come to represent release—the final sleep that knits up souls, the sleep that cannot be had by a Nick Adams haunted by the nightmare of his wounding, by an old man living with a nameless dread ("A Clean Well-Lighted Place"), or by a Frazer ridden with physical pain. The despair that lies at the bottom of so many of the Hemingway protagonists leads either to passive suffering or to a defiant seeking of violence.

When we reach *The Old Man and the Sea,* we seem to have come a long way from the early works, but there is a pattern into which all of them fall. It is true that the old man is the only hero who is not left alone, at the end of the story, with death or despair. He is old and womanless and humble. Yet in him we have a blending of the two dominant motifs—the matador and the crucified.

At first glance it may not seem that what the matador represents is in the old man too. Yet just as the matador pits himself against the bull, so does Santiago pit himself against the great fish; in their killing they achieve a rebellion against death. In this combat both men must call upon their pride and courage, their skill and knowledge of their craft. Whereas the bullfight terminates with the

[2] Both Robert Jordan and Colonel Cantwell are invested occasionally with a vague Christ symbolism. And in a short early play of Hemingway's, "Today Is Friday," the Roman soldier's comment on the crucified Christ—"He was pretty good in there today"—echoes and reechoes throughout the works.

final sword thrust between the shoulders of the bull, the fight with the fish terminates with the thrusting of the harpoon into his heart. And the old man, his hands lacerated and mushy, raises himself out of his pain to bring down the harpoon, in the same way as the matador Maera in *Death in the Afternoon,* disregarding his broken wrist, goes in for the sixth time over the horns of the bull. Nevertheless, there are differences. The artificial setting of the bullfight, its spectators, and its ceremony leave one with the sense that this is but violence on exhibit, that it is not a natural struggle between man and animal, and that the emotions produced seem strained and self-induced. But Santiago's struggle with the fish is natural. As he says, he was born to be a fisherman and the fish was born to be a fish. The killing of fish is an old accepted livelihood. And the setting for Santiago's struggle is the most natural in the world: overhead move the sun and the stars and the moon; beneath sways the sea, *la mar;* and about the boat move the birds and fish. The sea is the old man's home and the others are his friends and brothers. The old fisherman himself—his skin blotched brown by the friendly sun, his eyes "the color of the sea," the scars on his hands "old as erosions in a fishless desert"—is part of this natural universe. It is a complete and closed universe, a friendly one—its Creator neither hostile nor beneficent but mysteriously just. And the old man talks to the fish and the birds and the stars just as primitive man might have done long ago.

Yet more remarkable than Santiago's killing of the fish is his suffering. (Santiago is Spanish for Saint James—the fisherman, apostle, and martyr from the Sea of Galilee.) Etched on the reader's mind is the image of the old man as he settled against the wood of the bow—the big fish towing, the cord tight across the old man's back—and took his suffering as it came, telling himself, " 'Rest gently now against the wood and think of nothing.' " "The old man rode gently with the small sea and the hurt of the cord across his back came to him easily and smoothly." Suffering and gentle and wood blend magically into an image of Christ on the cross. Then as he was pinned to the bow, dreaming for a few minutes of the lions on the long yellow beach, he woke suddenly with a jerk, the line burning his right hand, his left without feeling. He leaned against the line and tried to brake it, while it burned his back and cut deeply into his left hand. "Just then the fish jumped making a great bursting of the ocean . . . jumped again and again." The straining line pulled the old man face down into the slice of dolphin at the bow. He got his head out of the fish, which was nauseating him, and rose slowly to his knees. Taking the strain with his left hand, he washed the dolphin off his face and let his bleeding right hand trail clean in the salt water, reassuring himself the while, " 'Pain does not matter to a man.' " The fish circled slowly, while "the old man was wet with sweat and tired deep into his bones" and his hands were mushy and he was seeing only in flashes and he was feeling himself go. It was then that he prepared for the kill, pitting "all his pain and what was left of his strength and his long gone pride" against the agony of the fish. When he thrust and pushed his harpoon into the fish's heart, "Then the fish came alive, with his death in him, and rose high out of the water showing all his great length and width and all his power and beauty. Then he fell into the water with a crash that sent spray over the old man and all of the skiff." For a moment after the death of the fish, the tension relaxed, but the pain continued and then the sharks came. " 'Ay,' he said aloud. There is no translation for this word and perhaps it is just a noise such as a man might make, involuntarily, feeling the nail go through his hands and into the wood." He fought the sharks through the afternoon, into the evening and the night, until he was almost dead; but the "pain of life" in his hands and shoulders told him otherwise. He fought until he was weaponless. Then he knew he was beaten and turned the skiff home. The sharks bit into what was left of the great fish, but the old man did not heed them. He was past everything now. Finally sailing into the little harbor, making the boat fast, and stepping ashore, he shouldered the mast and started to climb. "It was then that he knew the depth of his tiredness," as he looked back at the head and the white skeleton of the great fish. He climbed again, bearing his mast like a heavy cross, "and at the top he fell and lay for some time with the mast across his shoulder." He got up again. Then reaching his shack, he put the mast against the wall and lay down on his bed. The next morning the boy found him—"his face down on the newspapers with his arms out straight and the palms of his hands out."

Yet that afternoon the old man was dreaming of the lions on the white beaches of Africa. The dream may represent, as Philip Young has suggested, not only a nostalgic return to the strength of one's youth but also a desire for immortality—like the meaning of the frozen leopard on the summit of Kilimanjaro. Despite the suffering and seeming defeat of the old man, the final effect is that of a triumph which is invested not with the violent ritualized quality of the bullfights of *Death in the Afternoon* or the uneasily insistent and belligerent note of *Green Hills of Africa*, but with a warm autumnal glow. The old man beating off the sharks is like life rebelling against death—as though the old man and the great fish who are lashed together and steering as one toward home, just as earlier they had been bound by the "pain of life," have become the symbol of life; while the sharks (scavengers like the vultures and hyena who are symbols of death in "The Snows of Kilimanjaro") have become the death which must be resisted even though it will win.

Combined with this triumph is a tenderness not usually found in Hemingway's work. For all of Hemingway's glorifying of love between man and woman, too much of the author seemed involved, as Edmund Wilson and Philip Young have noted, with a repudiation of woman. But now in the relation between man and boy, Hemingway achieves a new gentleness. This turning to male companionships seems characteristically American, recalling the paired Huck Finn and Jim, Natty Bumppo and Chingachgook, Ishmael and Queequeg. Curiously, with the exception of Ishmael, they are all variations of primitives. And in Santiago Hemingway has created as fine a primitive as the twentieth century has revealed, one who seems worthy of comparison with Mark Twain's Huck Finn or Jim. But the old man is more richly endowed than most primitives: bearing the name of Saint James, who was fisherman and martyr, he strangely unites the matador and the crucified.

Melvin Backman

CLINTON S. BURHANS, JR.

The Old Man and the Sea: Hemingway's Tragic Vision of Man

I

In *Death in the Afternoon,* Hemingway uses an effective metaphor to describe the kind of prose he is trying to write: he explains that

> if a writer of prose knows enough about what he is writing about he may omit things that he knows and the reader, if the writer is writing truly enough, will have a feeling of those things as strongly as though the writer had stated them. The dignity of movement of an iceberg is due to only one-eighth of it being above water.[1]

Among all the works of Hemingway which illustrate this metaphor, none, I think, does so more consistently or more thoroughly than the saga of Santiago. Indeed, the critical reception of the novel has emphasized this aspect of it: in particular, Philip Young, Leo Gurko, and Carlos Baker have stressed the qualities of *The Old Man and the Sea* as allegory and parable. Each of these critics is especially concerned with two qualities in Santiago—his epic individualism and the love he feels for the creatures who share with him a world of inescapable violence—though in the main each views these qualities from a different point of the literary compass. Young regards the novel as essentially classical in nature; Gurko sees it as reflecting Hemingway's romanticism; and to Baker, the novel is Christian in context, and the old fisherman is suggestive of Christ.[2]

[1] Ernest Hemingway, *Death in the Afternoon* (New York, 1932), p. 183.

[2] On the other hand—though not, to me, convincingly—Otto Friedrich, "Ernest Hemingway: Joy Through Strength," *The American Scholar,* XXVI (Autumn, 1957), pp. 470, 513-30, sees Santiago's experience as little more than the result of the necessities of his profession; Philip Young, *Hemingway* (New York, 1952), p. 100; Leo Gurko, "The Old Man and the Sea," *College English,* XVII, 1, 14 (Oct., 1955); Carlos Baker, *Hemingway* (Princeton, 1956), p. 299.

Such interpretations of *The Old Man and the Sea* are not, of course, contradictory; in fact, they are parallel at many points. All are true, and together they point to both the breadth and depth of the novel's enduring significance and also to its central greatness: like all great works of art it is a mirror wherein every man perceives a personal likeness. Such viewpoints, then, differ only in emphasis and reflect generally similar conclusions—that Santiago represents a noble and tragic individualism revealing what man can do in an indifferent universe which defeats him, and the love he can feel for such a universe and his humility before it.

True as this is, there yet remains, I think, a deeper level of significance, a deeper level upon which the ultimate beauty and the dignity of movement of this brilliant structure fundamentally rest. On this level of significance, Santiago is Harry Morgan alive again and grown old; for what comes to Morgan in a sudden and unexpected revelation as he lies dying is the matrix of the old fisherman's climactic experience. Since 1937, Hemingway has been increasingly concerned with the relationship between individualism and interdependence;[3] and *The Old Man and the Sea* is the culminating expression of this concern in its reflection of Hemingway's mature view of the tragic irony of man's fate: that no abstraction can bring man an awareness and understanding of the solidarity and interdependence without which life is impossible; he must learn it, as it has always been truly learned, through the agony of active and isolated individualism in a universe which dooms such individualism.

II

Throughout *The Old Man and the Sea,* Santiago is given heroic proportions. He is "a strange old man," [4] still powerful and still

[3] This direction in Hemingway's thought and art has, of course, been pointed out by several critics, particularly by Edgar Johnson in the *Sewanee Review,* XLVIII, 3 (July-Sept., 1940) and by Maxwell Geismar in *Writers in Crisis* (Cambridge, Mass., 1942). With prophetic insight, Johnson says that "the important thing about Hemingway is that he has earned his philosophy, that he has struggled to reach it, overcome the obstacles to attaining it. . . . He has earned the right to reject rejection. For the good, the gentle, and the brave, he now tells us, if they do not try to stand alone and make a separate peace, defeat is not inevitable. His life-blood dripping into the bottom of the boat, Harry Morgan realized it at the end of his career. Philip Rawlings realized it in the blood and terror and tragedy and splendor even of a dying Madrid. Hemingway has realized it there too, and the realization may well be for him the very beginning of a new and more vital career."

[4] Ernest Hemingway, *The Old Man and the Sea* (London, 1952), p. 10.

wise in all the ways of his trade. After he hooks the great marlin, he fights him with epic skill and endurance, showing "what a man can do and what a man endures" (p. 64). And when the sharks come, he is determined " 'to fight them until I die' " (p. 116), because he knows that " 'a man is not made for defeat. . . . A man can be destroyed but not defeated' " (p. 103).

In searching for and in catching his big fish, Santiago gains a deepened insight into himself and into his relationship to the rest of created life—an insight as pervasive and implicit in the old fisherman's experience as it is sudden and explicit in Harry Morgan's. As he sails far out on the sea, Santiago thinks of it "as feminine and as something that gave or withheld great favors, and if she did wild or wicked things it was because she could not help them" (p. 27). For the bird who rests on his line and for other creatures who share with him such a capricious and violent life, the old man feels friendship and love (pp. 26, 46). And when he sees a flight of wild ducks go over, the old man knows "no man was ever alone on the sea" (p. 59).

Santiago comes to feel his deepest love for the creature that he himself hunts and kills, the great fish which he must catch not alone for physical need but even more for his pride and his profession. The great marlin is unlike the other fish which the old man catches; he is a spiritual more than a physical necessity. He is unlike the other fish, too, in that he is a worthy antagonist for the old man, and during his long ordeal, Santiago comes to pity the marlin and then to respect and to love him. In the end he senses that there can be no victory for either in the equal struggle between them, that the conditions which have brought them together have made them one (p. 92). And so, though he kills the great fish, the old man has come to love him as his equal and his brother; sharing a life which is a capricious mixture of incredible beauty and deadly violence and in which all creatures are both hunter and hunted, they are bound together in its most primal relationship.

Beyond the heroic individualism of Santiago's struggle with the great fish and his fight against the sharks, however, and beyond the love and the brotherhood which he comes to feel for the noble creature he must kill, there is a further dimension in the old man's experience which gives to these their ultimate significance. For in killing the great marlin and in losing him to the sharks, the old man learns the sin into which men inevitably fall by going far out beyond her depth, beyond their true place in life. In the first night of his struggle with the great fish, the old man begins to feel a loneliness and a sense almost of guilt for the way in which he has caught him (p. 48); and after he has killed the marlin, he feels no pride of accomplishment, no sense of victory. Rather, he seems to feel almost as though he has betrayed the great fish; "I am only better than him through trickery," he thinks, "and he meant me no harm" (p. 99).

Thus, when the sharks came, it is almost as a thing expected, almost as a punishment which the old man brings upon himself in going far out "beyond all people. Beyond all people in the world" (p. 48) and there hooking and killing the great fish. For the coming of the sharks is not a matter of chance nor a stroke of bad luck; "the shark was not an accident" (p. 99). They are the direct result of the old man's action in killing the fish. He has driven his harpoon deep into the marlin's heart, and the blood of the great fish, welling from his heart, leaves a trail of scent which the first shark follows. He tears huge pieces from the marlin's body, causing more blood to seep into the sea and thus attract other sharks; and in killing the first shark, the old man loses his principal weapon, his harpoon. Thus, in winning his struggle with the marlin and in killing him, the old man sets in motion the sequence of events which take from him the great fish whom he has come to love and with whom he identifies himself completely. And the old man senses an inevitability in the coming of the sharks (p. 101), a feeling of guilt which deepens into remorse and regret. "I am sorry that I killed the fish . . ." (p. 103), he thinks, and he tells himself that "You did not kill the fish only to keep alive and to sell for food. . . . You killed him for pride and because you are a fisherman" (p. 105).

Earlier, before he had killed the marlin, Santiago had been " 'glad we do not have to try to kill the stars' " (p. 74). It is enough, he had felt, to have to kill our fellow creatures. Now, with the inevitable sharks attacking, the old man senses that in going far out he has in effect tried "to kill the sun or the moon or the stars." For him it has not been "enough to live on the sea and kill our true brothers"; in his individualism and his need and his pride, he has gone far out "beyond all people," beyond his true place in a capricious and indifferent world, and has thereby brought not only on himself but also on the great fish the forces of violence and destruction. " 'I shouldn't have gone out so far, fish . . . ,' " he declares. " 'Neither for you nor for me. I'm sorry, fish' " (p. 110). And when the sharks have torn away half of the great marlin, Santiago speaks again to his brother in the sea: " 'Half-fish,' he said. 'Fish that you were. I am sorry that I went too far out. I ruined us both' " (p. 116).

The old man's realization of what he has done is reflected in his apologies to the fish, and this realization and its implications are emphasized symbolically throughout the novel. From beginning to end, the theme of solidarity and interdependence pervades the action and provides the structural framework within which the old man's heroic individualism and his love for his fellow creatures appear and function and which gives them their ultimate significance. Having gone eighty-four days without a catch, Santiago has become dependent upon the young boy, Manolin, and upon his other friends in his village. The boy keeps up his confidence and hope, brings him clothes and such necessities as water and soap, and sees that he has fresh bait for his fishing. Martin, the restaurant owner, sends the old man food, and Perico, the wineshop owner, gives him newspapers so that he can read about baseball. All of this the old man accepts gratefully and without shame, knowing that such help is not demeaning. "He was too simple to wonder when he had attained humility. But he knew he had attained it and he knew it was not disgraceful and it carried no loss of true pride" (pp. 9-10).

Santiago refuses the young boy's offer to leave the boat his parents have made him go in and return to his, but soon after he hooks the great marlin he wishes increasingly and often that the boy were with him. And after the sharks come and he wonders if it had been a sin to kill the great fish, the old man thinks that, after all, "everything kills everything else in some way. Fishing kills me exactly as it keeps me alive." But then he remembers that it is not fishing but the love and care of another human being that keeps him alive now; "the boy keeps me alive, he thought. I must not deceive myself too much" (p. 106).

As the sharks tear from him more and more of the great fish and as the boat gets closer to his home, the old man's sense of his relationship to his friends and to the boy deepens: "I cannot be too far out now, he thought. I hope no one has been too worried. There is only the boy to worry, of course. But I am sure he would have confidence. Many of the older fishermen will worry. Many others too, he thought. I live in a good town" (p. 115). In the end, when he awakens in his shack and talks with the boy, he notices "how pleasant it was to have someone to talk to instead of speaking only to himself and to the sea" (p. 125). This time he accepts without any real opposition the boy's insistence on returning to his boat, and he says no more about going far out alone.

This theme of human solidarity and interdependence is reinforced by several symbols. Baseball, which the old man knows well
and loves and which he thinks and talks about constantly, is, of
course, a highly developed team sport and one that contrasts im-
portantly in this respect with the relatively far more individualistic
bullfighting, hunting, and fishing usually found in Hemingway's
stories. Although he tells himself that "now is no time to think of
baseball" (p. 37), the game is in Santiago's thoughts throughout his
ordeal, and he wonders about each day's results in the *Gran Ligas*.

Even more significant is the old man's hero-worship of Joe
DiMaggio, the great Yankee outfielder. DiMaggio, like Santiago,
was a champion, a master of his craft, and in baseball terms an old
one, playing out the last years of his glorious career severely handicapped by the pain of a bone spur in his heel. The image of
DiMaggio is a constant source of inspiration to Santiago; in his
strained back and his cut and cramped left hand he, too, is an old
champion who must endure the handicap of pain; and he tells himself that he "must have confidence and . . . be worthy of the great
DiMaggio who does all things perfectly even with the pain of the
bone spur in his heel" (p. 66).

But DiMaggio had qualities at least as vital to the Yankees as his
courage and individual brilliance. Even during his own time and
since then, many men with expert knowledge of baseball have considered other contemporary outfielders—especially Ted Williams of
the Boston Red Sox—to be DiMaggio's equal or superior in terms
of individual ability and achievement. But few men have ever
earned the affection and the renown which DiMaggio received as a
"team player"—one who always displayed his individual greatness
as part of his team, one to whom the team was always more important than himself. It used to be said of DiMaggio's value as a
"team player" that with him in the line-up, even when he was
handicapped by the pain in his heel, the Yankees were two runs
ahead when they came out on the field. From Santiago's love of
baseball and his evident knowledge of it, it is clear that he would
be aware of these qualities in DiMaggio. And when Manolin remarks that there are other men on the New York team, the old man
replies: " 'Naturally. But he makes the difference' " (p. 17).

The lions which Santiago dreams about and his description in
terms of Christ symbols further suggest solidarity and love and
humility as opposed to isolated individualism and pride. So evoca-
tive and lovely a symbol is the dream of the lions that it would

be foolish if not impossible to attempt its literal definition. Yet it seems significant that the old man dreams not of a single lion, a "king of the beasts," a lion proud and powerful and alone, like the one from which Francis Macomber runs in terror, but of several young lions who come down to a beach in the evening to play together. "He only dreamed of places now and of the lions on the beach. They played like young cats in the dusk and he loved them as he loved the boy" (p. 22). It seems also significant that the old man "no longer dreamed of storms, nor of women, nor of great occurrences, nor of great fish, nor fights, nor contests of strength, nor of his wife" (pp. 21-22)—that is that he no longer dreams of great individualistic deeds like the one which brings violence and destruction on him and on the marlin. Instead, the lions are "the main thing that is left" (p. 65), and they evoke the solidarity and love and peace to which the old man returns after hunting and killing and losing his great fish.

These qualities are further emphasized by the symbolic value of the old fisherman as he carries the mast crosslike up the hill to his shack and as he lies exhausted on his bed. His hands have been terribly wounded in catching the great marlin and in fighting the sharks, and as he lies sleeping "face down on the newspapers with his arms out straight and the palms up" (p. 122), his figure is Christ-like and suggests that if the old man has been crucified by the forces of a capricious and violent universe, the meaning of his experience is the humility and love of Christ and the interdependence which they imply.

Such, then, are the qualities which define man's true place in a world of violence and death indifferent to him, and they are the context which gives the experience of the old fisherman its ultimate significance as the reflection of Hemingway's culminating concept of the human condition—his tragic vision of man. For in his understanding that "it is enough to live on the sea and kill our true brothers," the fellow creatures who share life with us and whom he loves, the old man is expressing Hemingway's conviction that despite the tragic necessity of such a condition, man has a place in the world. And in his realization that in going alone and too far out, "beyond all people in the world," he has ruined both himself and also the great fish, the old man reflects Hemingway's feeling that in his individualism and his pride and his need, man inevitably goes beyond his true place in the world and thereby brings violence and destruction on himself and on others. Yet in going out too far and alone, Santiago has found his greatest strength and courage and dignity and nobility and love, and in this he expresses Hemingway's view of the ultimate tragic irony of man's fate: that only through the isolated individualism and the pride which drive him beyond his true place in life does man develop the qualities and the wisdom which teach him the sin of such individualism and pride and which bring him the deepest understanding of himself and of his place in the world. Thus, in accepting his world for what it is and in learning to live in it, Hemingway has achieved a tragic but ennobling vision of man which is in the tradition of Sophocles, Christ, Melville, and Conrad.

III

It is not enough, then, to point out, as Robert P. Weeks does, that "from the first eight words of *The Old Man and the Sea* . . . we are squarely confronted with a world in which man's isolation is the most insistent truth." [5] True as this is, it is truth which is at the same time paradox, for Santiago is profoundly aware that "no man was ever alone on the sea." Nor is the novel solely what Leo Gurko feels it is—"the culmination of Hemingway's long search for disengagement from the social world and total entry into the natural" (p. 15). If the old man leaves society to go "far out" and "beyond all people in the world," the consciousness of society and of his relationship to it are never for long out of his thoughts; and in the end, of course, he returns to his "good town," where he finds it pleasant "to have someone to talk to instead of speaking only to himself and to the sea." To go no further than Santiago's isolation, therefore, or to treat it, as Weeks does, as a theme in opposition to Hemingway's concern with society, is to miss the deepest level of significance both in his novel and in Hemingway's writing generally.

For, surely, as Edgar Johnson has shown, the true direction of Hemingway's thought and art from the beginning and especially since 1937 has been a return to society—not in terms of any particular social or political doctrine, but in the broad sense of human solidarity and interdependence. If he began by making "a separate peace" and by going, like Santiago, "far out" beyond society, like the old man, too, he has come back, through Harry Morgan's " 'no

[5] Robert P. Weeks, "Hemingway and the Uses of Isolation," *University of Kansas City Review*, XXIV, 125 (Winter, 1957).

man alone,' " Philip Rawlings's and Robert Jordan's "no man is
an island," and Santiago's "no man is ever alone on the sea," with
a deepened insight into its nature and values and a profound awareness of his relationship to it as an individual.[6]

In the process, strangely enough—or perhaps it is not strange at
all—he has come back from Frederic Henry's rejection of all abstract values to a reiteration for our time of mankind's oldest and
noblest moral principles. As James B. Colvert points out, Hemingway is a moralist: heir, like his world, to the destruction by science
and empiricism of nineteenth-century value assumptions, he rejects
equally these assumptions and the principle underlying them—that
intellectual moral abstractions possess independent supersensual
existence. Turning from the resulting nihilism, he goes to experience
in the actual world of hostility, violence, and destruction to find in
the world which destroyed the old values a basis for new ones—
and it is precisely here, Colvert suggests, in reflecting the central
moral problem of his world, that Hemingway is a significant moralist.[7]

But out of this concern with action and conduct in a naturalistic universe, Hemingway has not evolved new moral values; rather,
he has reaffirmed man's oldest ones—courage, love, humility, solidarity, and interdependence. It is their basis which is new—a basis
not in supernaturalism or abstraction but hard-won through actual
experience in a naturalistic universe which is at best indifferent to
man and his values. Hemingway tells us, as E. M. Halliday observes, that "we are part of a universe offering no assurance beyond the grave, and we are to make what we can of life by a
pragmatic ethic spun bravely out of man himself in full and steady
cognizance that the end is darkness." [8]

[6] This development in Hemingway's thought and art is further illustrated
in a story which he wrote in 1939 and which, prompted by the recent Cuban
revolution, *Cosmopolitan*, CXLVI, 4 (April, 1959), pp. 78-83, has reprinted.
"Nobody Ever Dies!" is the story of a Spanish-speaking young man and a
girl who have given themselves with selfless devotion to the cause of social
liberty in a revolt in Cuba. The young man is trapped and killed by govern-
mental forces, and the girl faces the torture of questioning with "a strange
confidence. It was the same confidence another girl her age had felt a little
more than five hundred years before in the market place of a town called
Rouen."

[7] James B. Colvert, "Ernest Hemingway's Morality in Action," *American
Literature*, XXVII (Nov., 1955), pp. 372-85.

[8] E. M. Halliday, "Hemingway's Ambiguity: Symbolism and Irony,"
American Literature, XXVIII (March, 1956), p. 3.

Through perfectly realized symbolism and irony,[9] then, Hemingway has beautifully and movingly spun out of an old fisherman's great trial just such a pragmatic ethic and its basis in an essentially tragic vision of man; and in this reaffirmation of man's most cherished values and their reaffirmation in the terms of our time rests the deepest and the enduring significance of *The Old Man and the Sea.*

Clinton S. Burhans, Jr.

[9] Halliday's comment on Hemingway's ironic method is particularly applicable to *The Old Man and the Sea:* "the ironic gap between expectation and fulfillment, pretense and fact, intention and action, the message sent and the message received, the way things are thought or ought to be and the way things are—this has been Hemingway's great theme from the beginning; and it has called for an ironic method to do it artistic justice" (*ibid.,* p. 15).

KEIICHI HARADA

The Marlin and the Shark: A Note on *The Old Man and the Sea*

"I tried to make a real old man, a real boy, a real sea and a real fish and real shark. But if I make them good and true enough they would mean many things. The hardest thing is to make something really true and sometimes truer than true."—Ernest Hemingway (*Time* [Pacific edition], Dec. 13, 1954)

What makes that very simple story, *The Old Man and the Sea,* an esthetically satisfying work of art is the fact that Hemingway recognizes the value of "multi-layeredness" of literature as a basis of a "good" and "true" work of art and uses it in his novels. In this novel, he utilizes a great variety of images, symbols, and archetypal patterns which make the novel a rich one and which allow many interpretations.

This short essay is an attempt to develop some of the symbolic images in the novel into their full meanings and thus to see what Hemingway has done in representing a reality.

OF THE OLD MAN AND THE OCEAN

As we know from such great literary works as the *Odyssey, Moby Dick,* or "The Rime of the Ancient Mariner," a great number of writers have used the sea as something that reveals deep realities of man and the universe. It is a place where man's destiny and identity are sought after, dramatized, and clarified. However, these realities are revealed only when man is involved in and participates in the life of the sea. Hemingway also seems to have held such an idea of the sea in composing his masterpiece, *The Old Man and the Sea.* Thus, for Santiago, the ocean is not an objectifiable place for exploitation, as it seems to the younger fishermen, but is considered as a personality, which he considers in terms of femininity.[1] It is feminine because of its wantonness and because it em-

[1] Page 10. All the page references to the novel in the text are to *The Old Man and the Sea* (New York: Charles Scribner's Sons, 1952).

bodies both kindness and cruelty. But more. It is so, because it contains in itself so many elements of fertility and possibility, as many myths of woman demonstrate, as to be deep enough to hide in its depth a never-heard-of or never-seen-of great fish that Santiago eventually meets; wide enough to make it possible for the old man to travel into the region where the unknowable and unknown secrets of reality can be known and experienced; and large enough to allow him to live in eternity. Such a notion of the sea may be more strongly substantiated when we realize that the old man is a lonely figure when he is engaged in the act of fishing. The novel opens with the sentence: "He was an old man who fished alone in a skiff in the Gulf Stream" (p. 9). It is true that the aloneness of Santiago is one forced from the outside by more realistic circumstances: that is, his best and only companion, Manolin, had to leave him because the boy's father decided that the old man, who had not been able to catch any fish for over a month, was *salao,* the worst form of unlucky, and forced the boy to leave him. However, in a deeper level of meaning, it is only natural and logical that the old man should be alone, for, as we shall see more fully later, he has made up his mind to fish "far out" in order to achieve the task "that which he was born for," as he again and again vows in the course of his fishing voyage. For a fisherman of his character, the vow is a serious one, for all his honors and glories as a fisherman depend upon whether he can perform the task perfectly. No matter what kind of suffering and trial he has to go through he has to fulfill his destiny, and thus the act of performing the task becomes a kind of ritual. Each individual has his own sense of destiny and the task should be met by himself and for himself. There is no one else capable of this undertaking or allowed to participate in this ritualistic procedure. It is a sort of esoteric religious rite where the particular individual has to face his holy destiny. In the course of various trials and sufferings, the old man wishes that the boy could be with him to help, but it is not to be permitted, for he alone has to endure the sufferings to fulfill his destiny. Thus, the ocean becomes a place where the old man searches his own identity through the act of pursuing the fish.

OF THE LIONS AND THE BONE SPUR

The most obvious pattern in the structure of the novel is that of the alternation of dream-memory and actual experience. This is also the device, as any reader of Hemingway may notice, that is employed in such a story as "The Snows of Kilimanjaro." This device is generally an attempt to clarify man's present conditions by contrasting the past with the present. The experiences of the past are not meaningless and useless facts but are often "recaptured" by the self through the discriminating and organizing process of the mind in order to establish one's self-identity. Associations and remembrances do not take place at random but are directed toward such an end.

The most recurrent image in the dream of Santiago is that of lions. Whenever he dreams, they almost always appear. Besides, he

no longer dreamed of storms, nor of women, nor of great occurrences, nor of great fish, nor fights, nor contests of strength, nor of his wife. He only dreamed of places now and of the lions on the beach. They played like young cats in the dusk and he loved them as he loved the boy (p. 27).

And he wonders why the lions are "the main thing that is left" (p. 73). It is also the question that arises in the mind of the reader. Let alone the Freudian interpretations, we may understand this image in connection with the idea of primitivism, which has been a constant resort of Hemingway from *The Sun Also Rises* onward. The primitive scenes as contrasted to man-made societies in Hemingway's works seem to play the role of a giver of strength and purity. Harry's dream in "The Snows of Kilimanjaro" is a case in point. Among his various dreams, that of the life among the snowy mountains brings forth not only the vitality he once possessed, but also the cleansing power of nature when he remembers that "the snow was so bright it hurt your eyes." [2] In a similar fashion, Santiago dreams of the lions on the beaches of Africa. The long golden beaches and the white beaches are "so white they hurt your eyes" (p. 27). The lions and the whiteness of beaches that live in his happy memories have become part of the personality of the old man and give him a purity to his purpose and sense of vitality that drives him toward the goal "that which he was born for."

Another important image is that of DiMaggio. It does not live in his memories and dreams as the lions do, but it is fully alive in his consciousness. The old man loves baseball as some other heroes of Hemingway love bullfighting. In fact, just as the lions are "the main thing that is left" in his dreams, so is baseball all he has left when he is on his way home after a long-endured fight with the fish (p.

[2] "The Snows of Kilimanjaro" in *Great Modern Short Stories* (New York: The Modern Library, 1942), p. 267.

114). And whenever he thinks of baseball, there inevitably appears the figure of DiMaggio. He is a great baseball player and worthy of the old man's admiration. Santiago feels closer to him the more because his father was also a fisherman and he can certainly understand how a fisherman like Santiago feels. But the most important factor in DiMaggio that attracts the old man's attention is the bone spur that DiMaggio is supposed to have. It is precisely this bone spur that has made DiMaggio transfigured to something more than a mere hero. It comes to have a symbolic significance to the mind of the old man. To him DiMaggio symbolizes a man who both endures sufferings and achieves greatness. Notice that it is almost always when the old man faces crises and hard trials that he remembers DiMaggio. He has become not only a source of Santiago's strength and vitality but also an absolute criterion and directing source of his action. The old man decides that he "must be worthy of the great DiMaggio who does all things perfectly even with the pain of the bone spur in his heel" (p. 75). When he feels weakness within himself during the long struggle against the great fish, his mind turns to DiMaggio and he asks himself: "Do you believe the great DiMaggio would stay with a fish as long as I will stay with this one?" With an affirmative answer, "I am sure he would," he then goes on fighting with renewed strength (p. 75).

This takes us further to another plane of significance in the novel: the significance of the image of the "bone spur." The classic analogy of the image is fairly obvious, the tradition of which, I believe, underlies the theme of the novel in many ways. It reminds us, for instance, of Odysseus' scar, Achilles' wound, or of one of the anagnorisis scenes in Sophocles' *Oedipus Tyrannus*. The significance of the analogy lies: (1) these heroes are all "noble" characters and do the actions of "proper magnitude," as Aristotle points out, and (2) the scars on their feet are used to bring about their own identity in one way or another. We need not push this second analogy of *anagnorisis* too much, for no Aristotelian definition is applicable in a strict sense to any contemporary literary works. Rather, it is advisable to use a loose definition and analogy. Therefore, the word is here so used as to mean broadly "a discovery." Now what strikes the old man concerning DiMaggio is, as we have seen, that the latter, despite his pain in his heel, endured the sufferings and achieved greatness. His bone spur is a reminder of the nobleness of an action and of "what a man can do and what a man endures" (p. 73). Thus the image of a hero in his memory and consciousness helps formulate his present identity and discover his possibility.

This fact becomes more significant when we notice that, during his pursuit of the great fish, his hand becomes cramped and his back starts to ache. Whenever he feels that "the hands and the back hurt truly" (p. 107), he remembers DiMaggio's bone spur. Whatever he does, he wishes to follow the example of DiMaggio. His mere past memory of a hero now becomes part of himself. The pain in his hands and back may remind us of the image of Christ, as Professor Carlos Baker points out. But we may not be far wrong to take it that it is a constant reminder to the old man of the limitation of finite human being and thus helps him attain humility by way of the recognition of a classic idea of *hubris,* the point of which we shall discuss in our next section.

OF THE MARLIN AND THE SHARK

When Santiago declared that he would go "far out," he felt "confident" because the day was the eighty-fifth day and it meant to his mind a lucky day. The prospect of the day seemed to be a smiling one. Far out in the sea, he finally succeeds in hooking the great fish. But it is not until he has been taken farther out on the ocean by the fish that he realizes how big the fish is. He has never "seen a greater, or more beautiful, or a calmer or more noble thing than" this fish (p. 102). As he continues his fight, his respect for the greatness and dignity of the fish increases. He loves the fish as if it were his own brother, and yet he is determined to kill him. This determination and subsequent actions of his come from his sense of destiny. This decision is founded on his firm feeling that he is to show "what a man can do and what a man endures" and to fulfill the task "that which he was born for."

At this point, it may be helpful to notice two phases of time structure in the old man's consciousness. His being a fisherman is predetermined, so to speak, as far as we are made known of him in the novel. But, on the other hand, what saves him from being a mere victim of the past and making predetermination is what may be called his existential time consciousness. In the early stage of his fishing voyage, he shows a defiance to a deterministic and fatalistic attitude. His failure of catching fish for the past eighty-four days casts a doubt on his confidence. This doubt makes him say, "Only I have no luck any more." If it is true, it would be a fatal blow to a fisherman. But then he immediately rejects such a notion and tells himself, "But who knows? Maybe today. Every day is a new day" (pp. 36-37). Again, when he recognizes the "greatness and glory" of the fish, his determination to kill him is strengthened the more for it. Hemingway describes the mind of Santiago at this moment as follows:

"I told the boy I was a strange old man," he said. "Now is when I must prove it." The thousand times that he had proved it meant nothing.

Now he was proving it again. *Each time was a new time and he never thought about the past when he was doing it* (p. 73; italics are mine).

The characteristic of this kind of pursuit, as Professor Hans Meyerhoff points out, "enables the individual to live within the dimension of a permanent 'now,' without past or future." [3] Thus we see Santiago, in his pursuit of the fish, being given vitality and driven by the image of the lions and DiMaggio, and, at the same time, freed from any deterministic sense of the past and united to a permanent "now."

As the story proceeds, the real issue of Santiago's pursuit becomes clearer. The fish he has hooked ceases to be a mere physical object. It comes to symbolize something which belongs to a different realm of existence. This is a wholly new experience for the old man in his long years of life as a fisherman. Until he faces this fish, he has never seen or heard of such a great and beautiful fish. And he feels that "there is no one worthy of eating him from the manner of his behavior and his great dignity" (p. 83). The old man's wisdom and long years of experience prove to be useless, because the experience is a *Begegnung* with something which transcends the "limit-situation" of a physical and temporal being which is necessarily bound by finitude and time. This is precisely the reason why the old man repeatedly expresses his desire to share the fate with the fish. What the image of DiMaggio does to him in his memory and consciousness, the fish does in actuality. He feels he is not "worthy of eating him," but nevertheless he tries to kill him. He has to kill him because it is a kind of sacrifice to complete the ritual, and the sacrifice is absolutely necessary to attain a rebirth through death. Either one of them has to die for that purpose. Or possibly both. Thus he cries, "Come on and kill me, I do not care who kills who" (p. 102), and later, "If I were towing him behind there would be no question. Nor if the fish were in the skiff, with all dignity

[3] *Time in Literature* (Berkeley and Los Angeles, 1955), p. 70.

gone, there would be no question either . . . let him bring me in
if it pleases him. I am only better than him through trickery . . ."
(pp. 109-10). As these words of the old man show, Santiago's pursuit has now become a quest: a quest for the union with the
transcendental, that he nor anyone else has ever seen or ever been
able to see. Now it makes no difference which one dies as long as he
succeeds in the quest. He does succeed. The pursuer and the pursued have become one. Temporality is united with eternity.

But the fact remains that Santiago belongs to the temporal order
of time. He has to pay the price for what he has done and for what
he got. Already, at the beginning of the novel, we seem to discern a
tragic flaw when he tells the boy that he intends to go "far out" to
fish. The region where he hooked the great fish is that where no
other fishermen can be seen, or, more symbolically understood,
where no earthly being is permitted to enter. Whether he has committed the act consciously or not matters little. He has overstepped
the boundary of man's finite and limited nature. The act may be
interpreted more as a *hubris* than as a sin. For the concept of sin in
a Christian context involves some conscious act or motivation,
while *hubris* does not necessarily have to do with it. For example,
we may argue that the Moira was too severe on Oedipus for he has
really nothing to do with the making of his own fate. But just the
same, it is a *hubris,* and he has to take the responsibility.[4] Indeed,
that the old man has gone "too far out" is partly the responsibility
of the fish that has towed the fishing boat and Santiago toward the
heart of the ocean. And that he killed the fish thus "far out" on
the sea comes from a clear and simple reason, not wholly his own
responsibility that he was born a fisherman and nothing else, the
fact of which he cannot help himself. But just the same, he has to
pay the price for the glory. In this twentieth-century novel, the
Nemesis takes the shape of the sharks. After he has achieved the
act of greatness, the union with the eternal and the transcendental,
he turns his boat toward the land, the home of temporality, futility,
and fixedness. It is then that the old man has to face a great enemy,
the sharks. Just like the Furies haunting the doomed Orestes, the
sharks seem to be determined to prevent the old man from taking
the prize of his fighting out of the sacred region. It is as if these
sharks were the mortuary divinities who are angered by the sacri-
legious attempt of the old man to expose the unknowable face to

[4] Cf. Philip Wheelwright, "The Guilt of Oedipus," in *The Burning Fountain: A Study in the Language of Symbolism* (Bloomington, Indiana, 1954),
p. 229.

those in the temporary and finite order. That exhilarated joy of the old man was something attained by his plunging into the abyss of an eternal "now." But after the moment of this exhilaration, the old man is reminded of his actual predicament. He lives in time. And the goal of time is death and destruction. The sharks are the symbol of "time." They are the incarnation of "Devouring Time," and Santiago finally learns, with Shakespeare, that "nothing 'gainst Time's scythe can make defense" (Sonnet XII). He is now forced to learn the reality of man's existence. He says to the fish, "I shouldn't have gone out so far, fish, neither for you nor for me, I'm sorry, fish" (p. 121). He recognizes that he has transgressed his limitation, that he has to meet the consequences of his *hubris*. Now, at last, he would have admitted to the full the truth of the lesson of the *Oresteia,* that "By suffering man learns."

However, he is not "defeated," despite the fact that he has been "beaten," as he himself admits, by his violation of the sacred code. He pronounces that "nothing" beat him really and that his only fault was that he "went out too far" (p. 133). It is because he has learned "by suffering," and he now *knows* the truth that the penalty of his *hubris* is the loss of his supreme identity in an eternal order. "Mistah Kurtz" died in failure. But to the mind of Marlow, he was a victor because Kurtz had pronounced a "judgment" upon the "horror" to the abyss of human existence. In the same way, Santiago has learned much in a few days of fishing voyage through much suffering, and he is now able to pronounce a judgment upon the inscrutable human existence and man's destiny: he has "gone too far out." His failure has thus turned out to be his victory.

Keiichi Harada

APPENDIX

APPENDIX

A Checklist of Hemingway Criticism

NOTE: The following checklist is founded on Professor Maurice Beebe's bibliography, published in the Hemingway Number of *Modern Fiction Studies,* Volume I, Number 3, August, 1955. The general format of the original has been followed, as well. The passage of intervening years and a search of various foreign periodicals have led to a considerable enlargement of the version of 1955. In this task the editor has had the valuable assistance of Mr. James Adams.

I. GENERAL

Abramov, A., "Molodost veka," *Internatsionalnaya Literatura,* No. 6 (1935), 141.

————, "Novoye v amerikanskoi dramaturgii," *Teatr,* Nos. 2-3 (1939), 39-50.

Adams, J. Donald, "Ernest Hemingway," *English Journal,* XXVIII (1939), 87-94.

————, *The Shape of Books to Come,* New York, 1944, pp. 103-13.

————, "Speaking of Books," *New York Times Book Review,* Sept. 21, 1952, p. 2.

Adams, Richard P., "Sunrise Out of the Waste Land," *Tulane Studies in English,* IX (1959), 119-31.

Aldridge, John W., *After the Lost Generation,* New York, 1951, pp. 23-43.

————, "Hemingway: The Etiquette of the Berserk," *Mandrake,* II (Autumn-Winter, 1954-55), 331-41.

Allen, Hugh, "The Dark Night of Ernest Hemingway," *Catholic World, CLII* (1940), 522-29.

Alsop, Joseph, "A Cuban Visit with Hemingway," *New York Herald Tribune,* Mar. 9, 1960, p. 18.

Antonini, Giacomo, "Hemingway grande e meno grande," *La Fiera Letteraria,* No. 3 (Jan. 16, 1955), 1-2.

————, "Hemingway, uno dei maestri della letteratura americana," *La Fiera Letteraria,* VIII (Sept. 27, 1953), 1-2.

Astre, G.-A., *Hemingway par lui-même,* Paris, 1959.

Atkins, John Alfred, *The Art of Ernest Hemingway: His Work and Personality,* London, 1952.

Backman, Melvin, "Hemingway: The Matador and the Crucified," *Modern Fiction Studies,* I (Aug., 1955), 2-11.

Baker, Carlos, "The Hard Trade of Mr. Hemingway," *Delphian Quarterly,* XXIII (July, 1940), 12-17.

――――, "Hemingway's Wastelanders," *Virginia Quarterly Review,* XXVIII (Summer, 1952), 373-92.

――――, *Hemingway: The Writer As Artist,* Princeton, N.J., 1952; second edition, enlarged, 1956.

Bardacke, Theodore, "Hemingway's Women," McCaffery (see below), pp. 340-51.

Barea, Arturo, "Not Spain But Hemingway," *Horizon,* III (May, 1941), 350-61.

Barnes, Lois L., "The Helpless Hero of Ernest Hemingway," *Science and Society,* XVII (1953), 1-25.

Bartlett, Phyllis, "Other Countries, Other Wenches," *Modern Fiction Studies,* III (Winter, 1957-58), 345-49.

Bataille, Georges, "Hemingway à la lumiere de Hegel," *Critique,* IX (March, 1953), 195-210.

Bates, H. E., *The Modern Short Story: A Critical Survey,* London, 1943, pp. 167-78.

Beach, Joseph Warren, *The Twentieth-Century Novel: Studies in Technique,* New York and London, 1932, pp. 532-37.

――――, *American Fiction 1920-1940.* New York, 1941, pp. 69-119.

――――, "How Do You Like It Now, Gentlemen?" *Sewanee Review,* LIX (Spring, 1951), 311-28.

Beach, Sylvia, *Shakespeare and Company,* New York, 1956, pp. 33, 77-83, 121, 127, 130.

Beatty, Jerome, Jr., "Hemingway vs. *Esquire,*" *Saturday Review of Literature,* XLI (Aug. 23, 1958), 9-11, 36.

Beaver, Joseph, "Technique in Hemingway," *College English,* XIV (March, 1953), 325-28.

Beebe, Maurice, "Criticism of Ernest Hemingway: A Checklist with an Index to Studies of Separate Works," *Modern Fiction Studies,* I (Aug., 1955), 36-45.

――――, editor, *Configuration Critique D'Ernest Hemingway,* Paris, 1957 (*La Revue des Lettres Modernes,* Vol. IV, No. 31-34, 4ᵉ Trim. 1957).

Bienkowski, Zbigniew, "Opowiadania Hemingwaya," *Tworczosc,* No. 8 (Aug., 1956), 153-57.

Bishop, John Peale, "Homage to Hemingway," *New Republic,* LXXXIX (Nov. 11, 1936), 39-42. [Reprinted: CXXXI (Nov. 22, 1954), 109-11; Malcolm Cowley, editor, *After the Genteel Tradition,* New York, 1937, pp. 186-201; and Edmund Wilson, editor, *Collected Essays of John Peale Bishop,* New York, 1948, pp. 37-46.]

――――, "The Missing All," *Virginia Quarterly Review,* XIII (Summer,

1937), 107-21. [Reprinted: *Collected Essays* . . . , pp. 66-77; and McCaffery, pp. 292-307.]

Bleiman, M., "Poeziya borby i gumanizma," *Iskusstvo i Zhizn,* No. 5 (1939), 15-17.

Bluefarb, Samuel, "The Sea—Mirror and Maker of Character in Fiction and Drama," *English Journal,* XLVIII (Dec., 1959), 501-10.

Breit, Harvey, "Talk with Ernest Hemingway," *New York Times Book Review,* Sept. 7, 1952, p. 20.

Brown, Deming, "Hemingway in Russia," *American Quarterly,* V (1953), 143-56.

Burgum, Edwin Berry, *The Novel and the World's Dilemma,* New York, 1947, pp. 184-204. [Reprinted: McCaffery, pp. 308-28.]

Burnam, Tom, "Primitivism and Masculinity in the Work of Ernest Hemingway," *Modern Fiction Studies,* I (Aug., 1955), 20-24.

Bury, John P., "Hemingway in Spain," *Contemporary Review,* No. 1118 (Feb., 1959), 103-5.

Campoamor, Fernando G., "Homenaje Cubano a Hemingway," *Boletín Comisión Nacional Cubana de la UNESCO,* V (Sept., 1956), 11-13.

Cargill, Oscar, *Intellectual America: Ideas on the March,* New York, 1941, pp. 351-70.

Carpenter, Frederic I., "Hemingway Achieves the Fifth Dimension," *Publications of the Modern Language Association,* LXIX (Sept., 1954), 711-18; collected in his *American Literature and The Dream.*

Carsensten, Broder, "Evelyn Waugh und Ernest Hemingway," *Archiv für das Studium der Neueren Sprachen,* CXC (Feb., 1954), 193-203.

Cecchi, Emilio, *Americana: Raccolta di Narratori,* Ed. E. Vittorini, Milan, 1947.

Cimatti, Pietro, "L'altro Hemingway," *Fiera Letteraria,* XIII (June 8, 1958), 6.

Cohn, Louis H., *A Bibliography of the Works of Ernest Hemingway,* New York, 1931.

Colvert, James B., "Ernest Hemingway's Morality in Action," *American Literature,* XXVII (Nov., 1955), 372-85.

Cooke, Alistair, "Hemingway: Master of the Mid-West Vernacular," *Manchester Guardian Weekly,* Nov. 11, 1954, p. 7.

Corin, Fernand, "Steinbeck and Hemingway—A Study in Literary Economy," *Revue Des Langues Vivantes,* XXIV (Jan.-Feb., 1958), 60-75; (Mar.-Apr., 1958), 153-63.

Cousins, Norman, "For Whom the Bells Ring," *Saturday Review of Literature,* XLII (Aug. 22, 1959), 18.

Cowley, Malcolm, "Ernest Hemingway: A Farewell to Spain," *New Republic,* LXXIII (Nov. 30, 1932), 76-77. [Reprinted: M. D.

Zabel, editor, *Literary Opinion in America,* New York, 1937, pp. 506-11.]

——, "Hemingway at Midnight," *New Republic,* CXI (Aug. 19, 1944), 190-95.

——, "Hemingway and the Hero," *New Republic,* CXI (Dec. 4, 1944), 754-58.

——, " 'Mister Papa': Porträt eines Nobelpreisträgers," *Der Monat,* VII (Dec., 1954), 204-10.

——, "A Portrait of Mister Papa," *Life,* XXV (Jan. 10, 1949), 86-101. [Reprinted: McCaffery, pp. 34-56.]

——, editor, *The Portable Hemingway,* New York, 1944.

Crovi, Raffaele, "Vittorini, l'America e la giovane letteratura italiana," *Galleria,* IV (Dec., 1954), 307-13.

D'Agostino, Nemi, "Ernest Hemingway," *Belgafour,* XI (Jan., 1956), 54-73.

——, "The Later Hemingway," *Sewanee Review,* LXVIII (Summer, 1960), 482-93.

Daiches, David, "Ernest Hemingway," *College English,* II (May, 1941), 725-36.

Daniel, Robert, "Hemingway and His Heroes," *Queen's Quarterly,* LIV (Winter, 1947-48), 471-85.

D'Argo, Silvio, "Hemingway," *Paragone,* No. 22 (Oct., 1951), 77.

Dawson, William, "Ernest Hemingway: Petoskey Interview," *Michigan Alumnus Quarterly Review,* LXIV (Winter, 1958), 114-23.

Dewing, Arthur, "The Mistake about Hemingway," *North American Review,* CCXXXII (1931), 364-71.

Dinamov, S., "Roman Khemingueya o voine," *Internatsionalnaya Literatura,* No. 7 (1936), 165.

Dorgelès, Roland, "Ce rude Hemingway," *Figaro Littéraire,* No. 509 (Jan. 21, 1956).

Drummond, Ann, "The Hemingway Code as Seen in the Early Short Stories," *Discourse: A Review of the Liberal Arts,* I (Oct., 1958), 248-52.

Druzin, V., "V poiskakh nastoyashchevo cheloveka," *Rezets,* No. 18 (1938), 22.

Duesberg, Jacques, "Grandeur et décadence d'Ernest Hemingway," *Synthèses,* VI (Dec., 1951), 90-91.

——, "Une victoire par k.o. technique," *Synthèses,* VII (Mar., 1953), 219-22.

Duffy, Charles, "Ernest Hemingway," *Sprache und Literatur Englands und Amerikas: Lehrgangs vorträge der Akademie Comburg,* II (1957), 151-64.

Eastman, Max, "Bull in the Afternoon," *New Republic,* LXXV (June 7, 1933), 94-97. [Reprinted: *Art and the Life of Action,* New York, 1934, pp. 87-101; and McCaffery, pp. 66-75.]

Edel, Leon, "The Arft of Evasion," *Folio,* XX (Spring, 1955), 18-20.

————, and Philip Young, "Hemingway and the Nobel Prize," *Folio*, XX (Spring, 1955), 18-22.

Ekström, Kjell, "Ernest Hemingway," *Samtid och Framtid*, X (1953), 153-58.

Erval, François, "Transformations de Hemingway," *Temps Moderne*, VIII (Jan.-Feb., 1953), 1248-53.

Fadiman, Clifton, "Ernest Hemingway: An American Byron," *Nation*, CXXXV (Jan. 18, 1933), 63-64.

Fedin, K., "O knigakh Khemingueya," *Internatsionalnaya Literatura*, Nos. 7-8 (1939), 217.

Fenton, Charles A., *The Apprenticeship of Ernest Hemingway: The Early Years*, New York, 1954.

————, "Ernest Hemingway: The Young Years," *Atlantic Monthly*, CXCIII (Mar., 1954), 25-34; (Apr., 1954), 49-57; (May, 1954), 39-44. [The first part of the above book.]

————, "No Money for the Kingbird: Hemingway's Prizefight Stories," *American Quarterly*, IV (Winter, 1952), 339-50.

Fitzgerald, F. Scott, "How to Waste Material: A Note on My Generation," *Bookman*, LXIII (May, 1926), 262-65.

Flanagan, John T., "Hemingway's Debt to Sherwood Anderson," *Journal of English and Germanic Philology*, LIV (Oct., 1955), 507-20.

Forssell, Lars, "Den heroiska stilen. Några anteckningar till Hemingway," *Bonniers Litterära Magasin*, XXII (1953), 43-47.

Fouchet, Max-Pol, "Hemingway: un catcheur avec des myosotis dans le ventre," *Figaro Litteraire*, IX, I (Nov. 6, 1954), 5.

Freedman, Richard, "Hemingway's Spanish Civil War Dispatches," *Texas Studies in Literature and Language*, I (Summer, 1959), 171-80.

Frid, Y., "Rasskazy Khemingueya," *Literaturnoye Obozreniye*, No. 18 (1939), 49.

Friedman, Norman, "Criticism and the Novel: Hardy, Hemingway, Crane, Woolf, Conrad," *Antioch Review*, XVIII (Fall, 1958), 343-70.

Friedrich, Otto, "Ernest Hemingway: Joy Through Strength," *American Scholar*, XXVI (Autumn, 1957), 470, 518-30.

Frohock, W. M., *The Novel of Violence in America, 1920-1950*, Dallas, 1950, pp. 167-99. [Reprinted: McCaffery, pp. 262-91.]

Fussell, Edwin, "Hemingway and Mark Twain," *Accent*, XIV (Summer, 1954), 199-206.

Gary, Romain, "Le retour du champion," *Nouvelles Littéraires*, No. 1306 (Sept. 11, 1952).

Geismar, Maxwell, *Writers in Crisis: The American Novel Between Two Wars*, Boston, 1942, pp. 39-85. [Reprinted: McCaffery, pp. 143-89.]

Gérard, Albert, "Ernest Hemingway," *Revue des Langues Vivantes*, XXI (Feb., 1955), 35-50.

————, "Hemingway's Lehrjahre," *Revue des Langues Vivantes,* XXIII (Feb., 1957), 89-91.

Goodheart, Eugene, "The Legacy of Ernest Hemingway," *Prairie Schooner,* XXX (Fall, 1956), 212-18.

Gordon, Caroline, "Notes on Hemingway and Kafka," *Sewanee Review,* LVII (1949), 215-26.

Gray, James, *On Second Thought,* Minneapolis, 1946, pp. 74-82. [Reprinted: McCaffery, pp. 226-35.]

Grebstein, Sheldon, "Controversy," *American Scholar,* XXVII (Spring, 1958), 229-31.

Grinberg, I., "Chto zhe dalshe?" *Zvezda,* No. 3 (1937), 190.

————, "Geroi beryotsya za oruzhiye," *Rezets,* Nos. 9-10 (1939), 28-30.

Gullon, Ricardo, "Las novelas de Hemingway," *Insula,* VII (Nov. 15, 1952), 5.

Gurko, Leo, "The Achievement of Ernest Hemingway," *College English,* XIII (April, 1952), 368-75.

Guth, Paul, "En pêchant l'espadon en compagnie d'Hemingway," *Figaro Littéraire,* IX, I (Nov. 6, 1954), 5.

Guttman, Alan, "Mechanized Doom: Ernest Hemingway and the Spanish Civil War," *Massachusetts Review,* I (May, 1960), 541-61.

Haas, Rudolf, "Zum Todesmotiv im Werk Hemingways," *Die Neueren Sprachen,* VIII (Oct., 1959), 455-65.

Halliday, E. M., "Hemingway's Ambiguity: Symbolism and Irony," *American Literature,* XXVIII (March, 1956), 1-22.

————, "Hemingway's Hero," *University of Chicago Magazine,* XLV (May, 1953), 10-14.

————, "Hemingway's In Our Time," *Explicator,* VII (March, 1949), item 35.

————, "Hemingway's Narrative Perspective," *Sewanee Review,* LX (Spring, 1952), 202-18.

Happell, Hokolaus, "Ausserungen Hemingways zur Darstellung der Wirklichkeit und Wahrheit," *Archiv für das Studium der Neueren Sprachen,* CXCI (Feb., 1954), 204-13.

————, "Ein Beitrag zur 'discipline' in Hemingways Stil," *Die Neueren Sprachen,* VI (Dec., 1957), 583-87.

Harris, Robert T., "Plausibility in Fiction," *Journal of Philosophy,* XLIX (Jan., 1952), 5-11.

Hart, Robert C., "Hemingway on Writing," *College English,* XVIII (March, 1957), 314-20.

Hartwick, Harry, *Foreground of American Fiction,* New York, 1934, pp. 151-59.

Hatcher, Harlan, *Creating the Modern American Novel,* New York, 1935, pp. 228-33.

Hemingway, Ernest, "A Letter from Ernest Hemingway," *Saturday Review of Literature,* XXXV (Sept. 6, 1952), 11.

Hemphill, George, "Hemingway and James," *Kenyon Review*, XI (Winter, 1949), 5060. [Reprinted: McCaffery, pp. 329-39.]

Hicks, Granville, *The Great Tradition*, New York, 1933, pp. 273-76.

———, "The Shape of a Career," *Saturday Review of Literature*, XLI (Dec. 13, 1958), 16, 38.

———, "Twenty Years of Hemingway," *New Republic*, CXI (Oct. 23, 1944), 524-26.

Hoffman, Frederick J., *The Modern Novel in America 1900-1950*, Chicago, 1951, pp. 89-103.

———, "No Beginning and No End: Hemingway and Death," *Essays in Criticism*, III (January, 1953), 73-84.

———, *The Twenties: American Writing in the Postwar Decade*, New York, 1955, pp. 66-76 and *passim*.

Holman, C. Hugh, "Hemingway and Emerson, notes on the Continuity of an Aesthetic Tradition," *Modern Fiction Studies*, I (Aug., 1955), 12-16.

———, "Hemingway and Vanity Fair," *Carolina Quarterly*, VIII (Summer, 1956), 31-37.

Holmes, John C., "Existentialism and the Novel: Notes and Questions," *Chicago Review*, XVIII (Summer, 1959), 144-51.

Holthusen, Hans Egon, "Hemingways Darstellungkunst," *Universitas*, X (March, 1955), 257-60.

Hotchner, A. E., "Hemingway Talks to American Youth," *This Week Magazine*, October 18, 1959, 10-11, 24-26.

Ishi, Ichiro, "Understanding of E. Hemingway," *Hototogisu*, V (Feb., 1956), 12-13.

Jameson, Storm, "The Craft of the Novelist," *English Review*, LVIII (1934), 28-43.

Johnson, Edgar, "Farewell the Separate Peace," *Sewanee Review*, XLVIII (1940), 289-300. [Reprinted: McCaffery, pp. 76-108.]

Johnson, James, "The Adolescent Hero: A Trend in Modern Fiction." *Twentieth Century Literature*, V (Apr., 1959), 3-11.

Karst, Roman, "Casus Hemingway," *Tworszosc*, XI (1955), 98-106.

Kashkeen, Ivan, "Alive in the Midst of Death," *Soviet Literature*, No. 7 (1956), 160-72.

———, "Dve novelly Khemingueya," *Internatsionalnaya Literatura*, No. 1 (1934), 93.

———, "Ernest Hemingway: A Tragedy of Craftsmanship," *International Literature*, V (1945), 76-108.

———, "Ernest Kheminguei," *Internatsionalnaya Literatura*, Nos. 7-8 (1939), 319-20.

———, "Hemingway on the Path to Mastery," *Voprosi Literaturi*, No. 6 (Sept., 1957), 184-204.

Kazin, Alfred, *On Native Grounds*, New York, 1942, pp. 327-41. [Reprinted: McCaffery, pp. 190-204.]

Kinnamon, Kenneth, "Hemingway, the *Corrida*, and Spain," *Texas Studies in Language and Literature*, I (Spring, 1959), 44-61.

Kirstein, Lincoln, "The Canon of Death," *Hound and Horn,* VI (1933), 336-41. [Reprinted: McCaffery, pp. 59-65.]

Knoll, Robert E., *Robert McAlmon, Expatriate Publisher and Writer* (University of Nebraska Studies), Lincoln, Nebr., 1957.

Koreichuk, A., "Literatura velikovo amerikanskovo naroda," *Internatsionalnaya Literatura,* Nos. 7-8 (1939), 236.

Kreymborg, Alfred, "Exit Vachel Lindsay—Enter Ernest Hemingway," *Literary Review,* I (Winter, 1957-58), 202-19.

Labor, Earle, "Crane and Hemingway: Anatomy of Trauma," *Renascence,* XI (Summer, 1959), 189-96.

Lange, Per-Adolf, "Hemingways poesi," *Bonniers Litterära Magasin,* XXVII (Feb., 1958), 133-38.

Las Vergnas, Raymond, "Hemingway prix Novel," *Hommes et Mondes,* IX (Dec., 1954), 143-45.

————, "Un Classique américain: Hemingway," *Nouvelle Littéraires,* No. 1418 (Nov. 4, 1954), 1.

Leighton, Lawrence, "An Autopsy and a Prescription," *Hound and Horn,* V (1932), 519-39.

Levin, Harry, "Observations on the Style of Ernest Hemingway," *Kenyon Review,* XIII (Autumn, 1951), 581-609.

Lévy, Yves, "Hemingway, chevalier du Graal," *Preuves,* IV (Dec., 1954), 60-63.

Lewis, Wyndham, *Men Without Art,* London, 1934, pp. 17-40.

Littell, Robert, "Notes on Hemingway," *New Republic,* LI (Aug. 10, 1927), 303-6.

Loeb, Harold, *The Way It Was,* New York, 1959, pp. 259-98.

Loggins, Vernon, *I Hear America,* New York, 1937, pp. 134-38.

Lovett, Robert M., "Ernest Hemingway," *English Journal,* XXI (1932), 609-17.

McCaffery, John K. M., editor, *Ernest Hemingway: The Man and His Work,* Cleveland, 1950.

McClennan, Joshua, "Ernest Hemingway and His Audience," *Michigan Alumnus Quarterly Review,* LIX (Summer, 1953), 335-40.

McCole, C. J., *Lucifer At Large,* New York, 1937, pp. 153-72.

McCormick, John, "Hemingway and History," *Western Review,* XVII (Winter, 1953), 87-98.

McCullers, Carson, "The Flowering Dream: Notes on Writing," *Esquire,* LII (Dec., 1959), 162-64.

Magny, Claude-Edmonde, *L'Âge du Roman Americain,* Paris, 1948, pp. 159-77.

Maurois, André, "Ernest Hemingway," *Revue de Paris,* LXII (March, 1955), 3-16.

Mendelson, M., "Amerikanskaya literatura v poiskakh obraza nastoyashchevo cheloveka," *Znamya,* No. 3 (1947), 176-77.

Miller-Budnitskaya, "Ernest Kheminguei," *Internatsionalnaya Literatura,* No. 6 (1937), 219.

———, in O. Berestov, "Vecher E. Khemingueya," *Rezets*, No. 7 (1939), 24.

Mingulina, A., "Ernest Kheminguei," *Kniga i Proletarskaya revolyutsiya*, No. 8 (1937), 125.

Mohrt, Michel, "Hemingway, les héros et les dieux," *Table Ronde*, No. 606 (Dec., 1952), 122-28.

Moloney, Michael F., "Ernest Hemingway: The Missing Third Dimension," in Harold C. Gardiner, editor, *Fifty Years of the American Novel*, New York, 1952, pp. 183-96.

Moore, Harry T., "An Earnest Hemingwaiad," *Encounter*, X (June, 1958), 15-18.

Morris, Wright, "The Ability to Function: A Reappraisal of Fitzgerald and Hemingway," *New World Writing*, No. 13 (June, 1958), 34-51.

Muller, Herbert J., *Modern Fiction: A Study in Values*, New York, 1937, pp. 395-402.

Nakaza, Gensuke, "Hemingway and the Sea," *Bulletin of the Arts and Sciences Division, University of Ryukus*, IV (June, 1959), 1-28.

Nemerovskaya, Olga, "Sudba amerikanskoi novelly," *Literaturnaya Uchyoba*, No. 5 (1935), 102.

———, "V poiskakh geroizma," *Znamya*, No. 6 (1938), 277.

Nozaki, Takashi, "An Embodiment of Sensibility—The Works of Ernest Hemingway," *Studies in English Literature* (English Literary Society of Japan), XXXVI (Oct., 1959), 93-108.

O'Faolain, Sean, *The Vanishing Hero: Studies in Novelists of the Twenties*, London, 1956, pp. 135-65.

O'Hara, John, et al., "Who the Hell Is Hemingway?" *True*, XXXVI (Feb., 1956), 14-19.

Oldsey, Bernard S., "Hemingway's Old Men," *Modern Fiction Studies*, I (Aug., 1955), 32-35.

Orrok, Douglas Hall, "Hemingway, Hugo, and Revelation," *Modern Language Notes*, LXVI (Nov., 1951), 441-45.

Paolini, Pier F., "Lo Hemingway dei Grandi Racconti," *Letterature Moderne*, VI (Nov.-Dec., 1956), 742-50.

Papajewski, Helmut, "Die Frage nack der Sinnhaftigkeit bei Hemingway," *Anglia*, LXX (1951), 186-209.

Parker, Dorothy, "The Artist's Reward," *New Yorker*, V (Nov. 30, 1929), 258-62.

Parks, Edd Winfield, "Hemingway and Faulkner: The Pattern of Their Thought," *Dagens Nyheter*, Feb. 12, 1956, 4-5 (in Danish).

———, "Faulkner and Hemingway: Their Thought," *South Atlantic Bulletin*, XXII (March, 1957), 1-2.

Paul, Elliot, "Hemingway and the Critics," *Saturday Review of Literature*, XVII (Nov. 6, 1937), 3-4. [Reprinted: McCaffery, pp. 109-13.]

Pesis, B., "Pyataya kolonna," *Literaturnoye Obozreniye*, No. 11 (1939), 33-36.

Phillips, William, "Male-ism and Moralism," *American Mercury*, LXXV (Oct., 1952), 93-98.

——, "Sherwood Anderson's Two Prize Pupils," *University of Chicago Magazine*, XLVII (Jan., 1955), 9-12.

Platonov, A., "Navstrechu lyudyam," *Literaturny Kritik*, No. 11 (1938), 171.

Plimpton, George, "Hemingway—Dix Conseils aux Jeunes Ecrivains," *Arts*, No. 662 (March 19-25, 1958), 1, 45; No. 663 (March 26– April 1, 1958), 1, 3; No. 664 (April 2-8, 1958), 3.

——, "Ernest Hemingway," *Paris Review*, XVIII (Spring, 1958), 61-82.

Poore, Charles, editor, *The Hemingway Reader*, New York, 1953.

Praz, Mario, "Hemingway in Italy," *Partisan Review*, XV (1948), 1086-1100.

——, "Un giovane narratore americano," *La Stampa* (June, 1929).

Richardson, H. Edward, "The 'Hemingwaves' in Faulkner's 'Wild Palms,' " *Modern Fiction Studies*, IV (Winter, 1958-1959), 357-60.

von Rosen, Björn, "Hemingway och de gröna bergen," *Bonniers Litteräre Magasin*, XXIII (Dec., 1954), 800-4.

Rosenfeld, Paul, *By Way of Art*, New York, 1928, pp. 151-63.

Ross, Lillian, "How Do You Like It Now, Gentlemen?" *New Yorker*, XXVI (May 13, 1950), 36, 38-40, 42-56.

Rubin, Louis D., Jr., "Modern Novelists and Contemporary American Society: A Symposium," *Shenandoah*, X (Winter, 1959), 3-31.

Russell, Peter, editor, *An Examination of Ezra Pound*, New York, 1950, pp. 73-76.

Samuels, Lee, *A Hemingway Checklist*, New York, 1951.

Sanders, David, "Ernest Hemingway's Spanish Civil War Experiences," *American Quarterly*, XII (Summer, 1960), 133-43.

Sapin, Louis, "Hemingway—un colosse qui triomphe des éléments et des hommes," *Arts*, No. 62 (March 19-25, 1958), 4; No. 63 (March 26–April 1, 1958), 3.

Savage, D. S., *The Withered Branch: Six Studies in the Modern Novel*, London, 1950, pp. 23-43.

Schorer, Mark, "Mr. Hemingway and His Critics," *New Republic*, CXXXI (Nov. 15, 1954), 18-20.

Schwartz, Delmore, "Ernest Hemingway's Literary Situation," *Southern Review*, III (1938), 769-82. [Reprinted: McCaffery, pp. 114-29.]

——, "The Fiction of Ernest Hemingway," *Perspectives USA*, No. 13 (Autumn, 1955), 70-88.

Shockley, Martin Staples, "Hemingway's Moment of Truth," *Colorado Quarterly*, V (Spring, 1957), 380-88.

Sigaux, Gilbert, "Avec Hemingway," *Preuves*, III (Feb., 1953), 95-99.

——, "La sua ricerca," *La Fiera Letteraria*, VIII (Sept. 27, 1953), 1-2.

CHECKLIST OF CRITICISM   289

Slochower, Harry, *No Voice Is Wholly Lost,* New York, 1945, 32-40.
Snell, George, *Shapers of American Fiction,* New York, 1947, pp. 156-72.
Soria, R., "The American Writer and the European Tradition; Ernest Hemingway, the Man and His Work," *Revista di Letteratura Moderne* (July-Sept., 1951), 377-85.
Spilka, Mark, "The Death of Love in *The Sun Also Rises,*" in Charles Shapiro, editor, *Twelve Original Essays on Great American Novels,* Detroit, 1958, pp. 238-56.
Spivey, Ted R., "Hemingway's Pursuit of Happiness on the Open Road," *Emory University Quarterly,* XI (Dec., 1955), 240-52.
Startsev, A., "Novoye dekadentstvo," *Literaturnaya Gazeta,* Oct. 20, 1936.
Stein, Gertrude, *The Autobiography of Alice B. Toklas,* New York, 1933, pp. 261-71.
Suarez, Silvano, *El Esqueleto del Leopardo,* La Habana, 1955.
Sylvester, Harry, "Ernest Hemingway: A Note," *Commonweal,* XXV (Oct. 30, 1936), 10-12.
Thody, Philip, "A Note on Camus and the American Novel," *Comparative Literature,* IX (Summer, 1957), 243-49.
Thorp, Willard, *American Writing in the Twentieth Century,* Cambridge, Mass., 1960, pp. 185-95.
Todd, Harold W., Jr., "Natural Elements in Hemingway's Novels," *Wingover,* I (Autumn-Winter, 1958-1959), 25-27.
Trilling, Lionel, "Hemingway and His Critics," *Partisan Review,* VI (Winter, 1939), 52-60.
V., P. D., "Gli eroi a metà di Hemingway non piacciono a Hollywood," *La Fiera Letteraria,* No. 22 (June 1, 1952), 8.
Vallete, Jacques, "Dernier État de Hemingway," *Mercure de France,* No. 1703 (Jan., 1953), 151-56.
Von Blumenberg, Hans, "Die peripatie des Mannes: Über das Werk Ernest Hemingways," *Hochland,* XLVIII (Feb., 1956), 220-33.
Wagenknecht, Edward, *Cavalcade of the American Novel,* New York, 1952, pp. 368-81.
Waggoner, Hyatt H., "Ernest Hemingway," *Christian Scholar,* XXXVIII (June, 1955), 114-20.
Wagner, Vern, "A Note for Ernest Hemingway," *College English,* XVIII (March, 1957), 327.
Warren, Robert Penn, "Ernest Hemingway," *Kenyon Review,* IX (Winter, 1947), 1-28. [Reprinted: Introduction to Modern Standard Authors edition of *A Farewell to Arms,* New York, 1949; John W. Aldridge, editor, *Critiques and Essays on Modern Fiction,* New York, 1952, pp. 447-73; and M. D. Zabel, editor, *Literary Opinion in America,* New York, 1951, pp. 447-60.]
Waugh, Evelyn, "The Case of Mr. Hemingway," *Commonweal,* LIII (1950), 97-98.

Weeks, Robert P., "Hemingway and the Spectatorial Attitude," *Western Humanities Review,* XI (Summer, 1957), 277-81.

———, "Hemingway and the Uses of Isolation," *University of Kansas City Review,* XXIV (Dec., 1957), 119-25.

West, Ray B., Jr., "Ernest Hemingway: Death in the Evening," *Antioch Review,* IV (1944), 569-80.

———, "Ernest Hemingway: The Failure of Sensibility," *Sewanee Review,* LIII (Jan.-March, 1945), 120-35. [Reprinted: William Van O'Connor, editor, *Forms of Modern Fiction,* Minneapolis, 1948, pp. 87-101.]

———, *The Short Story in America, 1900-1950,* Chicago, 1951, pp. 85-106.

Wheelock, John Hall, editor, *Editor to Author: The Letters of Maxwell Perkins,* New York, 1950, pp. 77-80, 90-91, 94-99, 117-19, 152-57, 174-75, 200-7, 234-36, 264-65.

White, William, "Father and Son: Comments on Hemingway's Psychology," *Dalhousie Review,* XXXI (Winter, 1952), 276-84.

White, William, "On Collecting Hemingway," *American Book Collector,* VII (Nov., 1956), 21-23.

Whitfield, E., "Hemingway: The Man," *Why,* I (April, 1953), 10-19.

Wilson, Edmund, Introduction, Hemingway's *In Our Time,* New York, 1930.

———, "Hemingway: Bourdon Gauge of Morale," in his *The Wound and the Bow,* London, 1941, pp. 214-42. [Reprinted: *Eight Essays,* New York, 1954, pp. 92-114; and McCaffery, pp. 236-57.]

———, "Pismo sovetskim chitatelyam o Khemingneya," *Internatsionalnaya Literatura,* No. 2 (1936), 151-54.

———, *The Shores of Light,* New York, 1953, pp. 115-24, 339-44, 616-29.

Wyrick, Green D., "Hemingway and Bergson: the Élan Vital," *Modern Fiction Studies,* I (Aug., 1955), 17-19.

———, "The World of Ernest Hemingway: A Critical Study," *Emporia State Research Studies,* II (Sept., 1953), 3-32.

Young, Philip, *Ernest Hemingway,* New York, 1952.

———, "Hemingway: A Defense," *Folio,* XX (Spring, 1955), 20-22.

———, "Hemingway's *In Our Time,*" *Explicator,* X (April, 1951), item 43.

———, cf. Edel, Leon, above.

Zavaleta, Carlos E., "La novela de Hemingway," *Estudios Americanos,* XVI (July-Aug., 1959), 47-52.

Zielinski, Bronislaw, "Hemingway: A Polish Writer," *Poland,* No. 7 (July, 1959), 30.

Anonymous, "A Visit with Hemingway," *Look,* XX (Sept. 4, 1956), 23-31.

II. STUDIES OF INDIVIDUAL WORKS

Across the River and into the Trees
> Baker, *Hemingway*, pp. 264-88.
> Beach, "How Do You Like It Now, Gentlemen?" pp. 311-17.
> Beaver, Joseph, " 'Technique' in Hemingway," *College English*, XIV (March, 1953), 315-28.
> Oppel, Horst, "Hemingway's *Across the River and into the Trees*," *Die Neueren Sprachen*, Heft 11 (1952), 473-86.
> Politzer, Heinz, "Der neue Hemingway," *Die Neue Rundschau*, I (1951), 136-39.
> Prescott, Orville, *In My Opinion: An Inquiry into the Contemporary Novel*, Indianapolis, 1952, pp. 65-71.
> Raymund, Bernard, "Old Soldier Goes Sour," in Atkins, pp. 240-45.
> Rosenfeld, Isaac, "A Farewell to Hemingway," *Kenyon Review*, XIII (Winter, 1951), 147-55.
> Seyppel, Joachim H., "Two Variations on a Theme: Dying in Venice (Thomas Mann and Ernest Hemingway)," *Literature and Psychology*, VII (Feb., 1957), 8-12.
> Stephens, Robert O., "Hemingway's *Across the River and into the Trees*: A Reprise," *University of Texas Studies in English*, XXXVII (1958), 92-101.
> Young, *Ernest Hemingway*, pp. 87-93 and *passim*.

A Day's Wait
> Baker, *Hemingway*, p. 134.
> Hüllen, Werner, "Geschräche ohne Verstehen: Versuch einer Deutung von Ernest Hemingways Kurzgeschichten 'A Day's Wait' und 'Cat in the Rain,' " *Die Neueren Sprachen*, VI (Sept., 1957), 432-39.

Alpine Idyll
> Baker, *Hemingway*, pp. 119-21.

The Battler
> Bache, William, "Hemingway's 'The Battler,' " *Explicator*, XIII (Oct., 1954), item 4.
> Young, *Ernest Hemingway*, pp. 8-11.

Big Two-Hearted River
> Baker, *Hemingway*, pp. 125-27.
> Baker, Sheridan, "Hemingway's Two-Hearted River," *Michigan Alumnus Quarterly Review*, LXV (Feb. 28, 1959), 142-49.
> Young, *Ernest Hemingway*, pp. 15-20.

A Canary for One
> Baker, *Hemingway*, pp. 137-38.

Capital of the World
> Wilson, "Hemingway: Bourdon Gauge of Morale," pp. 136-37.

Cat in the Rain
  Baker, *Hemingway,* pp. 135-36.
  Hüllen, Werner, cf. *A Day's Wait,* above.
A Clean, Well-Lighted Place
  Bache, William B., "Craftsmanship in 'A Clean, Well-Lighted Place,'" *Personalist,* XXXVII (Winter, 1956), 60-64.
  Heilman, Robert B., *Modern Short Stories: A Critical Anthology,* New York, 1950, pp. 390-92.
  Kroeger, F. P., "The Dialogue in 'A Clean, Well-Lighted Place,'" *College English,* XX (Feb., 1959), 240-41.
  Warren, pp. 5-6.
  West, *The Short Story in America,* pp. 97-98.
The End of Something
  Parker, Alice, "Hemingway's 'The End of Something,'" *Explicator,* X (March, 1952), item 36.
  Whitt, Joseph, "Hemingway's 'The End of Something,'" *Explicator,* IX (June, 1951), item 58.
  Young, *Ernest Hemingway,* pp. 5-6.
A Farewell to Arms
  Aldridge, *After the Lost Generation,* pp. 6-10.
  Antonini, Giacomo, "Addio alle armi venticinque anni dopo," *La Fiera Letteraria,* IX, I (March 21, 1954).
  Baker, *Hemingway,* pp. 94-116.
  Beach, *American Fiction,* pp. 84-89.
  Burgum, pp. 184-86.
  Daniel, pp. 478-83.
  Editors, "Hemingway's *A Farewell to Arms,*" *Explicator,* III (Nov., 1944), item 11.
  Ford, Ford Madox, Introduction, Modern Library edition, New York, 1932.
  Galantière, Lewis, "The Brushwood Boy at the Front," *Hound and Horn,* III (1930), 259-62.
  Hackett, Francis, "Hemingway: *A Farewell to Arms,*" *Saturday Review of Literature,* XXXII (Aug. 6, 1949), 32-33.
  Halliday, "Hemingway's Narrative Perspective," 209-11.
  Herrick, Robert, "What is Dirt?" *Bookman,* LXX (Nov., 1929), 258-62. [See reply by H. S. Canby, 641-47.]
  Hoffman, *The Modern Novel in America,* pp. 98-100.
  ———, *The Twenties,* pp. 70-72, 194-95, and *passim.*
  Moses, W. R., "Water, Water, Everywhere: *Old Man* and *A Farewell to Arms,*" *Modern Fiction Studies,* V (Summer, 1959), 172-74.
  Russell, H. K., "The Catharsis in *A Farewell to Arms,*" *Modern Fiction Studies,* I (Aug., 1955), 25-30.
  Savage, pp. 32-36.
  Warren, *passim.*

West, Ray B., Jr., and Stallman, R. W., *The Art of Modern Fiction*, New York, 1949, pp. 622-33.

Young, Philip, "Hemingway's *A Farewell to Arms*," *Explicator*, VII (Oct., 1948), item 7.

————, *Ernest Hemingway*, pp. 60-66 and *passim*.

Fathers and Sons

Young, *Ernest Hemingway*, pp. 32-34.

Fifty Grand

Young, *Ernest Hemingway*, pp. 36-37.

For Whom the Bell Tolls

Aldridge, *After the Lost Generation*, pp. 34-38.

Backman, pp. 6-9.

Baker, *Hemingway*, pp. 223-63.

Barea, Arturo, "Not Spain But Hemingway," *Horizon*, III (May, 1941), 350-61.

Beach, *American Fiction*, pp. 89-93, 112-19.

————, "How Do You Like It Now, Gentlemen?" pp. 322-28.

Bessie, Alvah, "Hemingway's *For Whom the Bell Tolls*," *New Masses*, XXXVII (Nov. 5, 1940), 25-29.

Burgum, pp. 197-204.

Cargill, pp. 367-70.

Carpenter, pp. 714-17.

Fadiman, Clifton, "Ernest Hemingway Crosses the Bridge," in T. J. Gates and A. Wright, editors, *College Prose*, Boston, 1942, pp. 416-21.

Fenimore, Edward, "English and Spanish in *For Whom the Bell Tolls*," *English Literary History*, X (1943), 73-86. [Reprinted: McCaffery, pp. 205-20.]

Frankenberg, Lloyd, "Themes and Characters in Hemingway's Latest Period," *Southern Review*, VII (1942), 776-88.

Frohock, 192-204.

Geismar, pp. 79-84.

Gray, *passim*.

Gurko, pp. 372-73.

Halliday, "Hemingway's Narrative Perspective," pp. 214-16.

Isherwood, Christopher, "Hemingway, Death, and the Devil," *Decision*, I (Jan., 1941), 58-60.

Lewis, Sinclair, Introduction, Limited Editions Club Edition, Princeton, N.J., 1942.

Mellers, W. H., "The Ox in Spain," *Scrutiny*, X (June, 1941), 93-99.

Moynihan, William T., "The Martyrdom of Robert Jordan," *College English*, XXI (Dec., 1959), 127-32.

Savage, pp. 36-43.

Schorer, Mark, "The Background of a Style," *Kenyon Review*, III (Winter, 1941), 101-5.

Sickels, Eleanor M., "Farewell to Cynicism," *College English*, III (Oct., 1941), 31-38.

Snell, pp. 166-71.

Trilling, Lionel, "An American in Spain," in William Phillips and Philip Rahv, editors, *Partisan Reader*, New York, 1946, pp. 639-44.

West, "Ernest Hemingway: Death in the Evening," pp. 575-80.

Young, *Ernest Hemingway*, 75-86 and *passim*.

The Gambler, The Nun, and The Radio

Baker, *Hemingway*, pp. 141, 249.

Schwartz, pp. 775-76.

Young, *Ernest Hemingway*, pp. 38-41.

In Another Country

Brooks, Cleanth, Purse, John T., and Warren, Robert Penn, *An Approach to Literature*, 3rd edition, New York, 1952, pp. 104-6.

Davis, Robert Gorham, *Instructor's Manual for Ten Modern Masters*, New York, 1953, pp. 26-27.

Ludwig, Jack Barry, and Poirier, W. Richard, *Instructor's Manual to Accompany "Stories: British and American,"* Boston, 1953, pp. 12-13.

Short, Raymond W. and Sewell, R. B., *A Manual of Suggestions for Teachers Using "Short Stories for Study,"* revised edition, New York, 1950, pp. 22-24.

Indian Camp

Orvis, Mary, *The Art of Writing Fiction*, New York, 1948, pp. 26-27.

In Our Time

Happel, Nikolaus, "Chapter V aus Hemingways Kurzgeschichtenband *In Our Time*," *Archiv für das Studium der Neueren Sprachen*, CXCI (April, 1955), 324-25.

Young, Philip, 'Hemingway's *In Our Time*," *Explicator*, X (April, 1952), item 43.

The Killers

Brooks, Cleanth, and Warren, Robert Penn, *Understanding Fiction*, New York, 1944, pp. 316-24.

Daniel, pp. 471-78.

Evans, Oliver, "The Protagonist of Hemingway's 'The Killers,' " *Modern Language Notes*, LXXIII (Dec., 1958), 589-91.

Jaffe, Adrian H., and Scott, Virgil, *Studies in the Short Story*, New York, 1949, pp. 208-13.

Kempton, Kenneth Payson, *The Short Story*, Cambridge, 1947, pp. 39-41, 110-12, 126.

Morris, William E., "Hemingway's 'The Killers,' " *Explicator*, XVIII (Oct., 1959), item 1.

Sampson, Edward C., "Hemingway's 'The Killers,' " *Explicator,* XI (Oct., 1952), item 2.

Short, Raymond W., and Sewell, R. B., *A Manual of Suggestions for Teachers Using "Short Stories for Study,"* New York, 1950, pp. 24-26.

Weeks, R. P., "Hemingway's 'The Killers,' " *Explicator,* XV (May, 1957), item 53.

Young, *Ernest Hemingway,* pp. 20-22.

The Light of the World

Baker, *Hemingway,* pp. 140-41.

Young, *Ernest Hemingway,* pp. 22-23.

My Old Man

Davis, Robert Gorham, *Instructor's Manual for Ten Modern Masters,* New York, 1953, pp. 25-26.

Now I Lay Me

Barrows, Herbert, *Suggestions for Teaching "15 Stories,"* Boston, 1950, pp. 7-9.

The Old Man and the Sea

Atkins, pp. 227-30.

Backman, 9-11.

Baker, *Hemingway* (1956 edition only), pp. 289-328.

————, *"The Old Man and the Sea,"* in Edward Wagenknecht, *Preface to Literature,* Boston, 1950, pp. 341-44.

Barnes, pp. 1-8.

Burhans, Clinton S., Jr., *"The Old Man and the Sea:* Hemingway's Tragic Vision," *American Literature,* XXXI (Jan., 1960), 446-55.

Cotten, L., "Hemingway's *The Old Man and the Sea," Explicator,* XI (May, 1953), item 38.

Cournot, Michel, "Le Vieil Homme et la Mer," *Nouvelle Revue Française,* I (Feb., 1953), 351-53.

Dupee, F. W., "Hemingway Revealed," *Kenyon Review,* XV (Winter, 1953), 150-55.

Fagan, Edward R., "Teaching Enigmas of *The Old Man and the Sea,"* *English Record,* VIII (Autumn, 1957), 13-20.

Frohock, W. M., "Mr. Hemingway's Truly Tragic Bones," *Southwest Review,* XXXVIII (Winter, 1953), 74-77.

Gurko, Leo, *"The Old Man and the Sea,"* *College English,* XVII (Oct., 1955), 11-15; *English Journal,* XLIV (Oct., 1955), 377-82.

Happel, Nikolaus, "Stilbetrachtung an *The Old Man and the Sea,"* *Die Neueren Sprachen,* Heft 2 (1956), 71-78.

Harada, Keiichi, "The Marlin and the Shark," *Journal of the College of Literature* (Aryama Gakuin University, Tokyo), 1960, pp. 49-54.

Moses, cf. *A Farewell to Arms,* above.

Portuondo, José Antonio, "The Old Man and Society," *Americas,* IV (1952), 42-44.

Schorer, Mark, "With Grace under Pressure," *New Republic,* CXXVII (Oct. 6, 1952), 19-20.

Spector, Robert D., "Hemingway's *The Old Man and the Sea,*" *Explicator,* XI (March, 1953), item 38.

Waldmeir, Joseph, "Confiteor Hominem: Ernest Hemingway's Religion of Man," *Papers of the Michigan Academy of Science, Arts, and Letters,* XLII (1956 Meeting), 349-56.

Young, *Ernest Hemingway,* pp. 93-105.

The Short Happy Life of Francis Macomber

Baker, *Hemingway,* pp. 186-91.

Beck, Warren, "The Shorter Happy Life of Mrs. Macomber," *Modern Fiction Studies,* I (Nov., 1955), 28-37.

Crane, R. S., "On 'The Short Happy Life of Francis Macomber,' " *English "A" Analyst* (Northwestern University English Department), Number 16.

Davis, Robert Gorham, *Instructor's Manual for Ten Modern Masters,* New York, 1953, pp. 27-29.

Ennis, Lambert, " 'The Short Happy Life of Francis Macomber,' " *English "A" Analyst,* Number 9.

May, Merrill M., "Macomber as Hero," *English "A" Analyst,* Number 10.

Orvis, Mary, *The Art of Writing Fiction,* New York, 1948, pp. 99-101, 129-32.

Ross, Woodburn O., and Wallace, A. Dayle, *Short Stories in Context,* New York, 1953, pp. 310-14.

Sale, William M., Jr., Hall, James, and Steinmann, Martin, Jr., *Critical Discussions for Teachers Using "Short Stories: Tradition and Direction,"* Norfolk, 1949, pp. 40-44.

Wagner, M. J., "A Note on the Ending of the Story," *English "A" Analyst,* Number 9.

West, Ray B., Jr., "Three Methods of Modern Fiction," *College English,* XII (Jan., 1951), 194-96. [Reprinted: West and Stallman, *The Art of Modern Fiction,* pp. 259-62.]

———, *The Short Story in America,* pp. 99-101.

Young, *Ernest Hemingway,* pp. 41-46, 168-69.

The Snows of Kilimanjaro

Angstrom, Alfred, "Dante, Flaubert, and 'The Snows of Kilimanjaro,' " *Modern Language Notes,* LXV (1950), 203-5.

Bache, William B., *"Nostromo* and 'The Snows of Kilimanjaro,' " *Modern Language Notes,* LXXII (Jan., 1957), 32-34.

Baker, *Hemingway,* pp. 191-96.

Dworking, Martin S., "A Dead Leopard and an Empty Grail," *The Humanist,* XIII (July-Aug., 1953), 164-65.

Gordon, Caroline, and Tate, Allen, *The House of Fiction,* New York, 1950, pp. 419-23.

Lynskey, Winifred, *Reading Modern Fiction,* New York, 1952, pp. 266-68.

O'Connor, William Van, "Two Views of Kilimanjaro," *History of Ideas News Letter,* II (Oct., 1956), 76-80.

Orrok, pp. 441-45.

Tetlock, W. W., Jr., "Hemingway's 'The Snows of Kilimanjaro,' " *Explicator,* VIII (Oct., 1949), item 7.

Walcutt, Charles C., "Hemingway's 'The Snows of Kilimanjaro,' " *Explicator,* VII (April, 1949), item 43.

Young, *Ernest Hemingway,* pp. 45-50.

The Sun Also Rises

Adams, pp. 119-31.

Aldridge, *After the Lost Generation,* pp. 30-32.

Backman, pp. 3-4.

Baker, *Hemingway,* pp. 75-93.

Beach, *American Fiction,* pp. 79-83, 105-8.

Burgum, pp. 191-92.

Canby, Henry Seidel, Introduction, Modern Library Edition, New York, 1930.

Cargill, pp. 354-58.

Cohen, Joseph, "Wouk's *Morningstar* and Hemingway's *Sun,*" *South Atlantic Quarterly,* LVIII (Spring, 1959), 213-24.

Daiches, pp. 728-31.

Farrell, James T., *The League of Frightened Philistines,* New York, 1945, pp. 20-24.

Frohock, pp. 169-76.

Gurko, pp. 369-70.

Halliday, "Hemingway's Narrative Perspective," pp. 203-9.

Hoffman, *The Modern Novel in America,* pp. 95-98.

———, *The Twenties,* pp. 72-74, 80-85, and *passim.*

Levy, Alfred J., "Hemingway's *The Sun Also Rises,*" *Explicator,* XVII (Feb., 1959), item 37.

McCormick, pp. 90-98.

Scott, Arthur L., "In Defense of Robert Cohn," *College English,* XVIII (March, 1957), 309-14.

Snell, pp. 162-63.

Spilka, pp. 238-56.

Wood, Dean C., "The Significance of Bulls and Bullfighters in *The Sun Also Rises,*" *Wingover,* I (Fall-Winter, 1958-1959), 28-30.

Young, *Ernest Hemingway,* pp. 54-60.

Ten Indians

Thurston, Jarvis, *Reading Modern Short Stories,* New York, 1955, pp. 15-16, 22, 171-76.

The Three-Day Blow
  Millett, Fred B., *Reading Fiction,* New York, 1950, pp. 65-66, 114-15, 261-62.
To Have and Have Not
  Aldridge, *After the Lost Generation,* pp. 32-34.
  Baker, *Hemingway,* pp. 203-22.
  Cargill, pp. 363-66.
  Chamberlain, J. R., "Literature," in Harold E. Stearns, editor, *America Now,* New York, 1938, pp. 36-47.
  Geismar, pp. 72-76.
  Halliday, "Hemingway's Narrative Perspective," pp. 211-14.
  Johnson, pp. 295-300.
  Paul, *passim.*
  Schwartz, pp. 777-82.
  Young, *Ernest Hemingway,* pp. 70-73 and *passim.*
Torrents of Spring
  Baker, *Hemingway,* pp. 37-42.
  Young, *Ernest Hemingway,* pp. 52-54.
The Undefeated
  Baker, *Hemingway,* p. 122.
  O'Brien, Edward J., *The Short Story Case Book,* New York, 1935, pp. 262-323.
  West, *The Short Story in America,* pp. 91-95.
A Way You'll Never Be
  Young, *Ernest Hemingway,* pp. 23-26.

AMERICAN CENTURY SERIES

Distinguished paperback books in the fields of literature and history, covering the entire span of American culture.